Edith Landmann-Kalischer

OXFORD NEW HISTORIES OF PHILOSOPHY

Series Editors
Christia Mercer, Melvin Rogers, and Eileen O'Neill (1953–2017)

*

Advisory Board
Lawrie Balfour, Jacqueline Broad, Marguerite Deslauriers, Karen Detlefsen,
Bachir Diagne, Don Garrett, Robert Gooding-Williams, Andrew Janiak,
Marcy Lascano, Lisa Shapiro, Tommie Shelby

*

Oxford New Histories of Philosophy provides essential resources for those aiming to diversify the content of their philosophy courses, revisit traditional narratives about the history of philosophy, or better understand the richness of philosophy's past. Examining previously neglected or understudied philosophical figures, movements, and traditions, the series includes both innovative new scholarship and new primary sources.

*

PUBLISHED IN THE SERIES

Mexican Philosophy in the 20th Century: Essential Readings
Edited by Carlos Alberto Sánchez and Robert Eli Sanchez, Jr.

Sophie de Grouchy's Letters on Sympathy: *A Critical Engagement with Adam Smith's* The Theory of Moral Sentiments
Edited by Sandrine Bergès and Eric Schliesser. Translated by Sandrine Bergès

Margaret Cavendish: Essential Writings
Edited by David Cunning

Women Philosophers of Seventeenth-Century England: Selected Correspondence
Edited by Jacqueline Broad

The Correspondence of Catharine Macaulay
Edited by Karen Green

Mary Shepherd's Essays on the Perception of an External Universe
Edited by Antonia Lolordo

Women Philosophers of Eighteenth-Century England: Selected Correspondence
Edited by Jacqueline Broad

Frances Power Cobbe: Essential Writings of a Nineteenth-Century Feminist Philosopher
Edited by Alison Stone

Korean Women Philosophers and the Ideal of a Female Sage: Essential Writings of Im Yungjidang and Gang Jeongildang
Edited and Translated by Philip J. Ivanhoe and Hwa Yeong Wang

Louise Dupin's Work on Women: *Selections*
Edited and Translated by Angela Hunter and Rebecca Wilkin

Edith Landmann-Kalischer: Essays on Art, Aesthetics, and Value
Edited by Samantha Matherne. Translated by Daniel O. Dahlstrom

Edith Landmann-Kalischer

Essays on Art, Aesthetics, and Value

Edited and with an Introduction by
SAMANTHA MATHERNE

Translated by
DANIEL O. DAHLSTROM

OXFORD
UNIVERSITY PRESS

Oxford University Press is a department of the University of Oxford. It furthers
the University's objective of excellence in research, scholarship, and education
by publishing worldwide. Oxford is a registered trade mark of Oxford University
Press in the UK and certain other countries.

Published in the United States of America by Oxford University Press
198 Madison Avenue, New York, NY 10016, United States of America.

© Oxford University Press 2024

All rights reserved. No part of this publication may be reproduced, stored in
a retrieval system, or transmitted, in any form or by any means, without the
prior permission in writing of Oxford University Press, or as expressly permitted
by law, by license, or under terms agreed with the appropriate reproduction
rights organization. Inquiries concerning reproduction outside the scope of the
above should be sent to the Rights Department, Oxford University Press, at the
address above.

You must not circulate this work in any other form
and you must impose this same condition on any acquirer.

CIP data is on file at the Library of Congress

ISBN 978–0–19–768205–0 (pbk.)
ISBN 978–0–19–768204–3 (hbk.)

DOI: 10.1093/oso/9780197682043.001.0001

Paperback printed by Marquis Book Printing, Canada
Hardback printed by Bridgeport National Bindery, Inc., United States of America

Contents

Series Editors' Foreword	vii
Translator's Acknowledgments	ix
Notes on the Text and Translation	xi
Introduction by Samantha Matherne	xiii
Chronology	lxi
Primary and Secondary Sources	lxiii

THE THREE ESSAYS

On the Cognitive Value of Aesthetic Judgments	3
On Artistic Truth	64
Philosophy of Values	115
Translator's Afterword	199
Lexicon	203
Bibliography	213
Index	221

Series Editors' Foreword

Oxford New Histories of Philosophy (ONHP) speaks to a new climate in philosophy.

There is a growing awareness that philosophy's past is richer and more diverse than previously understood. It has become clear that canonical figures are best studied in a broad context. More exciting still is the recognition that our philosophical heritage contains long-forgotten innovative ideas, movements, and thinkers. Sometimes these thinkers warrant serious study in their own right; sometimes their importance resides in the conversations they helped reframe or problems they devised; often their philosophical proposals force us to rethink long-held assumptions about a period or genre; and frequently they cast well-known philosophical discussions in a fresh light.

There is also a mounting sense among philosophers that our discipline benefits from a diversity of perspectives and a commitment to inclusiveness. In a time when questions about justice, inequality, dignity, education, discrimination, and climate (to name a few) are especially vivid, it is appropriate to mine historical texts for insights that can shift conversations and reframe solutions. Given that philosophy's very long history contains astute discussions of a vast array of topics, the time is right to cast a broad historical net.

Lastly, there is increasing interest among philosophy instructors in speaking to the diversity and concerns of their students. Although historical discussions and texts can serve as a powerful means of doing so, finding the necessary time and tools to excavate long-buried historical materials is challenging.

Oxford New Histories of Philosophy is designed to address all these needs. It contains new editions and translations of significant historical texts. These primary materials make available, often for the first time, ideas and works by women, people of color, and movements in philosophy's past that were groundbreaking in their day, but left out of traditional accounts. Informative introductions help instructors and students navigate the new material. Alongside its primary texts, ONHP also publishes monographs and collections of essays that offer philosophically subtle analyses of understudied topics, movements, and figures. In combining primary materials and astute philosophical analyses, ONHP makes it easier for philosophers, historians, and instructors to include in their courses and research exciting new materials drawn from philosophy's past.

ONHP's range is wide, both historically and culturally. The series includes, for example, the writings of African American philosophers, twentieth-century Mexican philosophers, early modern and late medieval women, Islamic and Jewish authors, and non-western thinkers. It excavates and analyses problems and ideas that were prominent in their day, but forgotten by later historians. And it serves as a significant aid to philosophers in teaching and researching this material.

As we expand the range of philosophical voices, it is important to acknowledge one voice responsible for this series. Eileen O'Neill was a series editor until her death, December 1, 2017. She was instrumental in motivating and conceptualizing ONHP. Her brilliant scholarship, advocacy, and generosity made all the difference to the efforts that this series is meant to represent. She will be deeply missed, as a scholar and a friend.

We are proud to contribute to philosophy's present and to a richer understanding of its past.

Christia Mercer and Melvin Rogers
Series Editors

Translator's Acknowledgments

For originally suggesting the project of translating these essays and for her cheerful encouragement, critical eyes, and valuable suggestions during the process, I am immensely grateful to Samantha Matherne. For support for this translation, Samantha and I would like to thank Harvard University and the Dean's Competitive Funds for Promising Scholarship. For help with the translation, we would also like to thank master stylist Ian Dunkle and Eugenie Schleberger Dahlstrom. For assistance with the lexicon, we would like to thank Maximillian Dahlstrom. For her careful reading of a penultimate draft and for her suggestions, we would also like to thank the Oxford University Press Series Editor Christia Mercer. We are also grateful to Senior Editor Peter Ohlin for his advice and encouragement and for the assistance of Paloma Escovedo, Alex Rouch, Madison Zickgraf, and other members of the production staff at Oxford University Press. We are also grateful to Andrew Butler and Jordan Kokot for their help with the index and final editing.

Notes on the Text and Translation

What follows is our policy on the use of brackets and our manner of citing the original pagination within the translation.

Brackets: With one exception, all brackets and wording in them have been provided by the editor or translator. Brackets are used to identify German words that have been translated, for example, "fading [*Abklingen*]" or "paradigm [*Typus*]," and, very sparingly, to provide supplementary wording for purposes of readability, for example, "Modern grownups seldom succeed in retrieving in its pristine state the world of children and of peoples more at home in nature, a world that is also still in them [modern grownups]" or "But it [what is psychologically true] may not be sheer phantasy either." Brackets are also used to provide translations of Greek, Latin, French, and German titles, phrases, and passages, for example, "*Geschichte der Kunst des Alterthums* [History of the Art of Antiquity]" or "*veritas est norma sui et falsi* [truth is the norm of itself and the false]." Yet another use of brackets, confined to footnotes, is to supply otherwise undocumented references or commentary on a passage's context, for example, "[Landmann-Kalischer is likely referring to the work of Karl Rohwedder-Ruge (1865–1940)]" or "[A *biblia pauperum* [Paupers' Bible] was a late medieval picture book of biblical events]." The sole exception here, that is, the only place where the translator or editor is not the source of the wording in brackets, is Landmann-Kalischer's own introduction of brackets within a passage from Kant (the cited passage precedes footnotes 37 and 38 in "On the Cognitive Value of Aesthetic Judgments" (p. 19), where we call attention to the fact that the brackets are in the original).

Original Pagination: Embedded throughout the translation are numbers surrounded by vertical lines, referring to the original German pagination of the respective essay. Thus, for example, "|264|" on the opening page of the Introduction to "On the Cognitive Value of Aesthetic Judgments" refers to Edith Landmann-Kalischer (1905), "Über den Erkenntniswert ästhetischer Urteile. Ein Vergleich zwischen Sinnes- und Werturteilen," *Archiv für die gesamte Psychologie*, p. 264. Similarly, "|458|" on the first page of the second essay, "On Artistic Truth," refers to Edith Landmann-Kalischer (1906), "Über künstlerische Wahrheit." *Zeitschrift für Ästhetik und Allgemeine Kunstwissenschaft*, p. 458. And so on.

Introduction

Samantha Matherne

> Beauty should be considered a property of things.
> —"On the Cognitive Value of Aesthetic Judgments"

> Just as we would never see our face were it not for a mirror, so, too, we would never see our own inner life opposite us—were it not for the mirror of art.
> —"On Artistic Truth"

> Just as objects have a determinate, physical weight, independent of how light or heavy they seem to one or the other person today or tomorrow, so, too, they have a determinate inner weight, an objectively determinable value, independent of how light or heavy they may be found to be by X or Y in the 9th or 19th century.
> —"Philosophy of Values"

> We have to determine logic, ethics, and aesthetics very simply as sciences of the true, good, and beautiful.
> —"Philosophy of Values"

Reading these words may well mark the first time you have encountered the ideas of the German philosopher Edith Landmann-Kalischer (1877–1951).[1] In fact, picking up this volume may be the first time you have even seen the name "Edith Landmann-Kalischer." Though lamentable, the story of her neglect is familiar: as a Jewish woman, she was marginalized in the German philosophical scene of the early twentieth century. She had to leave Germany to pursue her PhD in Zurich because German universities did not grant PhDs to women at the time. She spent most of her adult life in Switzerland,

---

[1] Although her given name is "Kalischer" and married name is "Landmann," she uses "Landmann-Kalischer" to refer to herself in the three essays included in this volume, and I follow suit.

geographically isolated from the philosophical communities in Germany and Austria, because that is where her husband's job was. And though she returned to Germany after her husband's suicide in 1931, Hitler's rise to power in 1933 foreclosed the possibility of her remaining there, and she returned to Switzerland for the remainder of her life.

Yet, happily, as is also becoming a familiar story,[2] in spite of these barriers, Landmann-Kalischer published an extraordinary body of philosophical work. Indeed, she developed one of the most original and wide-ranging programs in aesthetics and value theory in Germany in the first half of the twentieth century. Navigating between the trends toward psychology, phenomenology, and Neo-Kantianism, she offered innovative analyses of beauty, art, goodness, and truth. In so doing, she defended a picture of our world as one that is replete with aesthetic, moral, and epistemic values, and of our lived experience as animated by the apprehension of those values. Long overdue, Landmann-Kalischer deserves recognition alongside more familiar names like Edmund Husserl, Martin Heidegger, and Ernst Cassirer, as an early twentieth-century German philosopher who merits our attention still today.

This volume represents a landmark step in the effort to recover the philosophy of Landmann-Kalischer: it is the first time that her work has been translated into English. It includes a translation of three of her early essays: "On the Cognitive Value of Aesthetic Judgments: A Comparison of Sensory Judgments and Value Judgments" ["Über den Erkenntniswert ästhetischer Urteile. Ein Vergleich zwischen Sinnes- und Werturteilen"] (1905), "On Artistic Truth" ["Über künstlerische Wahrheit"] (1906), and "Philosophy of Values" ["Philosophie der Werte"] (1910).[3] These essays serve as a cohesive and accessible introduction to the systematic view of aesthetic, moral, and epistemic value that she develops in the first decade of the 1900s.

---

[2] See, for example, the work of the philosophers collected in *Women Philosophers in the Long Nineteenth Century: The German Tradition*, ed. Dalia Nassar and Kristin Gjesdal (Oxford: Oxford University Press, 2021); the new translation of Gerda Walther's *Toward an Ontology of Social Communities* (1923), ed. and trans. Sebastian Luft and Rodney Parker (Berlin: De Gruyter, forthcoming); the essays in the *Oxford Handbook of Nineteenth-Century Women Philosophers in the German Tradition*, ed. Dalia Nassar and Kristin Gjesdal (Oxford: Oxford University Press, forthcoming), and the essays in the *Oxford Handbook of American and British Women Philosophers in the Nineteenth Century*, ed. Lydia Moland and Alison Stone (Oxford: Oxford University Press, forthcoming).

[3] Citations are to the pagination of the translation/original. CV: "On the Cognitive Value of Aesthetic Judgments"; AT: "On Artistic Truth"; and PV: "Philosophy of Values."

And in them, we find an innovative intervention in aesthetics and value theory that speaks as much to the concerns of her day as it speaks to us now.

But what were the concerns of her day? The philosophical discussions at the turn of the twentieth century in Germany were animated by perennial philosophical questions about the nature of mind, reality, knowledge, and value. However, the answers to these questions were steeped in philosophical trends that emerged over the course of the nineteenth century.

Looming large in the background was the revolutionary philosophy of Immanuel Kant.[4] Wary of unfounded metaphysical claims, Kant developed a 'critical' philosophy, which was meant to determine the boundaries of what we can and cannot know. To this end, Kant drew a distinction between two realms: the realm of appearances (phenomena), which we can cognize, and the realm of things in themselves (noumena), which we cannot cognize. In the *Critique of Pure Reason* (1781/87), he argued that instead of setting its sights on metaphysical knowledge of noumena, philosophy should set its sights on 'transcendental' insight into the a priori conditions that make appearances and our experience of them possible. He then broadened this transcendental program in the *Critique of Practical Reason* (1788) and the *Critique of the Power of Judgment* (1790), offering an account of the a priori insight we can have into the nature of morality and freedom, in the former, and into beauty and teleology, in the latter.

Though influential, at the turn of the nineteenth century, two major schools of philosophy emerged that challenged the Kantian approach: Romanticism and German idealism. Contrary to the Kantian account of knowledge as bounded, these philosophers argued that it is possible for us to arrive at absolute knowledge. And contrary to the Kantian picture of reality as divided between appearances and things in themselves, they defended a unified view of reality as one. In this spirit, the Romantics, like Friedrich von Hardenberg (Novalis), Friedrich Hölderlin, and the Schlegels (August, Friedrich, and Dorothea), offered a grand vision of art as holding the key to our most profound knowledge of reality.[5] Meanwhile German idealists, like Johann Gottlieb Fichte, Friedrich Schelling, and G. W. F. Hegel, defended ambitious

---

[4] For an introduction to Kant's philosophy, see Ernst Cassirer, *Kant's Life and Thought*, trans. James Haden (New Haven, CT: Yale University Press, 1983), and Paul Guyer, *Kant* (London: Routledge, 2006).

[5] For an introduction to German Romanticism, see Dalia Nassar, *The Romantic Absolute* (Chicago: University of Chicago Press, 2013), and Keren Gorodeisky, "19th century Romantic Aesthetics," The Stanford Encyclopedia of Philosophy, ed. Edward N. Zalta, https://plato.stanford.edu/archives/fall2016/entries/aesthetics-19th-romantic/, 2016.

metaphysical systems of the absolute, in which art, religion, and philosophy figured as our path to absolute knowing.

For all their grandeur, these Romantic and idealist ideas were met by much skepticism in Germany. This skepticism was motivated, in part, by a comparison with the natural sciences: whereas the natural sciences appeared to be advancing knowledge by remaining anchored in facts and experience, these philosophical systems seemed to be epistemically adrift in speculation. Challenging the Kantian, Romantic, and idealist precedents, toward the middle of the nineteenth century, so-called positivists, such as Richard Avenarius and Ernst Mach, called for a new empiricist approach to knowledge. According to the positivist program, we need to relinquish the idea that knowledge can be derived a priori and embrace the insight from the natural sciences that knowledge is derived a posteriori on the basis of facts and experience.[6]

While the positivists sought to put philosophy methodologically on a par with natural science, many worried that doing so lost sight of the distinctive contribution that philosophy, and philosophy alone, can make. In order to recover this distinctive philosophical contribution, in the 1870s a set of philosophers declared the need to go "back to Kant!"[7] This rejoinder to Kant coalesced into the Neo-Kantian movement that would dominate much of German academic philosophy until 1920. Though the Neo-Kantians were sympathetic to the idea that philosophical knowledge should be grounded in facts and experience, and hence wary of metaphysical speculation, they were equally wary of positivism and called for a return to Kant's transcendental method. According to the Kantian transcendental method, though philosophy should take facts and experience as its starting point, philosophy has the distinctive task of elucidating the a priori conditions that make these facts and experience possible. Over the next decades, the so-called Marburg School of Hermann Cohen, Paul Natorp, and Ernst Cassirer, and the so-called Southwest School of Wilhelm Windelband and Heinrich Rickert, would carry this program forward, offering a transcendental analysis of the facts and experience of nature, culture, and value.

---

[6] For an introduction to Avenarius, see Norman Kemp Smith, "Avenarius' Philosophy of Pure Experience: I," *Mind* XV, no. 57 (1906a): pp. 13–31 and "Avenarius' Philosophy of Pure Experience: II," *Mind* XV, no. 58 (1906b): pp. 149–160, and to Mach, see Paul Poljman, "Ernst Mach," *The Stanford Encyclopedia of Philosophy*, ed. Edward N. Zalta, <https://plato.stanford.edu/archives/win2020/entries/ernst-mach/>, 2020.

[7] For an introduction to Neo-Kantianism, see Frederick Beiser, *The Genesis of Neo-Kantianism* (Oxford: Oxford University Press, 2014).

In addition to the rise of Neo-Kantianism, the 1870s witnessed a landmark moment in the emerging field of academic psychology: Wilhelm Wundt established the first experimental psychology lab in Leipzig in 1879.[8] And at the end of the nineteenth century, many in Germany came to conceive of the project of philosophy as of a piece with the project of psychology: the project of understanding mental phenomena, mental processes, and consciousness. Indeed, at the end of the nineteenth century, many of the leading thinkers, like Carl Stumpf (who founded the Berlin Institute of Experimental Psychology in 1893), Alexius Meinong (who founded the Graz Psychological Institute in 1894), and Theodor Lipps (who founded the Academic Society for Psychology in Munich in 1895), worked at the intersection of philosophy and psychology.

As part of this trend toward philosophical psychology, in 1874 Franz Brentano published *Psychology from an Empirical Standpoint* in which he advocated for an empirical method for studying mental phenomena and consciousness, which he called 'descriptive psychology'. This method catalyzed a new field in philosophy that would have a profound impact on the trajectory of German thought in the early twentieth century: the field of phenomenology. Indeed, Brentano's descriptive psychology became a touchstone for the early and disparate forays into phenomenology by Husserl in the *Logical Investigations* (1900/01), as well as by members of the Graz School (or "Austrian phenomenologists"), such as Meinong, Christian von Ehrenfels, Stephan Witasek, Auguste Fischer, Mila Radaković, and Wilhelmine (Benussi-)Liel,[9] and by the Munich phenomenologists, such as Alexander Pfänder and Johannes Daubert.[10] However, the field of

---

[8] For an introduction to psychology in Germany, see Ch. 8 of John Greenwood, *A Conceptual History of Psychology*, 2nd ed. (Cambridge: Cambridge University Press, 2015).

[9] For reference to this group as the 'Graz School', see Barry Smith (in "Pleasure and Its Modifications: Witasek, Meinong and the Aesthetics of the Grazer Schule," in *The Philosophy of Alexius Meinong*, ed. L. Albertazzi, Axiomathes 7, no. 1–2 [1996]: pp. 203–232), Venazio Raspa (in *The Aesthetics of the Graz School* [Berlin: De Gruyter, 2013]), and Ingrid Vendrell-Ferran (in "On the Analogy between the Sensing of Secondary Qualities and the Feeling of Values: Landmann-Kalischer's Epistemic Project, Its Historical Context, and Its Significance for Current Meta-Ethics," in *Philosophy of Value. The Historical Roots of Contemporary Debate: An Overview*, ed. Beatrice Centi, Faustino Fabbianelli, and Gemmo Iocco [Berlin: De Gruyter, forthcoming]). For reference to this group as 'Austrian phenomenology', see Robin Rollinger (in *Austrian Phenomenology: Brentano, Husserl, Meinong, and Others on Mind and Object* [Berlin: De Gruyter, 2008]). For discussion of the women in the Graz School, with special focus on Fischer, see Eva Mayer, "Anfänge des Frauenphilosophiestudiums in Graz ab etwa 1900 am Beispiel der Meinong-Schülerin Auguste Fischer (1867–1958)," in *Logical, Ontological, and Historical Contributions on the Philosophy of Alexius Meinong*, ed. Mauro Antonelli and Marian David (Berlin: De Gruyter, 2014): pp. 161–82.

[10] Later members of the Munich and (later) Göttingen School include Theodor Conrad, Hedwig Conrad-Martius, Roman Ingarden, Max Scheler, Edith Stein, and Gerda Walther. For discussion of the Munich School of phenomenology, see Alessandro Salice, "The Phenomenology of the Munich

phenomenology soon divided between those who continued to adhere to an empirical method and those who, following Husserl's 'transcendental turn' in *Ideas Pertaining to a Pure Phenomenology* (1913), embraced a transcendental method in phenomenology, which brought it, in many ways, closer to Neo-Kantianism.

It is in this philosophical milieu in which the boundaries between philosophy and psychology were blurred and phenomenology was emerging that Landmann-Kalischer began her career. In 1901 she completed her dissertation *Analyse der ästhetischen Contemplation (Plastik und Malerei)* [Analysis of Aesthetic Contemplation (Sculpture and Painting)] under the supervision of Ernst Meumann, a philosopher and psychologist, who had worked as an assistant in Wundt's lab. In the dissertation, she focused on the Kantian concept of aesthetic experience as a form of contemplation, and she set for herself the "task of determining and analyzing the psychological process [*Vorgang*]" that contemplation involves (*Analyse* 5, my translation). She continued to pursue this task in her first two articles, "On the Cognitive Value of Aesthetic Judgments" and "On Artistic Truth," offering an analysis of the psychological process involved in our experience of beauty and art, respectively. And in the "Philosophy of Values," she broadened this program to include an analysis of the processes involved in our experience of value more generally, beauty, goodness, and truth included. Over the course of these three essays, which form the centerpiece of this volume, Landmann-Kalischer made a striking and systematic contribution in aesthetics and value theory, which was as responsive to psychology and phenomenology as it was to the Kantian and post-Kantian trends that shaped the trajectory of German philosophy in the nineteenth century.

By way of an initial introduction to her philosophical views, in the rest of this section, I briefly outline her philosophical method and core philosophical commitments—an outline I then fill out in more detail in subsequent sections.

Let's begin with Landmann-Kalischer's philosophical method. From the start, Landmann-Kalischer rejects a transcendental or speculative method in favor of an empirically grounded one. As she frames her aims in "On the Cognitive Value of Aesthetic Judgments,"

---

and Göttingen Circles," *The Stanford Encyclopedia of Philosophy*, ed. Edward N. Zalta, <https://plato.stanford.edu/archives/win2020/entries/phenomenology-mg/>, 2020.

> in order to avoid any misunderstanding, it is necessary for me . . . to state . . . that I refrain here from any metaphysical aim. I want merely to describe the factual state of things. (CV 42/305)

Notice that in this passage she characterizes her empirical approach in terms of a 'description' of the factual state of things. Here, she implicitly aligns her approach with Brentano's method of descriptive psychology.[11] And in the three essays included in this volume, she focuses her attention on deploying the method of descriptive psychology to describe the mental phenomena involved in our experience of aesthetic, moral, and epistemic value.

However, Landmann-Kalischer does not rest content with analyzing the subjective side of our experience of value. She also endeavors to offer an account of the objective side of value, which addresses the question of what aesthetic, moral, and epistemic value are. In other words, she asks, What are the beauty, goodness, and truth that we experience?

What is more, she pairs this subjective and objective analysis of value with a methodological commitment to analyzing aesthetic, moral, and epistemic value in a way that draws on experimental sciences, such as experimental psychology. She asks, for example, what experimental psychology might tell us about the illusions or deceptions we can undergo in our experience of beauty, truth, and goodness, as well as about the relationship among value, properties of objects, and responses in subjects.

In the end, though Landmann-Kalischer takes her methodological cue from the Brentanian conception of descriptive psychology, she extends this approach in further objective and empirically informed directions. In this way her method represents a dynamic moment in the wake of Brentano—a moment in which the effort to describe our lived experience of aesthetic, moral, and epistemic value is animated by both the desire to remain true to the 'things themselves' and the desire to proceed in an empirically grounded way.

Turning now to her philosophical contributions, in these three essays, she defends an original and systematic position in value theory and aesthetics[12] that rests on two main claims: the first about the nature of value and the second about our experience of value.

---

[11] I discuss her relationship to Brentano and early phenomenology at more length in §2.
[12] I discuss her relationship to philosophical aesthetics in Germany at more length in §3.

First, regarding the nature of value, she argues that aesthetic, moral, and epistemic value (i.e., beauty, goodness, truth) are in the world, rather than merely in the eye of the beholder. In defending this realist view of value, she rejects a variety of more subjectivist accounts of value. In philosophical aesthetics, for example, Kant had argued that beauty is only 'as if' a property of objects. And in value theory more generally the Neo-Kantian, Jonas Cohn, and Brentanians, like Meinong[13] and von Ehrenfels, had denied that value is a property of things.[14] Against these subjectivist positions, Landmann-Kalischer defends a realist position, according to which aesthetic, moral, and epistemic values are properties of things. Indeed, she advocates for an understanding of aesthetics, ethics, and logic as 'sciences of value', which have the task of clarifying what kinds of properties of things beauty, goodness, and truth are.

Second, regarding our experience of value, Landmann-Kalischer weaves together two ideas. On the one hand, she argues that our experience of value involves feeling. When I, for example, experience a painting as beautiful, a courageous act as morally good, or a statement as true, *per* Landmann-Kalischer, this experience involves some kind of affective response, some feeling, in me.

On the other hand, she claims that our experience of value is cognitive and objective. She casts this point, more specifically, in terms of our judgments about value being cognitive and objective. In this vein, she claims

[13] However, partially under the influence of Landmann-Kalischer, Meinong eventually gives up this subjectivist position in favor of a realist position. See, for example, his claim that "Landmann-Kalischer's remarks on the 'cognitional value' of the feeling, which appear to me today, contrary to my first impression, as far as their main idea is concerned, to be the most important thing that has been put forward so far for the justification of the position which is to be sketched here" (Meinong, "Für die Psychologie und gegen den Psychologismus in der allgemeinen Werttheorie," *Logos. Internationale Zeitschrift für Philosophie der Kultur* 3 [1912]: pp. 1–12: 10; translated by Maria Reicher-Marek, "Dispositionalist Accounts of Aesthetic Properties in Austro-German Aesthetics," *Paradigmi. Rivista di critica filosofica* 3 [2017]: pp. 71–86: 82). See also his claim, "I myself owe to the essay "Über den Erkenntniswert ästhetischer Urteile" [On the Cognitive Value of Aesthetic Judgments], despite initial fundamental reservations, substantial stimulations for the conceptions which are now, in the present writing, developed in some more detail" (Meinong, "Über emotionale Präsentation," *Sitzungsberichte der philosophisch-historischen Klasse der Kaiserlichen Akademie der Wissenschaften in Wien* 183 [1917]: pp. 415–16: 131–32; translated by Reicher-Marek, "Dispositionalist Accounts," p. 82). See Maria Reicher, "Value Facts and Value Experiences in Early Phenomenology," in *Values and Ontology*, ed. Beatrice Centi and Wolfgang Huemer (Frankfurt: Ontos, 2009): pp. 105–35 and "Ästhetische Werte als dispositionale Eigenschaften: 1905–2014," *Deutsches Jahrbuch Philosophie* 8 (2016): pp. 961–74 and Reicher-Marek, "Dispositionalist Accounts" for discussion of the aesthetics and value theory of Brentano and the Graz School (Meinong, Witasek, von Ehrenfels) and Landmann-Kalischer's influence on Meinong.

[14] In the introduction to "On the Cognitive Value of Aesthetic Judgments," Landmann-Kalischer canvasses these positions and indicates her sympathy with Brentano's view of value as a property of things.

that judging an object to have value involves cognizing value as a property of that object. And in cases where the object is, in fact, valuable, she claims our value judgments are objective. For example, granting that a painting like Rachel Ruysch's *Still Life with Bouquet of Flowers and Plums* is beautiful, when I judge it to be beautiful, on Landmann-Kalischer's view, this judgment is cognitive and objective. In defending this position, Landmann-Kalischer rejects a popular view of value judgments as relative, indexed to an individual or community. Against such relativism, she argues that just as we can arrive at objective judgments about physical properties of objects, so, too, can we arrive at objective judgments about the value properties of objects. So although, on her view, our experience of value is affective, feelings are not a barrier, but a path to cognition and objectivity.

In Landmann-Kalischer's "On the Cognitive Value of Aesthetic Judgments," "On Artistic Truth," and "Philosophy of Values," we ultimately find a philosophically and methodologically unified approach to aesthetic, moral, and epistemic value that contests the philosophical orthodoxy of her day. In her method, she rejects the transcendental and idealist approaches of Kant and the post-Kantians in favor of an empirical approach in keeping with philosophical-psychology and early phenomenology. And in her philosophical views, she eschews subjectivist, relativist, non-cognitivist, and idealist theories of value in the air, in favor of a realist account of value and a sophisticated account of our experience of value, as involving affective, cognitive, and objective dimensions.

While Landmann-Kalischer's vision of value represents an innovative contribution to German philosophy at the turn of the twentieth century, this vision is relevant still. For in these essays, we find her addressing questions in value theory and aesthetics that remain pressing for us. Are beauty, goodness, and truth real or merely subjective? Does our experience of value involve feeling? Can our experience of value lead to knowledge? Is a science of value possible? Landmann-Kalischer offers a powerful and profound answer to these questions—an answer this volume invites us to give its philosophical due.

In the rest of the Introduction, my goal is to provide more biographical and philosophical background on Landmann-Kalischer and to offer a reader's guide to the three essays included in this volume. In §1, I provide a biographical sketch of her life. In §§2-3, I take a closer look at the philosophical commitments that shape the three essays. In §2, I expand on her relation to the phenomenological movement and in §3 on her relation to philosophical aesthetics in Germany. In §§4-6, I offer an overview of the main philosophical theses and arguments she defends in "On the Cognitive Value of Aesthetic Judgments," "On Artistic Truth," and "Philosophy of Values," respectively. Readers might want to return to these sections before reading each essay.

§1. Landmann-Kalischer's Biography

Edith Kalischer was born to a Jewish family in Berlin in 1877, the youngest daughter of the banker Moritz Kalischer and Henriette Skolny. During her school years, she studied at the *Realkursen für Mädchen* [Real Courses for Girls], which had been founded by the feminist Helene Lange in 1889. Since at that time German universities did not recognize diplomas from the *Realkursen*, but Swiss universities did, in 1897 she enrolled at the University of Zurich for her undergraduate work. Ironically, being enrolled at Zurich allowed her to visit classes at the University of Berlin, where she took philosophy courses with Carl Stumpf, Georg Simmel,[15] Max Dessoir, and Gregor Itelson. In addition to philosophy, she studied psychology, art history, and archaeology.

Having decided to pursue a PhD in philosophy, she had little choice but to remain at the University of Zurich: German universities did not grant PhDs to women at the time. She completed her dissertation, *Analyse der ästhetischen Contemplation (Plastik und Malerei)* [Analysis of Aesthetic Contemplation (Sculpture and Painting)] in 1901 under the supervision of the philosopher and psychologist Ernst Meumann.

During her doctoral work, she met the economist Julius Landmann, whom she married in 1903. The couple had three children, Georg Peter, who became a classicist; Eva, who died from bone tuberculosis at the age of eighteen; and Michael, who became a philosopher. The family moved where Julius's career took them: living first in Bern (1906-1910) while he worked as a leading figure at the Swiss National Bank, then in Basel where he took up a post as a professor of economics at the University of Basel (1910-1927), and finally in Kiel where he taught at the University of Kiel (1927-1931).

---

[15] See Edith Landmann, "Erinnerung an Simmel von Edith Landmann," in *Buch des Dankes an Georg Simmel; Briefe, Erinnerungen, Bibliographie*, ed. Kurt Gassen and Michael Landmann (Berlin: Duncker und Humboldt, 1958): pp. 208-10 for her recollections about studying with Simmel and Stumpf.

After finishing her dissertation, Landmann-Kalischer did not obtain an academic post. She was, instead, expected (and, indeed, threatened)[16] to perform her duties as a wife and mother. Nevertheless, she actively participated in the philosophical world through her correspondence[17] and written work, publishing articles and book reviews in journals, including *Archiv für die gesamte Psychologie* (which was founded in 1903 by several of Wundt's former students), and the *Zeitschrift für Ästhetik und Kunstwissenschaft* (which was founded in 1906 and edited by Max Dessoir). Her early publications make contributions in aesthetics and value theory, and they include the three essays in this volume, as well as lengthy book reviews, for example, of Theodor Lipps's *Grundlegung der Ästhetik* [Foundation of Aesthetics] (1903) and Emil Lask's *Die Logik der Philosophie und die Kategorienlehre* [The Logic of Philosophy and the Doctrine of Categories] (1911) and *Die Lehre vom Urteil* [The Doctrine of Judgment] (1912).

During World War I, she turned her attention toward issues in epistemology and the nature of knowledge. These efforts culminated in her book, *Die Transcendenz des Erkennens* [The Transcendence of Cognizing], which was published in 1923, but which she had completed a manuscript of as early as 1916.[18] In *Transcendenz*, Landmann-Kalischer offers an account of the acts and objects of cognition, as well as the relation of 'transcendence' that holds between them. And in defending her view, she positions her account of cognition against the transcendental idealist views of Kant, the

---

[16] In her diaries from 1912 to 1914, she reports the following response from Julius when she proposed going to Davos to pursue some philosophical work without the children: "To my question if he knew the Touristenhotel in Davos, the answer came clearly and calmly: 'If you do this and something happens to Georg Peter over the next few years, I will kill you.' Everything was silent. I had the feeling that something terrible had happened. I couldn't move a limb. I tried to get a hold of myself, to accept this, to make clear to myself: so here too. In connection with the mood of the past days this meant: nowhere roots, nowhere sympathy, nowhere love" (trans. in Susanne Hillman, *Wandering Jews: Existential Quests between Berlin, Zurich, and Zion* [ProQuest Dissertations & Theses Global, 2011]: p. 312; cited originally in Korinna Schönhärl, "'Wie eine Blume die erforen ist'—Edith Landmann als Jüngerin Stefan Georges," in *Stefan George. Dichtung—Ethos—Staat. Denkbilder für ein geheimes europäisches Deutschland*, ed. Bruno Pieger and Bertram Schefold (Berlin: Verlag für Berlin-Brandenburg, 2010): pp. 207–42: 213.

[17] She corresponded, for example, with Meinong between 1905 and 1916 (see Meinong, *Philosophenbriefe. Aus der wissenschaftlichen Korrespondenz*, ed. Rudolf Kindinger [Graz: Akademischen Druck- U. Verlagsanstalt, 1965]: pp. 154–98). Much of her correspondence is held at the Stefan George Archiv in Stuttgart.

[18] See Johannes Riedner,, "Edith Landmann als philosophische Interpretin und Zeugin Stefan Georges. Zu Problemen der Assimilation im George-Kreis," in *Marburger Forum* 3(4) (2002): pp. 1–14 for the argument that features of *Transcendenz* anticipate some of Heidegger's views in *Being and Time*. See also her mention of Heidegger in "Wissen und Werten," in *Schmollers Jahrbuch für Gesetzgebung, Verwaltung und Volkswirtschaft im Deutschen Reich* 54(2) (1930): pp. 95–111: 98.

Neo-Kantians, and Husserl, on the one hand, and a kind of transcendental realist view endorsed by positivists, on the other.[19]

The 1910s also marked an important turning point in Landmann-Kalischer's life, as she became part of the *George-Kreis* (George-Circle), a circle of artists and intellectuals that gathered around the German poet Stefan George.[20] As a poet, George was a staunch critic of the realist trend in German literature and partially responsible for the emergence of aestheticism in Germany around the turn of the twentieth century. He advocated for a new form of German poetry, which was lyrical and symbolist in style and inspired by classical, anti-modernist, aristocratic, and mystical ideals. And in 1892 he founded a new literary magazine, *Blätter für die Kunst*, as a forum for writers and academics to publish work in keeping with his vision for a new German literary aesthetic.

The *George-Kreis* emerged in this milieu, with George assuming the role of a "*Meister*" and his adherents forming an intimate circle around him. Though intellectually vibrant, the *George-Kreis* was problematically shaped by George's privileging of men over women,[21] as well as his anti-Semitism and eventual sympathy for National Socialism (he died in 1933).[22] Membership of the *George-Kreis* was ever evolving, but its early members included the poet Karl Wolfskehl; the philosopher Ludwig Klages; the literary scholar Friedrich Gundolf; the jurist and author Berthold Vallentin and his wife, Diana; the art historian and poet (and only woman to publish in *Blätter*) Gertrud Kantorowicz; the painter and designer Melchior Lechter; and the industrialist and poet Robert Boehringer.

The Landmanns briefly met George in 1908 at Lechter's studio and were gradually drawn into the *George-Kreis*. George visited the Landmanns in Basel for the first time in 1913 and continued to visit them every year for

---

[19] She later returns to themes from *Transcendenz* in "Wissen und Werten" (1930) in which she discusses knowledge of value and its role in 'cultural science' (*Kulturwissenschaft*), using the economist Werner Sombart (the author of *Der moderne Kapitalismus* [The Modern Capitalism]) and Max Weber as her foils. For discussion of this piece and sociological themes in it, see Gesine Lenore Schiewer, "Das Problem des Politischen in der Philosophie Edith Landmanns. Diskussionen im Umfeld von Wertphilosophie, Gestalttheorie und Wissenssoziologie," in *Das Ideal des schönen Lebens und die Wirklichkeit der Weimarer Republik. Vorstellungen von Staat und Gemeinschaft im George-Kreis*, ed. Roman Koster et al. (Berlin: Akademie-Verlag, 2009): pp. 77–96: 87–90.

[20] For more on George and the *George-Kreis*, see Robert Norton, *Secret Germany: Stefan George and His Circle* (Ithaca, NY: Cornell University Press, 2002) and Gunilla Eschenbach, *Imitatio im George-Kreis* (Berlin: De Gruyter, 2011).

[21] For discussion of the women in the *George-Kreis*, see the essays in Ute Oelmann and Ulrich Raulff, eds., *Frauen um Stefan George* (Göttingen: Wallstein Verlag, 2010).

[22] For discussion of George's anti-Semitism and sympathy for National Socialism, see Norton (2002): pp. 155–56, 704–5, 726, 729.

several weeks each summer until 1927. It seems Landmann-Kalischer fell in love with George at some point during this period and the intensity of her devotion to him is evidenced in the diaries she kept during this period, published posthumously as *Gespräche mit Stefan George* [Conversations with Stefan George]. Though he did not return her affection, George nevertheless relied on her as a kind of unpaid literary assistant. And beginning in the late 1910s, she devoted significant intellectual attention to working out George's philosophical significance. In 1920 she anonymously published a revised version of a manuscript she had written in 1918 in honor of George's fiftieth birthday, *Georgika. Das Wesen des Dichters* [Georgika: The Essence of the Poet]. In *Georgika* she offered a theory of poetry and its distinction from other art forms, as well as an account of what she took to be the pedagogical, aesthetic, and ethical value of George as a model poet.[23] In some ways, this account of poetry serves as a complement to the account of sculpture and painting that she initially offered in her dissertation. However, certain themes reflect the ways in which her philosophical outlook had been shaped by George in the intervening decades, such as worries about modern literature, the role of poetry in 'creating a people', and the connection of poetry to the 'ideal' of humanity. She wrote another published work about George's account of the relationship between human beings and the earth in "Mensch und Erde" [Human Being and Earth] (1945) and two other posthumously published works focusing on his ethical program and classical vision, titled "Georges Wiedererweckung der Griechen" [George's Reawakening of the Greeks] (1955) and *Stefan George und die Griechen. Idee einer neuen Ethik* [Stefan George and the Greeks: Idea of a New Ethics] (1971).

Though Landmann-Kalischer remained close to George until his death in 1933, she appears to have begun distancing herself from him at the end of the 1920s. Long familiar with George's anti-Semitism, she reports that after objecting to George's sympathy for National Socialism given its 'brutality', George replied, "When I think of what Germany faces in the next fifty years, this whole Jewish thing in particular is not so important to me."[24] Far from indifferent to the fate of Jews in Germany, in 1933 Landmann-Kalischer distributed to her friends a piece titled "Omaruru: To the German Jews Who Stood with the Secret Germany," in which she discussed the threat posed

---

[23] See Daniel Dahlstrom, "Edith Landmann-Kalischer," in *The Oxford Handbook of Nineteenth-Century Women Philosophers in the German Tradition*, ed. Kristin Gjesdal and Dalia Nassar (Oxford: Oxford University Press, forthcoming) for an overview of *Georgika*.

[24] Norton, *Secret Germany*, p. 726.

by National Socialism for German-Jews and the need to emigrate somewhere like Vaduz (in Lichtenstein), San Marino (in Italy), or Omaruru (in Namibia), as well as her own complicated attitudes toward being Jewish and German.[25] Though her proposal was panned as naive, it marked her first attempt to think through the possibility of emigration and the prospects of Zionism—themes she would continue to return to (see, e.g., her manuscript "Assimilation and Zionismus" [1948] in her *Nachlass*[26]) and that informed her heralding of the independence of Israel in 1948.

The early 1930s were a time of upheaval in Landmann-Kalischer's life. In 1931 Julius, who suffered from depression, committed suicide. In 1933 George died, and Hitler came to power. Though she had moved back to Germany after Julius's suicide, given the threat of National Socialism, she decided to return to Switzerland, where she would live out the rest of her life. During the next two decades, she retained a close friendship with the painter and designer Gertrud Kantorowicz, who also lived in Basel. And in 1939, due to the worsening climate in Germany, she invited the classical philologist Renata von Scheliha to live with her. The two lived together until von Scheliha emigrated to the United States in 1948. Shortly after visiting von Scheliha in New York in 1950/51, Landmann-Kalischer died due to complications from an operation.

Throughout her last decades in Switzerland, Landmann-Kalischer continued to write philosophy and book reviews (occasionally under the pseudonym Marius Müller) and gave lectures at the *Volkshochschule* in Basel. She explored various ideas in this period ranging from Homer and the *Odyssey* to the possibility of a Jewish settlement outside of Germany. However, she also continued to pursue topics in aesthetics, publishing *Grundzüge einer Lehre vom Schönen* [The Outline of a Doctrine of the Beautiful] in 1940, which was an early draft of her final book, which was published posthumously, *Die Lehre vom Schönen* [The Doctrine of the Beautiful] (1953).[27] In this book she develops a systematic account of the nature and creation of artistic beauty in general, as well as of beauty internal to particular artistic media, including

---

[25] For discussion of "Omaruru" and her attitude toward Jewish emigration, see Michael Philipp, "Die Thematisierung des 'Jüdischen' im George-Kreis vor und nach 1933," in *"Verkannte brüder"? Stefan George und das deutsch-jüdische Bürgertum zwischen Jahrhundertwende und Emigration*, ed. Gert Mattenklott, Michael Philipp, and Julius H. Schoeps (Hildesheim: Georg Olms Verlag, 2001): pp. 201–218; Ulrich Raulff, *Kreis ohne Meister: Stefan Georges Nachleben* (München: Beck, 2009): pp. 150–52; Schiewer, "Das Problem," pp. 90–93; and Hillman, *Wandering Jews*, pp. 382–85.

[26] https://www.wlb-stuttgart.de/sammlungen/stefan-george-archiv/bestand/nachlaesse-george-kreis/teilnachlass-edith-landmann/.

[27] See Dahlstrom, "Edith Landmann-Kalischer," for an overview.

poetry, painting, and architecture. And she returns to many of the themes from the beginning of her career by exploring the relationship beauty has to goodness and truth and the importance of beauty in an ideal human life.

Over the course of her adult life, in spite of the challenges she faced as a Jewish woman writing philosophy in German, Landmann-Kalischer built an impressive oeuvre that reflected her ongoing commitment to exploring what aesthetic, moral, and epistemic value are, and why they matter in our lives and in our world. With this biographical sketch in place, I shall now narrow my focus to the three early essays included in this volume: "On the Cognitive Value of Aesthetic Judgment," "On Artistic Truth," and "Philosophy of Values." In the next two sections, I take a closer look at the philosophical background of these essays, focusing on her relationship to phenomenology and to philosophical aesthetics in Germany, in §2 and §3 respectively. I then turn to a detailed discussion of each essay in §§4-6.

§2. Landmann-Kalischer and Phenomenology

As I noted earlier, Landmann-Kalischer began her career at an exciting moment in German philosophy when the field of phenomenology first emerged amid the psychology, Neo-Kantianism, and positivism prevalent at the turn of the twentieth century. Indeed, as a mark of its nascence, early on philosophers interested in classic phenomenological issues, such as the nature of consciousness, lived experience, and intentionality, were more likely to present themselves as engaged in a kind of psychology, rather than in phenomenology per se. In her early work, Landmann-Kalischer was no exception: although she references 'phenomenology' a couple of times in "Philosophy of Values,"[28] her explicit point of orientation is psychology. But her philosophical-psychology is one that takes its cue from the vision of descriptive psychology laid out by Brentano that catalyzed the phenomenological movement. To the extent that we can label someone a 'phenomenologist' who takes Brentano's descriptive psychology as their starting point, Landmann-Kalischer can thus be classified as an early phenomenologist.

---

[28] See, for example, PV 171–72/63, where she references a "purely phenomenological treatment of thinking and acting." She also engages with Husserl's distinction between 'ideal' and 'real' sciences in the *Logical Investigations* in PV 182–83/74–76. However, in *Die Transcendenz des Erkennens* Husserl is a major foil for her. (In her diaries, she also records meeting Husserl for a 'tea hour' in late 1927/early 1928).

And appreciating the phenomenological strain in her thought is helpful for understanding her method and the contribution that she aims to make in the three essays included in this volume.

This said, Landmann-Kalischer's relationship to phenomenology is complex. She did not belong to the Munich or Göttingen Circles of phenomenology, nor did she adhere to Husserl's transcendental phenomenology. Indeed, given her interdisciplinary inclinations and location in Switzerland, she did not clearly belong to any single philosophical school in Germany or Austria, phenomenological or otherwise. Nevertheless she can be fruitfully situated among a group of thinkers known variously as the 'Graz School' or 'Austrian phenomenologists,' which included Meinong and Meinong's students, von Ehrenfels, Witasek, Fischer, Radaković, and (Benussi-) Liel.[29] Wary of the reductive attitude of the positivists and the transcendental orientation of the Neo-Kantians, these thinkers took as their starting point the descriptive psychology that Brentano laid out in *Psychology from an Empirical Standpoint*. And while they offered descriptive accounts of mental phenomena and lived experience, they also paid close attention to the objects we experience and became well known for their 'object theory' [*Gegenstandstheorie*].

Though Landmann-Kalischer was geographically distant from this group, the Brentano-inspired work of Meinong, von Ehrenfels, and Witasek served as one of her major touchstones in the first decade of her career.[30] Indeed, in the three essays included in this volume, we find her pursuing an approach that in many ways parallels the descriptive psychology and object theory developed in the Graz School.

In adopting this approach, she commits herself to an empirical method—a commitment that she will affirm later in *Die Transcendenz des Erkennens* (1923), in which she explicitly rejects the transcendental method of phenomenology that Husserl defends in *Ideas* (1913). However, like the members

---

[29] There is some question as to what extent the Graz School can be considered an early school of phenomenology (see Vendrell-Ferran, "On the Analogy"). Here, I characterize them as a phenomenological school to the extent that they take their cue from Brentano's method of descriptive psychology.

[30] She also corresponded with Meinong from 1905 to 1916 (see Meinong [1965]: pp. 154–98). For a discussion of the relationship between Landmann-Kalischer's value theory and that of Brentano and Meinong, see Vendrell-Ferran, "Tatsache, Wert und menschliche Sensibilität: Die Brentanoschule und die Gestaltpsychologie," in *Feeling and Value, Willing and Action*, ed. Marta Wehrle and Maren Ubiali (Cham: Springer, 2014): pp. 141–62 and "On the Analogy." See note 13 regarding Landmann-Kalischer's influence on Meinong's later value theory. For a discussion of the relationship between her aesthetic theory and that of Brentano, Meinong, and von Ehrenfels, see Reicher, "Ästhetische Werte" and Reicher-Marek, "Dispositionalist Accounts."

of the Graz School, she also extends the Brentanian method in dynamic directions as part of her effort to elucidate value. And it is against this dynamic Brentanian backdrop that she develops the theory of aesthetic, moral, and epistemic value that she defends in her early philosophy.

In order to further clarify these phenomenological dimensions of her project, let's consider how a Brentanian conception of, one, the subject matter and, two, the method of descriptive psychology shape her approach, as well as how she innovates this program in her work.

Beginning with the subject matter of descriptive psychology, in *Psychology from an Empirical Standpoint*, Brentano characterizes descriptive psychology as the "science of mental phenomena" (*Psychology from an Empirical Standpoint*, 19). By 'mental phenomena', Brentano has in mind conscious mental acts or lived experiences [*Erlebnisse*], for example, acts of perceiving, thinking, or feeling. Seminal to Brentano's conception of mental phenomena is the claim that they involve 'intentionality' or directedness toward objects. Insofar as this is the case, within Brentano's framework, if we are to make sense of mental phenomena, then we cannot just investigate the subjective side of mental phenomena, that is, the conscious, mental acts involved; we also need to heed the objective side of mental phenomena, that is, the intentional objects of those acts.

In keeping with this conception of the subject matter of phenomenology, Landmann-Kalischer conceives of descriptive psychology as a science of mental phenomena (see, e.g., AT 104/495, PV 171–72/63). And she inherits Brentano's conception of mental phenomena as having both a 'subjective' and 'objective' side:

> it is... correct for us to distinguish a subjective and an objective side in every lived experience. Sensing, representing, feeling, and willing [*Empfinden, Vorstellen, Fühlen, Wollen*] are, in each case, a mental, subjective lived experience; the sensed, represented, felt, and willed [*das Empfundene, Vorgestellte, Gefühlte, Gewollte*] are something objective [*Objektives*]....
> Act and content [*Akt und Inhalt*] can be distinguished ... in every mental lived experience [*psychisches Erlebnis*]. (PV 146/35)[31]

---

[31] She also explores the relationship between the subjective and objective sides of lived experience at length in *Die Transcendenz des Erkennens*, where she investigates the relations of intentionality and transcendence between the two.

For Landmann-Kalischer, then, descriptive psychology has as its subject matter both the subjective side of lived experience (conscious mental acts) and the objective side of lived experience (the objects that we are conscious of). For example, from Landmann-Kalischer's perspective, were I to analyze the perception of Ruysch's *Still Life with Bouquet of Flowers and Plums* as a descriptive psychologist, I would need to attend not only to the mental act of perceiving the painting (the subjective side) but also to the painting perceived (the objective side). And in her early work, Landmann-Kalischer orients herself, in particular, toward the subjective and objective sides of our lived experience of aesthetic, moral, and epistemic value. In this spirit, she analyzes, on the subjective side, the conscious mental acts involved in our experience of beauty, goodness, and truth, and, on the objective side, the beauty, goodness, and truth that we experience.

Let's turn now to the influence of Brentano's method on Landmann-Kalischer and how she updates it. For Brentano, descriptive psychology should be methodologically understood as a kind of science, which studies mental phenomena 'from an empirical standpoint.' However, he contrasts the method of descriptive psychology with the 'genetic' method that is typically deployed in psychology. According to Brentano, the 'genetic' method of psychology aims at a causal explanation of mental phenomena. By contrast the descriptive method endeavors to 'describe' mental phenomena as they are given in "inner perception" (*Descriptive Psychology*, pp. 31–32; see also *Psychology from an Empirical Standpoint*, pp. 29, fn1). As Brentano envisions it, the descriptive psychologist proceeds by noticing, analyzing, and classifying those given mental phenomena, with the goal of determining the general laws that govern them (*Descriptive Psychology*, pp. 31–32).

Although many of Brentano's early followers were sympathetic to the method of descriptive psychology, some, like the members of the Graz School, objected that this method could not do justice to the objective side of mental phenomena. Indeed, many regarded this methodological shortcoming as related to an ambiguity in Brentano's view about whether the objects that mental phenomena are directed at are ultimately immanent or transcendent with respect to consciousness. In response, Meinong and his followers sought to develop the objective side of the Brentanian project; hence the prominence of 'object theory' in the Graz School.[32]

---

[32] See Meinong's "On Objects of Higher Order and Their Relationship to Internal Perception" (1899) (in *Alexius Meinong Gesamtausgabe*, Vol. II, ed. Rudolf Halle, trans. Schubert Kalsi, 1978: pp. 137–208) and "The Theory of Objects" (1904) (in *Realism and the Background of*

Landmann-Kalischer's method betrays an affinity with both Brentano and the development of descriptive psychology in the Graz School. In keeping with Brentano, she eschews metaphysical approaches to mental phenomena in favor of an empirically based approach, modeled on natural science. And she regards the method of descriptive psychology as particularly apt for investigating the subjective side of lived experience: to understand mental phenomena, we should take as our starting point the 'facts' of our lived experience,[33] and proceed to "analyze the complex of consciousness, classif[y] their elements, and draw up lawful relations between them" (AT 104/495).[34]

However, as for members of the Graz School, according to Landmann-Kalischer, a complete science of mental phenomena requires that we also investigate the objects these mental phenomena relate to. For this reason, she claims that in addition to descriptive psychology, we need "objective sciences" that investigate the objects of consciousness (PV 170/62). Landmann-Kalischer has an encompassing and controversial view of what the relevant 'objects' and 'objective sciences' are. For in addition to acknowledging physical objects that are investigated by physical sciences, she treats values, like beauty, goodness, and truth, as objects that are to be investigated by 'sciences of value'. And it is in this spirit that she casts aesthetics as the 'science of beauty', ethics as the 'science of the good', and logic as the 'science of the true' (see PV 170/62).

This said, she nevertheless claims that descriptive psychology is a 'presupposition' of these sciences of value (PV 170/62). On her view, these objective sciences of value are to take as their starting point our lived experience of value, and their task is to elucidate the valuable objects and law-governed relations among valuable objects that we experience. For Landmann-Kalischer, it is thus the pairing of objective sciences of value with descriptive psychology that is required to do justice to the subjective and objective sides

---

Phenomenology, ed. R. M. Chisholm [Atascadero, CA: Ridgeview, 1991]: pp. 76–117). In addition to 'object theory', others sought to clarify the objective side in light of the content-object (*Inhalt-Gegenstand*) distinction (see, e.g., Twardowski's *On the Content and Object of Presentations* [1894], trans. R. Grossmann [The Hague: M. Nijhoff, 1977] and Husserl's *Logical Investigations* [1900/01]: Volume 2, trans. J. N. Findlay [London: Routledge, 1973]).

[33] See, for example, PV 144/32, 175-76/68–69; CV 42/304.

[34] She is, however, critical of Brentano's reliance on 'inner perception' (see PV 79–80/72–73). She objects that inner perception can only make us aware of a narrow set of mental phenomena, that outer perception can be as certain as inner perception, and that when Brentano relies on inner perception as evidence of the correctness of judgment, his view is circular because he treats correctness of judgment as the criterion of evidence.

of the mental phenomena involved in value; hence a pairing that the science of such mental phenomena ultimately calls for.

In addition to expanding the Brentanian vision along these objective lines, as I noted earlier, Landmann-Kalischer's approach to phenomenology is marked by a commitment to drawing on experimentally informed sciences, like experimental psychology, in order to elucidate mental phenomena. For example, she argues that experimental psychology can shed light on the stimulus-response pairings manifest in our lived experience, as well as on the conditions in which deception or illusion might arise. However, in keeping with her Brentanian outlook, Landmann-Kalischer does not think that the sorts of causal explanations of mental phenomena offered in experimental psychology should supplant those offered through descriptive psychology. She, instead, sees these efforts as complementary insofar as they illuminate the subjective and objective sides of mental phenomena and their relation. And this picture of an empirically informed phenomenology is one of the distinctive marks of Landmann-Kalischer's program in these three essays—a program that in many ways prefigures models of phenomenology informed by psychology and cognitive science today.[35]

In the three essays included this volume, Landmann-Kalischer thus offers a theory of aesthetic, moral, and epistemic value that is innovatively informed by a Brentanian conception of descriptive psychology and that, in many ways, parallels the efforts of the members of the Graz School. And insofar as she takes her creative cue from this Brentanian approach, these three essays represent a dynamic moment in early phenomenology, as Landmann-Kalischer defends an empirically informed account of value that is meant to do justice as much to our lived experience of value, as to value itself.

§3. Landmann-Kalischer and German Philosophical Aesthetics

In addition to their contribution to value theory, the three essays in this volume represent Landmann-Kalischer's groundbreaking work in aesthetics. Indeed, over the course of these essays, she develops a systematic and

---

[35] See, for example, the work of Shaun Gallagher, Alva Noë, Evan Thompson, and Dan Zahavi. See also the journal *Phenomenology and the Cognitive Sciences*, edited by Shaun Gallagher and Dan Zahavi.

original aesthetic theory, which challenges the major programs in German philosophical aesthetics dominant at the turn of the twentieth century.

As I noted in §1, foundational to her aesthetic theory is an argument to the effect that beauty is something that is in the world, rather than merely in the eye of the beholder, and that our aesthetic experience is a site of pleasure, cognition, and knowledge. To appreciate the ingenuity of her position, I want to consider it against the backdrop of the aesthetic theories of Immanuel Kant, Neo-Kantianism, Romanticism, German idealism, and philosophical-psychologists that she offers an alternative to.[36]

In the *Critique of the Power of Judgment* (1790), Kant laid out an influential aesthetic theory that set the agenda for philosophical aesthetics in Germany in the century to come. Central to Kant's aesthetics is an analysis of judgments of the beautiful. According to Kant, aesthetic judgments are a distinctive kind of judgment: unlike 'cognitive' judgments, which are based on a property of objects, judgments of the beautiful are 'aesthetic' judgments, which are based on our feeling of pleasure in an object. For Kant, then, beauty is not to be understood as a property of objects that we cognize, but rather as a predicate we attribute to objects when they bring about a certain feeling of pleasure in us. Famously, Kant characterizes this feeling of pleasure as one that is 'disinterested', that is, not based on our interest or desire for the object, and that has its source in contemplation.

However, also famously, Kant argues that even though judgments of the beautiful are based on pleasure, they are not private, but rather universally shareable. That is to say, *per* Kant, when we judge something to be beautiful, we think that everyone else should agree with that judgment. For example, from Kant's perspective, when I judge Ruysch's *Still Life with Bouquet of Flowers and Plums* to be beautiful, I am not judging the painting to be beautiful 'for me'; I am judging it to be beautiful 'for us', and I think everyone should agree with my judgment. Central to Kant's defense of this universalist picture of judgments of the beautiful is a transcendental analysis of the a priori conditions that reflect what all human beings share in common, which make it possible for us to share judgments of the beautiful in this way.

In his aesthetics, Kant thus rejects a cognitive picture of aesthetic experience in favor of a hedonic picture, according to which aesthetic experience

---

[36] In *Georgika* (Heidelberg: Weiss, 1920, revised edition in 1924) Landmann-Kalischer also engages with Nietzsche's aesthetics, especially with his notions of the Apollonian and Dionysian in *On the Birth of Tragedy* (see Dahlstrom, "Edith Landmann-Kalischer," for discussion).

is based on a distinctive kind of disinterested pleasure that has its source in contemplation. However, he also rejects a kind of subjectivism about judgments of the beautiful that would treat them as a purely private affair in favor of a transcendentally grounded conception of them as universally shareable. Carrying forward the Kantian project later in the nineteenth century, Neo-Kantians, such as Hermann Cohen, Wilhelm Windelband, and Jonas Cohn,[37] endorsed this transcendental approach to aesthetics and this gloss of aesthetic experience in hedonist and universalist terms.

Though influential, Kant's aesthetics was not without its rivals. In the late eighteenth and early nineteenth centuries, the Romantics, like Novalis and the Schlegels, and German idealists, like Schelling and Hegel, offered a powerful alternative to Kantian aesthetics, according to which beauty and art are paths to cognition and knowledge after all. Hegel, for example, argued that alongside religion and philosophy, art is one of the cultural ways in which the 'absolute' reveals itself to us, and that it is through our engagement with beautiful art that we come to know absolute truth.[38] In defending this cognitivist program, the aesthetics of Romanticism and German idealism harkened back to a pre-Kantian moment in German aesthetics in which rationalists, like Alexander Baumgarten, defended a view of aesthetic experience as a source of cognition.[39] However, the Romantics and German idealists couched this cognitivist insight in a broader idealist system in which art constitutes a way of knowing the 'absolute'.

Veering away from the transcendental approach of Kant and the metaphysical trappings of Romanticism and German idealism, philosophical aesthetics in Germany in the later nineteenth century veered increasingly in psychological directions. In this vein, Brentano and Brentanians, like Meinong, von Ehrenfels, and Witasek, offered accounts of the conscious mental acts and objects intended in aesthetic experience.[40] Early on, for example, Meinong analyzed aesthetic experience in terms of an emotional,

---

[37] For a discussion of Neo-Kantian aesthetics, see Paul Guyer, "What Happened to Kant in Neo-Kantian Aesthetics? Cohen, Cohn, and Dilthey," *The Philosophical Forum* 39(2) (2008): pp. 143–76 and Robert Clewis, "Aesthetic Normativity in Freiburg: Jonas Cohn as an Alternative to Kant," *History of Philosophy Quarterly* 39(2) (2022): pp. 183–97.

[38] See Lydia Moland, *Hegel's Aesthetics: The Art of Idealism* (Oxford: Oxford University Press, 2019) for an overview of Hegel's aesthetics.

[39] Landmann-Kalischer connects Baumgarten and German idealism together along these lines at the outset of "On Artistic Truth" (AT 64–65/457–58).

[40] For a discussion of the aesthetic theory of the Graz School of Meinong, von Ehrenfels, Witasek, among others, see Reicher, "Value Facts," Reicher-Marek, "Dispositionalist Accounts," and the essays collected in Raspa, *The Aesthetics of the Graz School*.

rather than a cognitive mental act, and aesthetic properties, like beauty, in subjectivist terms.[41] Meanwhile Witasek developed a robust aesthetic theory in which he analyzes aesthetic experience in hedonic terms, and aesthetic properties, like beauty, as 'ideal', rather than 'real'.[42]

In a different psychologically inspired vein, Robert Vischer, Johannes Vokelt, and Theodor Lipps offered accounts of aesthetic experience that turned on the notion of empathy [*Einfühlung*].[43] According to this empathy-based theory, aesthetic experience involves a psychological process in which we project our inner experiences, which are accompanied by pleasure or displeasure, onto objects, and experience them as beautiful or ugly as a result.

Though this overview by no means exhausts the landscape of philosophical aesthetics in Germany in the nineteenth century, these Kantian/Neo-Kantian, Romantic, German idealist, and psychological trends were the most influential for Landmann-Kalischer's composition of the three essays included in this volume. Indeed, much of the originality in Landmann-Kalischer's position stems from the ways in which she draws on the insights from these traditions that she sees as apt, while discarding what she deems unfruitful.

From the Kantian tradition, as is evident already in her dissertation, Landmann-Kalischer is sympathetic to a conception of aesthetic experience as involving 'contemplation' and 'disinterested' pleasure. However, she rejects the Kantian claim that aesthetic experience is not cognitive. Instead, in keeping with the tradition of Baumgarten, Romanticism, and German idealism, she argues that judgments of the beautiful are cognitive in nature, and that our experience of art is conducive to cognition and truth. That said, she also eschews the metaphysical approach of the Romantics and German idealists, as well as the transcendental approach of Kant and the Neo-Kantians, in favor of a psychologically inspired approach. But, unlike many of the other psychological aestheticians who endorsed a subjectivist theory of beauty, she pairs this psychological analysis of the mental acts involved in

---

[41] See note 13 for discussion of Landmann-Kalischer's influence on his later more realist position.
[42] For a discussion of Witasek's aesthetics, see Smith, "Pleasure and Its Modifications," Raspa's Introduction to *The Aesthetics of the Graz School* and Reicher-Marek "Dispositionalist Accounts."
[43] As noted earlier, Landmann-Kalischer wrote a lengthy review of Lipps's *Grundlegung der Ästhetik* [Foundation of Aesthetics] in 1903. For a discussion of psychological aesthetics in Germany, see Christian Allesch, *Geschichte der psychologischen Ästhetik* (Göttingen: Verlag für Psychologie, 1987) and "Fechner, Brentano, Stumpf. A Controversy on Beauty and Aesthetics," *Paradigmi. Rivista di critica filosofica* 3 (2017): pp. 11–23 and Paul Guyer, *A History of Modern Aesthetics*, Vol. 3 (Cambridge: Cambridge University Press, 2014), Ch. 1, who also addresses its influence outside of Germany, for example, on Vernon Lee and Ethel Puffer.

aesthetic experience together with a realist account of beauty as something that is in the world.

In her aesthetics, Landmann-Kalischer thus defends a systematic position in which she synthesizes a hedonist commitment to aesthetic experience involving a feeling of disinterested pleasure, a cognitivist commitment to aesthetic experience involving cognition and knowledge, and a realist commitment to beauty as a property of things, rather than something we merely project onto things. In so doing, she not only offers a sweeping alternative to the orthodox Kantian, idealist, and psychological aesthetics prevalent in Germany at the time but also a vision of aesthetic experience, beauty, and art that bears on our contemporary interest in these issues.

Over the past two sections, I have situated the three essays included in this volume against the backdrop of Landmann-Kalischer's relationship to early phenomenology and to philosophical aesthetics in Germany. With this background in mind, in what follows I turn to the substance of these essays and offer an overview of the major theses and arguments that she develops in each. As I noted earlier, these sections are intended as a prelude to each essay and readers are invited to return to these sections in advance of reading each essay.

§4. "On the Cognitive Value of Aesthetic Judgments"

In "On the Cognitive Value of Aesthetic Judgments," Landmann-Kalischer is motivated by two main sets of questions.[44] The first is a set of questions about the nature of beauty. Should beauty be understood as merely in the eye of the beholder? Or should beauty be understood as something that is in some sense part of the world? The second is a set of questions about the nature of our aesthetic experience of beauty. Is this experience cognitive or non-cognitive in nature? And does pleasure play a constitutive role in it?

As she indicates in the Introduction and Chapter 1, Landmann-Kalischer's primary target in this piece is, what she terms, a 'subjectivist' answer to these

---

[44] For another discussion of this essay set against the backdrop of contemporary questions about 'demarcation' (what if anything distinguishes the aesthetic domain from the cognitive and moral domains) and 'normativity' (what if any kind of normativity does the aesthetic domain involve), see Samantha Matherne, "Edith Landmann-Kalischer on Aesthetic Demarcation and Normativity," *British Journal of Aesthetics* 60(3) (2020): pp. 315–34.

questions.⁴⁵ In response to the question about the nature of beauty, the subjectivist claims that beauty is not a property of an object; it is, instead, something that subjects project onto objects. As for the second question, the subjectivist maintains that aesthetic experience involves judgments that are not cognitive, but rather expressive of how a subject feels.

Taking aim at these subjectivist positions, in "On the Cognitive Value of Aesthetic Judgments" Landmann-Kalischer argues that beauty should be understood in realist terms as a property of objects and that our experience of beauty is at once hedonic and cognitive in nature. As the subtitle to this article suggests ("A Comparison of Sensory Judgments and Value Judgments"), in order to defend her position, Landmann-Kalischer employs a secondary quality analogy.⁴⁶ In pursuing this strategy, she anticipates the strategy that John McDowell and David Wiggins deploy toward the end of the twentieth century: motivating the idea that value is, in some sense, part of the 'fabric of the world' by likening value to secondary qualities, like color.⁴⁷

There are two aspects to Landmann-Kalischer's secondary quality analogy. First, in order to help motivate the realist claim that beauty is a property of objects, she argues that it is a real property of objects in the way that sensory qualities, like color, are real properties of objects. Second, in order to help motivate the cognitivist claim, she argues that just as we can make cognitive judgments about sensory qualities on the basis of sensations, we can make cognitive judgments about beauty on the basis of a feeling of pleasure. Let's take a closer look at these realist, cognitivist, and hedonist aspects of her view of beauty, and how the secondary quality analogy bears on them.

4.1 Realism about Beauty

Landmann-Kalischer is a realist about beauty to the extent that she claims that beauty is a property of objects.⁴⁸ However, she qualifies her realism by

---

⁴⁵ As representatives of subjectivism, in the Introduction she singles out Alexius Meinong (at least in his early work), Georg Simmel, Christian von Ehrenfels, Joseph Kreibig, Jonas Cohn, and Max Weber.

⁴⁶ For Witasek's response to her secondary quality analogy, see "Über ästhetische Objektivität," *Zeitschrift für Philosophie und philosophische Kritik* 157 (1915): pp. 87–114, 179–99.

⁴⁷ See John McDowell, "Values and Secondary Qualities" and "Aesthetic Value, Objectivity, and the Fabric of the World," in *Mind, Value, and Reality* (Cambridge, MA: Harvard University Press, 1998): pp. 112–50 and David Wiggins, "A Sensible Subjectivism," in *Needs, Values, Truth: Essays in the Philosophy of Value* (Oxford: Blackwell, 1987): pp. 185–211.

⁴⁸ Two other notes on her theory of beauty in "On the Cognitive Value of Aesthetic Judgments." First, as emerges in Chapter 6, she conceives of beauty as a 'basic quality' that can be specified into

claiming that beauty is also "subjectively conditioned": it is a property that is, in some sense, dependent upon subjects (CV 7–8/267). Landmann-Kalischer thus rejects the view that in order for a property to be real it must be entirely mind-independent, and she endorses a realism that is consistent with properties that are, in some sense, mind-dependent.

In order to spell out how beauty can be at once real and subjectively conditioned, Landmann-Kalischer appeals to the idea that beauty is a response-dependent property of an object: it is a property of an object that brings about an appropriate response in appropriate observers in appropriate conditions.[49] In keeping with a tradition in aesthetics that reaches back to the eighteenth century, Landmann-Kalischer identifies the appropriate response as a feeling of pleasure. More specifically, in a Kantian vein, she identifies it as a 'pure' or 'disinterested' feeling of pleasure, which amounts to a feeling of pleasure that is motivated not by the subject's personal interests or desires, but by the object (CV 10/270). She understands the relation between beauty in the object and this feeling of pleasure to be a 'law-governed' relation of dependence (CV 14/275). And she devotes a lengthy analysis to what an appropriate observer in appropriate conditions amounts to. For example, she highlights the various ways in which our interests, prejudices, moods, and so on, might give rise to aesthetic 'deceptions' or 'illusions' (*Täuschungen*) in which we think our pleasure is motivated by the object, when it is, in fact, motivated by something other than the object (see Section II, Chapters 3 and 4). And ultimately, for Landmann-Kalischer, once we think of beauty along these response-dependent lines, then we have a model for understanding how beauty can be at once real and subjectively conditioned: it is real because it is a property of an object and it is subjectively conditioned because this property stands in a lawfully governed relation to a disinterested feeling of pleasure.

To repeat, in order to motivate this view of beauty, Landmann-Kalischer appeals to the idea that beauty is a response-dependent property of objects

---

"different forms, modifications, or kinds of beauty. . . . The graceful and dignified, the grotesque and lovely, the sentimental and naïve, the comic and tragic" (CV 58–59/323). In other words, she conceives of beauty as a determinate with many determinables. Second, she treats beauty as a property that has its 'foundation' in other sensible qualities of an object (CV 16–17/278–79). This view finds echoes in Sibley's treatment of aesthetic properties as grounded in non-aesthetic properties in "Aesthetic Concepts," *Philosophical Review* 68(4) (1959): pp. 421–50.

[49] Reicher-Marek, "Dispositionalist Accounts" frames Landmann-Kalischer's position in terms of 'dispositionalism' and discusses it in the context of the aesthetics of Bolzano and members of the Graz School, like Meinong, Witasek, and von Ehrenfels.

in the way that secondary qualities are. Take color, for example. On her view, color is a property of an object that brings about an appropriate response, viz., a sensation, in appropriate observers in appropriate conditions.[50] Beauty, she claims, should be understood in analogous response-dependent terms. The reason she appeals to this analogy is because she thinks that many of us are already inclined to think that even though color is response-dependent, it is still something real that we can make true or false judgments about. And she hopes to parlay our sympathy for this view of color into sympathy for a similar view of beauty as at once real and subjectively conditioned, qua a response-dependent property of an object.

4.2 Cognitivism and Hedonism about the Aesthetic Experience of Beauty

Landmann-Kalischer pairs this realist account of beauty with a cognitivist and hedonist account of our aesthetic experience of beauty. Her account is cognitivist to the extent that she thinks aesthetic experience involves us making truth-apt judgments in which we attribute beauty to objects. And her account is hedonist to the extent that she takes these cognitive judgments to be based on a feeling of pleasure we have in response to the object. As I just noted, this latter feature of Landmann-Kalischer's view belongs to a long-standing tradition in aesthetics that takes our immediate response to beauty to be a feeling of pleasure. And in this regard, she agrees with the subjectivist: aesthetic experience begins with a subject's feeling pleasure in response to an object. However, she argues that it is a mistake to draw the non-cognitivist conclusion that aesthetic experience merely expresses a subject's liking for something. Instead, she argues that although aesthetic experiences involve pleasure, this pleasure serves as the basis for us making cognitive judgments in which we attribute beauty to objects. And it is this "cognition through feeling" that she takes to be at the heart of aesthetic experience (CV 14/275).

In the course of defending this position in Chapter 2 ("Feeling and Cognition"), Landmann-Kalischer argues that the subjectivist makes the assumption that feelings are a "purely subjective element of consciousness,"

---

[50] More specifically, she analyzes color and other secondary qualities as properties of objects that "rest upon properties of objects that we can only grasp indirectly in the chemical laboratory" (CV 17/278).

that is, that feelings refer to the subject's state alone and not to the object (CV 13/273). However, she argues that we should recognize a difference between a "subjectively conditioned" feeling, which refers to a private state of the subject, and an "objectively conditioned" feeling, which refers to an object (CV 15/276). And she insists that although some feelings, like feeling gloomy, are subjectively conditioned, the feeling of disinterested pleasure that beauty brings about in us is objectively conditioned.

According to Landmann-Kalischer, once we recognize that our feeling of pleasure in the beautiful is objectively conditioned, then a path opens up for understanding how the aesthetic experience of beauty could involve cognition. For, on her view, the feeling of pleasure we have in response to beauty serves as the basis for us cognizing the beauty of an object. Landmann-Kalischer analyzes this cognition, more specifically, in terms of us making a cognitive judgment in which we attribute beauty to the object and which can be true if the object is beautiful.

Once again pursuing the secondary quality analogy, Landmann-Kalischer argues that we should think of these aesthetic judgments about beauty as the counterparts of perceptual judgments about secondary qualities. For just as in the perceptual domain we make cognitive judgments in which we attribute, say, a color to an object on the basis of the sensation that it brings about in us, in the aesthetic domain we make cognitive judgments in which we attribute beauty to an object on the basis of the feeling of pleasure that it brings about in us. And just as a perceptual judgment, like 'The flower is orange' can be true if the flower has the property of being orange, an aesthetic judgment, like 'Ruysch's *Still Life with Bouquet of Flowers and Plums* is beautiful' can be true if the painting has the property of being beautiful. In this way, Landmann-Kalischer motivates the idea that aesthetic judgments about beauty can be true and objective.

This said, Landmann-Kalischer does not think that every aesthetic judgment is true and objective. She, instead, devotes Section II to an analysis of the ways in which our aesthetic judgments can fail to be, in her words, 'objectively valid', 'correct', or 'reliable'.[51] To this end, she explicates a set of negative

---

[51] In this discussion, she distinguishes between two different forms of aesthetic judgments: judgments of a 'subjective' form ('I like X') and judgments of an 'objective' form ('X is beautiful') (CV 20/281). And she lays out the criteria for making 'reliable' judgments of both forms. However, in "Philosophy of Values," she argues that the subjective form is 'derivative' of the 'objective form', and, for this reason, I shall focus on the objective form here (PV 163–64/54).

and positive conditions that we must meet in order to make an objectively valid judgment of the form 'X is beautiful'.

In the negative vein in Chapter 4, Landmann-Kalischer argues that an objectively valid aesthetic judgment is one in which we are not deceived or subject to aesthetic illusion. And she devotes an illuminating discussion to various psychological, physiological, and physical sources of aesthetic illusion and deception. She traces many of these illusions back to us having a mistaken grasp of what sort of pleasure we are feeling: we judge something to be beautiful because we think our pleasure is motivated by the object, when the pleasure is, in fact, motivated by extraneous factors, like our personal preferences, prejudices, or moods. And her thought is that just as we are deceived in taking a straight stick in water to be curved, so, too, are we deceived when we take an object to be beautiful under the influence of extra-aesthetic factors like these. For Landmann-Kalischer, then, the negative criterion for making an objectively valid aesthetic judgment is to not be taken in by aesthetic illusions.

In Chapter 5, Landmann-Kalischer then turns to the positive criteria of a true aesthetic judgment, which she identifies as the criteria any judgment must meet to be objective. In this vein she claims that objectively valid judgments must not only be consistent with the formal claims of logic but also agree with other judgments. Landmann-Kalischer alights on four sets of judgments an objectively valid aesthetic judgment can agree with: the individual's own aesthetic judgments about the same object over time and in different circumstances; the individual's aesthetic judgments about other objects; aesthetic judgments of other human beings; and judgments in science, including judgments in psychological aesthetics about sources of aesthetic illusion (see CV 48–49/312).[52] And on her view, the degree of objective validity that an aesthetic judgment has will turn on the degree of agreement that is operative.

For Landmann-Kalischer, then, although aesthetic experience begins with a feeling of pleasure in response to an object, this is not where aesthetic experience ends. On her view, this pleasure serves as the basis for us making cognitive judgments about the beauty of objects. And it is this "cognition through feeling" that she takes aesthetic experience to ultimately involve (CV 15/276).

---

[52] She, once again, draws on the secondary quality analogy to illustrate what this sort of agreement looks like by comparing the aesthetic case with symmetrical forms of agreement that are involved in sensory judgments, viz., agreement with the person's other judgments internal to the same sense, with their judgments across multiple sense modalities, with other people's sensory judgments, and with judgments in science about sensory qualities (CV 44/307).

Stepping back, in this article, as part of her argument against subjectivist approaches to aesthetics, Landmann-Kalischer deploys a secondary quality analogy in which she likens beauty to secondary qualities, like color. Drawing on this analogy, she defends a realist view of beauty to the effect that beauty is a response-dependent property of an object that is at once real and subjectively conditioned. She also advances a view about aesthetic experience to the effect that it involves making cognitive judgments about the beauty of objects on the basis of a feeling of pleasure they bring about in us. In defending this latter view, she incorporates hedonism into a cognitivist theory of aesthetic judgment, and she lays out standards she thinks we need to hold ourselves accountable to if we aspire to objectivity in the aesthetic domain.[53]

§5. "On Artistic Truth"

In the second essay in this volume, "On Artistic Truth," Landmann-Kalischer continues to develop her cognitivist program in aesthetics, this time defending a cognitivist thesis about art. To this end, she argues that our experience of art is cognitive insofar as art conveys a distinctive truth to us about "subjective reality," that is, the reality of consciousness, mental phenomena, and lived experience (AT 68/460).

In the Introduction, Landmann-Kalischer situates this cognitivist approach to art in a long-standing tradition in German aesthetics, which treats art as a vehicle for cognition and truth. She notes that this cognitivist orientation animated the early efforts in German aesthetics, for example, in the work of Johann Christoph Gottsched and Baumgarten, and was carried forward in the efforts of Romantics and German idealists, like Schelling and Hegel. However, in spite of this cognitivist precedent in German aesthetics, Landmann-Kalischer notes that there is a powerful exception: the aesthetics of Kant. For Kant, Landmann-Kalischer claims, "any sort of cognition

---

[53] It is perhaps worth noting that on Landmann-Kalischer's view, although aesthetic judgments must be made on the basis of feelings of pleasure, we could make another kind of cognitive judgment about beauty on the basis of concepts. Indeed, she takes this sort of conceptual judgment to be the kind that is operative in the science of aesthetics, which she discusses at more length in "Philosophy of Values." So, in order to make aesthetic judgments in which we cognize beauty, feeling is required. However, we can make conceptual judgments in which we cognize beauty for which feeling would not be required.

through art was out of the question" (AT 65/458).[54] And in spite of the cognitivist precedent in German aesthetics, Landmann-Kalischer argues that at the outset of the twentieth century aesthetics has "overwhelmingly gone back to Kant" (AT 66–67/459). It is precisely this sort of Kantian non-cognitivism that Landmann-Kalischer takes aim at in her cognitivist theory of art.

At the center of Landmann-Kalischer's cognitivist view of art is the claim that art provides us with cognition of a certain sort of truth. However, unlike the German idealists who identified this truth as truth about the 'absolute', she describes it as truth about 'subjective reality'. In order to develop this claim, in Section Two ("Objective and Subjective Reality"), she distinguishes between two sorts of reality: 'objective' reality, which is the reality of the external world outside of us, and 'subjective' reality, which is the reality of the mental world within us. So understood, subjective reality encompasses the reality of the subjective side of mental phenomenal: the reality of our conscious mental acts or lived experience. Although she thinks that art can disclose to us truths about objective reality, she argues that this is something 'contingent', rather than essential to the nature of art (CV 83–84/476). What is essential to art, on her view, is that it conveys truths about subjective reality:

> Art . . . mirrors and portrays the mental world. . . . Just as we would never see our face were it not for a mirror, so, too, we would never see our own inner life opposite us—were it not for the mirror of art. Only art exhibits it for us. Only through art can we come to know it. (AT 70–71/463)

In Section Three ("The Elements of Subjective Reality and their Mirroring in Art"), Landmann-Kalischer proceeds by distinguishing five basic 'elements' of subjective reality, that is, domains within consciousness, and exploring how art enables us to cognize truths that pertain to each of these elements. The five elements include sensory states (sense impressions, gestalts, and perceptions); representations of memory; representations of phantasy (defined as the deliberate representation of something that does not exist); combinations of representations (involved in the representation of what is probable and necessary, and association); and feelings. She argues that in ordinary life these elements are usually so entangled with our cognitive and practical ends that we tend to not focus on them in their own right. In art,

---

[54] See §3 of this introduction for a lengthier discussion of Kant's aesthetics.

however, she claims that we are able to divorce these elements from their further cognitive or practical roles and explore them on their own terms. And she maintains that in virtue of 'mirroring' these elements to us, art can provide us with cognition of them. To this end, she lists a litany of different ways that painting, sculpture, music, poetry, tragedy, comedy, novels, fairy tales, and more can teach us about what it is like to, say, have a particular sensation, recall something from the past, fantasize a particular outcome, represent something as probable or inevitable, associatively connect two things together, or feel a certain affect. With this analysis, Landmann-Kalischer thus endeavors to show that far from art just giving rise to feeling in us, art provides us with cognitive insight into various truths about subjective reality and mental phenomena.

However, in Section Four ("Results"), Landmann-Kalischer notes that this might not seem to be something that is particularly distinctive about art. After all, psychology, including the descriptive psychology that is phenomenology, also purports to give us cognition of subjective reality and mental phenomena. Does art, then, just give us the same kind of cognition that we could get by doing psychology instead?

In this concluding portion of the article,[55] Landmann-Kalischer makes the case that art gives us a kind of cognition about subjective reality and mental phenomena that psychology cannot give us. There are two significant differences she adduces to this end, which concern the form and content of the cognition at issue.

Beginning with the cognition involved in psychology, she argues that this cognition ultimately has a 'discursive' or 'conceptual' form (AT 104/495). She claims that descriptive psychology, for example, proceeds by 'analyzing' and 'classifying' mental phenomena in order to "draw up lawful relations between them" (AT 104/495). Through this sort of analysis, classification, and ascertaining of laws, Landmann-Kalischer claims that descriptive psychology 'translates' what is "intuitively given ... into concepts" (AT 104/495). Insofar as this is the case, Landmann-Kalischer thinks that when we cognize

---

[55] At the close of the article, Landmann-Kalischer devotes a discussion to the relationship between truth and beauty. There, she argues that truth and beauty have a 'correlative relationship': "the contents of the concepts of truth and beauty partly coincide. They stand to one another in a correlative relationship. Art needs truth in order to be able to have an effect; psychological truth needs art in order to be discovered" (AT 112–13/504). However, she also claims that beauty is a "more encompassing concept" than truth because, even though all art must be 'true' to have an 'effect', not all art 'aims' at truth as its "main effect" (see AT 112–14/504–505). As an example, she cites Medieval art, which primarily aims at 'devotion', rather than truth (AT 112–13/504).

subjective reality and mental phenomena through descriptive psychology, our cognition ultimately has a 'discursive' or 'conceptual' form.

As for the content of the cognition we arrive at through psychology, Landmann-Kalischer argues that the sort of truths that we cognize are ultimately of a general form. For example, the sort of analysis, classification, and ascertaining of laws involved in descriptive psychology is supposed to provide us with cognition of the laws that govern particular classes of mental phenomena (e.g., representations, judgments, and emotions), and how they relate to one another.

In art, by contrast, Landmann-Kalischer claims that the cognition involved has an 'intuitive' form (AT 104/495). To this end, she argues that art does not translate something intuitively given into something conceptual, but rather stays at the level of intuition and finds a way to intuitively present something we are intuitively given in an artistic medium. As she puts it, art provides us with a '*Gegenbild*', an "image that is a counterpart to what is mentally given, leaving it as is" (AT 104/495). Since she takes this model to apply to all artistic media, the sort of counterpart image she has in mind should be understood in loose enough terms to encompass what we can intuitively grasp through our various sense modalities (and, though she does not say this explicitly, presumably also through our imagination, e.g., when we read literature or poetry). And, on her view, the cognition involved in art is ultimately 'intuitive' in form because it involves us grasping mental phenomena in this intuitive way.

Regarding the content of artistic cognition, Landmann-Kalischer contends that art discloses to us 'individual', rather than general truths (AT 106/497). By an 'individual truth', she has in mind the truth conveyed about a particular mental phenomenon in a particular work of art. From Landmann-Kalischer's perspective, a work of art is not supposed to convey to us general truths about a class of mental phenomena; it is supposed to convey to us an individual truth about a particular mental phenomenon. For example, instead of giving us a general truth about sensations or feelings in general, a work of art might give us an individual truth about a particular sensation of blue or a particular feeling of calm. And she thinks that a work of art can give us an individual truth as a kind of truth to the extent that the way a particular mental phenomenon is displayed in the work of art 'agrees' with the mental phenomenon given to inner perception (AT 106/497). Each work of art, on her view, can thus disclose an individual truth to the extent that it presents us with a counterpart image, a *Gegenbild*, that agrees with a particular mental phenomenon.

For Landmann-Kalischer, then, although psychology, including descriptive psychology, and art both provide us with cognition of mental phenomena, art accomplishes something that psychology cannot: art gives us an intuitive, rather than discursive grasp of mental phenomena and art conveys to us individual, rather than general, truths about them. It is for this reason that she claims, as we saw above, that 'only art' can help us 'see' our 'inner life'.

Over the course of "On Artistic Truth," Landmann-Kalischer thus builds her case against a Kantian non-cognitivist account of art by arguing that art not only gives us cognition of subjective reality, but also that art gives us a distinctive kind of cognition of subjective reality that not even psychology or phenomenology can give us.

This cognitivist approach to art serves as a counterpart to the cognitivist approach to the experience of the beautiful that she defends in "On the Cognitive Value of Aesthetic Judgments." And between these two essays, Landmann-Kalischer endeavors to show that the aesthetic domain is neither a merely subjective domain, nor a merely affective domain, but a domain in which we come to cognize beauty and learn distinctive truths about our lived experience.

§6. "Philosophy of Values"

In "On the Cognitive Value of Aesthetic Judgments," Landmann-Kalischer hints at the ways in which she takes her view to generalize beyond aesthetic value to other values, like moral and epistemic value.[56] However, it is not until "Philosophy of Values" that she explicitly tackles this project and defends a fully systematic account of beauty, goodness, and truth. This said, the "Philosophy of Values" also doubles as a lengthy review of the influential psychologist Hugo Münsterberg's 1908 book, *Philosophy of Values*. Indeed, she devotes the First Part of the essay to the book review before turning to her own positive position in the Second Part. Though valuable as a critique of Münsterberg's systematic approach to value theory, this review also lays the groundwork for the positive position that she defends in the Second Part. In what follows, I offer some background on Münsterberg and her review in

---

[56] See, for example, her concluding remarks at CV 62–63/327–28.

the First Part, before turning to a discussion of the positive position in value theory that she defends in the Second Part.

6.1 "First Part": Critique of Münsterberg's *Philosophy of Values*

Since Münsterberg's philosophical work is not widely known today, before turning to Landmann-Kalischer's critical remarks, I shall provide a bit more by way of background on him and his *Philosophy of Values*. (For readers who would prefer to focus only on her positive views, feel free to skip to the next section.)

Hugo Münsterberg (1863–1916) was a German-American psychologist, who is best known for his pioneering work in applied psychology. He did his PhD in psychology under Wilhelm Wundt at the University of Leipzig, and after acquiring a medical degree from the University of Heidelberg, he founded the second psychology lab in Germany. In 1892 William James invited him to establish an experimental psychology lab at Harvard, and in 1895 he was appointed a full professor at Harvard, where he spent the remainder of his career. In his work, he focused particularly on the application of psychology to industrial settings and its potential economic implications;[57] to forensic settings and its implications for eyewitness testimony, false confessions, and interrogations;[58] to education and its implication for child development; and to psychiatric settings and its implications for clinical practices. Though famous now for his psychological work, Münsterberg was also active as a philosopher. He was specifically interested in philosophical questions about the nature and source of value and what different types of fundamental values there are. *Philosophy of Values* represents Münsterberg's philosophical effort to answer these questions.[59]

---

[57] See, for example, Hugo Münsterberg, *Psychology and Industrial Efficiency* (Boston: Houghton Mifflin, 1913).

[58] See, for example, Münsterberg, *On the Witness Stand: Essays on Psychology and Crime* (Garden City, NY: Doubleday, 1908).

[59] Münsterberg first defends his theory of value in the German text, *Philosophie der Werte. Grundzüge einer Weltanschauung* [*Philosophy of Values: Basic Features of a Worldview*] (Leipzig: J. A. Barth, 1908), which is the text Landmann-Kalischer reviews. But he quickly followed this up with an English version of his view, *The Eternal Values* (Boston: Houghton Mifflin, 1909.) Though the core of his system remains the same across these two texts, the German version includes a more sustained engagement with German thinkers, like Wilhelm Windelband, Heinrich Rickert, and Edmund Husserl, whereas the English version includes a more sustained engagement with American thinkers, like James and other pragmatists. Münsterberg offers a brief overview of *The Eternal Values* in "The Opponents of Eternal Values," *Psychological Bulletin* 6(10) (1909): pp. 329–38.

As Landmann-Kalischer points out in the outset of her review, in the *Philosophy of Values* Münsterberg endeavors to develop a systematic theory of value that cuts a middle path between two other approaches to value (see PV 116/2). The first approach is an empirical approach to value, which identifies particular individuals or groups of individuals (e.g., societies or cultures) as the source of value and treats value as something that is relative to those individuals or groups of individuals. The second approach is a Platonic approach, which takes the source of value to be something that transcends human beings altogether and treats value as something that is 'absolute' in this sense. According to Münsterberg, neither approach is adequate. Against the Platonic view, Münsterberg argues that value does not have its source in something that transcends subjects altogether. Instead, he embraces, what Landmann-Kalischer describes as a 'critical' or 'Kantian' position, according to which value is, in some sense, "subjectively conditioned" (PV 116/2). However, he takes issue with the claim that value has an empirical source in actually existing subjects or groups of subjects. According to Münsterberg, value has a 'supra-personal' source, i.e., a source in something that all subjects share in common (see PV 119–20/5–6). And once we acknowledge this supra-personal source, he maintains that we have reason to regard value as something that is absolute, rather than relative.[60]

Münsterberg divides the *Philosophy of Values* into two parts: in Part I, he offers an idealist theory of value in general, and in Part II he defends a view of the different fundamental types of unconditioned values.[61] At the heart of his idealist account of value in Part I is an analysis of the 'supra-personal' source of value. More specifically, Münsterberg argues that value has its source in a 'supra-personal' will that all human beings, in some sense, share in common. He claims that this 'supra-personal' will is characterized by a certain "fundamental act of will": the act of willing "that there is a world" (quoted at PV 120/6). For Münsterberg, what 'willing that there is a world' amounts to is willing that we find coherence in our lived experience, rather than chaos. So he takes it to be the case that all human beings, in some sense, volitionally aim at finding the sort of coherence in experience that amounts to there being a 'world'.

---

[60] At the outset of the review, Landmann-Kalischer draws out the parallels and contrasts between Münsterberg's 'critical' approach to value and the 'critical' approach to value defended by the Neo-Kantian Wilhelm Windelband (PV 116–21/2–7).

[61] For a detailed review of Münsterberg's position, as well as some critical objections, see also G. E. Moore's review of *Philosophie der Werte, International Journal of Ethics* 19(4) (1909): pp. 495–504.

Münsterberg, in turn, claims that this volitional aim is satisfied when we are able to find 'identity' across our lived experiences, such that the content of one lived experience "recurs as something identical" in another lived experience (quoted at PV 123–24/10). For example, suppose in the morning, I look out the window and see an oak tree in front of my house, and then later in the day I see the same oak tree after I return from a walk. In this case, the content of my lived experience, the oak tree, would 'recur as something identical'. From Münsterberg's point of view, this sort of recurrence of something identical across experience is an instance of the realization of the volitional aim 'that there is a world' because it is an instance in which I find the sort of coherence across experience that this aim requires.

Deploying this picture of the supra-personal will in order to make sense of value, Münsterberg argues that value is whatever enables the 'satisfaction' or 'realization' of the volitional aim 'that there is a world'. In his words, "This recurrence [of something identical] ... fulfills our expectation, and precisely this recurrence generates that satisfaction that we call 'value'" (quoted at PV 123–24/10). Contra the Platonic approach, then, Münsterberg claims that the source of value does not transcend human beings, but rather depends on our will: value just is whatever satisfies the volitional aim 'that there is a world'. However, contra the empirical approach, he claims that this will is not something that varies from person to person, or group to group, but is rather a will that is supra-personal and characterizes something that all subjects share in common. And it is because there are certain fixed things that satisfy this supra-personal will that Münsterberg takes value to be something that is 'absolute'.

In Part II of the *Philosophy of Values*, Münsterberg offers an account of, what he takes to be, the four fundamental types of values: logical, ethical, aesthetic, and metaphysical (e.g., religious and philosophical) values. According to Münsterberg, each of these values involves a fundamentally different way of finding coherence or identity across experiences and each value is, in this sense, 'self-sufficient' and 'autonomous' from the other values (see PV 123–24/10, 126–27/13–14). In elucidating these four fundamental values, Münsterberg specifies in each case a unique way in which identity is found to recur and the will is thus satisfied. And he explores a range of ways in which each value is instantiated in life and culture.

Beginning with his view of logical values, Münsterberg claims that the relevant recurrence of identity is in lived experiences of what 'exists', for example, objects and persons. He claims that these identities are ones that we grasp in 'cognition', whether this cognition takes place in everyday contexts or in the context of natural science or history. Turning to aesthetic values, Münsterberg takes the relevant recurrence of identity to involve lived experiences of a kind of 'harmony' or 'unity' in diversity. Though he includes natural beauty and art under the umbrella of aesthetic values, he also extends this category to include love (which involves finding harmony between individuals) and happiness (which involves finding harmony among our inner drives). As for ethical values, Münsterberg connects them to the recurrence of identity that occurs in lived experiences of what something aims at becoming and what something becomes. Under this heading, he includes the recurrence of identity experienced in the growth of plants and animals, progress in human society, self-development, the economy, law, and morality. Finally, he construes metaphysical values as ones that are connected to the recurrence of identity that occurs in our lived experience of the relations of logical, aesthetic, and ethical values to one another. According to Münsterberg, these sorts of identities are ones that we apprehend through lived experiences that arise in the context of religion or philosophy, insofar as various religious or philosophical 'convictions' provide us with a way of grasping some sort of fundamental unity between logical, aesthetic, and ethical values, for example, as established by God or as having another metaphysical source.

In addition to this analysis of each value, Münsterberg, in a Kantian vein, argues that these values are 'constitutive' of the 'objective world' (see PV 117/ 3). That is to say, these values are what make the objective world possible in the first place because these values are what enable the sort of coherence required for there to 'be a world'. Münsterberg thus commits himself to the idealist position that the world does not exist independently from value altogether, but is rather constituted through value. However, since each of these values is 'self-sufficient' and 'autonomous', Münsterberg is committed to there being four worlds that are constituted through each of these values. (Hence Landmann-Kalischer's description of his position as 'the doctrine of the four worlds'.)

Though Landmann-Kalischer is sympathetic to Münsterberg's attempt to find a middle path between a relativist and Platonist theory of value, she raises a battery of objections to his view. However, I shall focus on three of these objections, which are particularly salient with respect to the positive agenda she sets for her own theory of value in the second part of the essay.

The first objection concerns Münsterberg's positing of the supra-personal will as the source of value (see Part I, Section 2). According to Landmann-Kalischer, the supra-personal will is nothing but an "arbitrary metaphysical assumption" on Münsterberg's part (PV 121/8). Indeed, Landmann-Kalischer claims that Münsterberg arrives at this notion by 'hypostasizing' a genuine epistemological commitment we have to finding coherence in experience into the 'metaphysical' 'reality' of a supra-personal will (PV 121/8). And she objects that this sort of reasoning has "a similarity to the dubious course of thoughts in the ontological proof of God" insofar as it slides from a legitimate epistemological claim about how we necessarily think to, what she takes to be, an illegitimate metaphysical claim about something that exists (PV 121/8). If we are to develop a viable theory of value, Landmann-Kalischer insists that we cannot give in to metaphysical speculation of this sort.

The second objection pertains to Münsterberg's claim that the four fundamental values are entirely independent from one another and constitute four distinct worlds (see Part I, Section 3). Landmann-Kalischer is sympathetic to the idea that each of these values is 'self-sufficient' in the sense of not being able to be derived from one another. However, she insists that, "Self-sufficiency is one thing, independence another" (PV 126/13). And she argues that if we consider the relations between the values, then we find that there is an asymmetrical dependence relation between them such that aesthetic, ethical, and metaphysical values presuppose logical value, but not vice versa. She takes this to be the case because she thinks that what we aesthetically, ethically, or metaphysically value is something in the existing world, but this existing world is constituted through logical value (more on this later).[62] And once we recognize this dependence, Landmann-Kalischer claims that instead of taking there to be four worlds constituted by each value, we can recognize that there is a single existing world, which is initially constituted through logical value, and which encompasses aesthetic, ethical, and metaphysical value '*within*' itself (PV 131/18).

---

[62] In addition to the presupposition argument I am considering here, she argues that logical value is more fundamental than the other values, one, because the sort of identity that Münsterberg takes to be crucial to each value is, in fact, a logical concept (PV 127–28/14–16); two, because we can conceive of a world in which aesthetic, ethical, or dogmatic values are 'canceled' but not a world in which logical values are 'canceled' since logical values "represent the minimum of existence" (PV 131–33/19–20), and, three, because there is an asymmetry in the sort of continuity between how logical values manifest in life and culture and a discontinuity in how the other values manifest in these two domains (PV 132–34/20–22).

The third objection targets Münsterberg's notion of logical value (see Part I, Section 4). According to Landmann-Kalischer, Münsterberg utilizes an overly restricted notion of logical value. As we have seen, on Münsterberg's view, logical value is responsible for the sort of coherence we find in cognition and for the constitution of the existing world. However, Landmann-Kalischer points out that Münsterberg operates with a 'mechanistic' conception of cognition and the existing world, which treats cognition as a process in which we cognize the 'causal' relations between objects and persons and which constitutes being as a "value-free, mechanistically conceived nature" (PV 137/25, 140/28). But she objects that this mechanistic conception fails to do justice to the 'scope' and 'polymorphous' nature of logical value and cognition (PV 136/24). On her view, logical value encompasses the various 'functions' that enable us to establish the "interconnectedness of things" in 'thinking' or 'cognition', which can happen as much in a mechanistic, as in an aesthetic, ethical, or metaphysical context (PV 136/24). And she argues that appreciating the more capacious nature of logical value and cognition paves the way toward a unified picture of the existing world as one in which values are 'located' (PV 141/29).[63]

If we are to find an alternative to empirical-relativism, on the one hand, and absolute-Platonism, on the other, Landmann-Kalischer claims that we need to embrace another philosophy of values.

6.2 "Second Part": Landmann-Kalischer's Philosophy of Values

In the Second Part of "Philosophy of Values," Landmann-Kalischer defends her alternative theory of value.[64] She frames her alternative in terms of the question of whether there is any way to account for the 'objectivity' or 'objective validity' of our value judgments. If neither the Platonist nor the

---

[63] Landmann-Kalischer notes that Münsterberg suggests that we can search for unity from the metaphysical perspective, for example, from a religious point of view; however, she objects that this unity "remains a postulate that cannot be fulfilled" because the metaphysical perspective "ignor[es] or den[ies] the value of existence and interconnections" established by some of the other values (PV 141–42/30).

[64] See Vendrell-Ferran, "On the Analogy," for a discussion of the value theory Landmann-Kalischer develops in this article in comparison with the value theories of Meinong and the Munich phenomenologist Max Scheler, as well as a discussion of the relevance of her views in contemporary debates in meta-ethics about the secondary quality analogy and value, the apprehension of value through intentional feelings rather than emotions, and the connection between affective responses and knowledge of values.

Münsterberg-style idealist is right, should we follow subjectivists and relativists in denying the possibility of the objectivity of value judgments altogether?

Landmann-Kalischer highlights two reasons that we might be tempted to think that objective value judgments are not possible. In the first place, there is widespread and seemingly intractable disagreement in people's value judgments (see PV 153/43). This is true on an interpersonal level: what one person finds beautiful leaves another cold, just as what one person deems ethically right, another deems ethically wrong. This is also true on a social and cultural level: what one society regards as ugly, another praises as beautiful, and what one culture treats as just, another condemns as unjust. And unlike in other domains where it seems possible for us to move from a place of disagreement to consensus, the disagreements over value seem to be intractable. *Prima facie*, then, this sort of disagreement about value suggests that it is not something we can be objective about.

In the second place, Landmann-Kalischer argues that the role feelings play in value judgments might also give us reason to think they cannot be objective. As is clear in Section I ("Introduction"), Landmann-Kalischer endorses an affective view of value judgments, according to which "we ascribe value to objects on the basis of feelings that they arouse in us" (PV 144/33). This idea should be familiar from "On the Cognitive Value of Aesthetic Judgments," where she argues that our judgments of the beautiful are grounded in a feeling of disinterested pleasure we have in response to an object. In "Philosophy of Values" she generalizes this point to all value judgments: whether we are making a judgment about logical, aesthetic, or ethical value, this judgment is made on the basis of a feeling we have in response to an object, understood in broad enough terms to include material objects, events, persons, actions, and sentences. However, if feeling plays a constitutive role in value judgment, given that feeling, it might seem, is irreducibly subjective, then these value judgments must be irreducibly subjective as well (see PV 145/34).

Nevertheless, in spite of the fact of widespread, intractable disagreement about value and the central role feeling plays in our experience of value, Landmann-Kalischer argues that value judgments can, indeed, be objective. And she uses what remains of the "Philosophy of Values" to make her case.

In Section II ("On the Psychology of the Emotional Sphere"), Landmann-Kalischer tackles the worry that value judgments cannot be objective because they are based on feelings. According to Landmann-Kalischer, this sort of worry is motivated by a tendency to construe feeling as an entirely subjective mental phenomenon. And she canvasses various reasons for this view of feeling: feeling is presumed to be a wholly subjective state of consciousness (II.1), feeling seems too closely connected to the I (the self) (II.2), feeling appears too dependent on the response of the I in the moment (II.3), feeling is seemingly not reproducible (II.4), and it does not look like feeling stands in law-governed connections to fixed stimuli (II.5).

Though she addresses these concerns one by one, here I shall flag a certain through-line between her argument and her earlier argument in "On the Cognitive Value of Aesthetic Judgments": this account of feeling rests on the false premise that all feelings are irreducibly subjective.

Recall that in "On the Cognitive Value of Aesthetic Judgments," Landmann-Kalischer distinguishes between subjectively conditioned feelings that refer to the subject and objectively conditioned feelings that refer to the object. Picking up on this distinction in "Philosophy of Values," she labels a subjectively conditioned feeling an 'emotion' [*Affect*] and an objectively conditioned feeling a 'pure feeling' [*Gefühle*] (see II.2). And she argues that although it is the case that emotions are subjective states that are inextricably bound up with the I, pure feelings are disinterested, hence distanced from the I and oriented to the object on its own terms. Far from it being the case that all feelings are irreducibly subjective, she thus holds up pure, disinterested feelings as ones that refer to objects.

The next move in Landmann-Kalischer's argument is the claim that we can make objective value judgments on the basis of such pure, disinterested feelings (see Section III: "Objectivity of Value Judgments"). Landmann-Kalischer's first step in this direction is to clarify what sense of objectivity she is and is not working with. She begins by setting aside three conceptions of objectivity: a Humean view, according to which objectivity is a matter of certain mental states, viz., sensations, "enter[ing] into consciousness outfitted with [reality]"; a mind-independent view according to which objectivity means "independence from the human being"; and a view according to which objectivity requires "universal agreement of judgments" (PV 163/54). In contrast with these three views, she defines objectivity as a 'task' that we strive to reach through our judgments (PV 162/53).

In order to clarify what she means by objectivity as a task, Landmann-Kalischer sharpens her picture of the process involved in making value judgments. To this end, she argues that we need to distinguish between two kinds of value judgments and attendant forms of objectivity. The first is a 'primary' value judgment in which we judge something to be true, beautiful, or good on the basis of an immediate feeling we have in response to it (PV 163–64/54–55). And she claims that a primary value judgment is objective in its 'sense' [*Sinn*] because it 'means' or 'intends' an object (PV 163–64/54–55). As we might make the point, these primary judgments are 'truth-apt'.

The second kind of value judgment is an objectively 'correct' value judgment, which we make on the basis of reflecting or 'working' on a primary judgment and determining that the judgment 'X is true (good or beautiful)' is 'warranted' (PV 164/55). According to Landmann-Kalischer, an objectively correct value judgment is objective in its 'content' [*Inhalt*] because this objectivity has been 'acquired' or 'won' through a process in which we determine the judgment is warranted by an object (PV 164/55). On her view, this second type of value judgment is thus not just truth-apt, but true. And it is this latter sort of objectivity that Landmann-Kalischer has in mind when she talks about the task of objectivity: it is the objectivity that value judgments have when we have worked out their warrant.

To unpack what sort of warrant the task of objectivity requires, Landmann-Kalischer argues that although we should take consistency with other experiences and judgments into account (as she does in "On the Cognitive Value of Aesthetic Judgments"), the "ultimate warrant" for a value judgment is the value of an object: is it because a sentence is true, an action is good, or a painting is beautiful that our value judgments about them are warranted (PV 165/56). However, if the ultimate warrant for a value judgment is the value of an object, then in order to 'win' objectivity for our value judgments, we need to have a grasp of what it is for an object to be true, good, or beautiful. And this latter task, Landmann-Kalischer claims, is a special task that falls to logic, ethics, and aesthetics understood as "sciences of value" (PV 167–68/62). For Landmann-Kalischer, then, if we are to achieve objectivity in our value judgments, we need logic, ethics, and aesthetics to develop as sciences that give us insight into what the true, good, and beautiful are, qua properties of objects that bring about disinterested feelings in us. And in sketching what these sciences of value involve, she again deploys the secondary quality analogy,[65] arguing that just as a science like optics clarifies what color is, qua a property of an object that brings about sensation in us, so, too, should logic, ethics, and aesthetics clarify what the true, the good, and the beautiful are, respectively, qua properties of objects that bring about disinterested feelings

---

[65] For discussion of Landmann secondary quality analogy in the context of this article and its significance in meta-ethics, see Vendrell-Ferran, "On the Analogy."

in us (see PV 170–72/59).[66] And in what remains of Section III, Landmann-Kalischer fills out her account of the task of the sciences of value (III.2) and the fulfillment of this task as it stands in logic (III.2.a), ethics (III.2.b), aesthetics (III.2.c), and religious dogmatics (III.2.d).

In detailing what she takes to be the task of a science of value, she positions her account against two other accounts of what a science of value might amount to. The first is a 'psychological' science of value that is concerned with describing the sort of mental acts we engage in when we take something to be valuable (PV 170–72/63). She includes under this heading "purely phenomenological" treatments of such mental acts, as well as other psychological approaches (PV 170–72/63). Given the descriptive aims of a wholly psychological science of value, she claims that it sets aside questions about whether these mental acts are 'correct', that is, whether they track the value of objects (PV 170–72/62).

By contrast, the second kind of science of value is a 'normative' one that focuses on what we 'should' find to be true, good, or beautiful, whether we, in fact, do so or not (PV 170–72/63). Here, she primarily has in mind the normative science of value developed by the Southwest Neo-Kantian Wilhelm Windelband.[67]

Contrasting her approach to the sciences of value with these two alternatives, Landmann-Kalischer says:

> in the sciences of value we are looking at neither sciences of thinking, feeling, and acting nor even sciences of how, in view of some higher purpose, one is supposed to think, feel, or act. Instead we have to determine logic, ethics, and aesthetics very simply as sciences of the true, good, and beautiful. Psychology would accordingly be merely the presupposition, merely the preparation for these objective sciences; normative science would be merely the consequence, merely the application of them. (PV 170–72/62–63)

So, unlike the psychological science of how we, in fact, think, feel, and act in relation to value, and the normative science of how we should think, feel,

---

[66] Landmann-Kalischer also addresses the fact that values appear to have more complicated 'presuppositions' than the properties that condition secondary qualities like color, but she thinks that this is a challenge for the sciences of value, rather than a reason to be skeptical (PV 167–68/59).

[67] She develops an extended critique of Windelband's approach to the science of values at PV 172–78/64–70.

and act in relation to value, Landmann-Kalischer casts the sciences of value as sciences of what values are.[68] And it is in this sense that she describes aesthetics as the science of beauty, ethics as the science of the good, and logic as the science of the true. At the same time, in a phenomenological spirit, she insists that the starting point of these sciences should be the 'fact' of our lived experience of "values as properties of things" (PV 176–77/68–69, 143/32). In laying out her vision of the sciences of value, we thus find Landmann-Kalischer filling out her picture of what a full-blown account of the objective side of mental phenomena calls for, qua an investigation of what values are as the real objects of our value judgments.

Having articulated the task of the sciences of value, Landmann-Kalischer then surveys how logic, ethics, aesthetics, and dogmatics have fared with respect to this task. She holds up logic as the most advanced of these sciences, having alighted on axioms, which are articulated through symbolic logic, as the objective basis of our objectively correct judgments of the true.[69] By contrast, she indicates that ethics, aesthetics, and dogmatics have advanced to a lesser degree in identifying what the objective basis of the good, the beautiful, and religious value are.[70] Nevertheless, she argues that in any scientific field, we should expect false starts and false theories to be part of the scientific progress—the sciences of value being no exception (see PV 188/81). She thus presents the shortcomings in ethics, aesthetics, and dogmatics not as reasons to be skeptical of their possible success, but rather as a mark of their relatively nascent state and the work ahead.

In what remains of "Philosophy of Values," Landmann-Kalischer addresses systematic questions about the relationship that values have to 'being' (Section IV) and the relationship that values have to one another (Section V), thus returning to many of the points she criticizes Münsterberg for in her review. In these sections, she expands on the sense in which she takes logical value to be the only value that has 'constitutive significance' with respect

---

[68] She takes the normative sciences to be a 'consequence' of the science of value as she envisions it insofar as this normative science addresses what we 'should' value given a 'mental mechanism' we possess, "as a consequence of which we necessarily seek every value and flee every non-value" and in accordance with which "all our actions are oriented toward the side of pleasure and turned away from displeasure" (PV 177/69, 198/92).

[69] In this discussion, she addresses questions about what justifies these logical axioms and criticizes Brentano's account of the evidence of inner perception (PV 178–81/71–74) and Husserl's claim that these axioms cannot be derived from any empirical facts (PV 181–83/74–76).

[70] However, she claims that aesthetics has made some headway, for example, in mathematically determining certain forms like circles, golden segments, and serpentine lines as beautiful or Aristotle determining certain tragic forms as beautiful (PV 188/81).

to being (see PV 190–94/84–88). She casts this constitutive relationship as a "purely logical" relationship of dependence, such that were there no logical value, then "the existence of a world cannot be thought at all" (PV 190–91/84–85). And she criticizes a swath of idealist philosophers, including the German idealist Johann Gottlieb Fichte, the Neo-Kantian Henrich Rickert, and Münsterberg, for construing this constitutive significance in metaphysical rather than logical terms (see PV 190–91/85–88).

Meanwhile, in Section V she considers the ways in which the various values relate to one another. On the one hand, she argues that ethical, aesthetic, and religious values asymmetrically depend on logical value (see PV 195/99, 197/91). Not only do these values depend on the existence of a world that is constituted through logical values, but also in order to make judgments about these values we depend on the standards of judgment provided by logic. On the other hand, she insists that these values are 'self-sufficient', that is, they cannot be reduced to one another, and are 'irreplaceable', that is, they cannot 'compensate' for one another (PV 194–95/88). In the latter vein, she claims, "No amount of goodness or moral rigor relieves us from taking account of aesthetic values, no wisdom can take the place of acting morally" (PV 194/88). At the same time, she claims that each of us will nevertheless have to "take sides" and 'choose' among these values in our own lives, and "be humble" about those choices (PV 195/89).

With this analysis of the relation among the true, good, and beautiful, Landmann-Kalischer brings the "Philosophy of Values" to a conclusion, having offered a value theory that is an alternative to relativism, Platonism, and Münsterberg-style idealism. At the heart of her alternative is a systematic theory of value, which rests on an analysis of the possibility of objectivity about value; a realist theory of value; a vision of logic, ethics, and aesthetics as sciences of value; and a view of how values relate to the world and to one another. And it is this systematic theory of value that she holds up as a more promising account of value that is at once grounded in lived experience and in science.

Conclusion

In the three essays included in this volume, Landmann-Kalischer develops an ambitious program in aesthetics and value theory that addresses many of the most persistent questions about what beauty, art, goodness, and truth are, and how we experience them. In so doing, she paints a picture of our experience of value as a site in which feeling can lead to knowledge and in which we can aspire to objectivity. She pairs this picture of lived experience of value with a picture of our world as value-laden, rather than value-less. As is perhaps only fitting, by engaging with these ideas, we have the opportunity to experience something of value in our world that we have too long lost sight of: the philosophy of Edith Landmann-Kalischer.[71]

---

[71] I would like to thank Daniel Dahlstrom, Kristin Gjesdal, and Sebastian Luft for invaluable feedback on this Introduction.

Chronology

1877	Born in Berlin to Moritz and Henriette, September 19.
1894–97	Attends the "Realkursen für Mädchen," which was founded by Helene Lange in 1889.
1897	Enrolls as an undergraduate at the University of Zurich to study philosophy, psychology, art history, and archaeology. Visits the University of Berlin and takes courses with Carl Stumpf, Georg Simmel, Max Dessoir, and Gregor Itelson.
1901	Completes her dissertation, *Analyse der ästhetischen Contemplation (Plastik und Malerei)* [Analysis of Aesthetic Contemplation (Sculpture and Painting)] under the supervision of Ernst Meumann at the University of Zurich.
1903	Marries the economist Julius Landmann.
1905	Publishes "On the Cognitive Value of Aesthetic Judgments." Her son, Georg Peter, is born. Publishes a book review of Theodor Lipps's *Grundlegung der Ästhetik* [Foundation of Aesthetics].
1906	Publishes "On Artistic Truth." The Landmanns move to Bern. Her daughter, Eva, is born.
1907	Publishes a review of Max Dessoir's *Ästhetik und allgemeine Kunstwissenschaft* [Aesthetics and General Art History].
1908	The Landmanns meet Stefan George.
1910	Publishes "Philosophy of Values." The Landmanns move to Basel.
1912	Travels to Italy (Verona, Venice, Rome, Naples, Pompeii, Padua, Catania, Syracuse, and Segesta).
1913	Publishes a review of Emil Lask's *Die Logik der Philosophie und die Kategorienlehre* [The Logic of Philosophy and the Doctrine of Categories] and *Die Lehre vom Urteil* [The Doctrine of Judgment]. Her son, Michael, is born. George visits the Landmanns in Basel for the first time.
1920	Anonymously publishes *Georgika. Das Wesen des Dichters* [Georgika: The Essence of the Poet] in honor of George's fiftieth birthday.

lxii CHRONOLOGY

1923 Publishes *Die Transcendenz des Erkennens* [The Transcendence of Cognizing].
1924 Publishes a revised edition of *Georgika*.
1925 Eva Landmann dies from bone tuberculosis.
1927 The Landmanns move to Kiel.
1927/28 Has a "tea-hour" with Husserl.
1931 Julius Landmann commits suicide.
1933 George dies. She circulates "Omaruru" to friends and writes a manuscript titled "Die Menschengestalt der Homerischen Götter" [The Human Form of Homer's Gods].
1939 Invites Renata von Scheliha to live with her in Basel. Lectures at the *Volkshochschule* in Basel: "*Eine Interpretation der Odyssey*" [An Interpretation of the *Odyssey*].
1940 Publishes *Grundzüge einer Lehre vom Schönen* [The Outline of a Doctrine of the Beautiful].
1944–49 Writes book reviews under the pseudonym of Marius Müller for the *Zuricher Bücherblatt*.
1948 Writes "Assimilation und Zionismus."
1950 Visits von Scheliha in New York.
1951 Dies due to complications from an operation.
1953 *Die Lehre vom Schönen* [The Doctrine of the Beautiful] is posthumously published.
1955 "Georges Wiedererweckung der Griechen" [George's Reawakening of the Greeks] is posthumously published in *Edith Landmann*, a volume edited by her son, Michael, which includes contributions by Margret Schuster, Wera Lewin, and Kurt Singer, among others.
1963 *Gespräche mit Stefan George* [Conversations with Stefan George] is posthumously published.
1971 *Stefan George und die Griechen. Idee einer neuen Ethik* [Stefan George and the Greeks: Idea of a New Ethics] is posthumously published.

Primary and Secondary Sources

Primary Sources

Kalischer, Edith. *Analyse der ästhetischen Contemplation (Malerei und Plastik).* Barth: Leipzig, 1902.

Kalischer, Edith. "J. Cl. Kreibig, Über den Begriff 'Sinnestäuschung.'" *Zeitschrift für Philosophie und Physiologie der Sinnesorgane* 120(2) (1903): pp. 197–203.

Landmann-Kalischer, Edith. "Über den Erkenntniswert ästhetischer Urteile. Ein Vergleich zwischen Sinnes- und Werturteilen." *Archiv für die gesamte Psychologie* 5(3) (1905): pp. 263–328.

Landmann-Kalischer, Edith. "Theodor Lipps, Grundlegung der Ästhetik. Ästhetik. Psychologie des Schönen und der Kunst. Erster Teil." *Archiv für die gesamte Psychologie* (Review) 5 (1905): pp. 213–27.

Landmann-Kalischer, Edith. "Über künstlerische Wahrheit." *Zeitschrift für Ästhetik und Allgemeine Kunstwissenschaft* 1 (1906): pp. 457–505.

Landmann-Kalischer, Edith. "Die moderne Ästhetik: Jonas Cohn, Konrad Lange, Karl Groos, Theodor Lipps, Witasek, Volkelt, Dessoir." *Preussische Jahrbücher* 130 (1907): pp. 410–30.

Landmann-Kalischer, Edith. "Max Dessoir, Ästhetik und allgemeine Kunstwissenschaft" (Review). *Archiv für die gesamte Psychologie* 9(1) (1907): pp. 50–61.

Landmann-Kalischer, Edith. "Theodor Lipps, Grundlegung der Ästhetik. Ästhetik. Psychologie des Schönen und der Kunst. Zweiter Teil." *Archiv für die gesamte Psychologie* (Review) 14 (1909): pp. 172–89.

Landmann-Kalischer, Edith. "Philosophie der Werte." *Archiv für die gesamte Psychologie* 18 (1910): pp. 1–93.

Landmann-Kalischer, Edith. "Kunstschönheit als ästhetischer Elementargegenstand." In *Beiträge zur Ästhetik und Kunstgeschichte*, edited by Edith Landmann-Kalischer, Gertrud Kuehl-Claassen, and Gertrud Kantorowicz. Berlin: Moeser, 1910: pp. 1–89.

Landmann-Kalischer, Edith, Gertrud Kuehl-Claassen, and Gertrud Kantorowicz, eds. *Beiträge zur Ästhetik und Kunstgeschichte.* Berlin: Moeser, 1910.

Landmann-Kalischer, Edith. "Jacob Segal, Psychologische und normative Ästhetik" (Review). *Archiv für die gesamte Psychologie* 20(4) (1911): pp. 162–63.

Landmann-Kalischer, Edith. "Käte Friedemann, Die Rolle des Erzählers in der Epik" (Review). *Archiv für die gesamte Psychologie* 20(4) (1911): pp. 163–64.

Landmann-Kalischer, Edith. "Erich Becher, Die Grundfrage der Ethik." *Archiv für die gesamte Psychologie* 20(4) (1911): p. 164.

Landmann-Kalischer, Edith. "W. M. Urban, Valuation, The Nature and Laws, Being an Introduction to the General Theory of Value" (Review). *Archiv für die gesamte Psychologie* 25(1) (1912): p. 31.

Landmann-Kalischer, Edith. "Emil Lask, Die Logik der Philosophie und die Kategorienlehre und Die Lehre vom Urteil" (Review). *Archiv für die gesamte Psychologie* 29 (1913): pp. 21–37.

Landmann, Edith. "H. Friedemann, Platon" (Review). *Preussische Jahrbücher* 161 (1915): pp. 331–41.

Landmann, Edith. *Georgika. Das Wesen des Dichters Stefan George.* Heidelberg: Weiss, 1920 (revised edition in 1924).

Landmann, Edith. *Die Transcendenz des Erkennens.* Berlin: Bondi, 1923.

Landmann, Edith. "Carl Spittelers poetische Sendung." *Schweizerische Monatshefte für Politik und Kultur* 3(7) (1923): pp. 334–52.

Landmann, Edith. "Wissen und Werten." *Schmollers Jahrbuch für Gesetzgebung, Verwaltung und Volkswirtschaft im Deutschen Reich* 54(2) (1930): pp. 95–111.

Landmann, Edith. "Stefan George. Das Neue Reich." *Logos* 20 (1931): pp. 88–104.

Landmann, Edith. "Die Menschengestalt der Homerischen Götter." *Festschrift für Karl Joel*, Basel (1934): pp. 165–84.

Landmann, Edith. "George und Nietzsche." *Die Tat* (1944): 2./3.12.

Landmann, Edith. "Mensch und Erde." *Neue Schweizer Rundschau* 13 (1945): pp. 624–32.

Landmann, Edith. "Interpretation eines Gedichtes: Ursprünge von Stefan George." *Trivium* 5 (1947): pp. 54–64.

Landmann, Edith. *Die Lehre vom Schönen.* Vienna: Amandus, 1952.

Landmann, Edith. "Georges Wiedererweckung der Griechen." In *Edith Landmann*, edited by Michael Landmann. Amsterdam: Castrum Peregini, 1955: pp. 7–33.

Landmann, Edith. "Erinnerung an Simmel von Edith Landmann." In *Buch des Dankes an Georg Simmel: Briefe, Erinnerungen, Bibliographie*, edited by Kurt Gassen and Michael Landmann. Berlin: Duncker und Humboldt, 1958: pp. 208–10.

Landmann, Edith. "Wem Du dein licht gabst bis hinauf zu dir." *Castrum Peregrini* 35 (1957): pp. 35–39.

Landmann, Edith. *Gespräche mit Stefan George*. Düsseldorf: H. Küpper, vormals G. Bondi, 1963.

Landmann, Edith. *Stefan George und die Griechen. Idee einer neuen Ethik*. Amsterdam: Castrum Peregrini, 1971.

Landmann, Edith, and Renata von Scheliha. *Eine Freundschaft im Zeichen Stefan Georges Briefe aus den Jahren 1934–1951*. Edited by Marianne von Heereman, Christiane Kuby, and Herbert Post. Berlin: Hentrich und Hentrich Verlag, 2022.

See also the bibliography in Landmann, Michael, ed. *Edith Landmann*. Amsterdam: Castrum Peregini: pp. 123–28, 1955.

Landmann-Kalischer's Teilnachlass is housed at the Stefan George Archiv at the Württembergische Landesbibliothek in Stuttgart, Germany. It includes her manuscripts, letters, journals, and other documents (https://www.wlb-stuttgart.de/sammlungen/stefan-george-archiv/bestand/nachlaesse-george-kreis/teilnachlass-edith-landmann/).

Secondary Sources

Bock, Claus Victor. "Edith Landmann." In *Besuch im Elfenbeinturm: Reden, Dokumente, Aufsätze*. Würzburg: Königshausen & Neumann, 1990: pp. 160–65.

Dahlstrom, Daniel. "Edith Landmann-Kalischer." In *The Oxford Handbook of Nineteenth-Century Women Philosophers in the German Tradition*, edited by Kristin Gjesdal and Dalia Nassar. Oxford: Oxford University Press, forthcoming.

Dutt, Carsten. "Edith Landmann—oder der poetologische Essentialismus des George-Kults." In *Frauen um Stefan George*, edited by Ute Oelmann and Ulrich Raulff. Göttingen: Wallstein Verlag, 2010: pp. 233–51.

Egypten, Jürgen. "Schwester, Huldin, Ritterin. Ida Coblenz, Gertrud Kantorowicz, and Edith Landmann. Jüdische Frauen im Dienste Stefan Georges." In *Zions Töchter: Jüdische Frauen in Literatur, Kunst und Politik*, edited by Andrea M. Lauritsch. Wien: Edition Mnemosyne, 2006: pp. 149–84.

Harada, Tetsushi. "Die Anschauliche Theorie als Fortsetzung der historischen Schule im George-Kreis: Edgar Salin unter dem Einfluss Edith Landmanns." In *Das Ideal des schönen Lebens und die Wirklichkeit der Weimarer Republik: Vorstellungen von Staat und Gemeinschaft im George-Kreis*, edited by Korinna Schönhärl, Bertram Schefold, Werner Plumpe, und Roman Köster. Akademie Verlag, 2009: pp. 195–210.

Hartung, Gerald. *Edith Kalischer*. In *Simmel-Handbuch: Leben—Werk—Wirkung*, edited by Jörn Bohr, Gerald Hartung, Heike Koenig, und Tim-Florian Steinbach. Stuttgart: J.B. Metzler, 2021: pp. 441–42.

Hillman, Susanne. *Wandering Jews: Existential Quests between Berlin, Zurich, and Zion*. ProQuest Dissertations & Theses Global, 2011.

Landmann, Michael. *Erinnerungen an Stefan George. Seine Freundschaft mit Julius und Edith Landmann*. Amsterdam: Castrum Peregrini Presse, 1980.

Landmann, Michael, ed. *Edith Landmann*. Amsterdam: Castrum Peregini, 1955.

Lewin, Wera. "Edith Landmann in Memoriam." In *Edith Landmann*, edited by Michael Landmann. Amsterdam: Castrum Peregini, 1955: pp. 64–68.

Matherne, Samantha. "Edith Landmann-Kalischer on Aesthetic Demarcation and Normativity." *British Journal of Aesthetics* 60 (3) (2020): pp. 315–34.

Matherne, Samantha. "Are Artists Phenomenologists? Perspectives from Edith Landmann-Kalischer and Maurice Merleau-Ponty." In *Horizons of Phenomenology*, edited by Patrick Londen, Philip Walsh, and Jeffrey Yoshimi. Springer, 2023: pp. 247–64.

Matherne, Samantha. "Trends in Aesthetics." In *The Oxford Handbook of Nineteenth-Century Women Philosophers in the German Tradition*, edited by Kristin Gjesdal and Dalia Nassar. Oxford: Oxford University Press, forthcoming.

Meyer, Ursula. "Edith Landmann-Kalischer." In *Philosophinnen-Lexikon*, edited by Ursula I. Meyer und Heidemarie Bennent-Vahle. Paderborn: FACH-Verlag, 1994: pp. 331–33.

Norton, Robert. *Secret Germany: Stefan George and His Circle*. Ithaca, NY: Cornell University Press, 2002.

Oestersandfort, Christian. "Landmann, Edith." *Stefan George und sein Kreis: ein Handbuch, Band 3*, edited by Achim Aurnhammer, Wolfgang Braungart, Stefan Breuer, and Ute Oelmann. Berlin: de Gruyter, 2021.

Philipp, Michael. "Die Thematisierung des 'Jüdischen' im George-Kreis vor und nach 1933." In *"Verkannte brüder"? Stefan George und das deutsch-jüdische Bürgertum zwischen Jahrhundertwende und Emigration,"* edited by Gert Mattenklott, Michael Philipp, and Julius H. Schoeps. Hildesheim: Georg Olms Verlag, 2001: pp. 201-18.

Raulff, Ulrich. *Kreis ohne Meister: Stefan Georges Nachleben*. München: Beck, 2009.

Reicher, Maria. "Value Facts and Value Experiences in Early Phenomenology." In *Values and Ontology*, edited by Beatrice Centi and Wolfgang Huemer. Frankfurt: Ontos, 2009: pp. 105-35.

Reicher, Maria. "Ästhetische Werte als dispositionale Eigenschaften: 1905-2014." *Deutsches Jahrbuch Philosophie* 8 (2016): pp. 961-74.

Reicher-Marek, Maria. "Dispositionalist Accounts of Aesthetic Properties in Austro-German Aesthetics." *Paradigmi. Rivista di critica filosofica* 3 (2017): pp. 71-86.

Riedner, Johannes. "Edith Landmann als philosophische Interpretin und Zeugin Stefan Georges. Zu Problemen der Assimilation im George-Kreis." *Marburger Forum* 3 (4) (2002): pp. 1-14.

Schiewer, Gesine Lenore. "Das Problem des Politischen in der Philosophie Edith Landmanns. Diskussionen im Umfeld von Wertphilosophie, Gestalttheorie und Wissenssoziologie." In *Das Ideal des schönen Lebens und die Wirklichkeit der Weimarer Republik. Vorstellungen von Staat und Gemeinschaft im George-Kreis*, edited by Roman Koster et al. Berlin: Akademie-Verlag, 2009: pp. 77-96.

Schönhärl, Korinna. "Transcendenz des Erkennens: Erkenntnistheoretische Grundlagen der wissenschaftlichen Methodendiskussion im George-Kreis." *Archiv für Kulturgeschichte* 91 (2) (2009): pp. 445-76.

Schönhärl, Korinna. "'Wie eine Blume die erforen ist'—Edith Landmann als Jüngerin Stefan Georges." In *Stefan George. Dichtung—Ethos—Staat. Denkbilder für ein geheimes europäisches Deutschland*, edited by Bruno Pieger und Bertram Schefold. Berlin: Verlag für Berlin-Brandenburg, 2010: pp. 207-42.

Schuster, Margaret. "Edith Landmann als Philosophin." In *Edith Landmann*, edited by Michael Landmann. Amsterdam: Castrum Peregini, 1955: pp. 34-48.

Singer, Kurt. "Erinnerung an die Georgika." In *Edith Landmann*, edited by Michael Landmann. Amsterdam: Castrum Peregini, 1955: pp. 50–57.

Vendrell-Ferran, Íngrid. "Tatsache, Wert und menschliche Sensibilität: Die Brentanoschule und die Gestaltpsychologie." In *Feeling and Value, Willing and Action*, edited by Marta Wehrle and Maren Ubiali. Cham: Springer, 2014: pp. 141–62.

Vendrell-Ferran, Íngrid. "On the Analogy between the Sensing of Secondary Qualities and the Feeling of Values: Landmann-Kalischer's Epistemic Project, Its Historical Context, and Its Significance for Current Meta-Ethics." In *Philosophy of Value. The Historical Roots of Contemporary Debate: An Overview*, edited by Beatrice Centi, Faustino Fabbianelli, and Gemmo Iocco. Berlin: De Gruyter, forthcoming.

THE THREE ESSAYS

On the Cognitive Value of Aesthetic Judgments

A comparison of sensory judgments and value judgments (1905)[1]

Overview of Contents

Introduction (Posing the question, theses; overview of the present status of the question)	263

Section I

Chapter 1. Feeling and value	268
Chapter 2. Feeling and cognition	272

Section II

Chapter 3. The subjective reliability of value judgments	281
Chapter 4. The objective reliability of value judgments	285
Chapter 5. The criteria for the correctness of sensory judgments and value judgments	304
Chapter 6. The qualities of aesthetic feeling	322

---

[1] [For an introduction to this essay, see §4 of Matherne's Introduction.]

Introduction

The question of the cognitive value of aesthetic judgments comprises two questions that need to be treated separately:

(1) the more general question whether the aesthetic judgment is a cognitive judgment (in the Kantian sense) at all;
(2) the more specific question whether and to what extent aesthetic judgments can be credited with trans-subjective validity [*übersubjektive Gültigkeit*].

In order to answer these questions, I attempt to demonstrate the three following theses by pointing out thoroughgoing analogies between sensory judgments and value judgments:

(1) The aesthetic valuation is carried out by means of an organ whose function and accomplishment are like that of sense organs. |264|
(2) With regard to its objective validity, aesthetic judgment is on the same level as sensory judgments.
(3) Beauty should be considered a property of things in the same sense as sensory qualities.

The most plausible conception of value, still represented today solely by Franz Brentano, is that value is a property of things. But in the present view of values, a view that is universal in science, they are regarded without exception as subjectively conditioned. Since this doctrine is familiar to everyone today, a more detailed account of it would not be necessary if it did not constantly appear to be disastrously conflated with another standpoint. The representatives of the subjectivist doctrine of values namely maintain not simply that value has the sort of subjectivity that it would share with all other properties of objects.[2] Instead, by emphasizing its subjectively conditioned character, they want precisely to separate value from the other properties of objects and give it, in contrast to the latter, an isolated and *sui generis* status. On the basis

---

[2] [Landmann-Kalischer may be thinking of the Kantian view that the objectivity of experience is guaranteed by universal and necessary subjective conditions of experience (see, e.g., pp. 273–74), or she may have in mind the properties of objects that are accessed by subjective sensory experience, e.g., an object's visible or tactile properties. In either case subjectivity of some sort is shared by the properties of objects but, at least according to what she deems the prevailing opinion, values are not on a par with those properties since their subjectivity is sui generis and non-cognitive.]

of—and at the same time along with—the [allegedly] self-evident, subjectively conditioned character that the value shares with all objects, they also maintain that value has its own status in relation to the being of things. Value judgments are for them not cognitive judgments.

Simmel probably stresses this standpoint more energetically than anyone else. "That objects, thoughts, events are valuable, that is never something to be read off their merely natural existence and content; and the order imposed on them in accord with values deviates the most from the natural order."[3] "There is the so to speak complete, objective being, determined in its reality from every side, and then the valuation that first approaches it, like light and shadows, which cannot stem from it itself but instead only from somewhere else."[4] "The valuation, as an actual psychological process, is a part of the natural world. But what we mean by it, its conceptual *sense*, is something standing on its own opposite this world and it is so little a part of the latter that it is rather the entire world regarded from a particular viewpoint."[5]

Von Ehrenfels also holds that value cannot be construed as a property |265| or capacity of objects but must be construed instead as a relation, "and, to be sure, of the category similar to the relation between a represented object and the representation directed at it, the relation between a judged object and the relevant judgment, and more of the same."[6]

The representation of the peculiar status of value seems to emerge from the following account by Meinong as well: "One ascribes... to a sound [the property of] being pleasant or displeasing with the very same ease that one ascribes to it [the property of] being high or low and it is commonly experienced that one must first draw the attention of the person judging to the subjectivity of attributes of the former sort. But then extra-sensory, e.g., aesthetic feelings also show this capacity, as I would put it, of being linked to purely intellectual determinations... This abbreviated procedure of attaching the feeling of value as an attribute to a mental object without further ado may comply well with practical needs. But that can change nothing about the *fact* that the feeling cannot be a property of the thing in question..." and so forth.[7]

---

[3] Georg Simmel, *Philosophie des Geldes* [Philosophy of Money], Leipzig: Duncker & Humbolt, 1900, p. 1.
[4] Ibid., p. 4.
[5] Ibid.
[6] Christian von Ehrenfels, *System der Werttheorie* [System of Value Theory], Leipzig: Reisland, 1897, p. 65.
[7] Alexis Meinong, *Psychologisch-ethische Untersuchungen zur Werttheorie* [Psychological-ethical Investigations for a Theory of Value], Graz: Leuschner & Lubensky, 1894, p. 26.

Kreibig expresses himself quite decisively: "What is nonetheless necessary is the founding determination that value is never a property or quality inhering in an object of the external world but is instead *solely* of a subjective nature."[8] Jonas Cohn makes the distinction explicit: "We confer a value; *we do not somehow assert an objectively determinable property*."[9] So, too, Max Weber: "Value judgments are ultimately based on determinate ideals and, for that reason, have a subjective origin."[10]

Independently of this general question of the epistemological [*erkenntnistheoretischen*] sense of the value judgment, answers have been given to the more specific question of the objective validity of value judgments. Indeed, although Kant explicitly says that the very |266| relation of the object to our feeling prevents the aesthetic judgment from being a cognitive judgment, he had already presupposed a common sensibility [*Gemeinsinn*] through which universality and necessity were nonetheless supposed to accrue to aesthetic judgments. When Cohn, building directly on Kant, speaks of value judgments' "mandate-character [*Forderungscharakter*]" ("the individual feels that a mandate, standing over his arbitrary will, compels him to acknowledge the value"), he likely gave expression in this way to today's universal conviction.[11] To my knowledge, only once has the attempt been made—namely, by Robert Eisler—to deny the mandate-character inherent in values and to derive from the subjectivity of valuation the merely subjective validity of value judgments as well. Eisler puts forward the proposition: "Beautiful is what pleases anyone or at any time has done so."[12] It is apparent that this proposition contradicts facts about the mind; a more detailed critique of it will ensue from the following accounts of the matter (see, too, pp. 283 and 320).

If we proceed to ask how the other authors brought the subjective doctrine of value into harmony with the mandate-character inherent in values, we do not get a completely satisfying answer. According to Simmel, the claims things make (on us) to value in determinate ways can be housed in the I no more than they can in the objects to which they refer. "There are norms for

---

[8] Josef Kreibig, *Psychologische Grundlegung eines Systems der Werttheorie* [Psychological Foundation of a System of Value Theory], Wien: Hölder, 1902, p. 6.
[9] Jonas Cohn, *Allgemeine Ästhetik* [General Aesthetics], Leipzig: Engelmann, 1901, p. 17.
[10] Max Weber, "Die 'Objektivität' sozialwissenschaftlicher und sozialpolitischer Erkenntnis [The Objectivity of Social Scientific and Social Political Cognition]." In *Archiv für Sozialwissenschaft und Sozialpolitik*, 19, 1904, pp. 22f.
[11] Cohn, *Allgemeine Ästhetik*, p. 37.
[12] Robert Eisler, *Studien zur Werttheorie* [Studies for Value Theory], Leipzig: Duncker & Humblot, 1902, p. 97.

subjectivity that are produced between us and things in such a way that they appear subjective when considered from [the perspective of] the natural state of the matter [*Sachlichkeit*], but appear objective when considered from [the perspective of] the subject, while in reality they form a third category, not capable of being put together from them."[13] He explains the concept of the objective value of things, indifferent to whether it is acknowledged by anyone, as metaphysical and constructs a third category for values between subjectivity and objectivity.[14]

Jonas Cohn is content with showing that there is a necessary gap in the proof of non-logical values and that there is no possible way around appealing to something that can only be experienced but not proven.[15] |267| According to Meinong, mistakes in regard to values refer only to mediated values. "If maintaining something's value [*Werthaltung*] comes about without an accompanying judgment, there is then no space for a mistake with regard to value."[16] The significance of the distinction between true and false value judgments can never go beyond the judgments that are presupposed in the relevant instance of maintaining something's value.[17] Von Ehrenfels acknowledges, to be sure, the possibility of deceptions even about what one holds to be valuable, and Kreibig explicitly declares that setting aright the popular skeptical claims ("value is something relative, through and through subjective, a private matter of the individual, capable of no generalization" and so forth) is part of the genuine purpose of his treatise.[18] Yet one looks in vain in the case of one author as in that of another for a principled stance toward the question of the extent and the degree to which value judgments can be true and false and can accordingly demand [*fordern*] from us acknowledgment or rejection—whether, like von Ehrenfels, one speaks of normal, outlived, and aspirational valuations or, like Kreibig, one grounds a theory of the development of value on the observations of modern biology. By drawing up law-governed processes in the development of valuations and value judgments, one can indeed acquire scientific truths about the domain

---

[13] Simmel, *Philosophie des Geldes*, p. 10.
[14] Simmel, *Philosophie des Geldes*, p. 12.
[15] Cohn, *Allgemeine Ästhetik*, pp. 40–42.
[16] Meinong, *Psychologisch-ethische Untersuchungen zur Werttheorie*, p. 81. [*Werthaltung* means literally 'holding a value' but in Meinong's discussion it frequently signifies 'maintaining some particular thing's value' such as a dowsing rod [*Wünschelrute*] or healing herb [*Heilkraut*]; see Meinong, *Psychologisch-ethische Untersuchungen zur Werttheorie*, p. 68.]
[17] Meinong, *Psychologisch-ethische Untersuchungen zur Werttheorie*, p. 76.
[18] Kreibig, *Psychologische Grundlegung eines Systems der Werttheorie*, p. 11.

of value, but without being able to establish the contrast of truth and error in the value judgments themselves.

The fact that all values are subjectively conditioned can no longer be disputed today. But the proper status of values relative to the being of things, a status that is maintained at the same time as this fact, is a different matter. If, while fully acknowledging that they are subjectively conditioned, we should nonetheless succeed in doing justice to the fact that values enjoy a trans-subjective validity without having recourse to a new category (like Simmel) or a metaphysical purpose of the world (like Lotze); and if we should succeed at this by placing value judgments on a par with judgments about the sensory qualities of things, judgments that are no less subjectively conditioned and no less trans-subjectively valid, |268| then this explanation would have the advantage over those others of simplifying instead of complicating the picture of the world. The value judgment would then be a cognitive judgment and value would no longer be contrasted with being but instead would become a *content* of being [*Seinsinhalt*] and would move into the place where the ancients and (following Democritus) Descartes, Locke, and Spinoza moved it, namely, into a place on a par with the sensory qualities of things.

Section I

Chapter 1. Feeling and Value

The representatives of the subjectivist doctrine of values have conceived of the subjective element on which they ground value in various ways. In regard to this question there has been a tendency of late to start out in an obviously one-sided way from moral judgments whose *meaning* essentially consists in their relation to future actions and, hence, to the will. This seems to be the only explanation of why so many authors see the subjective foundation of value judgment in the *will*. Höfler, von Ehrenfels, Schwarz, and Höffding, among others, agree in positing the value of the thing in its relation to desire. This definition, as something universal, is not tenable since the primary aesthetic and ethical judgments of taste contradict it.[19] This definition would be feasible only if one reduced these judgments as well to volitional

---

[19] The same holds also for Meinong's reduction of values to feelings of existence and judgment.

reactions—a reduction that, to my knowledge, has as yet been attempted nowhere. It would be easier to reduce all other values to the paradigm of judgments of taste than vice versa since desire, in every case, presupposes an acquaintance with the desired object [*Objekt*] as satisfying a need, or a conjecture that it will do so. But now since satisfaction of a need contains no volitional element, the value, as Meinong also emphasizes,[20] is not created by the desire but found by it to be there already. Accepting and rejecting objects [*Gegenstände*] is |269| the expression, not of the feeling of value but instead of the reaction of the will tied to this feeling. To be sure, things determine us to act only insofar as they are values for us and, for this reason, one may at least define a value as a power of motivation. This definition (found in Schwarz) may be legitimate as a conceptual equivalent but the value-creating principle is not provided by it. Von Ehrenfels is repeatedly compelled to reach back to the feeling determining the desire,[21] and since for him desire resolves itself into elements of feeling and representation, his definition is not inherently opposed to the theory of feeling anyhow.

Just as matters stand with the will, so they stand likewise with another subjective element to which value has been reduced: the *ideal* or *norm* of the subject. Erdmann, Stange, and Busse determine values as norms and the feeling of value as the expression of an agreement with the norm.

This doctrine also corresponds to the facts insofar as countless value judgments are in fact made on the basis of an ideal on the part of the subject. Thus, to seize upon merely one example, it is Novalis' own ideal against which he measures Goethe's work when he takes issue with the lack of any mood of ambivalence [*Dämmerungsstimmung*] in *Wilhelm Meister*. But immediate value judgments are so little dependent upon an ideal or a norm that every such dependence must be construed rather as a falsification of the value judgment. For the ideal is itself already a value and hence cannot be regarded as what forms values. An object that is measured against an ideal is no longer valued in an immediate way; such a judgment would instead have as its theme the connection of the object to a representation belonging to the subject, a representation that has, for its part, already been valued. Such a judgment would thus have the relationship of two values as its theme.

---

[20] Meinong, *Psychologisch-ethische Untersuchungen zur Werttheorie*, p. 15. So, too, Kreibig (*Psychologische Grundlegung eines Systems der Werttheorie*, p. 80): "All wanting is directed at the *realization* of values."

[21] For example, "Every valuation is a disposition of feeling" (von Ehrenfels, *System der Werttheorie*, p. 149).

We are content here with dismissing, on logical grounds, the two theories mentioned. The facts on which they are grounded, the complications that arise through the values' connection to the will and through their conflict with one another, as well as the deceptions regarding facts of value that arise through unconsciously indirect valuation are to be discussed in detail below. |270|

Hence, if a value judgment asserts neither a connection of its object to a representation already valued by us nor such a connection to our desires, then, along with the majority of psychologists, we will be able to see its content only in the object's connection to our feeling. To be sure, we will then have to see in the pure, disinterested judgment of taste the paradigm of the value judgment; we will have to see it accordingly, along with Kant, in the connection of an object to the subject and the subject's feeling of pleasure and displeasure.

In what follows we have only the primary, unmediated values in our sights. One might want to object to this restriction that the difference between primary and secondary values is not everywhere clear, that there may be objects that appear to be valued immediately while their value is in fact mediated solely by associations that have become unconscious. If this objection were made, the reply would have to be that although our cognition does not, to be sure, always suffice to classify an individual instance with infallible certainty under a conceptually produced group, this is itself no objection to the conceptual distinction itself insofar as the theoretical aim of the investigation appears to require and justify this distinction.

Now, of course, it is possible to think of a standpoint that would not count immediate ethical and aesthetic judgments of taste among value judgments at all, due to the way these judgments differ from all other judgments, in particular since the volitional element is missing in them. In this sense, Witasek, referring to aesthetic feeling, says that the application of the term 'value' to 'being pleased' by something or 'finding it pleasing' [*Gefallen*] is mistaken since it blurs the boundaries between essentially different mental components [*psychische Tatbeständen*].[22] Schwarz occupies a quite similar standpoint when he distinguishes the feeling of pleasure and displeasure from finding something pleasing as a *sui generis* state of consciousness, in other words, from maintaining something's value [*Werthalten*].[23] This is also essentially the standpoint of Meinong who characterizes feelings of value, in contrast to

---

[22] Stephan Witasek, "Wert und Schönheit [Value and Beauty]," *Archiv für systematische Philosophie VIII*, 1902, p. 164.

[23] Hermann Schwarz, "Gefallen und Lust [Being Pleased and Pleasure]," *Philosophische Abhandlungen, R. Haym gewidmet [Philosophical Treatises, dedicated to R. Haym]*, 1902, pp. 407–506.

feelings of representations, as feelings of judgment.[24] Now undoubtedly there are feelings of value that presuppose judgments, but I am unable to find within myself the mental component that |271| would require *necessarily* tying *every* feeling of value to an existential judgment. Meinong argues: "The pleasure aroused by the object cannot be itself the feeling of value, otherwise one could consider the thing valuable only as long as it arouses pleasure."[25] But if one considers something valuable without feeling pleasure, one does not thereby have some other mysterious feeling of value. One is then grounding a judgment about an object on a past or dispositional pleasure instead. In the distinction flagged by Meinong and by Witasek, I can see nothing other than the difference of judgments about inner perception from those about external objects. Thus I believe that all judgments about feelings of judgment could be traced back to the paradigm of the pure judgment of taste. Should an investigation, however, directed specifically at this not prove successful, a distinction in Witasek's sense might well be desirable. One could perhaps in this way reach back to the distinction emphasized by Plato in the *Philebus*, namely, the distinction between feelings of pleasure that are preceded by the painful need for them and those the lack of which is painless and goes unnoticed.

Without entering into this question in more detail, we can nevertheless recognize, without further ado, that pure judgments of taste are not found only in the domain of aesthetics. Not even all ethical judgments are mediated by the concept of the good; instead, certain relationships to the will are immediately liked and disliked, as Herbart has shown. Nourishment, habitation, ornamentation, health, knowledge—all from the domain dubbed 'autopathy' by Kreibig—are also immediately valued. A conscious connection to the subject's well-being and detriment [weal and woe: *Wohl und Wehe*], as Kreibig's presentation suggests, does not necessarily take place here.[26] |272|

---

[24] Meinong, *Psychologisch-ethische Untersuchungen zur Werttheorie*, pp. 22ff. [These pages of Meinong's essay refer to §9, a section entitled "The feeling of value as feeling of a judgment [*Urteilsgefühl*]." In this section he argues that the feeling of value refers back to a judgment that calls it up and produces the connection between it and the object of value.]

[25] Ibid., p. 22.

[26] Ibid., p. 22. The criterion, according to which something is valued autopathically, encompasses the poles of opposition: "good in the sense of initiating pleasure, for the subject valuing [this or that]" and "bad in the sense of initiating displeasure, for the subject valuing [this or that]." Correspondingly (ibid., p. 106), what is understood under the heading of heteropathy is the doctrine of the valuation of all given contents with respect to the polar opposites "good in the sense of initiating pleasure, for another subject" and "bad in the sense of initiating displeasure, for another subject." Finally, under the heading of ergopathy, Kreibig would have us understand the doctrine of the valuation of all given contents with respect to the opposites "beautiful" and "ugly" in the sense of initiating pleasure and initiating displeasure as pertaining purely, i.e., without referring to oneself as the subject or to another subject.

By contrast, I necessarily and fundamentally exclude here those values of a domain that more recent theoreticians of value like to treat—I mean economic values. Only objects that are already recognized in some direction or other as valuable, i.e., *only values* can enter into the economic exchange; and *all objects of value*[27] (whether they belong to the autopathic, heteropathic, or ergopathic domain) become economic values as soon as their possession has to be purchased by giving up other objects of value. All economic values are thus of a secondary nature; they express relations between objects of other domains of value. Even where values are seemingly newly *created* only in the economic domain, what the production still depends upon is only the *realization* of objects already recognized, in the representation of them, as autopathically, heteropathically, or ergopathically valuable. That no primary values are present here at all already follows from the fact that in economic life there is indeed a scale of values but no opposite of value. There are economically lesser values but no economic non-values.

Also to be excluded from the primary values is what is useful since it already presupposes a value in relation to which another object acquires value; the concept of utility is thus first derived from the concept of value.[28]

Chapter 2. Feeling and Cognition

The question now arises: are value judgments the sorts of judgments that have as their object [*Gegenstand*] the immediate relation of an object [*Objekt*] to the subject and the subject's feeling of pleasure and displeasure and just for that reason are not really cognitive judgments? Are they really incapable of designating a property of the object?

This construal of valuation is consistent as long as one continues to consider |273| feeling as the only purely subjective element of consciousness. From the time that feeling was introduced into psychology in general as a self-standing element of consciousness, it has always been regarded as a paradigm of subjectivity. Thus, more recent psychologists like Külpe, for example, distinguish it as a *state* of consciousness [*Bewußtseinszustand*] from

---

[27] *Objects of value*, i.e., valued objects of the external world [are meant here]; what has been said does not hold for values *of a mental sort* [*psychische Werte*]; these can never become economic values.
[28] See, too, Meinong, *Psychologisch-ethische Untersuchungen zur Werttheorie*, p. 13.

the *contents* of consciousness.[29] And Wundt merely expresses the predominant way of construing it when he says: "While representation always aims at external objects and, if it refers to one's own being, makes this itself into a theme of objective consideration, feelings remain subjective... They all refer to a state of the entity itself that feels, i.e., to a suffering or acting on the part of the I."[30]

Epistemologically, feeling is also conceived as the stimulus and point of departure for the radical separation of subject and object from the side of the subject. "However vaguely, indeterminately, and deficiently localized the lowest animal apprehends the mechanical, thermal, and chemical effects on its skin, the effects nonetheless appear from the outset as polar opposites to the manners of feeling in which the entity finds itself. It seizes upon itself in its feeling and finds, opposite itself, the contents of sensation as 'objective,' as not-I."[31] "Contents of sensation and feelings camp around two points, separated from one another."[32]

In my view, it is time to become skeptical of such purely subjective elements of consciousness.

If any constant direction of development in the history of epistemology can be affirmed at all, it surely consists in the fact that ever more elements for our world-picture are recognized as subjective. For centuries insight into the subjectively conditioned character of beings fostered doubt regarding the possibility of objective cognition in general. But since Kant has taught us to see |274| the essence and guarantee of an objective world in purely subjective elements of our mind, shouldn't we cast doubt on the "*purely* subjective" elements, i.e., those that could supposedly never, in all eternity, produce an objective world, or those opposite which no such world could supposedly ever appear as a correlate? If one reduces things in the positivistic sense to the sum of their qualities, and if these qualities are ultimately nothing but sensations or, adopting Mach's terminology, "elements" that one can imagine

---

[29] Compare Oswald Külpe, *Grundriß der Psychologie* [Outline of Psychology], Leipzig: Engelmann, 1893.

[30] Wilhelm Wundt, *Vorlesungen über Menschen- und Tierseele* [Lectures on the Human and the Animal Soul], Leipzig: Voss, 1897, p. 223. See, too, further quotations with the same content by Wundt and similar quotations by Lipps, Lehmann, and others in Johannes Orth, *Gefühl und Bewußtseinslage* [Feeling and State of Consciousness], Berlin: Reuther & Reichard, 1903, in the paragraph "Über das Subjektive als Kriterium des Gefühls [On the Subjective as Criterion of Feeling]," pp. 20–28.

[31] Ernst Laas, *Idealismus und Positivismus: Eine kritische Auseinandersetzung, Dritter Theil: Idealistische und positivistische Erkenntnistheorie* [Idealism and Positivism: A Critical Dispute, Third Part: Idealist and Positivist Epistemology], Berlin: Weidmann, 1884, p. 66.

[32] Ibid., p. 67.

[*sich vorstellen*] as constant connections of the objects to our sense organs, why should one not take the further step of construing the constant connection of an object to our feeling as a property of this object? Is not the epistemological separation of things' sensory qualities from the feeling they elicit perhaps just as incoherent and untenable as the separation of its primary from its secondary qualities? Why should being red count as a property of the thing but not being beautiful? One is keen to prove the dependency of values on the subject; but two hundred years ago Locke proved such a dependency for other objective properties of things as well.

The sole objection that von Ehrenfels advanced as counting against construing value as a property or capacity of the object (a property or capacity indirectly determined through the relation to our desiring and feeling) is the consideration that the value is then bound in its existence to the existence of the object. One could then no longer ascribe to an object a value independent of any temporal determination. But this in fact allegedly happens when, for example, a German patriot, currently alive, places a value on Hermann's victory in the Teutoburg Forest.[33] The choice of this example is unfortunate insofar as a battle cannot be evaluated immediately but only in view of its consequences. And, insofar as that view exhibits a relation, one can at most attribute to this value a legitimacy across different times. But, although the *valuation* is carried out in the present, precisely the use of language to which von Ehrenfels appeals would permit the value itself to be placed only in the past tense [*Präteritum*] of that battle that is long over. But this is quite decisively the case for |275| all unique values. The unique value of an object [*Objekt*] ceases with the existence of the object [*Gegenstand*] as much as all its other qualities do. Von Ehrenfels does not distinguish between real and represented value. The value can be *represented* in an object that does not exist just as much as the object itself and its other qualities can. To this extent it is in fact not tied to the *existence* but to the time-transcending essence of the object. But its realization depends upon the realization of the object.

It is above all the seemingly greater variability of feeling that leads to subjectifying it. Tetens had his eye on this when he distinguishes "sentiments" [*Empfindnisse*] as the feeling of "the subjective relationships and connections of objects and variations to *our present state*" from the feeling of "the relationships and connections in which the objects stand among

---

[33] von Ehrenfels, *System der Werttheorie*, p. 64.

themselves, the feeling of their objective relationships."[34] "A further distinction is made regarding a type of sensation or alteration that the feeling takes on in keeping with the different connections of the objects felt to the *present make-up of the soul* and its capacities and powers."[35] By way of elucidation, he adds: "Someone who has eaten his fill is disgusted by [the thought of] enjoying any further the food that awakens nothing but pleasure in someone who is hungry . . . after a few hours we grow weary of the music that now enthralls us." But we also find differences conditioned in this way by the momentary state of consciousness even in representations and sensations. For centuries, to be sure, from the time that these differences were emphasized by the Eleatics, they led to skepticism in general or, at least, to discrediting *sensory* cognition and to rationalism. But there has been some success in working on the fragmentary and at times distorted material that the senses provide such that today we nonetheless acknowledge the law-governed dependency of sensations on the object and accordingly the possibility of objective cognition through the senses. Given this success, why should we, based on the same seeming lack of law-governed dependency in the way feelings occur, consider any cognition through feelings |276| to be closed off? *Just as we distinguish between subjectively and objectively conditioned sensations, so, too, we may distinguish between subjectively and objectively conditioned feelings.* It is not—as commonly assumed—that determinate phenomena of consciousness justify the subjectivity and others the objectivity; it is instead the respective constellation within the individual phenomena of consciousness, the fact that law-governed dependencies obtain or fail to obtain, that decides on the subjective or objective origin of the respective appearance.

The view that properties of things are discerned through feeling appears especially paradoxical because science has labored for centuries precisely to purge cognizing of any elements of feeling.

What things signify for us, whether they bring us pleasure or suffering, did not enter into consideration for cognition of causes, for cognition of lawful connections generally, and hence, they had to be suspended. But it was, and continues without exception to be, not only the felt significance of things that science had to suspend for its work. Since cognition of lawful connections signifies, without exception, the formation of a sequence in which the

---

[34] Johannes Tetens, *Philosophische Versuche über die menschliche Natur* [Philosophical Essays on Human Nature], I, Leipzig: Weidmann, 1777, p. 190.
[35] Ibid., p. 184.

individual members are always connected to *one* quality alone, science had to abstract from the sensory qualities of things no less than from the values. For mechanics, the color of things is as irrelevant as thermal qualities are for optics. So, too, for the consideration of the anatomy of a flower, its aesthetic value is no less immaterial than its color.

Science had to battle animistic representations along with the theological and teleological consideration of things. Guilt and punishment were "deliberately misread" [*hineingelogen*] into things, elements were allowed to love and hate each other. In this way, too, feeling was a hindrance to science. But one easily sees that cognition by way of feeling, the cognition through feeling as an inner sense, of which we are speaking, has as little to do with importing representations of human feelings into things as it does with the teleological consideration of them. What we are discussing is perception; animistic representations are scientific, philosophical |277| or religious hypotheses. If I call a thing 'beautiful' or 'ugly,' 'good' or 'bad,' I no more import into the thing something alien to it than I do by asserting that it is blue. If we want to see a cognitive judgment in the value judgment, it is not scientific cognition that is meant but instead its foundation: cognition through perception.

In view of the significance that perceptual judgments have for conceptual cognition, an objection might be raised against this construal of value judgments precisely as a kind of perceptual judgment. The objection would go like this: the sensory properties of things, one could say, have a fundamental significance for conceptual cognition—first for recognizing things, then for concept formation; their beauty, by contrast, accomplishes nothing in this regard. And there's more. Sensory qualities have incomparably greater significance than values do, not only for practical, but also for scientific cognition. An entire world-view, the mechanistic world-view, constructs the world from elements to which the primary sensory qualities of solidity, extension, shape, and mobility are ascribed exclusively. But, the objection would continue, since only the primary properties form this sort of interconnectedness among themselves and since they are of such generality that one can derive all other qualities from them and can think the entire world constructed on them, placing primary and secondary qualities on the same epistemological level fails to recognize essential differences. How much more does placing tertiary qualities on the same level as well fail to do so!

As far as the first objection is concerned, one would be warranted to reply that the different sensory qualities have a completely different significance for recognizing things and for the concept of things. A color, for example, frequently performs a valuable service for recognizing things, but it is usually set aside in the process of concept-formation. By contrast, a thing's value is hardly helpful for recognizing things but quite essential for concept-formation. Only by means of it can the concept of certain things, e.g., any work of art, be grasped at all. As for the second objection, every religious system and a large number of philosophical systems are at odds with the mechanistic world-view. When Plato derives all other ideas from the idea of the good, when Lotze has the world striving to realize the good, when for Nietzsche (in the |278| *Birth of Tragedy*) the world can only be justified as an aesthetic phenomenon, all properties that are ascribed here to ethical and aesthetic values are the properties that according to the mechanistic construal of the world are the distinguishing marks of so-called primary qualities: permanence, interconnectedness among themselves, and derivability of all other qualities from them. Yet it has still not occurred to anyone to classify all objects according to their colors or the sounds they emit, let alone to explain the world on the basis of colors or sounds. Thus, in terms of their inner interconnectedness and universality, the secondary properties of things in each case stand *farther* from the primary properties than the tertiary qualities, the values, do. But if, viewed from the standpoint of the mechanistic construal of things, beauty appears as it were as a contingent phenomenon that could not have anything to do with the essence of things and the cognition directed at them, then it needs to be asked in turn what color has to do with it and whether the lawfulness of the beautiful could not be researched in aesthetics just as that of color is in optics. If one speaks of a complete being, determined in its reality on every side, which valuation would first approach like light and shadow, then this can be maintained, with even greater right, of the atomic world of mechanics, which colors, sounds, odors and so forth approach by first starting from the standpoint of the subject. For the sensory properties are no more derivable than value from being that is thoroughly determined in a causal way.

What could still speak against placing values on a par with sensory qualities is the fact [*Umstand*] that the construal of beauty first comes about through the mediation of sensory perception. Yet whether a property like color, odor, or taste rests upon properties of objects that we can only grasp indirectly in the chemical laboratory or, like beauty, on properties that we can grasp directly through other organs of sense, this would indeed amount to characterizing the latter phenomenon as dependent to a higher degree and stepping into the light later but it would not permit a lesser degree of being to be ascribed to it. Platner's observation[36] must, indeed, be conceded, namely, that the more complicated the sense organ and the more indirectly the |279| effect of the object on it is, the less pure and true the representations of it are. But this difference refers only to the empirical correctness of the judgments based upon it. For the emergence of a perception that is more mediated, as aesthetic perception is, many presuppositions are necessary, of which sometimes the one, sometimes the other fails to be realized. By this means, the number of possible deceptions is increased. But this circumstance proves nothing against the fact that, if the fulfillment of all conditions is presupposed, the perception—in our case, the aesthetic feeling—enters with the very same *immediacy*, certainty, and constancy as any other sense-organ's perception. The ethical evaluation of an action likewise exhibits an *immediate* connection of the feeling to the action, regardless of how complicated the activities on the part of the mind necessary for its construal (which does not happen solely through the senses) may be. It is precisely this immediacy that occasioned Hutcheson already two centuries ago to assume an "inner sense" for beauty. Today, on account of this immediacy, Gestalt-qualities can also be counted as a perception, although conceptually they presuppose a collection of individual perceptions. Just as these individual perceptions form the foundation for the perception of the whole, so the Gestalt-qualities (e.g., melodies) form the foundation for a new perception, beauty. Beauty is given with the perception of the Gestalt-quality just as little as the Gestalt-quality is given with the construal of the parts. Although the aesthetic apperception is there at the same time as the Gestalt-quality, it is nonetheless necessary to acknowledge the possibility theoretically that a melody can be grasped as such without its aesthetic character. Just as the perception of color and that of extension are two different perceptions (although the one cannot be had without the other), so the construal of the sounds in their relationship to one another that makes up the apperception of the melody is manifestly distinguishable from the simultaneous connection of this relationship to the feeling of pleasure and displeasure—which makes up the aesthetic apperception.

In all the places where value's distinctive status opposite things is maintained, one can put a color, odor, or sound in the place of the value each time.—In keeping with our intuitions, |280| the Kantian question of how

---

[36] See Arthur Wreschner, *Ernst Platner und Kants Kritik der reinen Vernunft* [Ernst Platner and Kant's Critique of Pure Reason], Leipzig: Pfeffer, 1893, p. 97.

judgments of taste are a priori possible would need to be raised precisely for judgments of the senses as well: "how is a judgment possible that, merely from *one's own feeling* of the pleasure an object affords—[from *one's own* sensation of the color]—independently of the concept of it, would judge that this pleasure—[this sensation]—inheres in the representation of the same object in *every other subject*, a priori, i.e., without needing to wait for the other's agreement."[37] Or: "It is an empirical judgment that I perceive and evaluate an object with pleasure—[as red]. But it is a judgment *a priori* that I find it beautiful—[red]—that is to say, that I am permitted to expect that gratification—[that color]—as necessary for everyone."[38] Allow me to seize upon one more example. Ehrenfels says "we do not desire things because we recognize that mystical, incomprehensible essence 'value,' but instead we attribute 'value' to things because we desire them."[39] When he says this, one can argue correspondingly that we do not see things because we recognize that mystical, incomprehensible essence of color and light in them; instead we attribute color and light to things because we see that color and light.

From the discussions of this chapter, it emerges clearly enough (so I hope) that, by laying claim to feeling as a source of cognition, we are not reverting to the Leibniz-Wolffian, intellectualist construal of feeling. Feeling remains for us an elementary quality of consciousness that, precisely through its uniqueness, conveys a thoroughly *sui generis* and by no means confused cognition, a cognition that could be given neither by an organ of the senses nor by thinking at all, let alone be given more clearly and more distinctly.

The question of the truth and falsity of value judgments will concern us at length in the following chapters. Yet from the foregoing, this much can already be inferred: if value-judgments stand on one level with sensory judgments, then the problem posed above (pp. 248f)—namely, how the acknowledgement of the subjectively conditioned character of values can be reconciled with the acknowledgement of |281| their mandate-character—leads back to a more general problem. In our construal of the matter, the claim of things to a determinate valuation is nothing other than the mandate inherent in true sensory judgments. Values' claim on being acknowledged is

---

[37] Kant, *Kritik der Urteilskraft* [Critique of the Power of Judgment], § 36. [Brackets and text in them here are interposed by Landmann-Kalischer into the cited text. Note, too, that the first use of 'object' is a translation of *Gegenstand* and the second use is a translation of *Objekt*. Kant's characterization of the latter as 'the same object' as the former suggests that, at least in this context, he treats them as synonyms.]
[38] Ibid., § 37.
[39] von Ehrenfels, *System der Werttheorie*, p. 2.

formed in no other way and has no other origin than the claim that sensory qualities have to be recognized. That this compelling character is also present for objectively false judgments is grounded in the sources of deception and likewise finds its analogue in the domain of the senses. To impart this or that value to an object is a matter of an individual's preference just as little as it is left to its arbitrary will to see this or that color.

Section II

Chapter 3. The Subjective Reliability of Value Judgments

In the preceding chapter we sought to suggest, through general reflections, that the epistemological status of values is on a par with that of things' sensory properties. But the justification of that parity depends on the answer to the more specific question of whether—and to what extent—the same degree of objective validity that can be ascribed to sensory judgments can be ascribed to aesthetic judgments. Hence, in what follows we attempt to draw out the analogy between sensory judgments and value judgments with respect to the kind and degree of their validity. In the process, detailed analogies will also afford themselves, thanks to which the construal of aesthetic feeling as a kind of sense organ appears justified.

Like sensory judgments, aesthetic judgments appear in two forms, in a subjective form ('this pleases me,' 'I see a blue') and an objective form ('this is beautiful,' 'this is blue'). Like a sensory judgment, the aesthetic judgment is made immediately and without reflection. It can neither be proven nor be refuted in its subjective form, and it can nonetheless be true or false.

We examine first the subjective form of sensory judgments and value judgments in which they present themselves as judgments of inner perception. In logic, even up to the present day, judgments of inner perception count |282| as evident and thus not open to a question of truth or falsity. Sigwart speaks of their "immediate," "absolute" certainty, their "self-evident validity."[40] Even a psychologist like Meinong considers "that

---

[40] Christoph Sigwart, *Logik*, Freiburg in Breisgau: Mohr, 1889, I, p. 391.

certainty and evidence that no other immediate knowledge of existence has in common with inner perception" to be characteristic of the latter.[41] And this holds for him not only for judgments with such universal content as 'I feel pain' or 'I see light.' Instead he specifically formulates a law of evidence for judgments of difference; for refutation of this law by the psychological facts themselves, see Schumann's "Contributions to the Analysis of Visual Perceptions."[42]

The most thoroughgoing examination of sensory judgments with respect to their validity is probably found in Stumpf's psychology of sound, to which I refer in what follows.

Stumpf distinguishes between the objective and subjective reliability [Zuverlässigkeit] of judgments. Under the latter, which first concern us here, he understands the reliability of a judgment in regard to the correct construal of sensations as such in contrast to the correct interpretation of them for external objects.[43] As factors of subjective reliability, he cites: certainty and exactness of the reproduction of the representation, degree of attentiveness, feelings, accompanying representations. The same inherent features also influence aesthetic judgment. Such a judgment easily confuses aesthetic and intellectual satisfaction; it is distracted by the contingent mood, the emotion, or the prejudice that obtains as the aesthetic impression is being taken up.

Now as certain as it is that all these factors also inhibit or advance the correct evaluation of the aesthetic feeling, it is just as evident on the other side that these factors influence not only the judgment about the feeling but also—and to a much higher degree—the feeling itself. Thus, in order to avoid redundancies, we will first discuss them when we go over the objective reliability of these judgments. |283|

Belonging squarely to the domain of subjective reliability is, by contrast, the case in which feelings factually on hand are colored over by others and thus not heeded. This phenomenon, which is very familiar from the domain of the senses, plays a great role in ethical and aesthetic feelings, particularly in education. We can become conscious of such feelings merely by their being named or merely by directing our attention to them. And this is

---

[41] Alexis Meinong, "Über Gegenstände der höheren Ordnung [On Objects of a Higher Order]," Zeitschrift für Psychologie 21 (1899): p. 212.
[42] Friedrich Schumann, "Beiträge zur Analysis der Gesichtswahrnehmungen [Contributions to the Analysis of Visual Perceptions]," III. Zeitschrift für Psychologie 30 (1902): pp. 331f.
[43] Carl Stumpf, Tonpsychologie [Psychology of Sound], Leipzig: Herzel, 1883, p. 31.

of the greatest significance for the individual just as it is for the education and development of feelings in the lives of peoples. When Winckelmann "discovered" ancient art, when Victor Hugo taught the French to love the monuments of their Gothic art, when Goethe disclosed a feeling for the Alps, they developed by these means the aesthetic feeling of their contemporaries. Ethical feeling can also be influenced in the same way. Thus, for example, the Sentimental Poets set not merely poetry but the entire life of the German people, particularly its ethical life, on a completely new path.[44] No one has given generally a satisfactory representation of the extent to which our ethical feelings develop under the influence of the conceptual emphasis. Compassion and devotion, like feelings in regard to oneself [*Selbstgefühl*] and rigidity, and religious sentimentality and Promethean defiance—all are developed in this [conceptual] manner from scarcely perceptible starting points to the greatest excess. The same role is played naturally by the case in reverse, in which one believes in the presence of feelings that are *not* present but reproduced [in the imagination], represented in a lively way, and artificially exalted under the influence of a wish, an ideal, or a mere belief. Thus, in many cases, under the influence of a religious suggestion, there is a feeling of sinning.

Hence, in the cases before us, we have false judgments of inner perception in relation to aesthetic and moral feelings, and these judgments have their analogue in the domain of the senses in 'mishearing' and 'overlooking' and in the falsification of the judgment of the senses through some preconceived opinion. What is already apparent here from the subjective unreliability of aesthetic judgments is, we may note in passing, the untenability of Eisler's position according to which the beautiful is supposed to be everything that is said to be pleasing.

The question now is what criteria are on hand to monitor the subjective reliability of individual judgments. |284| In the domains of the senses in which the stimuli and sensations form series of sequences, subjective reliability is measured by testing a series with the same adequate, external stimuli and under the same distorting, attendant conditions. In the aesthetic domain an investigation of this could perhaps be carried out by placing the same object before the person in the experiment, while systematically directing or

---

[44] ['Sentimental poets' refers to *Dichter der Empfindsamkeit*, a literary and musical style beginning in the mid-eighteenth century with Klopstock's *Oden* (1750) and Carl Philipp Emanuel Bach's *Versuch über die wahre Art das Klavier zu spielen* [Essay on the True Art of Playing Keyboard Instruments] (1753).]

diverting attention, producing accompanying representations, arousing determinate dispositions of feeling through contrasts, investigating the influence of the exercise, and so forth. Particularly for the evaluation of geometric figures, different but invariably prescribed viewpoints for their apperception would deliver interesting results.

The possibility of acquiring subjectively correct judgments is naturally not closed off by the fact that judgments are altered through more or less contingent co-determinations. As soon as the co-determinations are *discerned*, they can also be discounted or even eliminated. In the sensory domain, too, one must be content with the approximate assessment of the disturbing elements.[45] But we have no reason to assume from the analogy with the relationships on hand in sensory judgments that the exercise and with it the refinement of aesthetic judgment could continue without end. Based on existing experiments made in regard to the former [sensory judgments], the exercise ceases essentially to advance after reaching a certain level and hence it can be regarded as remaining the same.[46] Accordingly, one can speak roughly of a "maximal subjective reliability,"[47] i.e., not an absolute reliability but one that is greatest in proportion to other circumstances and individuals tested, and that proportionately approximates the ideal maximum.

Much can happen through practice and systematic education to reach this maximal subjective reliability of the aesthetic judgment. But psychological aesthetics is also of significance for this. The increasingly more precise familiarity with the specifically aesthetic mental state and the factors of its emergence is a precondition for the exclusion of anything extraneous and, along with that, for the possibility of subjectively reliable |285| judgments in general. What science achieves here for arriving at subjectively correct judgments is more important than one would have supposed for such a personal and complicated process. As the psychologists describe and analyze what they hold to be their aesthetic feeling, the typical aesthetic behavior is necessarily established through a mutual supplementation and honing [*Ergänzung und Abschleifung*], and its characteristic features can serve a layperson as signposts for subjectively correct judgments.

---

[45] Stumpf, *Tonpsychologie*, p. 46.
[46] Ibid., p. 47.
[47] Ibid., p. 47.

Chapter 4. The Objective Reliability of Value Judgments

Deceptions in Judgment

"Objective reliability is the reliability of a sensory judgment in which, along with the sensation, something objective is evaluated at the same time, or it is a judgment about sensations as signs of outer processes (stimuli)."[48] In the aesthetic domain the judgment takes leave of the fact that one is oneself pleased and, on the basis of that fact, asserts the beauty of the pleasing objects. Meanwhile, the attempt here to draw out the analogy runs up against a fundamental difficulty. Stumpf determines the sense of the objective reliability in more detail as follows: "To ask whether a sound that appears higher than another really is higher is to ask whether the tuning fork or string involved, whose vibrations occur simultaneously with this phenomenon of hearing, indicates quicker vibrations than another."[49] One sees that the question of what is really beautiful can have no analogous meaning. In some domains of the senses we are in a position of being able to compare the adequate stimuli of the sensations with the sensations themselves. In the aesthetic domain we completely lack anything of the sort. Most importantly, we have no names for the different kinds of feeling of beauty. All experimental ventures up to now have foundered on this point. The only one who has previously considered these differences is Lightner Whitmer who distinguished between liking symmetrical and liking asymmetrical proportions.[50] Since aside from this first attempt, no differentiations are made, |286| we do not know at all whether adequate aesthetic stimuli (i.e., firm connections between determinate feelings and determinate qualities) obtain; if such stimuli exist, we are not acquainted with them.

Many greet this fact of the matter as a compelling argument against putting sensory judgments and aesthetic judgments on the same level. Meanwhile, in no domain is the connection between stimulus and sensation given from the outset. Acoustics and optics were needed to be able to set up that sequence of stimuli so important for psychology. The invention of the thermometer was needed in order to be able to distinguish objective from subjective warmth. In addition, as Wundt supposes, the ability to arrange the world of sounds into a continuous series depends on the particular

---

[48] Stumpf, *Tonpsychologie*, p. 23.
[49] Ibid., p. 24.
[50] *Philosophische Studien*, herausgegeben von Wilhelm Wundt, Bd. 8 (1893) und Bd. 9 (1894), Leipzig: Engelmann.

fineness of the organ by virtue of which we can make out extremely fine gradations in the diversity of sounds.[51] "In the case of smell and taste the finer transitions of sensation are closed off from us." Thus, in the domain of the sense of smell we are still in exactly the same position as in the domain of aesthetics. We have objects from which different odors proceed, while we have no linguistic designation for their difference. We cannot produce *in nuce* the individual substances that have those odors, much less array them into a series. If so much work, streaming together from the most diverse realms of knowledge, was needed for the domains of the senses in order to set up the equivalence of two groups of sensation, why shouldn't this also be for aesthetic feelings the task of a science from which we might hope for a solution? It will be objected that aesthetics has already frequently taken on this task yet never solved it and that the way the problem is posed contains the unproven presupposition that firm connections generally exist between stimuli and sensations (aesthetic feelings), a presupposition that the popular acquiescence to the differences in taste resists. But that aesthetics up till now has still not solved that problem is no proof against the correct way of posing the problem. In addition, as far as individual differences in judgment are concerned, the constancy of the [aesthetic] judgment is, to be sure, an unproven presupposition |287| but a presupposition that it has in common with every science and that only its own progress can justify: this presumption just is the postulate that its object is generally cognizable. By distinguishing between subjective and objective beauty and drawing up the points of view that have to be applied in testing the correctness of any aesthetic judgment, the investigation that lies before us seeks precisely to decrease the muddled diversity of assertions that threatens to cut the threads of life off from aesthetics.

Since we cannot test the objective reliability of aesthetic judgments in the same way as we do for judgments regarding sounds and colors, in what follows we will introduce the process of theoretically determining the conditions of objectively reliable judgments, discussing the possible deceptions here in analogy with deceptions of the senses, and pointing out such deceptions in the history of aesthetic judgments. For now the objectively correct judgment accordingly remains a presupposition, an ideal, imaginary point that we must hope to be able to find by setting aside all causes of deceptions. Here we

---

[51] Wilhelm Wundt, *Beiträge zur Theorie der Sinneswahrnehmung* [Contributions to the Theory of Sensory Perception], Heidelberg: Winter, 1862, pp. 430, 432.

are compelled to follow Spinoza's maxim in reverse: not *veritas est norma sui et falsi* [truth is the norm of itself and the false] but instead *falsum est norma sui et veritatis* [the false is the norm of itself and the truth].

Subjective reliability presupposes objective reliability. Conditions of objective reliability are accordingly conditions for any reliability at all. Yet, since the conditions of subjective reliability have already been discussed, they are to be set aside here.

For sensory judgments as for aesthetic judgments, the conditions of objective reliability can be of a psychological, physiological, or material nature. On the presupposition that all deceptions of the senses are deceptions in *judgment*, the causes of the deception can be grounded in physical, physiological, and psychological circumstances.[52] The cause of deceptions can lie in a particular constellation of the |288] object—as in the case of the broken staff—or in the receiving organ's peculiar make-up—as in the case of contrasts and imitations—or in central conditions—cases of leading attention astray—as in the case of optical deceptions about comparison.

I would like to say here in advance that, as is the case for sensory deceptions, so, too, for aesthetic deceptions, the question often remains open which of the mentioned groups a false judgment belongs to and that the judgment, furthermore, can be false along several axes and, hence, can belong to different groups at the same time.

We begin with the central conditions of judgment and psychological deceptions.

Psychological Deceptions

The first condition for the correctness of an aesthetic judgment is without doubt the fact that it is actually an *aesthetic* judgment, that is to say, that it is pure, that it expresses nothing other than the feeling's *immediate* connection to the object. In countless cases, precisely this first, self-evident condition is not met. Just as a judgment about a tone's pitch becomes false if a judgment about its volume takes the place of the judgment about the quality, or just as judgments about spatial stretches are false if stretches other than those designated are compared with one another, so, too, in countless cases

---

[52] See Joseph Clemens Kreibig, "Über den Begriff 'Sinnestäuschung' [On the Concept 'Sensory Illusion']" *Zeitschrift für Philosophie und philosophische Kritik*, 120/2 (1902): pp. 197–203. [Landmann-Kalischer publishes a paragraph review of this essay in *Zeitschrift für Psychologie und Physiologie der Sinnesorgane* 32 (1903): p. 429.]

of aesthetic judgment an action or mood occasioned by the aesthetic object, a political or scientific theory, is evaluated in place of the aesthetic object itself. No distinction is made as to whether what is evaluated in the artwork is the artist's intention and talent, the material make-up of the artwork, or the artwork itself, whether as a whole or merely with respect to individual parts of it.

a. An art critic will praise works that laypersons pass over because the critic finds in them the announcement of a new fruitful direction or endowment. Not the artwork as such but its historical position is being evaluated. Thus, when Ruge first appeared with his paintings, it was not the accomplishment but the intention that caused a sensation.[53]

b. What is evaluated in an artwork is not the art but rather its object [*Gegenstand*]. Every history of art, music, and literature is full of judgments that stem from this source. |289| Even the greatest works of art have not escaped the clash of opinions thanks to this confusion. The ladies of Weimar found the interest paid to the fate of an innkeeper in *Hermann und Dorothea* an unseemly imposition. The gushing praise paid in the 17th century to paintings of flowers amounted for the most part to a love for flowers that corresponded to a mystical orientation of the mind. Insofar as they are directed at the entire style and express themselves as a fashion, differences in taste are also in part dependent upon such interest in the content. One also confuses aesthetic interest with interest in the content when one demands of the artwork that it fulfill spiritual needs and when one passes judgment on whether those needs are satisfied rather than on the artwork itself. Such is the case when an artwork is rejected because it has nothing to teach us, does not better us, or incorporates nothing supersensory. On the other hand, anyone who regards art as a "guilty pleasure" [*Nascherei*] and seeks nothing in it but "d'agréables distractions" will find the tragic power of Wagner or Michelangelo an unpleasant emotion. This was also one of the causes of the universal judgment against the so-called naturalism of the 1880s. And even someone who refuses to present art with any specific tasks will nonetheless easily become intolerant of a work whose idea directly contradicts a specific worldview that animates him. This

---

[53] [Landmann-Kalischer is likely referring to the work of Karl Rohwedder-Ruge (1865–1940).]

explains the judgments about tragedies whose heroes meet their demise without having committed any crime.

c. An artwork can also be beautiful in many directions; a musical piece can be praised for its themes, for the implementation of the themes, for the orchestration, and so on. A drama can have the beauty of a setting, lyric beauty, compositional beauty; a painting can have painterly beauty, the beauty of the sketch, poetic beauty. One part can succeed; another not. For all but the most cultivated, attention is usually limited to one or some of these factors, and they confuse their judgment about the part with a judgment about the whole.

The analogy of this large group of aesthetic deceptions with, for example, comparable optical deceptions also emerges clearly inasmuch as the deception disappears as soon as its cause is recognized and greater concentration on the object enters in.

Another form of psychological deception is the confusion of what is valued immediately and what is valued associatively. Just as |290| we believe we are seeing what stands in the closest associative conjunction with what is actually seen although it is either not given to the senses at all or something completely different is given—for which the psychology of the assertion has provided the most striking and most numerous examples—so, too, a factor that is in itself indifferent, indeed, distorting and contingent acquires a value when it appears in constant conjunction with valuable objects [Gegenständen]. Such is the value of relics; a relic only becomes deceiving when the value's origin is forgotten and the value is accorded to the object [Objekt] without connection to the value conveying it. Thus, a picture appeared beautiful that demonstrated the same "gallery tone" that time has leant the famous paintings of the old masters. So, too, the absence of color in sculpture became an aesthetic value because one found that the ancient sculptures most valued were devoid of color.[54]

Physiological Deceptions

Without doubt the polyvalence of the word 'pleasing' fosters to the utmost the confusions mentioned. But here, too, as usual, the deficiency of language is at the same time a deficiency of the matter. Relative to an object there are

---

[54] The last example is also found in Cohn, "Beiträge zur Lehre von den Wertungen [Contributions to the Doctrine of Valuations]," *Zeitschrift für Philosophie und philosophische Kritik*, 110, 1897, p. 240.

different feelings that are confused with one another and this happens so easily because, like many sensory qualities, they in fact pass over into one another in such a way that only a very sharpened focus of attention can distinguish them. The main reason for this fusion is probably to be sought in the fact that those extra-aesthetic feelings, particularly ethical feelings, are strongly cultivated, while aesthetic feelings are, by contrast, too often only slightly developed. They are thus colored over, as it were, by the former [ethical] feelings and, in order to make them tangible, one would have to invent aesthetic resonators. Thus, too, historically the pure concept of the aesthetic first emerges late, actually first with Kant; and, in art criticism, it is first emphasized with the appropriate sharpness by the Romantics. Both before and even after Kant, religious feelings, moral feelings, and feelings of a completely personal sort—in general all "higher feelings" are reckoned among the aesthetic feelings. Bolzano still speaks of God's beauty and finds that the portrait of someone familiar is more pleasing than that of someone unfamiliar. |291|

If the confusion of artist and artwork, of material and form, of part and whole was predominantly but not always solely of a logical nature, then with the distractions of the judgment that rest on such fusions of different feelings, one can be constantly vacillating as to whether the deceptions resulting from them should count as physiological or as psychological deceptions. In any case they already lead over to the physiological deceptions.

In the first place, the feeling's general disposition to make the correct evaluation of the aesthetic impression can be either favorable or unfavorable. Every *emotion* [*Affekt*] must be regarded generally as disturbing our receptivity to all sides [of an object] and conditioning false judgments. To be sure, by the fact that the emotion enhances the receptiveness to one side, it can sharpen the aesthetic organ in this direction and lead directly to the discovery of new values—a significance that emotions have for cognition, one that is still not sufficiently acknowledged at all. However, since this effect is exercised only on one side and the receptiveness in every other direction is correspondingly diminished, the emotion in most cases becomes the source of false judgments. If, for example, the tranquility of a landscape in the evening has an effect on a stormy soul, the aesthetic character of the landscape will emerge more clearly through the contrast than if this impression had met with soulful composure. But if, on the basis of this impression recorded in the [stormy] emotion, that landscape were judged to be particularly peaceful in comparison to others, the judgment in that case is falsified by the emotion.

In addition to this state of the soul, a determinate feeling toward the object to be evaluated aesthetically can generally have the effect of side-tracking the judgment. Since the tendency towards what is similar in new impressions dwells to a high degree in every feeling, an already deeply rooted aversion to the artwork's creator or a blind love for him will, for example, color the impression of the work from the outset. One can value every object from the standpoint of, so to speak, a 'yes' or a 'no.'

But even the aesthetically valued object itself can trigger feelings that fuse with the aesthetic feeling and influence the judgment. This is the case already discussed, in which liking or disliking the material make-up or content |292| of the artwork is mistaken for the feeling for or against the artwork itself.

If now one also adds that, prompted by an impression of one sort or another, one frequently finds oneself in an animated or crestfallen mood and judges as a result of this, without rightly knowing its aesthetic components, what results are mixtures in this domain that are completely similar to those that are familiar enough in the case of sense impressions, i.e., in the fusion of sensations of taste and touch [*Berührungs-*], temperature and tactility [*Tastempfindungen*].

In addition to emotions and feeling, there are orientations of the will that have to a high degree a distracting effect on immediate judgments of taste. An entity's prevailing tendency toward one side hinders, as emotion does, a receptiveness to *all sides*. With the *will's decision* for one value, values are transported from the realm of observation (in which they are only found and recognized) into that of the reality in which they first have to be newly created. While the thoughts dwelt easily next to one another in the realm of observation, and disinterested observation could do justice to the most diverse values, the first attempt to realize a value makes it apparent that things collide violently in space and that certain values are so opposed to one another that they cannot be realized at the same time. Hence the will's decision for *one* value produces so easily an artificial blindness to all others and directly produces an inversion of the valuation of those objects whose value contradicts the one wanted. This fact is important for the appreciation of a phenomenon that has its roots in it and that, at first glance, seems to contradict every law-governed process of disliking or liking something—I mean the phenomenon of the *"revaluation of values."*

It is already apparent on the first closer look [at this phenomenon] that even the wording bars the interpretation that it is a matter here of destroying and newly creating values. It is not that the value that the one thing had is taken from it and that a value is given to another thing that had no value. Instead, one thing that possesses a value x is weighed against another thing that has a value y, and, under the influence of a new |293| orientation of the will, the will's decision is validated that y is now made to count to the detriment of x which previously set the standard and suppressed y. It is only natural that in the one case as in the other the suppressed value is denigrated as much as possible, while its negative (that in which it is not x, not a value) is stressed as strongly as possible. This is how things go with ethical as well as with aesthetic values. An artwork cannot have idyllic and sublime, Apollonian and Dionysian beauty at the same time. An artist, however, who strives passionately after one of these very forms of beauty will be blind or unfair to the others. (Thus, artists who seek to realize a specific form of beauty in their works, in keeping with who they are essentially, are the ones most suspected of one-sidedness in their aesthetic judgment, regardless of how much natural capacity and exercise of their skills would otherwise appear to predispose them to be judges in judgments of taste.) A human being cannot simultaneously possess or want to possess the courage of a lion, the swiftness of a deer, and so on. Only the slightest part of what value a human being actually realizes and strives to realize depends on the greatness of the value which might have been assessed correctly one time and falsely another time relative to other values—it depends far more on the ideal which the person valuing is most predisposed to and has the most energy for. Thus all *choosing* of values goes beyond the object's immediate connection to feeling. The disinterested consideration does justice to all values equally. Such principled differences of value like those between Nietzsche and Christendom display a battle of values for the conquest of the will. All differences in judgment flowing from this battle are *derived* values and, as such, false or correct only in relation to the basic value. It is not true that uncivilized peoples' custom of murdering their old fathers would suddenly have become praiseworthy once one had introduced the power ideal into ethics. Instead, the negative value of ingratitude, the violation of human dignity, remains linked to this custom, while, on the other hand, the positive value, the affirmation of life expressed in it, was newly emphasized, discovered as it were, under the influence of a will oriented in this direction.

The depicted complication rests finally on the fact that a human being is not only a cognizing but also an |294| acting being, that he not only first finds values but also—and for the most part—realizes them himself. A clean division between the theoretical and practical side of his essence is rare. Yet there are also such clear-headed and rich natures in whom one finds a decisive orientation of the will and faithful devotion to an ideal, united with the distinct consciousness and acknowledgment that there are other, perhaps higher values that may, however, not be suited to the individual in question.[55]

In the domain of aesthetics we now have an exact analogue to the physiological deceptions in the domain of the senses. We have the analogue in all cases in which the aesthetic feeling is, so to speak, attuned to a determinate form of beauty and accordingly rejects as ugly any deviation from this form. What the first color is for the appearance of the second, the dominating style is for the aesthetic evaluation of a newly arriving style. The artwork then acts, not on a fresh, normal organ but instead on one already adapted to a different stimulus, one that is already prepared according to some orientation or other.

In this way each custom, each fashion, each style produces a constant predisposition of the organ through which each new impression is colored. Thus it was that the English theater necessarily came across as barbaric to Voltaire and to the French nation that was accustomed to the three unities. It is also possible—and for this the difference in the aesthetic organ's predisposition is responsible—that precisely what is disparaged in an artist is often what a later age reckons to be his greatest glory. It is supposed to be an expression of disdain when Quandt, passing judgment on Rembrandt in 1853, says that, being an etcher, Rembrandt accomplished nothing but a play of light and shadows. When Puvis de Chavannes made his appearance, he was berated as the *fou tranquille* [the quiet madman], and even Delacroix was scolded for precisely what gave him significance as a reformer.[56] So, too, the reproaches of Böcklin were directed |295| precisely at what appears to us today to be his contribution. "His seriousness is considered stubbornness, his naiveté affectation, his creativity tastelessness, his originality arbitrariness."[57] Interesting in this direction are Taine's and St. Beauves' judgments about Balzac since

---

[55] von Ehrenfels (*System der Werttheorie*, pp. 146ff) explains the battle for the existence of valuations by appealing to the limited amount of vital forces that accrue to each individual and that require that the presence of one valuation in an individual already hinders the emergence and growth of other valuations.

[56] For further examples, see Muther, *Geschichte der modernen Malerei* [Richard Muther, Geschichte der Malerei im 19. Jahrhundert [History of Painting in the Nineteenth Century], Bd. III, München: Hirth, 1893/94, p. 582] and Gurlitt, *Geschichte der deutschen Kunst im 19. Jahrhundert* [History of German Art in the Nineteenth Century] (1900). [Landmann-Kalischer is likely referring to Cornelius Gurlitt, *Die deutsche Kunst des neunzehnten Jahrhunderts: Ihre Ziele und Thaten*, in *Das Neunzehnte Jahrhundert in Deutschlands Entwicklung*, Band II, herausgegeben von Paul Schlenther, Berlin: Bondi, 1900].

[57] Alfred Lichtwark, "Urteile über Böcklin [Judgments about Böcklin]," *Zukunft*, Bd. 22 (1897): pp. 245–251.

they are particularly compelling and rest on the individual predisposition of the [respective] aesthetic organ. While the eyes of the one are fixed on the interconnectedness [of things], those of the other are fixed precisely on breaking through the latter, on the unforeseen and surprising. Thus Taine says: "... To be exact then is to be great. Balzac grasped the truth because he grasped the whole ... the same characters reappear; everything comes together ... on every page you embrace the entire human comedy; it is a landscape arranged such that it can be seen in its entirety at every turn...."[58] By contrast, St. Beuve says: "That pretense of grasping the whole eventually leads him to one of the most false ideas and, in my opinion, one that is the most contrary to the overriding interest; I have in mind the idea of making the same characters constantly re-appear from one novel to the other, like stooges already known. Nothing does more harm to the *curiosity* born of the *new* and to the *charm of the unforeseen*, which is the attraction of the novel. In the end one always finds oneself confronted with the same faces."[59]

If disappointing the very expectation (that is given with each predisposition) generally arouses displeasure, there is an exception to this phenomenon when, with the excessive fatiguing of the organ by the same stimulus, the disposition to perceive a specific quality flips over into the disposition to perceive its opposite. Just as the eye tired of green brings out the contrasting color itself, so the aesthetic feeling long nourished by one sort of form of beauty produces a need for its opposite. While the turnover of fashions is proof enough of this property of aesthetic feeling, we also find a continual iteration of this phenomenon in the history of individual arts. It also happens that, even before the contrasting phenomenon |296| emerges, the fatigue asserts itself all on its own. Thus, in architecture after the pinnacle of Palladio's time, a weariness with the master's serious forms vented itself in a gaudy mishmash [*Kunterbunt*] of imitations in a bizarre, exotic style.

---

[58] Hippolyte Taine, *Nouveaux essais de critique et d'histoire* [New Essays of Criticism and History], Paris: Hatchette, 1909, p. 24: ".... C'est donc être exact, que d'être grand. Balzac a saisi la vérité, parce qu'il a saisi les ensembles... Les mêmes personnages reparaissent; tout s'enchaîne... à chaque page vous embrassez toute la comédie humaine; c'est un paysage disposé de manière à être aperçu tout entier à chaque détour."

[59] Ferdinand Brunetière, *Évolution de la poésie lyrique en France au dix-neuvième siècle* [Evolution of Lyric Poetry in France in the Nineteenth Century, cited by Landmann-Kalischer as Histoire de la lyrique française au dix-neuvième siècle], II, Paris: Hatchette, 1895, p. 137n1: "Cette prétention de saisir les ensembles l'a finalement conduit à une des idées les plus fausses et, selon moi, les plus contraires à l'intérêt, je veux dire à faire sans cesse reparaître d'un roman à l'autre les mêmes personnages, comme des comparses déjà connus. Rien ne nuit plus à la *curiosité* qui fait du *nouveau* et à ce charme de *l'imprévu* qui fait l'attrait du roman. On se retrouve à tout bout de champ en face des mêmes visages."

In contrast to these deceptions based upon tempo and a sort of "fading" [*Abklingen*] are phenomena that, in the case of sensations, are called a "dawning" [*Anklingen*] and that likewise have, it seems to me, a distinct analogue in the aesthetic domain. Just as the sensory stimulus requires a determinate duration of effectiveness in order to call up the sensation adequate to it, and just as, before this is reached, various other stages of sensation make their appearance, so, too, the aesthetic stimulus does not immediately arouse the feelings adequate to it but other feelings instead, feelings frequently at odds with those adequate ones. The greater the complexity of the aesthetic organ, the longer is the duration of this period of dawning. It can last minutes, even hours. In the case of stimuli that have an effect only briefly, a frequent renewal of the stimulus substitutes for it [that duration]. The constancy of an aesthetic feeling in relation to the stimulus necessarily counts as a criterion for its adequacy. Yet with the first offering of an object, fluctuations appear almost incessantly while the judgment about an object is individually constant for a more or less short time. Thus, anyone who does not let this period of dawning pass before making the judgment is, without fail, exposed to errors. In fact one frequently finds among experts a mistrust of the first impression.

Moreover, even in the case of the so-called sensory feelings, e.g., the feelings tied to the sensations of tasting something, this dawning can be observed quite distinctly. If a new sensation of taste appears, it is usually not until the second or third time that it appears decisive for the feeling that from then on will be constantly conjoined with this sensation. So it is in the case of many delicacies (*haut-goût!*) and stimulants [*Genußmittel*] such as alcohol, tobacco, and so forth.

For the physiologically conditioned deceptions, we need to consider not only temporary alterations but also persisting imperfections in the function of the receptive organ. By an aesthetic organ, I mean the sum of those activities on the part of the soul |297| whose co-operative effect brings forth the aesthetic impression. Here, with Külpe, we distinguish between the direct and the associative factor.[60] With regard to the direct factor, i.e., the inherent features that first come into consideration for the construal of the sense-impressions underlying any aesthetic object, these are the same ones that are requisite for the formation of sensory judgments. Here then we need only point to the most important feature, the attentiveness to the sensory

---

[60] Oswald Külpe, "Der assoziative Faktor in der neueren Ästhetik [The Associative Factor in Recent Aesthetics]," *Vierteljahrsschrift für wissenschaftliche Philosophie 23/2* (1899): pp. 145–83.

impression, the concentration on it. It is superfluous to expand on how frequently people sin against this basis of all aesthetic feeling. It suffices to cite the following: reading a poem silently, letting oneself be lulled away by music into reveries, wandering from what is given in a painting or a sculpture to the object, taking away maxims for living from a drama, and so forth.

In order for the *associative factor* to work correctly, what is presupposed above all is a certain power of representing in general. Just as sculpture and painting pick out one inherent feature from the entire representation of things, choosing and structuring it so that the representation of the whole can be reproduced from this one feature,[61] and just as human beings or trees can be reproduced by a few dabs of color in a painting, so, too, entire characters, moods, past and future actions are developed by short dialogues in drama, and entire worlds of feeling are developed by mere sequences of sounds in music. It calls for a certain intensity and readiness of representations so that the requisite reproductions can appear with ease, certainty, and strength. Uncivilized peoples and children are unable to develop the representation of bodies from the two-dimensional image [*Flächenbilde*].

In addition to this formal side of the formation of the representation, the individual trove of representations is also significant in terms of its content for the aesthetic receptiveness. A greater wealth of representations and feelings, together with the capacity to form new ones from familiar ones, invariably expands the receptiveness. But, even apart from this fact, the representations' content itself comes into consideration since *completely alien* contents cannot be reproduced at all |298|; hence, the artwork [in such a case] must remain dead to the viewer. We constantly find ourselves in this situation in relation to cultures that are extinct or alien to us. This is often the case, for example, in relation to Japanese pictures where the portrayed action and the way of expressing feeling are unfamiliar to us. We also constantly find ourselves in this situation in relation to any artwork that has events of the day as its material and thus is forgotten along with these events, as is quite frequently the case for comedies, satires, and caricatures. This is probably the reason why they are regarded as less valuable, although the artistic achievement in them can be just as high as it is in a work that has something universally human as its theme. Every work of art that has to reckon mainly with representations that only a specific

---

[61] See my "Analyse der ästhet. Kontemplation" (Malerei und Plastik) ["Analysis of Aesthetic Contemplation" (Painting and Sculpture)], *Zeitschrift für Psychologie 28* (1902): pp. 199ff.

class of human beings find themselves to possess (e.g., a nation, a specific stripe of cultivated individuals) remains limited in its effect to this class. But when these representations are *actually placed* in such works of art, one cannot for this reason deny that these works are objectively beautiful. Moreover, only if the feeling of beauty is aroused through individually contingent associations (such as, for example, when through some connection to a contemporary event an old comedy comes to have an attractiveness that it was not placed there for) must this feeling of beauty be designated a subjective phenomenon and, in an objective sense, as a deception. The abstruseness of ascribing beauty as an objective property to a work that no one can any longer appreciate disappears perhaps more readily if one considers the fact that the aesthetic object, from the moment that it is not felt to be beautiful, is indeed not present in its entirety, that it then exists only as sounds when we cover our ears, as colors in the night, or as words in a language we do not understand.

> Maint joyeau dort enseveli
> Dans les ténèbres et l'oubli,
> Bien loin des pioches et des sondes . . .[62]

The work came to have its—now abstruse—form of being, only on account of that long-gone connection. If one wanted to deny it this essential property, its being would then not be conceivable at all.

For the normal function of the aesthetic organ, what comes into consideration, beyond representations, is the world of feeling, specifically, the capacity for |299| empathy. A human being who did not have this capacity at all would be capable of aesthetic impressions and judgment only to a minimal degree. But there may be few human beings who are capable of every [kind of] empathy. Being predisposed to specific feelings will hinder the reproduction of feelings opposed to these. When Maeterlink stigmatizes dramas like Othello as superficial art [*Vordergrundkunst*], this can only rest on the fact that he has become too indifferent to the soulful contents of such dramas and that those contents have become too alien to him for him to be able to reproduce them in a lively way. Entire ages are so dominated by a mood that artworks with a different feeling-content are no longer enjoyed at all and the satisfaction of

---

[62] [Charles Baudelaire, "Le guignon" ["Bad Luck"] in *Les Fleurs du Mal* (1857), p. XI: "Many a jewel sleeps buried / In darkness and obliviousness / Far from picks and probes."]

what is felt in that mood blinds them to other artistic deficiencies. In this way, Gothic's singular thought of allegorical forms [*formensinnbildlich*] excused all sorts of emptiness and meagerness in the execution.

Physical Deceptions

We come now to those deceptions of aesthetic judgments that, in analogy with sensory deceptions, we would like to call "physical" deceptions. We will speak of a physically conditioned deception where we have to look for the source of the deception in the aesthetic stimulus much as, in the domain of the senses, we have to look for it in the physical stimulus of the sensation. But we first have to determine the concept of aesthetic stimulus in more detail.

As in the psychology of the senses, so, too, we have to distinguish here between physical and physiological stimuli. The aesthetic object would correspond to the physical stimulus; the *construed* [*aufgefaßte*] object to the physiological stimulus (stimulus in the narrower sense). Should the adequate aesthetic stimulus in the narrower sense come about, it must be preceded by a series of mental activities that can themselves be sources of deceptions. Thanks to differences in the sensory and mental construal of the aesthetic object, different stimuli can be introduced for what is nonetheless objectively the same object. With the aesthetic organ functioning in a completely correct way, a mistaken construal of the sense-impressions underlying any aesthetic object will nonetheless bring about a judgment that is just as false as the judgment (correctly made in accordance with all the laws of seeing) |300| that the rod sitting halfway in water is bent. Only for this narrow interpretation of the concept of aesthetic stimulus will it be possible to find out unambiguously what the actual agreements and differences of aesthetic judgment are.

We will discuss first the deceptions that are conditioned by the different possible transitions from a physical to a physiological stimulus.

How manifold the possibilities of apperception of the physical stimulus can be emerges most distinctly for geometric figures. Lines present a different figure and come to have a different connection to one another, depending upon whether they are construed spatially or in terms of surfaces; they run from left to right and from above to below or vice versa, depending upon how these or those parts are grasped together into a unity. It is clear that, if these lines are to be judged aesthetically, one or the other sort of apperception must be made the basis. Only in this way does one acquire a unified stimulus, whose aesthetic evaluations by different persons are comparable to one another.

In the great majority of cases beauty rests on the perception of relationships[63] of sense-impressions to one another, but a different combination of elements is often possible. Hence, an object can sometimes be beautiful and sometimes ugly and sometimes both at once, depending upon how the connection of its parts is construed. In addition, it is possible for different forms of beauty to relate to one another in a mutually exclusive way, so that under certain circumstances only the negative value of a positively valuable object can come to be apperceived. One will never be able to call an object beautiful in the way that one calls a color blue; at best it will be beautiful in one connection, indifferent in another; but mostly the same thing that makes it beautiful in the one connection will make it ugly in the other. Fashion's ways of construing the human body deliver the most obvious evidence for this claim. Hair that lies smoothly is beautiful, for example, insofar as it allows the head's structure to emerge clearly; hair falling loosely on the forehead is beautiful insofar as it lends the face a gracious framework; the rococo dress and the Egyptian wig are beautiful insofar as they lend the entire |301| gestalt a linear, finished off character. To the extent, however, that the Egyptian wig, for example, conceals the head's structure, it is ugly or at least indifferent. But now since hair cannot be worn in all ways at once, each of the indicated fashions must be called simultaneously beautiful and ugly. Thus one need not at all explain the taste for the allonge wig solely on the basis of associations, as did Fechner who was obviously still under the impression of the immediate reaction against this style.[64] Even without this [appeal to associations], justice can be done to the positive as well as the negative aesthetic value of the allonge wig, if one goes back to the elements of their aesthetic effect. The necessity of the object's connection to the feeling is never in fact linked to the complicated beautiful objects but instead to the beautiful elements, and the aesthetic stimulus in the narrower sense must be designated first, before one can acquire comparable judgments.

Artworks should, of course, be put together in such a way that only *one* kind of sensory-mental construal would be possible and necessary relative to them. However, new difficulties surface here. Only in the rarest cases does the

---

[63] [Landmann-Kalischer may be thinking, not merely of 'relationships,' but of 'proportions' which is also a suitable translation of *Verhältnissen* here.]

[64] Gustav Fechner, *Vorschule der Ästhetik* [Introduction to Aesthetics], Leipzig: Breitkopf & Härtel, 1876, I, pp. 236ff.

artwork come into the art lover's [*Genießer*] sights immediately in the form that the artist planned. A piece of music needs the performance, a drama the stage, a poem the reciter; even painting and sculpture need the right set up, the right surroundings and lighting. Inserted between the artwork (in the form it had as it lived in the artist's soul) and the art lover are intermediary persons who complete the artist's creation with more or less success. False interpretations not only bring to naught the effect of valuable works but also elevate the effect of worthless works unjustifiably, as when an outstanding actor "occupies" a role that is in itself insignificant. Frequently, the phantasy of the art lover himself completes the achievement of developing the work lying before him in unfinished form as a book or as a score into a physiological-aesthetic stimulus. The greatest concentration is thus required in order to understand a piece of music |302|, to put the values of a picture's individual colors and space into the right connection to one another, to find the right standpoint in relation to a sculpture, to comprehend the composition of a novel, a drama—and yet the aesthetic stimulus in the narrower sense is only given when this happens. Here, too, an acquired habit of a certain manner of construing things can hinder a new kind of art from finding entry [into the world of art]. Anyone who was accustomed, for example, to distinguishing every little point in a picture necessarily saw a kind of chaos in impressionistic images that achieved spatial clarity only by being observed from a distance. Someone accustomed to Beethoven's treatment of themes could not follow a piece of music that is divided according to leitmotifs.

Another deception whose cause lies on the path from a physical to a physiological-aesthetic stimulus is based on the alteration that the content of sense impression undergoes through memory, i.e., by becoming the content of a representation. A large part of the "errors concerning values" rests on representations that are mostly incomplete, having been postponed in the face of the contents of sensations that are actually entering into consciousness. A proportional relationship of lines that the lay person imagines [*sich vorstellt*] to be agreeable will not hold up in his own judgment, once it is placed before his eyes. A chord, represented as impossible, can have a surprising effect once it is actually played.—That this state of affairs mostly takes place only among lay persons seems to me to speak against the view that, in the case of the *right* representation, a person feeling the relevant value would react differently to the representation than to the sense impression. Artists are able, after all, to decide about the value or disvalue of combinations of colors and the like from a mere representation [of them]. This is not to say, however, that there is no distinction at all between the aesthetic feeling which has mere representations as its presupposition and the aesthetic feeling that is tied to the original aesthetic stimulus. Rather: just as the representation of the sensation, although similar to it in quality and intensity, is nevertheless specifically different from it, so, too, aesthetic feelings, if they are tied only to representations of the aesthetic stimulus, no longer have its original liveliness. |303|

Deceptions about Intensity

We have to discuss now the deceptions about intensity, namely, those that result from the effects of Weber's law in the aesthetic domain.[65] Depending upon how one construes this law, it may be attributed to psychological, physiological, or physical deceptions. I attach it here to the physical deceptions, chiefly for the purpose of being able to discuss it in that context, albeit without hiding the fact that deceptions based, for example, upon the sensitivity to difference [*Unterschiedsempfindlichkeit*], insofar as they express the significance of a different preparedness of the receptive organ, should be counted among physiologically conditioned deceptions.

In the aesthetic domain neither the stimuli nor the sensations form series of sequences; [but] we can designate the range of sensitivity, for ear and eye, by determining the upper and lower aural limits and outermost limits of the visible spectrum, respectively. Hence, in the best case we can gather what that range is only through listing the stimuli that still awaken aesthetic feelings and those that no longer do so. The Aristotelian determination of being neither too small nor too large would be pertinent here. Fechner has already introduced the concept of an aesthetic threshold, as has Simmel in a more general rendition of it.[66] The upper aesthetic threshold would lie where the aesthetic impression became so strong that it would explode the framework of the aesthetic comportment and would evoke a general arousal of feelings. If Wagner was reproached for having an artistic effect on the senses that was too strong, then it was obviously a case of overstepping the upper

---

[65] ['Weber's law' is named as such and formulated as a mathematical proportion by Gustav Theodor Fechner in honor of his teacher Ernst Heinrich Weber. The law states that the smallest change in stimuli that can be perceived is proportional to the initial intensity of the original stimulus; see Gustav Fechner, *Elemente der Psychophysik* [Elements of Psychophysics], Leipzig: Breitkopf und Härtel, 1860, pp. 64f, 134–238.]

[66] Simmel, *Philosophie des Geldes*, pp. 256ff; Gustav Fechner, *Vorschule der Ästhetik*, pp. 49f.

aesthetic threshold for the one making that judgment. Enormous individual differences show up even at the extreme of the lower threshold. Just like the threshold of sensations, it can be suppressed considerably through practice. The increase in aesthetic demands made by the cultivated seems to stand in contradiction to this, but it nonetheless only proves their finer organ for the ugly and imperfect that goes hand in hand with their capacity to uncover the slightest beauties. |304|

Even more important than the range of sensitivity is the sensitivity to difference that is heightened, like the range, through practice. In terms of the correctness of the judgment the expert who can distinguish the work of an artist from that of his most faithful student or best counterfeiter stands above the lay person who admires the beauties of the master unfazed by the crudest imitation of them. Someone unfamiliar with Rembrandt finds a fullness of body and faithfulness to nature already in Raphael. Hence, the difference of judgment in different epochs and the appearance of the same judgments where only the same *proportions* of stimuli are objectively present. Such is the case when Giotto in the 14th century is called 'naturalistic' in precisely the same sense as Manet in the 19th century. Such is the case when Raphael is admired as soulful by the Nazarenes[67] whose eyes are schooled in the art of Classicism, while the English Pre-Raphaelites, whose phantasy was full of the paintings of the Quattrocentro [fifteenth-century Italian early Renaissance], found Raphael cold. In cases of differences in judgment, it is usually not made clear how a large series of aesthetic categories (on whose application the dispute turns in an individual case) are simply concepts of relation and refer to degrees of intensity. Such is the case if there is talk of richness, simplicity, clarity, and so forth. Indeed, it can perhaps be said that *all* aesthetic categories are designations not only of quality but at the same time of intensity.

Chapter 5. The Criteria for the Correctness of Sensory Judgments and Value Judgments

In the preceding chapter we sought to draw the analogy between deceptions, along with their conditions, for value judgments and those for sensory

---

[67] ['Nazarenes' is the derisive name given to an early nineteenth-century group of German Romantic artists who aimed to revive Christian art in the style of Dürer and Raphael.]

judgments. The question now is whether the analogy can be drawn and sustained [*durchführen*] for the positive criteria of both groups of judgment.

In what follows I venture to provide a brief schematic orientation regarding the criteria of truth for sensory judgments and value judgments. In order to avoid any misunderstanding, it is necessary for me, when I do this, to state in advance that I refrain here from any metaphysical aim. I want merely to describe the factual state of things. Like any science, epistemology, too, must make presuppositions, it must presuppose *one* truth |305| in order to be able to test or find another one. Hence, foregoing any preliminary consideration, I start out from the present state of what we are acquainted with and measure the truth of sensory judgments and of value judgments against it. Instead of any complicated defense of this method, allow me to refer to Spinoza's standpoint: "... *illa bona erit Methodus, quae ostendit, quomodo mens dirigenda sit ad datae verae ideae normam.*"[68]

The truth of sensory judgments and value judgments has no other criteria than those that also hold for the truth of all other judgments.

If the more or less hypothetical character of all truths is granted and if the judgment relative to acquiring that character satisfies the formal claims of logic, there is only one major criterion of its truth: its agreement with other judgments.

Now the application of this criterion to sensory judgments and value judgments seems at first to be at odds with the frequently emphasized immediacy of these judgments. Indeed, thanks precisely to this property, sensory judgments and value judgments typically stand out from scientific judgments which are constantly made in connection with other judgments and acknowledged as true only so long as they can obtain along with other, already supported judgments, without contradicting them. If scientific judgments' property of being dependent on one another designates at once their universal content which consists in asserting connections between things, then the peculiarity of sensory judgments and value judgments—that of being made independently and uninfluenced by another judgment—seems merely to express their invariably particular content. Just as they invariably refer to *one* object alone, so, too, their truth seems to depend solely on this object.

But in order to resolve this apparent contradiction, we need only remind ourselves of the fact that those immediate judgments form, to be sure, the

---

[68] "... that method will be good that shows how the mind is to be oriented to the norm of a *given true idea*." Spinoza, *Tractatus de Intellectus Emendatione. Opera, quae supersunt omnia.* II, Ed. H. E. Gottlob Paulus, Jena: In bibliopolio academico, 1803, p. 426.

foundation for every sensory judgment and value judgment but that those judgments laying claim to *objective* reliability—and it is only these that we have to do with here |306|—either are not made *simply* on the basis of the immediate impression or are nonetheless subjected to comparison after the fact and modified accordingly. Even the formation of scientific judgments—and precisely the most original—is frequently implemented in an entirely intuitive manner, with regard merely to the individual case presently at hand. But no one will doubt here that the truth of such judgments is corroborated only through agreement with other judgments.

That the criterion of agreement can also cooperate, consciously or unconsciously, in the formation of a judgment is familiar enough for sensory judgments. But an object, in spite of the dark, can be called not only 'blue' but also 'beautiful' without arousing any aesthetic pleasure. For value judgments as well, the subjective judgment 'this pleases me' is clearly distinguished from the objective judgment 'this is beautiful.' It is frequently the case that an object is judged to be beautiful that, at the moment, evokes no aesthetic pleasure or only a very weak degree of it. Conversely, even while being vibrantly pleased by something, one is often reserved about making a judgment about its beauty. Thus Brunetière says of the poets he intends to discuss: "I will praise to the heavens what I basically do not like at all but criticize energetically what delights me personally. . . . To enjoy something is one thing, but to judge it is quite another."[69] It is also acknowledged by modern value-theorists that the intensity of the current feeling of pleasure (or of desiring) is no measuring rod for the height of the value.[70]

In this anomaly that a source of cognition is declared inaccessible or completely overlooked on the basis of acquaintances [or things that we are acquainted with, *Kenntnisse*] that nonetheless stem solely from this very source, in this irksome relationship in which the pupil pummels the master with weapons that he could only have obtained from the master himself—precisely in this anomaly the chief analogy in the kind of validity found in sensory judgments to that of value judgments becomes apparent.

And it is apparent not only in the contradiction but also in its resolution.

Let us begin with the investigation of sensory judgments. For each individual sensory judgment, it is possible to distinguish four groups of

---

[69] Brunetière, *Évolution de la poésie lyrique en France au dix-neuvième siècle*, I, p. 25: "J'en louerai par dessus les nues, qu'au fond je n'aime guère, comme au contraire j'en critiquerai vivement, dont je fais moi-même mes délices. . . . Jouir est une chose, mais juger en est une autre."
[70] See, for example, von Ehrenfels, *System der Werttheorie*, p. 67 and in other places in the text.

judgments |307| with which it agrees or disagrees and on whose agreement or disagreement with it its validity can depend.

It can agree

(1) with other judgments of the same sense,
(2) with judgments of other senses,
(3) with other individuals' sensory judgments,
(4) with any other acquaintances with things that we may have, in particular our various sorts of scientific cognition of things.

The *first* principle, the agreement of the same sorts of sensory judgments, serves as a corrective to many, so to speak "normal" deceptions of the senses. If mountains in fog appear far away, clear weather shows them to be much closer. If land or water seems to be in motion, one's own act of standing still shows them to be inert. The rod, taken out of water, once again appears straight. If the contrasting color is removed, the background color re-emerges. The table that looks oblong from the side becomes round as soon as it is observed from above,[71] etc., etc. This principle, according to which one abstracts from the momentary sensation in all these cases and recognizes it as a deception, is that of contradicting the remaining experiences [*Erfahrungen*] of the same sense. A sensory judgment that lays claim to objective validity is made, not on the basis of a single impression, but on the basis of all the experiences of the sense regarding the relevant object. To be sure, to the extent that the representation of the thing works here with these experiences, this case belongs already under the fourth principle, the agreement of sensory judgments with our representations.

The *second* principle, the agreement of different sorts of sense impressions, has likely been overestimated previously in its significance for the correction of sensory judgments. Indeed—taken in the strict sense—impressions of different senses cannot agree or contradict one another at all. Only in two groups of cases is the assertion of the one sense significant for the assertion of another sense:

(1) Belonging to the first group are all the cases in which different sense impressions have been so associated with one another that their association makes up an essential part of the representation of the object.

---

[71] Stumpf (*Tonpsychologie*) calls judgments of this sort 'transferred' judgments.

Thus we will |308| believe we are having a hallucination if, standing in an open field, we hear loud talking without seeing anyone. Or we will believe that we are deaf if we see lips' movements without hearing a sound. Hence, even a negative sensory judgment would fall victim to doubt as a consequence of an association that has become fixed. But if we look closer at this case, it is evident that the meaning that one sense's assertion acquires here for the other succeeds only through the mediation of representations. The absence of expected sense impressions or the appearance of unexpected sense impressions is decisive for the objective judgment. Thus, this case also belongs, at least in part, to the fourth rubric.

(2) The second group are those cases in which two sense organs convey one and the same perception or rather stand in such contact that the sensations of both organs work together in one perception. This exceptional relationship occurs only for the senses of sight and touch in the way that they work together for the perception of space. Although the space of the eye and that of touch are naturally different spaces, the sense of sight is nonetheless monitored here by the sense of touch and vice versa, as a consequence of that relationship. The deception, demonstrated by Weber, about the number of compass points touching the skin, is merely one particular case of this relationship, and it proves that, for surface distances, the eye is sensitive in a more finely tuned way than the skin is.[72]

The principle of the agreement of different sorts of sense impressions thus overlaps partly with the principle named under (4) and is to be discussed in more detail there, but it is also grounded partly on an entirely special relationship of the organization of the senses.

We come now to the *third* principle: the agreement of sense impressions of different individuals. One sees that, with this principle, we have arrived at the *consensus gentium* [consensus of peoples], the "universality," that ancient epistemological crux that surfaces again and again in the history of epistemology, first as a skeptical determination of truth—truth is what appears to everyone in the same way (Aenesidemus)—and then as a criterion of truth.

---

[72] [Weber determined that when two points of a compass touching the skin are set close enough to one another, they are perceived as one point; the phenomenon is commonly called "the two-point threshold" or "spatial threshold."]

Many authors directly identify universality with objectivity. If, as we must do here, one sets aside Kantian universality—which is no empirical universality but is based instead on the concept of the "human in general"—then the |309| untenability of that position already follows from the fact that the spheres of the concepts of objectivity and universality do not coincide. There are universal judgments that are false and true judgments that are not universal. "Certainty about the constant relationship between the presupposed object and the subject, thus about the absolute sameness of the organization and sensory activity of everyone"[73] does not yet guarantee the objectivity of the judgment based upon it. If we relied upon these guarantors, we would still consider the cellar always colder in the summer than in the winter. On the other hand, we believe in the objective existence of certain overtones that can nonetheless be perceived by only a handful of exceptionally musical persons. Hence, universality alone cannot suffice in the least as a criterion of the truth of sensory judgments.

Moreover, agreement about the most rough and ready differences in sensation obtains *as a matter of fact*; such agreement reaches just as far as is necessary to secure the foundation for everyone's common concept of reality. Yet it does not extend to more refined distinctions generally, as is proven by every psychological investigation of a sensory domain. Indeed, anyone who wanted to claim that judgments about color by the color-blind are objectively false, and who appealed to the non-agreement of these judgments with the judgments of most other human beings as a criterion of truth for this, would be assaulting the judgment of the minority via the judgment of the majority. Why should what one person necessarily represents on the basis of individual organs not be objective in the same sense as what humanity necessarily represents as a consequence of its organization? "Why do the general and the enduring have a priority over the individual and the transient when it comes to objectivity? Or *is there no objective judgment about the singular and temporary?*"[74]

Let us assume for the moment that truth *ex definitione* cannot mean anything else but the agreement of someone's judgments among |310| themselves. It may be possible to conceive of a standpoint that, on that assumption, would deny that it is permissible to call individually constant judgments about sense-impressions false merely on account of their non-agreement

---

[73] Sigwart, *Logik*, p. 402 [Landmann-Kalischer paraphrases a bit here].
[74] Laas, *Idealismus und Positivismus*, p. 616.

with those of other people. Systems of judgments agreeing among themselves even with the most diverse starting points would then be possible. Such a standpoint would correspond to a particular fact about our psychology [dem psychischen Tatbestand], namely, that the mere non-agreement of our judgments with those of others is never able to convince us of an error unless that non-agreement is bound up with the demonstration of a contradiction within our own judgments. So, too, the agreement of our judgment with others' judgments cannot convince us of the truth of our own judgment if we still discover a contradiction in it with one of our other judgments. The suggested standpoint would also be fruitful to the extent that it permitted a concept of truth like ours to be upheld even for world-systems that would be constructed on an organization of senses completely different from ours. From this standpoint, the agreement of everyone would make no sense as a criterion of truth, and we would be able to uphold the distinction between true and false even for completely isolated individuals and thus secure the concept of an individual truth.[75]

But even if one cannot bring oneself to accept this standpoint, one will in any case have to hold fast to this much, that the criterion of universal agreement is valid at most for those judgments that concern the simplest sense-impressions and the most rough and ready sorts of distinctions. For all other judgments, another criterion is needed.

With this last point, we come to the *final* respect in which a judgment of the senses can agree with other judgments, namely, its agreement with our judgments about things in general. That this criterion must stand alongside the criterion of universal agreement, complementing it, is also assumed by Laas when he says: "Although double images, mirrorings, and echoes are perceived just as much by others, the inability to fit them into the world of things denies [them] objectivity."[76] |311|

We have already seen that a judgment's agreement—discussed under (2)—with the judgments of other senses, when precisely viewed, is also nothing other than its agreement with our other acquaintances [or the other things that we are acquainted with, *sonstigen Kenntnissen*]. This is likewise the case for the "transferred" judgments named under (1), in those cases in which the experience [*Erfahrung*] of the same sense, the experience correcting the judgment, is not made at the same time but instead is present only as

---

[75] This conception is found in Georg Simmel, *Kant*, Leipzig: Duncker & Humblot, 1904, pp. 174f.
[76] Laas, *Idealismus und Positivismus*, p. 456.

a representation. Along with the universal concept of a thing, various sorts of scientific cognition serve as criteria. We must be acquainted with the difference between the velocity of the propagation of sound and that of light in order to refrain from inferring from the later perception of thunder that lightning is temporally prior to thunder. We must be acquainted with the narrow confines of consciousness in order to know that the relationship of the subjectively construed sequence of perceptions does not stand in any fixed connection to the relationship of the sequence of the perceived, objective processes. We must know of the phenomena of fatigue and adaptation in order to refrain from inferring without further ado the cessation of the stimulus from the cessation of the sensation. More meaningful than these individual results is the acquaintance with stimuli and their numerical gradation that science has attained (albeit not yet for *all* sensory feelings by far). Indeed, for Stumpf in the definition cited above (see page 285), the content of a sensation's "really being so" means nothing else but its agreement with the stimulus.[77] As a criterion of truth, this agreement is distinct from the previously discussed criteria of truth in one essential regard. Those criteria—the experiences [*Erfahrungen*] of the same sense, those of other senses, the judgments made by other human beings, the other conceptually acquired experience [*Erfahrung*] of the objects from which the stimulus proceeds—can all be in consciousness during the formation of the judgment. They are not only operative as criteria after the fact. Instead, along with the immediate occasion |312| of the judgment (i.e., the sense impression itself), they comprise *factors* in the formation of the objective judgment and, indeed, factors of equal value that can be weighed against the momentary sense impression's power to be convincing. By contrast, the sense impression itself no longer comes into question opposite the cognizance of the stimulus. When this cognizance is at hand, it is so compelling that when it enters into a judgment, the judgment can no longer be called a sensory judgment at all. Hence, while the other agreements mentioned are factors in the formation of a judgment but never entirely sure-fire criteria of the judgment's correctness, the agreement with our scientific representations—the stimulus' determinative sway [*Kontrolle*] over the sensation—can be deemed purely and simply

---

[77] One could be tempted to see in the agreement of the sensory judgment with the stimulus nothing other than the agreement between judgments of different domains of the senses, which was rejected above as a criterion of truth (pp. 307f). But it is clear that, when equating two groups of sensations in this way, no connection at all occurs such that a judgment about the one sensation could *immediately* influence the judgment about the other. This can happen only when various sorts of scientific cognition are presupposed.

the criterion for the correctness of sensory judgments but not, by contrast, a factor in the formation of the judgment.

I would like finally to call to mind one further criterion of truth that has been put forward for judgments and for sensory judgments specifically. It has been said that a judgment is true if it can motivate an action useful to us. That the picture in the mirror is no real object is proven by the futility of attempting to grab hold of it. Yet on closer inspection this criterion also amounts to that of the agreement with other judgments. An inference is tied to a sensory judgment whenever the inference's correctness is tested as it were experimentally by the action performed and its [the inference's] correctness or incorrectness also yields the correctness or incorrectness of the premises. The truth of a sensory judgment is proven, according to this, by its agreement with those judgments that form a presupposition for our acting.

We come now to the criteria of value judgments.

The judgments with which a value judgment can agree or not agree are

(1) judgments of the same individual about the same object at another time and under other circumstances;
(2) judgments of the same individual about other objects;
(3) judgments of other human beings;
(4) judgments that have universal, specifically scientific representations for their object. |313|

What I would like to call the *natural* objectivity that applies to the aesthetic judgment is distinctly evident in the first principle, in the notion that contradictory judgments of the same individual cannot obtain together. Just as the bearers of an objective judgment are not the individual sense impressions but instead the sum of impressions that have been acquired of the object beyond the present sensation, so, too, what is decisive for the objective aesthetic judgment is not the individual feeling of pleasure but instead an entire series of impressions received from the object under different conditions. In this way the "temporary value" (in Ehrenfels' terminology) passes over into the "normal value," which refers to the average measure of factual dispositions for the feeling. Only frequent repetition of the impression protects against "occasional accompanying determinations" that can be found in the subject or in the object. Only those judgments reinforced by the agreement with judgments during different epochs of life would warrant being called objectively reliable in the highest sense of the term. When one speaks of the taste of an age, what is to be understood by this is mostly a falsification of the judgment by prevailing tendencies of feeling, representation, or will.

That one's own judgments about *other objects* can be considered criteria of judgment is expressed particularly in the course of comparing. The juxtaposition of different objects is of decisive significance for the correct judgment (see, too, the chapter on "objective reliability," pp. 303f above), especially for judgments that are capable of a gradual progression—and, as has been said, almost *all* aesthetic judgments are among these. Everything mediocre reveals its nature when something great outshines it. What is little regarded gains in value when it stands the test of time relative to masterpieces. The positive aesthetic judgment of a figure [sculpted] by Thorwaldsen must be modified relative to the likewise positive valuation of a Doryphoros.[78]

This modifiability of a judgment through judgments about other objects naturally emerges first for judgments about objects of the same genus [or genre, *Gattung*]. Whether and to what extent even judgments about completely different objects can be considered in this connection would be a matter for a particular investigation. It is doubtful to what extent the development of the understanding for one art |314| "trains in tandem" [*mitübt*] an understanding for other arts and natural beauties as well. Only to the extent that this was the case could one expect an influence of the one judgment on the other. There is without doubt a certain coherence or moral of aesthetic judgment that forbids someone who can appreciate a sculpture by Michelangelo from admiring a picture by Karl Becker or a popular tune.[79] It is doubtful, however, how far this goes and whether this influence also extends from the so-called pictorial arts to poetry and music and vice versa. A further question would be the extent to which judgments not only about concrete objects of a different genre but also about different aesthetic qualities can influence one another, whether, for example, the capacity to make correct judgments about pleasing proportions of lines could acquire an influence on the judgment about the expressive value of colors. The one-sided cultivation of the art of lines or of colors in individual artists and peoples perhaps goes hand-in-hand with a mutual independence of the judgments in this respect. One could perhaps approach such questions on an experimental basis. Their solution would also be of interest since it would provide

---

[78] [The references are to the Danish sculptor Bertel Thorvaldsen (1770–1844) and the ancient sculpture of *Doryphoros* [Spear Bearer] by Polycleitus.]

[79] [Karl Becker (1820–1900) is a painter of historical and mythical scenes, in classicist and neo-renaissance style.]

some insight into whether the aesthetic sense is to be considered a unified organ or not. Based on the analogy with the relationships at hand in sensory judgments, we have reason to suppose that aesthetic judgments about different objects, if they can in fact influence one another, are rooted in one unified organ [or] that they are at least of a less disparate nature than the judgments of different senses.

Whether the *agreement* of aesthetic judgments *with the judgments of other human beings* is real, whether it is possible, necessary, conclusive, desirable, is a question endlessly disputed like the analogous problem in the case of sensory judgments. Opposite the *de gustibus* [maxim][80] stands the appeal to the most diverse authorities; opposite subjective modesty stands the claim to universality.

In two directions the aesthetic and ethical judgments seem here to resist being put on the same level as sensory judgments. This parity seems as it were to unduly elevate value judgments and at the same time to underrate them. It seems to elevate them since the arbitrary aesthetic judgments seem still far removed from the universal agreement |315| that it is possible to arrive at for sensory qualities. It seems to underrate them since sensory judgments are, by contrast, denied the very *claim* to universal validity that aesthetic judgments are allowed. Just as human beings who are the most insecure on the inside tend to appear outwardly with the greatest self-assurance and arrogance, so the greatest claim on universal acknowledgement corresponds to the slighter degree of empirical universality which is all the aesthetic judgments have to show for themselves. And there's even more. Anyone not in agreement with our aesthetic judgment frequently falls prey at once to our scorn.

In order to deal first with this underrating, let us begin with aesthetic judgments' greater claim to universality, emphasized so acutely by Kant. This greater claim can be traced back to the fact that we connect an aesthetic judgment much more profoundly with the essence of the human being than we are inclined to do for a sensory judgment. Opinions differ on value judgments; the individuality, the originality of a personality is expressed in the person's value judgment. But a human being of the highest standing can share a sensory judgment with someone of the lowest standing, indeed, with an animal, and his own sensory judgments are for him merely the indifferent basis on which value judgments are first elevated as their sense and purpose. Thus we are indifferent to the sensory judgment of the person standing next to us that

---

[80] *De gustibus non disputandum est* [regarding tastes there should be no dispute].

diverges from ours, while differences in value judgment can make us seethe. This difference between sensory judgments and value judgments, meanwhile, does not justify any intrinsic contrast between these judgments. It results far more from an already-mentioned unique property of the aesthetic sense, namely, the far more extensively mediated character of its sensations, its dependency on representations and feelings, which also explains why it emerges individually later (see pp. 278/9).

Let us ask now about the matter of the apparent elevation of aesthetic judgments that comes from placing them on the same level as sensory judgments, i.e., the factual universality that is supposed to apply to value judgments to so much slighter a degree than it does to sensory judgments.

We have already demonstrated why a very large number of judgments cannot be in agreement. The constancy |316| of the connection between the object and the aesthetic feeling can only refer to aesthetic elements, but the judgments are mostly made in a universal form; they are not specified, either in relation to the specific form of beauty that they assert or in relation to the part of the object *of* which they assert this [specific form]. This and the difficulty of producing *physiologically* the same stimulus has hitherto prevented [researchers from achieving] satisfying findings regarding the degree to which judgments about aesthetic elements factually agree.

Nonetheless, this much can be said: Some judgments that rest upon the universally human organization, such as those about symmetry, will be assured of universal agreement. The Aristotelian "not too small and not too large," the Platonic unity in multiplicity, proportion and contrast would also likely be guaranteed as elements of a universally positive aesthetic effect. Even where we perceive a development of the aesthetic sense, such elementary agreements are still recognizable. Even the crudest tattoos rest upon the pleasure taken in what occupies the senses and in their function, something that is expressed in our ornaments, in decoration, and so forth. In addition, there are the experiential rules that are brought together in the doctrine of the individual art: in poetics, in tectonics,[81] in the doctrine of perspective, the doctrine of the "technique" of drama (a dimension that is actually its aesthetic and rightly so), and so forth. The doctrine of musical composition likely contains the richest material; what Herbart said of "musical doctrines

---

[81] [Originally a Greek term for architecture [*Baukunst*, the art of building], the term is applied by geologists to the structure of the earth's crust and in visual arts to signify the combination of architecture and painting. Landmann-Kalischer is presumably using it in the latter sense.]

that bear the strange name *basso continuo* [*Generalbaß*]" still holds today, namely, that they "are up to now the sole correct prototype on hand for a genuine aesthetics."[82]

If the unanimity in relation to these [aesthetic] judgments corresponds to the agreement that it was necessary to affirm even in the domain of the senses for the most rough and ready differences in sensation, the number of judgments that do not agree here [in the aesthetic domain] should also probably not be greater than there, if one takes into consideration the deceptions that are more frequent in the aesthetic domain (for reasons already treated in the previous chapter). Only in one direction is a greater divergence perhaps present. It seems, namely, that it is necessary for us to affirm, in the aesthetic domain, a development of the organ in the sense of [a capacity for] differentiating, not only (as for organs of the senses) in an individual life but |317| also in the life of peoples. And it seems that this differentiating has been carried out in part in completely different directions under the influence of different external circumstances, so that we ultimately believe that we are confronted in different cultures with completely different sorts of aesthetic feeling.

No one any longer believes today in the development of the sense of color, something that was announced with so much fanfare thirty years ago. Yet, even assuming that it was established that no development took place, one would not be compelled to assume something of this sort for the simple reason that objects lying before one's eyes were essentially always the same. By contrast, the *aesthetic* objects in relation to which the sense of beauty was supposed to have developed differ in time and place.

Aesthetic objects are present in nature and art.

Since nature as it changes presents no intrinsically new phenomena, the changes in the feeling for nature (changes that we must assume to find in history) will not be of a drastic sort. In fact, from a passing overview this much emerges, namely, that the change in the feeling for nature seems to indicate a belittlement of the lower aesthetic threshold [in the past] and a gradual conquest of ever new objects [*Gegenstände*] for the feeling more than it does a muddled difference in the valuation of the same objects [*Objekte*]. The striking differences that frequently tend to be cited [from history] consist essentially in the lack of any feeling in a place where it is strongly cultivated in us. If Alpine travelers in antiquity only knew how to complain about

---

[82] Johann Friedrich Herbart, *Sämmtliche Werke, Achter Band: Schriften zur Praktischen Philosophie, Erster Theil* [Complete Works, Volume 8: Writings on Practical Philosophy, First Part], herausgegeben von G. Hartenstein, Leipzig: Voss, 1851, p. 20.

the impassable and dreadful routes, if the romantic quality of nature's scenes never occupied them, and if Julius Caesar, when he returned to his legions in Gaul, used the time during the trip over the Alps to finish a text on grammar ('On analogy'),[83] and if the Minnesingers who took part in the Crusades left no noticeable impression of either the Italian or the Oriental landscape,[84] the preconditions of a disinterested aesthetic contemplation were obviously missing here. If the Greeks and the Romans almost without exception found attractive only those regions in the landscape that were comfortably inhabitable and |318| if they showed no sense for the desolate in nature,[85] what emerges from this is only the prevailing mood in them, one that inhibited the development of opposite feelings. And so, too, it is a matter of the aesthetic eye's different posture when the gaze in the Old Testament is directed at the whole of nature, while for other peoples it immerses itself lovingly in an individual part of nature.

The other aesthetic object that, in direct contrast with nature, is historically subject to the greatest changes is art. One might want to take exception straightaway to the attempt to derive the different development of the aesthetic sense from this difference in the object. If art objects are different, one might protest, this is, indeed, directly the consequence of differences in taste first. But if someone lodges this objection, it is necessary to reply that the development of art is by no means based only on aesthetic viewpoints. It would be an interesting task to find the purely aesthetic element in the development of individual forms of art; the answer would perhaps be surprising through its similarity across the most heterogeneous forms. But the fact is that the arts are essentially influenced in their development by motives that lie outside art. In architecture, the form is explained without exception—as in the case of Schnaase, for example—by what is necessary for the construction, by matters of practical facility, by the purpose of the building, by the religious view— *and* by aesthetic exigency.[86] The mimetic arts are likewise conditioned by

---

[83] Alexander von Humboldt, *Kosmos II*, Stuttgart und Tübingen: Cotta, 1847, p. 25.
[84] Ibid., p. 36.
[85] Ibid., p. 79.
[86] Compare the discussion about individual forms, e.g., pointed arches [*Spitzbogen*] and entrances [*Portal*] in Schnaase, *Grundzüge der Architektur des Mittelalters* [Basic Features of Medieval Architecture], Volume 4, Book 6, Chapter One. [*Grundzüge der Architektur des Mittelalters* is the title of Chapter One of Book 6: *Die Kunst des Mittelalters diesseits der Alpen* ["The Art of the Middle Ages This Side of the Alps"] of Volume 4: *Geschichte der bildenden Künste im Mittelalter* [The History of the Pictorial Arts in the Middle Ages]. This volume is the fourth volume of Carl Schnaase, *Geschichte der bildenden Künste* [History of the Pictorial Arts], Zweite, vermehrte und verbesserte Auflage; Vierter Band [second, enlarged and improved edition; fourth volume], Düsseldorf: Buddeus, 1871; for *Portal*, see pp. 91–93 and for *Spitzbogen*, see pp. 105–108.]

technique and theme [*Technik und Gegenstand*]. By the technique—after all, Semper wanted to derive all forms of style from the conditions of the material! By the theme—after all, everything that the artist has before him is conditioned by the entire culture of the age! The constant exercise of the organ on different objects [*Objekte*] must also lead to a different cultivation of it. And this difference brings forth a system of judgments that characteristically diverges from systems of a different cultural circle. Attending more closely to the conditions of the emergence of art objects would, in keeping with this last point, confirm Fechner's conjecture "that |319| most changes in taste depend ultimately on causes that do not belong to the domain of taste at all, but enter into it through the intermediary of association, entrenching and propagating themselves through habituation and transference [from another domain]."[87]

How far these differences extend to aesthetic elements or only to complex objects is utterly undecidable, given the complete lack of investigations of this matter. We must reckon in any case with the possibility that the aesthetic sense, in the course of much mutual agreeing, remains subject all the same to even greater differences among individuals than do the other organs of sense. If one does not want, in particular, to trace the historical differences in [views of] the agreeableness of intervals back to the emergence of a difference in the organ of hearing (so that the same interval in the 13th century presented a stimulus physiologically different from that in the 19th century), differences in the judgments about aesthetic elements would in fact show up here.

Hence, we see that there are judgments about which universal agreement reigns in the aesthetic domain as well as in the realm of organs of sensation. The greater number of aesthetic judgments not in agreement is explained partly by the fact that they mostly do not refer to aesthetic elements, but partly, too, perhaps by the aesthetic organ's greater complexity that enables its differentiation in directions completely different from one another.

But even if—and to whatever extent—agreements can be affirmed as *factual*, they nonetheless cannot serve as a *criterion* for the correctness of judgments. They cannot because, if the agreement is absolutely universal, there can also be no exception to it. Opposite judgments are then unthinkable and a criterion for the correctness of these judgments would have no sense or purpose. But if that agreement is not thoroughly universal, then it also cannot count as a criterion for the correctness of these judgments since every declaration that a judgment is false on the basis of this criterion would

---

[87] Fechner, *Vorschule der Ästhetik*, I, p. 254.

then amount in turn to an assault on the minority by the majority. |320|— This observation holds for universal agreement as a *criterion* of truth for the correctness of value judgments. It does not come into consideration at all as a factor in the formation of the judgment, since here, as in the case of sensory judgments, someone else's judgment can influence our own only indirectly, by prompting a re-examination.

We thus see ourselves also driven here to the standpoint already sketched for sensory judgments. That is the standpoint that the criterion for the truth and falsity of aesthetic judgments could in no case consist in universal agreement and, hence, that individual truth could nonetheless be accorded to individually constant judgments about which no universal agreement reigns, even if they should directly contradict those of others.

That this standpoint permits us to uphold the concept of truth even for entities organized in completely different ways is of incomparably greater significance for value judgments than for sensory judgments. We cannot come to any agreement at all with entities whose senses are organized in ways completely different from ours. Hence, their judgments are beyond our purview. And in this regard anomalies like color-blindness have more of a theoretical than practical significance. By contrast, in the case of the development of the aesthetic sense, carried out under the influence of different sorts of objects in completely different directions, we have no other possibility of acknowledging the objective beauty of entire systems of aesthetic judgment (whose presuppositions cannot be re-experienced by us or at least not immediately) than by decisively rejecting the criterion of universal agreement.[88] |321|

When we ask now what other criterion could take its place, it is apparent that "individual truth" could be accorded only to those judgments that are individually constant and agree among themselves. It is likewise apparent, however, that this agreement of an individual's aesthetic judgments among themselves presents no *complete* criterion. Constant mistakes in subjective reliability could be recognized only through experiments explicitly

---

[88] In our rejection of the *consensus gentium* [consensus of peoples] as a criterion of truth, we are agreeing with the standpoint of Avenarius as he critically engages specifically with the problem of judgments of the senses that contradict one another; see his *Der menschliche Weltbegriff* [The Human Concept of the World], Leipzig: Reisland, 1892, pp. 121–131. Yet, in contrast to Avenarius, we must hold fast to the distinction between mere perceptual judgments on the one hand and judgments as assertions about something objective on the other. Particularly in view of the manifold deficiencies (discussed above) to which the subjective as well as the objective reliability of value judgments are exposed, it does not seem appropriate to us to draw without qualification the same conclusions from Avenarius regarding the validity of value judgments that Robert Eisler derives from them.

directed at it; many a constant mistake in objective reliability (the physiological deceptions in particular) could only be discerned from a bird's eye perspective, at the end of a human being's life, or from a later epoch. Also, not all possible objects of the judgment are given to an individual. And it is less likely that an individual should always come directly into possession of those aesthetic judgments whose non-agreement with one of the individual's earlier judgments could prove its erroneousness. No other criterion than this incomplete one seems *factually* to obtain for the praxis of living. Aesthetic truth establishes itself, too, like scientific truth only in the battle of the ages. And can a theory set up new criteria that go beyond the factual?

The sole criterion of truth for judgments that was given in some domains of the senses and the one that also suffices in a practical sense is the agreement of the judgments with those judgments of ours that were acquired scientifically, their comparison with stimuli. This criterion is not for the time being at our disposal in the aesthetic domain for reasons already cited. Thus, we are dependent here upon the criterion of the agreement of a person's aesthetic judgments with one another and, as a means of supplementing it and setting aside individually constant mistakes, we have to make use, as an indirect criterion, of the path also embarked on in the present investigation, that of investigating each judgment with respect to the possible causes of its deceptiveness.

Now a criterion has also been put forward even for the truth of aesthetic judgments, a criterion that corresponds to the decision about the truth of a sensory judgment through the action grounded on it. This is the principle of good taste put forward by Fechner |322|: "A taste is good (or correct) if something good comes of it."[89] As is the case with the corresponding criterion for sensory judgments, here, too, it is the consequences tied to the judgment that are supposed to decide on its correctness. According to this principle, a positive value judgment about something unhealthy, immoral, internally untrue or not genuine would show itself to be false. One sees that it is the agreement with other value judgments that is made the criterion of truth of aesthetic judgments here. But this agreement cannot come into consideration for *purely* aesthetic judgments. The object of a purely aesthetic judgment stands completely outside the contexts in which the other value judgments put it. As an example of an incorrect judgment Fechner cites how the Chinese are gratified by their women's deformed feet. But this foot

---

[89] Fechner, *Vorschule der Ästhetik*, pp. 256ff.

pleases either immediately or not. If the foot pleases immediately, there is no awareness at all of its deformation (that would be autopathically evaluated in a decidedly negative way); it is pleasing, not in the context of the determination of its purpose, not as a foot, but instead as a gentle, light, fine shape in and for itself; the [experience of] being pleased is then accordingly tied to a stimulus that has nothing to do with the deformation at all. If the foot is not immediately pleasing, however, then it is so only through an associative chain, with other values, as a *sign* of nobility, wealth, privilege. The taste itself then is neither false nor correct; instead there is an error in the autopathic valuation, an error that the conveyed value participates in and that shows itself in its contradiction with values of the same domain. But an immediate aesthetic value judgment can *never* be shown to be false in terms of its agreement with autopathic or heteropathic disvalues.

Chapter 6. The Qualities of Aesthetic Feeling

Up till now we have spoken of the feeling of beauty as a unified feeling. Yet we were already required in several places to distinguish different forms of beauty. We call objects beautiful which affect us in a completely different manner |323| just as we call objects colored whose colors are completely different. In aesthetics one has for ages distinguished different forms, modifications, or kinds of beauty and there have been attempts to derive them in various ways from the beautiful. The graceful and dignified, the grotesque and lovely, the sentimental and naïve, the comic and tragic are treated as themes of aesthetics without their relationship to the beautiful ever having become entirely clear. Either, on the one hand, one derived them metaphysically as when Schasler has the ugly bring about the unfolding of the beautiful through the manifold world of beauty; when Rosenkranz has the beautiful make the transition into the comic through the ugly; so, too, when Ruge names the sublime, ugly, and comic stages of the dialectical process into which the beautiful enters; [or] Vischer calls the sublime and the comic the conflict of the features inherent in the beautiful. Or, on the other hand, one construed the modifications of the beautiful purely with respect to the material by reducing them to differences in the themes—as when Schiller defined the graceful as an expression of a beautiful movement of the soul and dignity as the expression of ethically great action. Or finally—like Herbart—one interpreted them as subjective arousals, "excitements of the mind" which can accompany the inherently calm aesthetic judgment even while alien to it.[90]

From our standpoint it would be easy to construe the modifications of the beautiful as qualities of beauty, analogous to the construal of individual colors as qualities of color. The question of how individual forms of beauty might have arisen objectively, would concern us here as little as the question of the origin of various smells and colors. It would only be a matter of ascertaining and (perhaps) bringing into a system the number of possible sensations of which the aesthetic sense would be capable and to which a determinate group of aesthetic objects would correspond each time. The obscurity that settled over the relationship of the beautiful to its modifications and that one sought to clear up through metaphysical explanations would be lifted to the extent that one coordinated this relationship of a large group of phenomena very familiar to us.

But with this the difficulty first begins. We may well suppose different forms of beauty as qualities of the aesthetic |324| sense, but it is still quite doubtful whether we have to see simple qualities of it in the modifications of the beautiful usually treated in aesthetics. Working on the aesthetic feeling as an organ of sense would have to begin by first basically drawing up the simple qualities. Thus, in what follows only an indication of the preliminary questions that surface in this regard may be permitted.

If one considers the modifications mentioned above, they seem to contain nothing other than different feelings that, stirred up by the process of aesthetic contemplation, enter into the feeling of beauty. The tragic appears as a sad theme [*Gegenstand*] treated or viewed aesthetically, the comic as a ridiculous theme treated or regarded likewise. We call an aesthetic object [*Objekt*] 'graceful' whose content is of an amiable nature, 'naïve' or 'idyllic' what portrays something simple, natural, and innocent as such. Even if the innocent were portrayed, for example, satirically or sentimentally, this posture of the artist towards his theme would alter the theme itself only for the observer; in the case of the sentimental portrayal, instead of the innocent, the longing

---

[90] [Max Schasler, *Aesthetik: Grundzüge der Wissenschaft des Schönen und der Kunst* [Aesthetics: Basic Features of the Science of the Beautiful and Art], Leipzig: Freytag/Prag: Kempsky, 1886, Erster Teil, pp. 19–23; Karl Rosenkranz, *Ästhetik des Häßlichen* [Aesthetics of the Ugly], Königsberg: Korntäger, 1853, pp. 9, 53, 61, 74; Arnold Ruge, *Neue Vorschule der Ästhetik: Das Komische* [New Introduction to Aesthetics: The Comic], Halle: Waisenhaus, 1837; Friedrich Theodor Vischer, *Vorträge, erste Reihe: Schöne und die Kunst* [Lectures, first series: Beauty and Art], Stuttgart: Cotta, 1898, pp. 174f, 195, 215; Friedrich Schiller, "Über Anmut und Würde [On Grace and Dignity]," *Neue Thalia*, 2. Jahrgang, 1793; Johann Friedrich Herbart, *Lehrbuch zur Einleitung in die Philosophie* [Textbook Introduction to Philosophy], Leipzig: 1850, 5 Aufl. S. 109.]

for innocence would be portrayed for him; the aesthetic process would remain the same. According to this interpretation, the modifications of the beautiful would be considered merely as supplements to the beautiful in the sense of Herbart, or as supplements in the same sense in which Schopenhauer construes the sublime [das Erhabene] as "an elevation [die Erhebung] above the known [erkannte] inimical relationship of the contemplated object to the will in general" and thus as a "supplement" through which the feeling of the sublime is distinguished from that of the beautiful.[91] If this is right, the modifications could not be construed as simple qualities but only as mixed phenomena. We have an analogue to such a mixed phenomenon in the domain of the senses, e.g., in the phenomenon of bodily pain. Even here there has not up to now been enough differentiation of how much of its uniqueness depends upon the quality of the sensation, how much on its intensity, its spatial expanse, its temporally rhythmic flow, and how much depends finally on its peculiar tone of feeling. |325|

Now, to be sure, each theme [Gegenstand] requires its own manner of artistic treatment. For the treatment of an object [Objekt] with a specific tone of feeling, there is in each art a form of portraying it corresponding to this tone. In this connection Rosenkranz has distinguished high or rigorous, intermediate, and easy or low styles. If rhythms, tempos, kinds of tone, and chord sequences employed for a funeral procession are other than those for a dance, if a different, higher degree of probability is required for tragedy than for comedy and so, too, a different construction of the action, a different characterization of the persons—something that, with the neglect of the aesthetic treatment of comedy, is still not sufficiently developed at all—one could perhaps see in these typically different forms (respectively dependent upon the tone of feeling of the theme) different fundamental qualities of aesthetic feeling. But if we look more closely at these forms of portraying things and their differences in the case of different themes, we find aesthetic elements that call up different feelings—corresponding to the theme—through empathy, while the process of the empathy itself remains the same. Construing the different rhythms, timbres, lines, and colors—in keeping with the difference in their felt-character respectively—as so many simple, aesthetic qualities would mean making a material factor into the principle for the division of aesthetic forms.

---

[91] See Arthur Schopenhauer, *Die Welt als Wille und Vorstellung* [The World as Will and Representation], I, Buch 3, zweite, durchgängig verbesserte und sehr vermehrte Auflage, Leipzig, Brockhaus, 1844, §39.

For the same reason, we may not base qualities of aesthetic feeling either on the different sensory impressions underlying the feeling of beauty or on the different mental processes that trigger them. One could, if one made those qualities foundational, attempt a division of aesthetic feelings in terms of acoustic or optic, simultaneous or non-simultaneous impressions, and so forth. But if one selects the difference in the processes triggered by the impressions as the principle of the division, one could distinguish between the sort of aesthetic feelings that arise through stirring up feelings (or, better, representations of feelings) or their general rhythms and the sort that arise through stirring up representations of themes (effects of art that are musical and portray things). All these divisions may be worth recommending for heuristic reasons. But once beauty is placed into a relation, it is not possible to ground any distinction [*Unterschied*] within the relation itself on a difference [*Verschiedenheit*] among its |326| fundaments.

Lipps seeks to ground the modifications of the beautiful on qualitative differences among the aesthetic feelings of value themselves.[92] For Lipps there are as many modifications of the beautiful as there are feelings that underlie the object's own unique value and have the character of being personally valuable. Pleasure and displeasure are, for him, simply colorings, recurring everywhere, of all possible feelings (p. 508). He distinguishes feelings of demand (quantity-feelings), feelings of slowness and quickness, of mass and the opposite, of simplicity and differentiation, depth and expanse. Factual differences among aesthetic impressions have undoubtedly been provided by this means, but to decide whether we additionally have to see in these complicated mental formations feelings at all, i.e., whether we have to see in them aesthetic, *purely* aesthetic feelings and basic qualities of them (in the sense of basic colors)—that would require a much more thoroughgoing analysis.

If we want to find simple qualities of the aesthetic feeling, we should seek them only in differences within the aesthetic process itself. One such unambiguous difference is that between the smooth and the inhibited flow of the process. Wherever the course of aesthetic contemplation is inhibited, displeasure and the impression of the ugly arise.[93] Hence, we would have to

---

[92] Theodor Lipps, *Grundlegung der Ästhetik* [Foundation of Aesthetics], Hamburg/Leipzig: Voss, 1903, pp. 506ff. [See Landmann-Kalischer's review in *Archiv für die gesamte Psychologie*, V, 1905: pp. 213–27.]

[93] Even Lipps concedes that the ugly consists in inhibiting the aesthetic process. The aesthetic conflict arises, he says, when the manifoldness asks for the apperception of unity and yet in turn forbids it. Such is the case for colors, sounds, rhythms lying extremely close to one another. But when, in addition, he inserts the ugly into the objectified feeling of the negation of life (ibid., p. 140), he then falls back into an explanation based upon the material.

regard the beautiful and the ugly in any case as basic qualities of the aesthetic sense. Insofar as both allow for degrees, one could be tempted to construe them as intensities. But things hold here in the same way as they do with the sensation of temperature. Although degrees and transitions take place, beautiful and ugly as qualities are still just as separate as cold and warm, black and white, high and low sounds. The last analogy might be the most pertinent one. For, although the neutral point in all |327| these domains is as far as possible from both qualities, it can still be produced *objectively* for the black-white and the warm-cold scales from both qualities by mixing them, while an intermediate sound can be produced by high and low sounds just as little as a neutral theme can be produced by [mixing] beautiful and ugly properties.

The differentiation of further qualities must be reserved for a separate individual investigation.

In the foregoing study we have tried to draw out the analogy between the sensations of the senses and aesthetic feelings and to support it specifically through the comparison between sensory judgments and aesthetic judgments in regard to their validity and the sources of deceptions in them. As a result, we have come to believe ourselves epistemologically justified in concluding that beauty is to be construed as a property of things in the same sense as sensory qualities are. With this conclusion we come in a strange circle back to the doctrine that was still dominant up to the end of the 18th century in regard to the relationship of feeling and sensation. Before one successfully managed at that time to distinguish between sensation and feeling in our sense, either one ascribed sensory qualities on the one side and the perfect and imperfect, the beautiful and ugly, the good and evil on the other side *in the same manner* to things as properties or in the same manner one denied them [this] and excluded them, as a product of the imagination, from the true cognition of things.[94] But today the proof |328| has

---

[94] The intermingling and equating of feelings and sensations also emerges clearly in the case of Spinoza (II, p. 74; *Ethics*, First Part, Supplement) when he says "... et rei alicuius naturam bonam, vel malam, sanam vel putridam et corruptam dicunt, prout ab eadem afficiuntur. Ex. gr. sc. motus, quem nervi ab objectis, per oculis repraesentatis, accipiunt, valetudine conducat, objecta, a quibus causatur, pulchra dicuntur, quae autem contraria cient, deformia. Quae deinde per naves [sic] sensum movent, odorifera, vel foetida vocant, quae per linguam, dulcia, aut amara, sapita aut insipida etc. Quae autem per tactum dura, aut mollia; aspera aut laevia etc. Et quae denique aures movent, strepitum, sonum, vel harmoniam edere dicuntur etc." [... and they call the nature of anything good or evil, healthy or putrid and spoiled according to how they are affected by it. For example, if the movement that the nerves take up from objects through the eye's representations is conducive to well-being, the objects by which it is caused are called beautiful [*pulchra*] but those that cause the contrary are called ugly [*deformia*]. Then they call those that move the senses through the nostrils [*nares*] fragrant or fetid, through the tongue, sweet or sour, flavorful or tasteless, etc. Then those through touch they call hard or soft, rough or smooth, etc. And whatever then moves our ears is called noise, sound, or harmony, etc.]

to proceed in reverse. While the subjectivity of sensations was proven at that time by showing that they were not distinct from feelings (see Locke, *Essay on Human Understanding*, II, chapter 4, §§17–18), so today it is necessary to demonstrate the objectivity of the properties of things grasped by feeling by placing them on a par with sensory qualities.

Now one might want to object that the analogies that have been drawn here are much too general to prove precisely that the *aesthetic* feeling can be put on the same level with organs of sense—since even if the aesthetic feeling agreed in individual points with the behavior of the organs of sense, what follows in this regard are only the general laws that governed the life of the soul, specifically the life of feeling in general. If one wanted to make this objection, I would have nothing against it. I have pointed on several occasions to the same behavior of being pleased in an elementary, ethical way. I do not doubt that all other feelings also appear in their elements with the same law-governed character as sensations and thus, like them, are capable of *legitimate objectification*. The more general validity of my thesis should not by any means undermine the proof conducted for the specific case.

(Entered on January 8, 1905.)

On Artistic Truth

1. Introduction[1]

German aesthetics has again and again come back to the thought that beauty and art yield cognition of some sort. First it was the truth of nature that was demanded of art, in keeping with the 17th century French revival of the theory of imitation. In the beginning of the 18th century Germans understood the theory in the sense of an uninspired naturalism of which the doctrine's major creator[2] was as innocent as God was of evil in the world. Following the French precedent, one reproached rhyme and opera for being untrue, since people are typically not in the habit of speaking or singing in verse. And what was wondrous in poetry appeared so wondrous at the time of this truth-fanaticism that Bodmer was forced to devote a work explicitly to its defense.

Along with truth in the sense of the naturalness of the portrayal, abstract truths were also demanded of art and poetry. Poetry belonged to "the beautiful sciences."[3] It was an *ars popularis*, intended to make truths of an abstract-theoretical or moral sort accessible to minds not capable of the higher, nobler sort of delight that is more removed from the senses, minds whose understanding is too limited to connect the manifold into a unity in *thought*. "To ready itself for a higher splendor, the understanding

---

[1] [For an introduction to this essay, see §5 of Matherne's Introduction.]
[2] [Landmann-Kalischer is likely referring to Johann Christoph Gottsched, who proposed a metaphysical foundation of ancient and French classicist literary rules, based in large part on considerations of imitation and verisimilitude, where mention of the utterly improbable, for example, angels and devils, should be kept to a minimum; see his *Versuch einer critischen Dichtkunst vor die Deutschen* [Attempt at a Critical Art of Literary Composition for the Germans], Leipzig: Breitkopf, 1729. Resistance to Gottsched's views—leading to a so-called *Dichterkrieg* ("Poets' War")—came from Swiss critic Johann Jakob Bodmer, who defended Milton's *Paradise Lost*; see his *Critische Abhandlung von dem Wunderbaren in der Poesie* [Critical Treatise of the Wondrous in Poetry], Zürich: Orell, 1740].
[3] ['Beautiful sciences' is a translation of *schöne Wissenschaften* which might also be translated as 'fine literature' [*belles lettres*] as the parallel to the 'fine arts' [*beaux artes, schöne Künste*].]

practices on the alluring."[4] Since the actions of human beings are grounded on representations, truth is of the highest importance for human beings; everything represented by the arts must accordingly be grounded in truth. Acquaintance with the world and human beings is supposed to deepen the arts; a freer, more elevated grasp and consideration of reality is supposed to instruct them.

Baumgarten took the great step of acknowledging artistic intuition as a *sui generis* cognition, but even he continued to orient |458| it so exclusively to conceptual cognition, at least in terms of its value, that he made it in turn fully dependent upon the latter and did not venture very far beyond the standpoint sketched above.[5] Goethe also gives art an essentially intellectual character when he labels 'beautiful' the things that reveal their (the things!) laws to intuition [and] when he makes it the artist's task to express, through stylization and idealization, the sense of nature and its supreme truth.

For the critical philosophy, which denied the objective nature of the beautiful and emphasized that the beautiful pleases without a concept, conveying any sort of cognition through art was also out of the question. According to Kant, an aesthetic judgment about the purposiveness of an object neither is grounded in any concept of it on hand nor does it provide one. Yet right after Kant, in Romantic and speculative aesthetics, the old thought of conveying a truth through art was revived with all its energy. Precisely on this point, the Hegelian aesthetic reconnects with Baumgarten. The entire Romantic and speculative aesthetic still sees in the beautiful the absolute in an intuitive form, the idea appearing in a limited way. Art is supposed to show the meaning of reality; it is supposed to make a concept intuitive; it is once again a preparatory stage to true cognition (Hegel); and aesthetics forms the entryway to philosophy since what a philosophical mind is can only be explained in it (Schelling). While Romantic aesthetics still stresses the peculiarity of "intellectual intuition" and "pure cognizing," i.e., the unique form in which various cognitions are conveyed by art, Hegelians fully return once again to the construal of art as a *biblia pauperum*.[6]

---

[4] [From Friedrich Schiller's poem *Die Künstler* ["The Artists"]; see Henry Wireman's translation in *The Poems of Schiller*, Philadelphia: Kohler, 1879, p. 83: "The mind, to face Truth's higher glances / Must swim some time in Beauty's trances".]

[5] Alexander Gottlieb Baumgarten, *Aesthetica*, Frankfurt an der Oder: Kleyb, 1750; *Aestheticorum, Pars altera* [Second Part of Aesthetics], Frankfurt an der Oder: Kleyb, 1758.

[6] [A *biblia pauperum* [*Paupers' Bible*] was a late medieval picture book of biblical events.]

Only now, in place of the shallow bits of worldly wisdom that art, as it was construed in the 18th century, taught, it was the great metaphysical truths of the Hegelian philosophy that were supposed to be conveyed by art to the poor in spirit.

Fiedler was the first to develop the positive and extremely fruitful core of the Baumgartian doctrine.[7] He would never tire of iterating that the artistic drive is a cognitive drive, that artistic activity is an operation of cognizing, that the artistic result is a cognitive result. Yet, more clearly than Baumgarten, he saw in the artist's intuitive cognizing a cognition that was *sui generis*, a self-sufficient and supremely significant cognition that is not in any way linked to conceptual cognition. The organ of this cognition is solely intuition and its mastering is the work of artists alone. |459|

In contrast to this course of thought, which has never been completely abandoned, modern aesthetics has overwhelmingly gone back to Kant. It sees in art the bearer of beauty, and in beauty a value. But its concept of value is detached from, or opposed to, any concept of cognizing.

Yet even in modern aesthetics there is talk of truth. A feeling of truth enters into the aesthetic impression, a feeling that demands an explanation. We feel that some works of art are true, that others are fake. We feel blessed by the truth that an artwork affords. The greatest artists are at the same time the truest and an artwork that we find to be fake is condemned.

On what is this feeling of truth grounded? What sort of cognition does an artwork convey?

Of the above-mentioned concepts of truth of earlier aesthetics, the most naturalistic concept is untenable because it rests upon the confusion of means and end, form and content. An artwork as a whole cannot be true or false. Only judgments are true or false. A judgment that agrees with other judgments is true. But with what is an artwork supposed to agree? It has its entire sense in being beautiful; in grasping it we behave not by cognizing but by feeling. It can no more be true or false than a human being or a flower can. When there is, nonetheless, talk of the truth of a verse, a song, a figure, or a building, this can only happen with the presupposition that a *what* and a *how* are distinguished, that one is speaking not of the truth of the entire artwork but only of a truth *in it*. Its truth can lie only in its

---

[7] [Konrad Fiedler, a major art theorist in the nineteenth century, developed a conception of 'aesthetic truth.' See, for example, "*Moderner Naturalismus und künstlerische Wahrheit* [Modern Naturalism and Artistic Truth]," in *Wissenschaftliche Beilage der Leipziger Zeitung* (1881); reproduced in *Schriften zur Kunst* [Writings on Art], hrsg. von Hans Marbach, Leipzig: Hirzel, 1896, pp. 133–82.]

content, its outcome, in the result of the process through which we take it up into ourselves, only in what it says, relates, shows, or expresses. In terms of its form, an operatic aria may be as untrue as the monologue in a drama, the rhyme in a poem, and any form of art at all. Yet the feeling that is expressed by it, the outcome of the process of contemplation stirred up by it, is true or false.

But, with the exception of the Baumgarten-Fiedler concept, none of the concepts of truth of earlier aesthetics can come into consideration as far as we are concerned. They cannot be considered because they all presupposed—in part explicitly, in part implicitly—that artistic truth is also attainable on a path other than that of the artwork. For those aestheticians, the truth that the artwork contains was a means of connecting the artwork itself with other domains of life in order to |460| explain and justify in this way its existence and its value. But the feeling of truth is so closely and internally conjoined with the aesthetic feeling that at least for purely methodological reasons, we must initially proceed from the assumption that there is a specifically aesthetic truth, a truth that can be conveyed, discovered, and discerned solely through art and on no other path. Any other truth that an artwork could somehow convey beyond this could call forth only the intellectual joy that every truth arouses and thus could only have the significance of an extra-aesthetic side effect for the artwork. If, however, the feeling of the truth of an artwork is an aesthetic feeling, then this truth must also have a specifically aesthetic content and it is the content of this specifically aesthetic truth that we seek.

Of what sort, then, can this content be? If, in keeping with our presupposition, it is supposed to be something new, something that we have no acquaintance with anywhere else and that is only discovered by art, on what basis then are we able to judge its truth or falsity? With what can it possibly agree?

2. Objective and Subjective Reality

Reality is one thing; consciousness of reality is another. Even the representatives of immanent philosophy who teach the inseparability of subject and object still distinguish objective reality from the mental world [*psychischen Welt*]. They distinguish the latter either as the social part of consciousness or as the internally agreeing system of everything perceivable and thinkable, the lawfulness of which forms the criterion for distinguishing what really is from hallucinations. Whether one presupposes that subject and object are originally one and undivided or whether one assumes that all given elements are originally subjective or originally objective—for each of these standpoints, the necessity of thinking of the contrast as unfolding in some way still obtains. The world of the mind always remains distinct from objective reality, not only practically but also theoretically. Since this contrast underlies the following accounts of the matter, we need to elucidate it briefly from a naive as well as an epistemological [*erkenntnistheoretischen*] standpoint.

For the naive consciousness, pervaded without exception by this contrast, the individual form in which consciousness appears, appears as the most universal fact |461|, one that sustains the difference between mental reality and objective reality. For the naive take on things, objective reality is something constant, something that first needs to be taken up sequentially and piecemeal by the individual subject. Each individual consciousness embraces only one segment of objective reality; it [the individual consciousness] is divided into a center and periphery and each element of reality that is to be taken up anew is exposed to individual deceptions. The naive take on things accordingly interprets this difference in such a way that mental reality is subordinated, as something individual and alterable, to objective reality as something lasting and grounded in itself. Objective reality here is identical with what is [*Seienden*]; mental reality with what is not [*Nichtseienden*], with what is "merely" thought.

If mental reality is thus only a segment of objective reality for the naive take on things, the reverse is the case for the epistemological consideration. Objective reality, considered epistemologically, is only a segment, only an element of mental reality. Considered epistemologically, objective reality is a concept, a system of judgments, the outcome of a ceaseless process through which the mental reality is worked over; hence, it is something created and something that needs to be created over and over. Mental reality is accordingly the raw material, as it were, for the structure of objective reality. Much of it [the mental reality] is taken over, just as it is, into the objective world, but most of it is transformed for this purpose in some direction or put into other combinations, while some of it, finally, is omitted from any application to that structure as completely unusable. In the psyche every representation is assimilated by the entire content of consciousness and hence is altered in its uniqueness. But while this is the case, as soon as the representation is recognized as true and is supposed to be elevated to being a component of the actually existing world, it is then detached, isolated from that nexus; its relationship to the sense impression is rigorously tested as is any other origin it may have, and it is worked over into a concept from specific viewpoints. If the representations are in this way subjected to a transformation in order to enter into the objective world, feeling is not permitted any entrance into this world or, rather, where it has managed to creep in, it is more and more driven away from it. [After having been] thoroughly amalgamated with objective reality in pre-scientific thinking and even deeply in scientific thinking, feeling is gradually driven back into its own world, the religious world. And even in this world it is ultimately indulged only to the extent that it is thought to be completely independent of objective reality and granted no influence on the latter. In this way |462| between mental and objective reality many sorts of deviations emerge that later need to be elucidated in detail. This much is clear, that the mental world, in its components as well as in the manner of its interconnections, is different from objective reality, and in part directly opposed to it.

The concept of objective reality stems initially from the naive and predominantly practical consciousness. It is the external world from which we receive sense-impressions, a world that acts on us for good and for ill, and that we, in acting, strive to act upon in turn; a world that resists our wishes, remains silent toward our dreams, and never and nowhere realizes [*realisirt*] our memories and phantasies. But this naive concept is by no means developed in a logically coherent manner. Its elements are not universally interconnected with one another nor is it free of the contradictions that arise from the fact that elements of mental reality protrude into it. Resolute work on this naive representation, the rigorous concept of objective reality, is the desideratum and product of science alone and is progressively realized by it alone. Between the two concepts there are many sorts of transitions. Each science proceeds from the concepts of pre-scientific and practical thinking; they protrude into every cultivated science, indeed, even into every coherent worldview. It is, in particular, a trademark of every childlike worldview that it builds elements of mental reality into the objective world despite the obvious contradictions that logical elaboration of them yields. The process of separating [the two concepts] is still relatively new and we are accustomed to say of such non-scientific constructs of the world that they contain poetic elements, just as we do of religious worldviews or philosophical systems that, for example, make the good the world's final purpose. We speak in terms of a distinction of poetry [*Dichtung*] and truth[8] and tend to chalk up to poetry everything that flatters the soul too much, everything that is too beautiful, too blissful, too enticing—to be real. Does poetry thus stand in opposition to objective reality?

The task of the following accounts of the matter is to show in detail that art and poetry stand in the same relationship of similarity, dissimilarity, and opposition to objective reality that we have already sketched for the mental world.

It is, to be sure, a naive and purely intellectual rather than aesthetic joy when we recognize things of nature in art, |463| when we come to know [*erkennen*] "that this is that and that is this."—Nonetheless, we cannot get over the fact that something is recognized in the artwork, that some sort of identity is felt through this. And perhaps only a small correction is needed to set aright in modern terms Aristotle's intellectualistic construal of the matter. In the artistic portrayal—we can perhaps thus say—we recognize not the things of nature but indeed our *representation* of them. And not only our representation of the things of nature but instead our representations, our feelings, our inner life in general.[9]

Art does not afford objective reality. It mirrors and portrays the mental world instead, and it is true insofar as it portrays that world faithfully, insofar as it succeeds in freeing the mental world from its entanglement with objective reality (which overreaches often enough precisely in naive consciousness) and in establishing it purely on its own terms.—Our age is perhaps in such need of art and beauty because the mental world has become so very hidden opposite the brute force of external reality. The life of the mind is given to us only through inner perception. Just as we would never see our face were it not for a mirror, so, too, we would never see our own inner life opposite us—were it not for the mirror of art. Only art exhibits it for us. Only through art can we come to know it. And we feel the truth of artistic contents in their agreement with the inner world.

---

[8] ["Poetry and Truth" is the subtitle of Goethe's biography *Aus meinem Leben: Dichtung und Wahrheit*, Bände 1–3, Tübingen: Cotta; 1811–1814.]

[9] [Landmann-Kalischer is likely referring to Aristotle's discussion of μιμεῖσθαι ('imitating') in *Poetics* 4 (1448b5–b24). Each instance of 'come to know' in this and the next paragraph is a translation of *erkennen*.]

3. The Elements of Subjective Reality and Their Mirroring in Art

In order to become acquainted in detail with the differences that obtain between mental and objective reality, we need to free up its components from their real [*realen*] interconnectedness and consider them psychologically.

We have already mentioned the most general property of the mental world, its individual form. This form underlies three different peculiarities of subjective reality that express, in psychological terms, the "narrowness of consciousness":

(1) mental reality contains only a segment of objective reality;
(2) the respective entire content of the mental reality is divided into a center and periphery; |464|
(3) each individual element of mental reality, in particular each new impression, is conditioned in its existence and its constitution by the respective entire constellation of consciousness.

If we look closer at how these peculiarities come to be expressed in the various zones of the mental world and for the various groups of mental elements and if we follow up how they are mirrored in art, we secure an overview of the various forms of artistic truth.

1. Sense Impressions, Gestalts, and Perceptions

If we apply the general distinctions to sensations and perceptions first, it is clear that perception is limited, that each time only one object or one complex of objects falls within its domain and that only one inherent feature of this object or complex appears in the center, the rest appearing in what we see indirectly. Perception targets a selection from the continuum of reality and only one element from what is selected moves in turn into the foreground. So, too, perception is ultimately colored, like any content of consciousness, by foregoing or simultaneous sense-impressions, representations or feelings—a state of being conditioned that appears as sense-deception when seen from the standpoint of objective reality. In the eye's reality, however, the staff in the water is broken, the mountains in the clear air are close enough to grab, the blurry white fleck on the water is a swan.

Now, all these properties of perception that distinguish them from what is perceived, from what is objectively given, make up their truth in the artistic reproduction.

That every artwork presents a segment [of reality] is self-evident, even if not quite so self-evident as it initially appears. After all, primitive art comes to terms with this self-evident necessity only reticently and with difficulty. It wants to show as much as possible, just as it is contained in the cognizing consciousness. Every primitive picture of a landscape not only shows infinitely more detail than a modern picture; it wants to allow as much as possible to be surveyed. If the typical form of the ancient picture of a landscape is the *veduta*,[10] then that of the modern is the corner of a garden. Each developed art—one need only think of Japanese art—consciously and deliberately presents the segment that primitive art and children's art accept only reluctantly. Anyone who has ever researched the portrayal of an action in the history of art knows the immense difficulty that the necessity of depicting only a segment creates for the portrayal. |465|

If every artwork presents a segment of objective reality, it also presents this segment with a definite arrangement and, to be sure, an arrangement with a center and periphery. The first requirement of any artistic composition is the obviousness of the arrangement [*Übersichtlichkeit*, that it can be taken in at a glance]. A symmetrical division accommodates the eye's natural construal of a surface and the famous compositional form of the half-circle is a reflection of the spatial schema in which the world stands before us. It should be noted here, to be sure, that this obviousness of the arrangement, if it is to remain artistically true, may not go too far, since the truth of the perception that is at issue here is canceled the moment the ordering of the space or colors in a picture becomes something that can be calculated intellectually or—in the case of overused schemata—is known in advance. The intellect then at once robs the perception of the possibility of artistic satisfaction by taking its work away from it and entering into its function.

Finally, in artistic portrayals, the sense-deceptions that can be corrected in the construction of objective reality also awaken the impression of truth. Indeed, painting typically develops by gradually taking visual deceptions up into the portrayal, while in all primitive art the attempt is made to reproduce

---

[10] [*Veduta*, the Italian word for 'vista,' is used to designate a type of detailed, large-scale visual depiction, typically of a town.]

in the picture the conceptually real world instead of the mentally real world. The progress of truth in painting rests upon the discovery, and upon the progress in application, of various sorts of perspective; portraying intersections, proportions, and so forth *in the right way* means presenting them as they appear to the eye, not as they are in reality. A large part of the truth in architecture and sculpture also rests upon this illusionism. A typical example of an impression that is, by contrast, untrue in this domain is the effect of a panorama that reckons with the eye's functions in a way that can never occur at once in real sensory perception.[11]

In addition to the inherent features cited, the reality of sensory perception also finds expression in art inasmuch as many *more* sensations appear in art than come into consideration for objective reality. For what else could it mean, that irksome fact that we possess such insufficient names |466| for differences in sensation, particularly, for sensations of colors? [The reason is that] language, indeed, exhibits the inventory of objective, not mental reality. Sensations deliver the most important material for the construction of the outer world but they are only employed insofar as they can be of service for cognition of objects and their changes. For this, finer grain differences in sensation are not commonly considered; these differences thus remain trapped in the mental world. Only music and painting have given objective expression to these, as it were, *surplus* sensations and their connections to one another. Painters have discovered in objects qualities of sensation scarcely anyone had previously been conscious of since they are irrelevant for the cognition of things or are even, like colored shadows, a direct disturbance. So, too, in general we only know the full scope and finer points of sensations of sound through music.

Summing up these considerations, it follows that sensations and perceptions are given in art just as they are in consciousness, when they do not yet or no longer serve as means of cognition, when the correction that thinking makes in them, for the purpose of the construction of objective reality, is not yet or no longer performed on them. Sensation is the material of cognition insofar as it is useful for the purposes of consciousness in the process of cognizing; it is agreeable or disagreeable insofar as it enters into the subjective common feeling as a component of it. It is aesthetically true or

---

[11] Adolf Hildebrand, *Das Problem der Form in der bildenden Kunst* [The Problem of Form in Pictorial Art], Strassburg: Heitz, 1893, Kap. III.

untrue insofar as it is taken up in and for itself, in its status as a mental fact and in its own connections to other sensations, and insofar as it is expressed accordingly.

One could object that what has been said here might hold for sensations alone but not for perceptions and, in particular, not for sense-deceptions. One could say that the deceptions in whose artistic reproduction we would want to find aesthetic truth are in fact only deceptions insofar as they contain cognitive judgments, just as any perception at all already contains in itself a judgment (Brentano's primary judgment of perception).[12] But to this objection it should be replied that we can scarcely encounter any contents of consciousness that are not being worked on in one way or another for cognitive purposes. The categories of the understanding after all may extend to all the contents of consciousness. We are nonetheless able to distinguish various degrees to which they serve cognition or the construction of the external world. Memory's representations, for example, doubtlessly serve cognition as memories, but if in an individual case they are not worked on, they serve in a supremely imperfect manner since, in keeping with their natural mental composition, they are, as means of cognition, |467| full of deceptions. So, too, in the sense-deceptions and their correction, the relationship between the processes recurs, that is to say, between processes that run their course purely according to laws of the psyche and those that are transformed for the particular purposes of cognition. Although perception already contains a cognitive judgment, this is nonetheless initially conditioned solely by mental *habit*, by the very forms of cognition that have developed as a habitual form of working on sense-impressions and have in the process, figuratively speaking, lost consciousness of their purpose. The judgment that underlies a specific sense-deception is thus not directed actually at cognition of the fact in question but instead has emerged solely from a mental habit. The sense-deception can accordingly be regarded, in contrast to its correction, as a component of the mental reality.[13]

---

[12] [Landmann-Kalischer likely has in mind Franz Brentano's claim that every perception is a judgment; see *Psychologie vom empirischen Standpunkt* II, ed. O. Kraus, 1874/1924, pp. 50–51, translated as *Psychology from an Empirical Standpoint*, ed. T. Crane and J. Wolff, trans. A. C. Rancurello, D. B. Terrell, and L. McAlister, London: Routledge, 1973/1995, p. 209.]

[13] The question arises whether art, by corresponding to the psychological laws of perception, precisely for that reason actually awakens the impression of *truth* [or] whether through this process it does not straightaway awaken the feeling of beauty and agreeableness far more. For the answer to this question, see the final section of the last chapter that treats the interconnectedness of beauty and truth.

2. Memory's Representations

If we pass from sensations and perceptions to *representations* and, indeed, to *memory's representations* first of all, the general phenomenon with which we have already become acquainted as a mark of mental reality recurs to an even higher degree here. The difference between the mind's being as such and its cognitive purpose comes to light here even more distinctly than in the case of perception. Indeed, it intensifies here to the point of being in open conflict. The purpose served by the life of representations takes place in a pronounced contradiction, in a constant battle with its own set of laws. The ideal of memory's representations—seen from the standpoint of cognition—is to copy perceptions with complete fidelity. The natural tendency of the life of representations is, by contrast, to move toward what typically differentiates representations from sensation.

Indeed, the depiction of memory's representations as weaker but generally faithful copies of direct sense-perceptions is generally acknowledged today to be "as off the mark as possible."[14] |468| It is also generally acknowledged that memory's representations are characterized far more by their *incompleteness*, when compared to sense-impressions, than by their weaker intensity. Here, too, the narrow confines of consciousness first necessitates a selection of impressions, followed by the emphasis on some elements of these selected impressions and the blurring of others, and finally the supplementation and alteration of what is retained through representations that are conditioned by the respective constellation of the mind. The result is a falsification in memory's representation [*Fälschung der Erinnerungsvorstellung*], a memory deception.

As for the question concerning the manner in which the content of memory's representations diverges in a law-like way from the sense impressions corresponding to them, at which places the gaps in the sense-impressions accordingly arise, and whether, how, and by what means those gaps are filled—this question is at the moment the subject of lively discussion by 'assertion'-psychology.[15] In general we can distinguish three principles by means of which the selection of impressions and that of their

---

[14] Wilhelm Wundt, *Grundriß der Psychologie* [Outline of Psychology], 4. Auflage, Leipzig: Engelmann, 1901, p. 299.

[15] [See, for example, William Stern (Hrsg.), *Psychologie der Aussage mit besonderer Berücksichtigung von Problemen der Rechtspflege, Pädagogik, Psychiatrie und Geschichtsforschung* [Psychology of the Assertion with Particular Consideration of Problems of the Justice System, Pedagogy, Psychiatry, and Historical Research], Band 2, Nr. 3. Leipzig: Barth, 1905.]

elements as well as their modification are determined. The impressions and elements of impressions are preserved by memory's representations, and gaps are filled by such representations where those impressions and elements of impressions either (1) are frequently repeated, (2) correspond to representations, to tendencies of feeling or willing that are already on hand, or (3) are accompanied by a strong feeling or interest.[16] Conditioned as they are by these inherent features, our memory's representations are little suited to afford a faithful picture of reality. We become aware of this fact often enough. We speak of a recollection's infidelity, of an embellishing memory, and so forth, and we reach back to perception as soon as we wish to make an exact determination.

In the same segment [of reality], however, and in the same modified way in which the sense-impressions (and, with them, objective reality) are given to us through memory's representations, we find them in turn in art.[17] |469|

In the first place, the selection of representations, with which art works, is immediately oriented not to objective reality but to mental reality. In this respect what is mentally real is the sum of representations that are familiar to us, as Avenarius formulates it in his *Critique of Pure Experience* [*Erfahrung*]. Depending upon individual life circumstances and lived experiences [*Erlebnisse*], only this or that segment of beings falls within [the scope of] consciousness. Art follows this mental reality completely. The conquest of a new domain for art is invariably only a sign that a new domain of life has found its way into the mental reality of the age. The materials of art are invariably drawn from the [age's] central interests. Art is religious or social, it paints farmers or women of high society, depicts heroes of love or war—in each case in keeping with the ruling interest of the age, the people, the class and so forth. Thus, the naturalism of the 1880s was true in comparison with the tradition of epigones of art dominating at that time, because naturalism drew its material from its age's domain of interests.

---

[16] Recollection [*Gedächtnis*] is generally conditioned by the attentiveness that was directed at the impression. The attentiveness itself, however, is determined by the inherent features cited above, and the same principles also govern the formation of associations; see Hermann Ebbinghaus, *Grundzüge der Psychologie* [Basic Features of Psychology], Leipzig: Veit, 1902, I, §48 and 49 and §§56ff.

[17] In his remarks on the problem of form in literary art [*Dichtkunst*], Riehl, as is well known, has already expanded [on the notion] that the poetic portrayal captures the manner of appearance of the image in memory (*Vierteljahrsschrift für wissenschaftliche Philosophie*, 21. Jahrgang, pp. 283–306; 22. Jahrgang, pp. 96–114). Nonetheless, the completely different viewpoint, under which the analogy is posited here, justifies a renewed engagement with it. ["Bemerkungen zu dem Probleme der Form in der Dichtkunst [Observations on the Problem of Form in Literary Art]," reprinted in Alois Riehl, *Philosophische Studien aus Vier Jahrzehnten* [Philosophical Studies from Four Decades], Leipzig: Quelle und Meyer, 1925.]

And it is not only this mental contemporaneousness that is mirrored in an artwork and that conditions its truth or untruth. These roles are also played by the mind's accentuation of one representation over and against the remaining representations, i.e., the significance attributed to that representation in proportion to the whole of consciousness. The artistic expression for this accentuation of the representation is the absolute intensive or extensive measure of an artwork.[18] The spatial dimensions of the surface of a picture, the length of a poem, or the intensity of the sound of a musical piece should not contradict the inner significance of its object. A lemon the size of a stein of beer or the portrayal of a Goethe or Beethoven as miniature porcelain figures would have a hollow and untrue effect to the point of being embarrassing; a Gothic church in miniature (like St. Maria della Spina in Pisa) does not allow the content of the feeling of the Gothic forms to arise at all and acts like a game, in contrast to the way that the *Romanesque* forms stand in contradiction of the expansiveness of the great Gothic cathedrals.

The fact that art follows the laws of the life of representations is apparent from the selection that is made among the representations and from the different accentuation that they undergo. Yet it is apparent even more clearly from the way the contents of the representations are given.

The first two principles, according to which memory's representations |470| are formed, are thus that memory holds fast to (1) impressions that continually recur in a regular way and (2) impressions corresponding to representations already on hand. These two principles find expression in art, the portrayer of the reality of the mind, inasmuch as its portrayals are not flawlessly faithful but instead more or less typical.

It has always been acknowledged as a fact and set up as a requirement that art lend its portrayals a typical [*typisch*] validity. And likewise, what conforms to the norm among nature's creations, the typical representative of its species, counts as beautiful. The concept of the paradigm [*Typus*] first entails that it captures, without individual determinateness, the ever-recurring and, hence, most frequent impressions that we get of objects of some species. If we nonetheless feel that some paradigms are true which, like Polycleitus' Canon, never exist anywhere in the reality of nature, this may perhaps ultimately lie in the fact that in it an idea of nature is revealed to us. But it probably lies closer [to the truth] to seek the explanation for it in the fact that the typical

---

[18] Max Dessoir, *Ästhetik und allgemeine Kunstwissenschaft* [Aesthetics and General Study of Art], Stuttgart: Enke, 1906, pp. 148–150.

portrayal of the object corresponds to the representation of it that we carry around in us.

That there are various degrees of stylization in art agrees with this point. As memory's representation distances itself more or less from perception, as it blurs a greater or lesser part of the elements of perception, and as it still contains this part—compared to what is centrally seized upon—to a higher or slighter degree of distinctness, so, too, the stylization of art displays various degrees. The typical truth can advance from the liveliest fullness to the heights of simplification. The limit for this artistic simplification lies in the very elements of the representation that are inseparable from the representation of an object, that are essential to it and characteristic for it. Thus, a body portrayed in painting or sculpture that shows no material characteristics of any sort invariably has the effect of being untrue.

But the concept of the paradigm not only entails that it corresponds to memory's representations, which have formed according to the principle of repetition, but also that it brings out the characteristic essence of an object. The paradigm of a lion is not only the lion that looks like most lions but, as Taine expresses it, "a mouthful of teeth on four legs"; it is the lion of which the properties essential to the species have been developed the most or elaborated the most by the artist. In this sense even a building or an object of a craft is typical if in its external form what it is for |471| comes to light. Let us recall here that property of recollection by virtue of which it prefers to hold fast to those impressions that correspond to representations already on hand. The representation of the lion stems for us not only from an image of its face; it is co-determined by everything that we know of its life and its place in the animal realm. Thus, if the image of the face of a lion is given to us in pictorial art, then in order to have the truth of what is paradigmatic it must not only contain its ever-recurring components but must emphasize among these components what allows the complete representation that we have of it to dawn on us.

The point is also clear in cases when we feel that the portrayal is untruthful. If the portrayal of a lion elaborates those properties that express its nature as a predator, i.e., what is paradigmatically true of it, then a portrayal that placed the purely sensual splendor of its mane in the center would be untrue to the sense of that paradigm.[19] For, what is not contained in our representation of

---

[19] Such a portrayal could still very well contain an artistic truth of another sort. Regarding this matter, see the last chapter.

the object has the effect of being a deviation and fake, regardless of how distinctly that property may be contained in the object itself. Van Dyck, for example, gives his figures proportions that do not occur anywhere and, hence, violate the paradigm in the sense of what invariably recurs. He is also untrue insofar as, in a portrayal like that of the mourning over Christ, he makes the center of gravity the depiction of a youth's beautiful body, whose corpse awakens in us representations completely different from those of the death of a moral person and divine human like Jesus Christ. Van Dyck is obviously not alone in sinning in this way against the second requisite of the paradigmatic portrayal. This holds even for the completely religious art of the *Cinquecento* [sixteenth-century Italy]. Despite also bringing out so much that is paradigmatically true to *intuition* with its interest in virtuosic treatment of spaces, bodies, and garments, it is untrue insofar as it deviates from its objective theme, when compared to the concentrated manner in which all the felt content [*ganze Gefühlsinhalt*] of a story of the New Testament is expressed in a portrayal by Duccio or Giotto.—For the same reason, Defregger's peasant girls would be fake even if they were nothing but color photographs, whereas a caricature can contain the utmost truth if only it captures what is contained in our representation of the object [*Gegenstand*]. |472| A sculpture, too, is untrue when, in the portrayal of a living human body, it flirts with the ideal of a smooth surface since that contradicts our representations. Architecture is untrue when it fashions "our proletarian houses as palaces, palaces as Swiss chalets, farmhouses as prisons, prisons as churches and churches as train stations."[20] It is also untrue when it adorns the flat ceiling of a room with three-dimensional [*plastisch*] figures or adorns a façade with paintings that give the illusion of a relief of ledges or any sort of architectural character that it does not possess. Craft objects, like beer steins adorned with figures of the Apostles, are untrue but so, too, are bronze chests finished off with painted cardboard or plaster of Paris, oil prints, woodcarving reliefs, and the like. In the latter cases the actual material of the object contradicts the very representation of the material that it seeks to awaken by the way it looks. Since the lack of truthfulness in such cases aims directly at deception, it has an effect just like a lie that has been uttered. In this connection, however, it should be noted that not every imitation of a decorative motif in some other material

---

[20] [Paul Schultze-Naumburg, "Die Gestaltung des Arbeiter-Wohnhauses [The Design of the Workers' House]," in *Die künstlerische Gestaltung des Arbeiter-Wohnhauses*, Zentralstelle für Arbeiter-Wohlfahrtseinrichtungen, p. 14. Konferenz (1905), Berlin: Heymann, 1906, p. 35.]

necessarily contains what is untrue from an aesthetic point of view. Gothic cabinets whose wood carvings imitate the purpose and material of an iron smith's trellis simply take over from another technology an extremely attractive decorative motif that does not contradict the technology of the wood carving. Because the motif taken over from another technology does not contradict its own technology, the Buchara rugs also do not offend our feeling of the truth, although they were invented as surrogates for the sumptuous wall paintings in Sasanian palaces.

Consideration of the third mark of memory's representations, that is, their strong accentuation of feeling, breaks down into two parts. The feeling is either a specific, affective comportment toward the object, or it is an interest, i.e., an attentiveness, that has concentrated on specific sides of the object. Interest as well as feeling in the narrower sense agrees in portraying the object from one point of view, in emphasizing specific properties, and in letting all others be blurred or be forgotten. Psychological experiments have taught or, better, they have confirmed that, even in the case of completely simple sense-impressions, e.g., such as colors, the quality is not retained if attention had been diverted to another inherent feature of the impression.[21] But the way an emotion colors the facts about events in memory to the point of distorting |473| and falsifying them is too familiar to everyone from personal experience to need any more detailed account.

Now this property of memory is of enormous significance for art. In the first place, the one-sidedness of the viewpoint—the ocular point, standpoint, impression-point, or however one dubs it—is not only a law of style for art but also a requisite of artistic truth. The prevailing interest, whether it be in contours, the values of color or light, large masses or detail, in features inherently psychological or in those of the appearance, determines the style. But every eclectic art that combines all viewpoints, all interests is devoid not only of style but of truth. It corresponds to what is conceptually [*dem begrifflich Seienden*], not to the mental reality. Unity of style is a postulate of artistic truth because it is a property of memory's representation.

More important for the question treated here than this one-sidedness that follows from the interest is the other unity of the artwork: namely, the unity

---

[21] Compare, for example, Narziß Ach, *Über die Willenstätigkeit und Denken* [On the Activity of Willing and Thinking], Göttingen: Vandenhoeck & Ruprecht, 1905.

of feeling. In its artistic portrayal every gestalt of poetry, painting, or plastic art is seen in terms of a determinate feeling, through which everything given [and] not given by it [the portrayal] is determined, precisely as is the case with memory's representation. Depending upon the viewpoint from which it is considered, the same actual gestalt comes to have a tragic, comic, or tragicomic character. The feeling that it arouses determines the portrayal of it. An artwork whose portrayal is not thoroughly guided by a feeling will never be able to take hold of anyone. So much has been said about disinterested gratification that the artist's stake in his work, which played a large role in earlier aesthetics,[22] has been forgotten. Yet only emotion sees things in a new light at all. Only a strong feeling, relative to a theme [*Gegenstand*], makes an artistically true portrayal of it possible since its representation lives in our memory only under the influence of such a feeling. Indeed, there are times when, while the reality of the present occasions constant fluctuations [in feelings], the distance of memory first makes clear even to us the dominating feeling that we bring to a theme.

We cannot enter here into the way in which the artist expresses his love and respect, hate and scorn for his figures. What matters here is only to show that a principle of configuration lies in this position of the feeling. Let me refer |474| to *Wahlverwandschaften* [Goethe's 1809 novel, *Elective Affinities*] as an example of the purest instance of configuring and nuancing the figures of a novel through the feeling the writer has towards them. The composition is completely focused on what is central; the whole is inspired by the love for Ottilie; everything is invented for its sake; everything is connected to it. Right from the outset, as gradually afterwards, Ottilie is talked about, along detours through Charlotte, Eduard, the captain, garden settings, and letters—truly, an introduction, regal like a sunrise. Step by step, before she appears herself, she illumines the others and the region. But the author introduces her only with expressions like "the splendid child," "the dear" or "the good" or "the beautiful girl." Everyone loves her. Her appearance gathers everything around her "through a gentle attraction as it were." Toward the conclusion, his love ascends to exaltation. The representation of saints performing miracles was certainly as far from this Olympian [Goethe] as it was from the minds of few humans; yet, to embellish her even in death, he lets her corpse still perform miracles. Alongside Eduard's hasty gestures, Charlotte's staid

---

[22] In particular for Bodmer and Breitinger; on this point, see Friedrich Braitmeier, *Geschichte der poetischen Theorie und Kritik* [History of Poetic Theory and Criticism], I, Frauenfeld: Huber, 1888.

gestures, Hauptmann's measured gestures, and the fuss [*Brimborium*] with which Luciane appears, Ottilie's inspired movements ceaselessly ascend like a tranquil and penetrating melody. The unity that the feeling we have for a human being gives him or her—perhaps the only unity that a human being possesses at all—is the unity that the artist gives his figures.

The uniformity and one-sidedness of the artistic standpoint (corresponding to memory's representations) naturally extends not only to the way the artist shapes human beings but also to the artistic or poetic theme [*Vorwurf*]. And one can distinguish entire kinds of art based upon the diversity with respect to this standpoint. Schiller has distinguished between the naive and the sentimental poet. Many more kinds could be inserted between these two major types and the diversity of possible standpoints can be illustrated by an image taken from [consideration of] the perspective. The naive poet corresponds to someone who stands at the same height as his object and across from it; someone else can stand at the same height but sketch the same object from the back; another while kneeling on the ground; a fourth from a bird's eye perspective, and so on in every nuance and direction. In this way the most diverse images arise, images that express to a very unequal degree what is conceptually and objectively called "the *essence* of the object." Many may even express the direct opposite of the latter and yet all would be artistically true as long as each is given only in itself, i.e., given correctly from the standpoint occupied. |475| With this image one can make clear an important difference between artistic truth and scientific and historical truth. A fixed ocular point is also required for acquiring a scientific truth. The difference from the artistic truth, however, lies in the fact that this ocular point *cannot* be chosen arbitrarily but is determined instead in each case by the purpose of [coming up with] an objective finding. Science also goes beyond the reality of perception by holding fast, via concepts and laws, to what is paradigmatic of the objects and processes. But the understanding deliberately chooses the viewpoint from which concept formation proceeds, while art, by fashioning paradigms, merely follows the psychological laws of memory. Thus, while every emotion is ruled out as a unifying point for scientific truth, the deliberately extreme standpoints that provide scientific observation with artificial means of assistance, like microscopes and telescopes, are useless for artistic truth. For the scientific finding, the gestalt of a plant may not be described from the perspective of a bird or a worm; rather the plant to be analyzed must be moved as a whole as well as successively in its individual parts into a position where it can be seen in the most distinct manner; it must be moved to the yellow surface[23] in each sense. It is an ever-recurring error in the history of aesthetics to attempt to lay down the unifying point of the artistic configuration as something fixed, while it is precisely the diversity of possible standpoints that distinguishes artistic truth from scientific truth. For those who theorize about art and demand that the artistically portrayed object express its "essence," its "idea," no mood, temperament, or idiosyncrasy of the artist is allowed to determine the standpoint from which the configuration proceeds. The artist is supposed to approach his object instead, they stipulate, with a completely determinate kind of construal that they call a state of "determinate determinability," "will-less cognition," or the like.[24] In the case of the art of painting, for example, this construal, common to classical as well as speculative aesthetics, has had the consequence of privileging sketching over painting and in fact the contour is objectively more characteristic for an object than its color. But this construal only lets *one* art count, namely, Classical art—just as, indeed, Goethe, too, the classicist, the *naive* poet, is indeed theoretically representative of the standpoint that demands that the essence and law of things be expressed in the artistic configuration of them. And it lets only *one* beauty count, the famous Winckelmannian beauty of clear water, the *one* |476| beauty of Wackenroder.[25] Yet entire genera of art like comedy, satire, caricature show that artistic truth can be gathered from quite inadequate standpoints.

If it were necessary for the "essence" of objects really to be expressed by the artistic truth, then—for a positivistic manner of thinking—this could only be grasped through a synthesis of all artworks and kinds of art. The truth would

---

[23] [Landmann-Kalischer's mention of a "yellow surface" [*gelben Fleck*] is probably a reference to the *macula lutea*, the yellowish area at the center of the retina near the optic disc that is responsible for visual acuity. When a person fixes her gaze on an object, the center of the macula and the object are in a straight line.]

[24] [The expression *bestimmte Bestimmbarkeit* [determinate determinability] is found in Fichte's *Wissenschaftslehre nova methodo* (published posthumously, based mostly upon students' notes) but cognate discussions can be found in various versions of his *Wissenschaftslehre*; see Johann Gottlieb Fichte, Sämtliche Werke, Band I, hrsg. von J. H. Fichte, Berlin: Veit, 1845, pp. 206–16, 403f, 497; given the context, Landmann-Kalischer is likely thinking of Schiller's variation on the notion in the Twenty-first letter of his *Aesthetic Letters*. *Das willenlose Erkennen* [will-less cognition] is a theme discussed at length by Friedrich Calker in his *Denklehre oder Logik und Dialektik* [Doctrine of Thinking or Logic and Dialectic], Bonn: Weber, 1822, pp. 204–35 and and by Schopenhauer in his *The World as Will and Representation*, Vol. I, Sectoins 34, 38, 41, and *passim*.]

[25] [Landmann-Kalischer is likely referring to Winckelmann's description of the Greek art of sketching and Winckelman's reference to a universal, original beauty [*allgemeine, ursprüngliche Schönheit*]; see Johann Joachim Winckelmann, *Geschichte der Kunst des Alterthums* [History of the Art of Antiquity], Dresden: Walther, 1764, erstes Buch, erstes Kapitel; Wilhelm Heinrich Wachenroder, *Herzensergießungen eines kunstliebenden Klosterbruders* [Outpourings of an Art-Loving Friar], Berlin: Unger, 1797; Leipzig: Diederich, 1904, p. 67.]

then be like a garden, like beauty as Friedrich Schlegel construes it; only the sum total of all its plants makes up the entire garden, the entire truth. In that case we could no more afford to miss the cutting, bitter irony of Wedekind than the Olympian eye of Goethe. But what matters to us here is not this truth found beyond the artworks, that first has to be abstracted from them. What we seek is only the content of the truth that each individual artwork contains. We have sought to prove that this truth relates to objective truth like the mind relates to reality.

Artistic truth, which is analogous to the image in memory, *can* also be an objective truth under certain circumstances. It *can* hit upon the essence of the object, it *can* uncover a side of the object that up to that point was still unknown. But for aesthetics this is only a contingent coincidence. That art captures what is also *objectively* essential in a phenomenon—perhaps even more frequently and consistently than something accidental—follows solely from the abstracting procedure of memory. The representation via memory initially holds fast, as we saw, to what regularly recurs and then to what corresponds to representations already on hand. Memory representations of this kind, however, are the material of concept formation and what is grasped by means of them frequently coincides with what is objectively characteristic of the essence of the object. Thus, artistic paradigms can approximate the conceptually cognized essence of objects and, since art follows memory representations of this kind, its truth partially coincides with objective truth. What *conforms to the norm* thus becomes an individual instance of artistic truth. By contrast, memory's representations that are conditioned by what we called the third mark of them, namely, their strong stress on feeling, stand in this regard in direct opposition to memory representations of the first sort. No guarantee of any kind is given that the feeling or interest emphasizes what is objectively essential in an object. The opposite is much more likely. If lofty artistic truth is thus also in the sort of portrayals that memory-representations of this kind manage to express, this proves that |477| that coincidence of artistic truth and objective truth was only an individual instance and that the latter [truth] may not be used to determine the former conceptually.

With respect to memory's representations, we had to distinguish two kinds of them. The peculiarity of the first kind is the fact that its representations are based upon the frequent recurrence of impressions and the correspondence of those impressions to representations already on hand. In its artistic portrayal, this first kind brought out the truth of what is typical, characteristic, or conforms to the norm. The other kind, whose structure was determined by feeling and interest, generated in its artistic reproduction the truth of the unity of feeling and style. This kind stood in no relation at all to objective truth or was directly opposed to it; the former kind, the truth of what is typical, coincided in part with it.

3. Phantasy's Representations

There is no sharp boundary between phantasy's representations and memory's representations. If the former are distinguished from the latter thanks to the deliberate synthesis of their elements, the passive form of phantasy's activity nonetheless immediately emerges from the usual functions of memory, and, under the influence of our feelings and our will, memory's images are transformed into phantasy's images. There is only a difference of degree between phantasy and memory. The former is merely a conscious exercise, using what the latter constantly provides unconsciously and non-deliberately.[26] As we saw, art faithfully follows memory's unconscious falsifications in such a way that, far from violating the truth, it first works out such truth. For this reason, when art completely surrenders to phantasy, it will be able to be just as true as or even truer than art that adheres closely to reality. In fact, the reconfiguration that real things undergo even in the artistic portrayal most faithful to nature is so enormous that phantasy's arbitrary additions are hardly worth considering alongside it. "In comparison to the human being who walks on the street, the human being in a picture is so remarkably something from a fable that the peculiarity signified by his horns and hooves completely disappears."[27] Whether a story is invented or whether it is the retelling of a real story is immaterial for its artistic truth, however it be considered, "... and it means roughly the same thing when we |478| say of images in dreams that they are as enchanting as real things or of real things that they are as enchanting as images in dreams."[28]

What drives the conscious formation of phantasy's representations are representations of a purpose and these are frequently definite ideas of a moral or philosophical nature, as in the fable or the didactic poem. But

---

[26] Compare Wundt, *Grundriß der Psychologie*, pp. 318–320.
[27] Julius Meier-Graefe, *Der Fall Böcklin* [The Case of Böcklin], Stuttgart: Hoffman, 1905, p. 23.
[28] *Blätter für die Kunst*, p. 7. Folge, herausgegeben von Carl August Klein, 1904. Italien und Niederland. Stoffkunst. Phantasiekunst [*Pages for Art*, 7th sequel, 1904, Italy and Netherlands. Art of material. Art of phantasy].

the chief role is played here once again by feeling whose significance in configuring memory's representations has, indeed, already surfaced. Art that is predominantly phantasy (the fairytale) could also be defined as the one that flatters feeling the most. For the most part, the viewpoint that provides the criterion for devising it [art that is phantasy] is none other than this: what is likely to delight the heart the most. It flatters every possible drive, from the love of splendor to the love of justice. One need only think of the proverbial "fairytale-like grandeur" of castles, gardens, repasts, precious stones, and materials in the Arabian fairytales. All feelings are intensified and they come into play with tragic ferociousness. But justice wins out. Fallen innocents are avenged; the guilty parties perish. All fairytales end happily. The proverbial closing sentence of German fairytales "and they lived splendidly and joyfully and, if they have not died, they still live so today"[29] corresponds to the closing line of the Arabian fairytales: "And so they lived until the destroyer of all joys, the one who severs all unions, sought them out. Praise to him who lives forever!" If one wanted to characterize the course of events, one could say simply that in a fairytale everything goes on as we would like it to go on. In a fairytale we feel free because it plays freely with the things that we stand powerless against in life, the things that we have been delivered to without any hope of rescue. In particular, alongside this longing for unlimited control of things, what is lived out in the fairytale is particularly the drive for surprises, for the extraordinary, for everything that breaks through the everyday and what is merely possible. Birds that speak and flying carpets, ghosts and magic caps that render someone invisible—all these are the devices of that world. Even in the events there is an adventurous change of places: the poor become rich, the rich poor, the slave becomes a princess; someone who just a moment ago stood on the beheading rug, suddenly sees herself with everything that she wished for.[30] Seen from the standpoint of a grown-up, even the naive

---

[29] [The English equivalent is, of course, "and they lived happily ever after." For examples of the German ending, see the final line of the Brothers Grimm's "Oll Rinkrank" in their *Kinder- und Hausmärchen* [Children's and Familiar Fairy Tales], Halle: Hendel, 1812, no. 196; the final line of Ludwig Bechstein's "Die verzauberte Prinzessin" [The Enchanted Princess] in his *Märchen* [Fairy Tales], Leipzig: Wigand, 1879, pp. 28f; and the final lines of several fairytales in Johann Georg von Hahn's *Griechische und Albanesische Märchen* [Greek and Albanian Fairy Tales], Leipzig: Engelmann, 1864, pp. 200, 227, 268, 348, 454, 709, 1049, 1262.]

[30] [More literally, 'suddenly sees herself at the goal of her wishes' [*wer eben noch auf dem Blutleder stand, sieht sich plötzlich am Ziel seiner Wünsche*]. Landmann-Kalischer is alluding here to a scene in one of the stories of *Fables of 1001 Nights*, specifically the story of the "Streichen der verschlagenen Dalilah und ihrer Tochter, Zainab die Gimpelfängerin," in *Die schönsten Geschichten aus 1001 Nacht*, Leipzig: Seemann, 1914, p. 160: "Dann führte er sie in den Diwan, . . . und brachte die Alte vor die höchste Gegenwart. Sowie nun der Kalif sie sah, befahl er, sie auf das Blutleder zu werfen; doch sie

animism expressed in phantasy's representations has an element of wishing. As Hermann Grimm once put it, "There lies in children of all times and all peoples a common stance |479| towards nature. They see everything as animated to the same degree. Woods and mountains, fires and stars, creeks and springs, rain and wind speak and harbor a good and evil will and mix it into human fates."[31] This animistic and anthropocentric construal of nature is the manner of thinking not only of children but also of all child-like peoples, and offshoots of it reach, as is familiar, far into the subtlest scientific thinking. As much as science sought to ban this kind of thinking—one thinks of modern positivists' battle against causality—it has nonetheless established itself just as ineradicably as a natural law of human thinking. And thus, the fairytale that is at home in this animated world expresses not only children's construal of the world but also the natural tendency of human thinking generally—a tendency that, if we want to secure objective reality, is like a prod that we must constantly resist.

It is not hard to see how the essential character of fairytale-like elements penetrates the depths of the most serious art, how the fairytale as a genre merely cultivates in the most perfect manner what every art lives from. Wondrous revelations and recognitions are a canonical component even of Greek tragedies, and English drama likewise flattered the wish for the extraordinary, having created "an entirely new race of beings, whose sorrows were more terrible than any sorrow man has ever felt, whose joys were keener than lovers' joys, who had the rage of the Titans and the calm of the Gods, who had monstrous and marvellous sins, who had monstrous and marvellous virtues . . ."[32] And don't things proceed in most novels just as we would like them to? Is the famed novel of Abbé Prévost—*Manon Lescaut*—anything other than a single sweet flattering of the highest dreams of love? And isn't it said also of Werther: "Each youth longs to love so, each maiden to be so loved?"

---

rief: 'Ich rufe deinen Schutz an, o Schuuman!'" See "The Tale of Shifts of Delilah-the-Wily and her Daughter, Zainab-the-Cheat," in *The Book of the Thousand Nights and One Night*, Volume 2, ed. J. C. Mardrus and E. P. Mathers, New York: Routledge, 1990, p. 519: "After the villainous Delilah is brought to the Khalifah, he first commands that she be thrown on the blood carpet, a mat made of leather for beheadings, but then pardons her."]

[31] [Jacob Grimm und Wilhelm Grimm, *Kinder und Hausmärchen*, 32. Auflage, Einleitung von Hermann Grimm, Berlin: Bardtenschlager, 1906: p. xxix.]

[32] Oscar Wilde, "The Decay of Lying," *Intentions*. Engl. Libr. Nr. 54, Leipzig: Heinemann & Balestier, 1905.

One could object that the worst and most mendacious novels are precisely the ones that correspond to our wishes and flatter our dreams. But these novels are untrue not because they do this but because they seek to enliven the truth wished for [*Wunschwahrheit*] by amalgamating it with the truth of what is probable, which they violate furthermore in the grossest manner, and because they want to persuade us that our wishes can be fulfilled in the framework of reality. The fairytale presents itself in every instance as a fairytale. A bad novel, by seeking to correspond to heterogeneous zones of consciousness, |480| must always contradict one sphere in order to do justice to another.

Romantic art in particular, in contrast to Classical art, is in turn a poetic composition of a wish [*Wunschdichtung*], as its preference for dreams and fairytales already demonstrates. And all poetry [*Dichtung*] without distinction is like the fairytale in its animation of nature. "Who else [but the poet] lets the storm rage in passions and lets the dawn glow in an earnest mind. . . ."[33] It makes no difference thereby whether one populates nature with fables' half-human entities or (with Chateaubriand) condemns these "requisites of the theater" and seeks nothing but the "mood" in nature—in the latter case as in the former, one is lending a human soul to nature, lending [a human soul] to it even where one seeks in it precisely the non-human, its being otherwise [*Anderssein*]. It is then the longing for redemption from oneself that one objectifies in nature.

For all their contrast with reality, the fairytale and everything in art that bears a fairytale-like character are still true in the deepest sense, indeed, so true that we can study the soul of a people nowhere better than in the fairytale. In the fairytale we feel the truth—and therein lies its unique appeal—precisely in contrast to reality. Because it depicts the world of phantasy's wishes, the freedom and innermost impulses of thinking, it assists mental capacities to live out what would otherwise wither away. For it was precisely these representations that had to be severely slashed and destroyed as much as possible since they were at the same time a hindrance to the construction of external reality and to practical life. Thus it is, from time immemorial, that one saw the realm of art and poetry mainly in phantasy, and that the wondrous counts as the object of poetry in the genuine sense: "Everything truly wondrous is of itself poetic" (Jean Paul). The example grossly overstates the point, but in it the essence of artistic truth could not be clearer. Here, too,

---

[33] [Goethe, *Faust—Vorspiel auf dem Theater*, Kap. 2.]

feeling is particularly sensitive to every untruth. Modern grownups seldom succeed in retrieving in its pristine state the world of children and of peoples more at home in nature, a world that is also still in them [modern grownups]. Almost all modern fairytale compositions—not to speak at all of shoddy works like "The Three Heron Feathers"[34] or "The Sunken Bell"[35]—are fake because they carry rational elements into the fairytale world. Thus, if we want to immerse ourselves in that world, we have to look to folk fairytales, myths, and legends.

Finally, as a species of phantasy's representations, I would like to call to mind certain representations in which it becomes particularly clear that the truth of art, even if its content coincides with objective reality and truth, still |481| has nothing to do with the latter. I am thinking of representations which we possess through anticipation. Every human being possesses representations of characters and human states that they have never themselves seen or experienced. Every child anticipates lived experiences of which the child is in reality still fully incapable. Such anticipated representations are poets' preferred material. "By way of anticipation, the poet creates characters that the reader finds apt even without encountering their prototypes."[36] Something true is created here, and a truth is felt without familiarity with the reality, on one side or the other.[37]

4. Combinations of Representations: The Probable, the Necessary, and the Conjunction of Representations in Lyric Poetry

Everything that has been said about memory's and phantasy's representations holds not only for individual objects but also for events and happenings. The way that things are conjoined with one another is also construed, recalled, and transformed in phantasy. The spatial-temporal conjunction of things is

---

[34] [Hermann Sudermann's verse drama, *Die drei Reihefedern* [The Three Heron Feathers], which premiered in Berlin in 1899 was a failure in the eyes of the public and critics; see Paul K. Whitaker, "A Key to Sudermann's 'Die drei Reihefedern,'" *Monatshefte* 48(2): pp. 78–87.]

[35] [Gerhart Hauptmann, *Die versunkene Glocke: ein deutsches Märchendrama* [The Sunken Bell: A Fairy Tale Play]," Berlin: Fischer, 1897, premiered in Berlin in 1896 to public and critical acclaim.]

[36] Jean Paul, *Vorschule der Ästhetik* [Introduction to Aesthetics], Stuttgart: Cotta, 1813, p. 435.

[37] Compare also Goethe to Eckermann (February 26, 1824): "I generally had joy simply in the portrayal of my inner world before I was familiar with the outer world. When I later found that in reality the world was just as I had thought it to be, it was irritating to me and I no longer had any pleasure in portraying it. . . ."

also an object of sensory perceptions and memory's representations. In the typical course of what happens, we witness the succession of day and night, morning and evening, youth and old age, summer and winter, happiness and neediness. The artistic portrayal follows these paradigms, indeed, it has directly made them into its object often enough; the sequence of seasons has found expression in painting, poetry, and even music. By contrast, artworks that provide the truth of a wish also go their own ways here. For them there is eternal youth and fountains of youthfulness, an eternal springtime, eternal love and eternal happiness. The golden age and a land of milk and honey are phantasy's ways of rewriting the natural course of what happens and doing so in ways that flatter every longing (and to that extent are artistically true).— This contains in principle nothing new.

But here we move from the material to the formal kinds of conjunction of things or their elements, and, with this, to the discussion of the concept which, set down by Aristotle, has ever since belonged |482| to aesthetics, in particular to poetics, as a secure possession: the concept of the probable.

(a) From the demand for unity, Aristotle derives the demand that an artwork portray, not what is true, but what is probable. Reality only delivers occurrences; if a completed action, according to the definition of tragedy, is supposed to be imitated, then the poet must assemble what is internally coherent; he must give not what actually happened but what could happen.[38] When the justification here is pushed back to some other aesthetic demand, moderns ground the demand for probability on the artist's intention of stirring, of having an effect on the imagination. The real is not necessary for this, but the impossible cannot be employed since it cannot be represented. Sulzer makes this point, as does Bodmer.[39] Witasek gives another version of this explanation, when he says that our feelings of partiality and empathy are oriented, as it were, to reality and thus react only to the possible.[40] Approaching the matter from the other side, Bodmer in turn defends the *merely* probable when he compares the poetic process with how telescopes and microscopes correct for objects too small or too distant for human sight.

---

[38] At least no other justification is found in the preserved parts of the *Poetics*. See, too, footnote 39 of Überweg's translation in the *Philosophische Bibliothek. Grundriss der Philosophie* [Philosophical Library: Outline of Philosophy], Vols. 1–2, seventh edition, Berlin: Mittler, 1886–88.

[39] "Der Poet bekümmert sich nicht um das Wahre des Verstandes; da es ihm nur um die Besiegung der Phantasie zu tun ist, hat er genug am Wahrscheinlichen" [The poet does not worry about what is understood to be true since for him it is only about conquering phantasy, should it be plausible enough]; Bodmer, *Critische Abhandlung von dem Wunderbaren in der Poesie*, p. 47.

[40] Stephan Witasek, *Grundzüge der allgemeinen Ästhetik* [Basic Features of Aesthetics in General], Leipzig: Barth, 1904, p. 393f.

Were poetry bound to the real, the future and the past would be closed off from it.

It is interesting that all these explanations construe the probable not as a self-standing effect of art but as a means to its effect. In order to have the artistic effect of unity, poetry should be truer than history; in order to make empathy possible, it should not move beyond what can be represented, i.e., the possible. It is indeed not in the slightest bit doubtful that these aesthetic inferences are correct. The artwork, which has already been compared so often with an organism, is akin to it also in this respect, namely, that the most diverse purposes are combined into a unity within it, that end and means are conjoined in it in such a way that each means is at the same time an end and each end is still a means. Thus, alongside the construal of the probable as one of the aesthetic means to its end, it would also be legitimate to see in the probable |483| a self-standing effect of art. The explanations mentioned consider the most diverse aesthetic aims of the artwork with the exception of the one lying closest to the probable: the truth-effect.

For us the probable can mean nothing other than what appears as true, what is psychologically and thus artistically true. The probable is the truth of art because it is *what appears as true*. It was necessary for this question to be considered from two sides: on one side, to what extent—one was compelled to ask—must what is real be reshaped in order to be suitable for the artistic portrayal, and, on the other side, to what extent must the purely fantastic approach reality? Starting from either side, one arrived at the probable. If one comes from reality, then the demand for probability means that art needs to portray the "merely" probable—if one comes from phantasy, then it means that the art must "at least" be probable. But with this it is precisely what is psychologically true that is glossed over from both sides. It does not coincide with the real—for how often does the real seem improbable; how often do we exclaim, facing something real: "that is not possible"? But it [what is psychologically true] may not be sheer phantasy either, something that contradicts the *vérités de raison* since this would be unimaginable [it could not be represented, it is *unvorstellbar*].

What kind of combinations appear individually as true cannot be said in general; it essentially depends on the content of the relevant representations. Sulzer says: "Occasionally things happen ... where an effect seems without cause. The power of representing is not eager to assume such things, even if they would still be quite certain."[41] When he says this, it is necessary to

---

[41] Johann Georg Sulzer, *Allgemeine Theorie der schönen Künste* [General Theory of the Fine Arts], Band 2, Leipzig: Weidmann, 1774, Article: Probability, pp. 1263–1266.

object to it that under some circumstances the power of representation willingly takes up the play of the most phantastic coincidences. The same coincidence can seem to us completely probable or entirely improbable, depending upon whether the content of the representations sounds credible to us or is believed by us only reluctantly. We are easily ready to believe the usual, normal, or agreeable; the strange, the extraordinary, and the tragic require stronger motivation in order to be held to be true. As for what contradicts too much either our wishes or the representations we have that have been nourished by what constantly recurs, it, too, must first be proven to us to be true in reality. This consideration brings us to necessity, the form of the artistic truth in tragedy. |484|

(b) In the sketch of characters and in the invention of the fable, what is probable commonly appears to be true. By contrast, in order to appear to be true, tragedy demands what is necessary in the course of its action. It does not suffice that one event *can* follow another or that an action *can* follow from a character. Instead we also want to see that it follows of *necessity*. In tragedy it is not so much the extraordinary that requires this strong means in order to move us to believe—since even if the extraordinary contradicts the truth of what is typical, it nonetheless accommodates all the more the natural longing of every unspent soul. What requires such measures is far more the tragic itself which, by its nature, clashes with consciousness. Only what is proven and comprehended is so firmly connected with all the other representations that it *must* be incorporated into this nexus. What happens with necessity according to our discerning eye also really happens based upon the presuppositions given. Tragedy thus requires necessity because, as far as its content is concerned, it resists being believed and thus needs the strongest means to compel belief nevertheless. Hence, in every tragedy, the feeling of inevitability goes hand in hand with the feeling of the tragic, so much so that tragedy is characterized almost as much by the former as it is by the latter. Whether the fate is prefigured by gods, oracles, or stars, whether it is placed in an individual human heart or in social contexts—each tragedy is a tragedy of fate and every possibility of a different development of things, of a gentler outcome, of a path leading to other destinations only surfaces in order for us to see all the more bitterly the necessity of the one path.

That the form of necessity in tragedy is really required by what is tragic in it, and not somehow by the form of the drama generally, can be proven by the fact that the epic with tragic content also requires this necessity but comedy does not. As for what primarily matters in the case of epics and narratives, one might consider Kleist's *Michael Kohlhaas* or his novellas in general. They are a kind of calculated exercise. Viewed in hindsight, they are straightforwardly explanations. They provide a kind of probability-calculation of the actions. And for every serious novel, the development of the action would have to be capable of being predicted by the science of psychology—if this were far enough along. By contrast, not only does comedy not need any necessity, it also requires only a very slight degree of probability. The more colorfully it proceeds, the better. It is either a poetic composition of a wish, and then needs no |485| other truth than that of the fairytale, or it is a comedy of characters or bourgeois comic play—in which cases its truth corresponds to what is in the foreground of consciousness, the truth of what is typical with a dash of a truth wished for. In what tragedy, in what serious theater play would we tolerate the sort of conclusion characteristic of a comedy, namely, the resolution of a conflict through a coincidence?

The difference between truth in tragedy and in comedy thus rests on the contrast of the feelings that underlie them. The high seriousness to which tragedy attunes us corresponds to the brute force of reality [*Realität*] at its peak, while the concentration of the feeling corresponds to that of the representations. By contrast, [the feeling in comedy is] the cheeriness that takes things lightly and likes to spread its wings, that is ready to believe what it hears and sees—as long as they nourish it.

From this nexus [of genres and feelings], it might be said in passing, it follows that poetic justice has its proper place in a poetic composition of a wish but that it is not required in the slightest in tragedy. For were what happens in tragedy fair, it would not be strictly tragic and there would be no need at all for necessity in order for us to believe it. So, too, poetic justice could be read into tragedies for the most part only by sacrificing necessity. But if everything happens with the strictest necessity, such that the truth of what is seen has penetrated us in the deepest way and the action nonetheless expresses what is fair and just to the highest degree, then an incomparable effect arises, one that we are familiar with only in very few works, such as *Wintermärchen*.[42] Objective and subjective reality seem to be reconciled; the profoundest essence of what happens in the world seems to be revealed; poetry appears as a "silent messenger of endless mysteries."[43]

---

[42] [Landmann-Kalischer is probably referring to Shakespeare's *A Winter's Tale*, not Heine's work by that name.]
[43] [Novalis, *Hymnen an die Nacht* [Hymns to the Night], 2, in *Schriften. Die Werke Friedrich von Hardenbergs*, Band 1, Stuttgart: 1960–1977, p. 132.]

The necessary conjunction of representations springs from the intellect directed at the formation of reality [*Realität*] as it is. It seeks, not only to attain what is real but, beyond that, to disclose what is not yet known. We take all kinds of things to be real that are not strictly proven, doing so on the basis of the semblance of the senses, on hearsay and on good faith [*Treu und Glauben*]. But we take to be necessary only what is demonstrated to be necessarily conjoined, whose reality is beyond any doubt—unless the presuppositions are contested. The necessary conjunction increases the reality [*Realität*] of what is conjoined. It is originally a conjunction of representations and the justification of transferring that conjunction to the interconnectedness of things has been doubted since Hume. Nevertheless, the postulate of some sort of law-likeness is still presupposed so much in every instance of cognition, that it can be provided in no other way than with this very [conjunction]. |486| All cognition aims at the necessary conjunction of the given, should this conjunction consist in an enormous causal series or in the rational dependence of every individual thing on a supreme concept in the Spinozistic sense.

In keeping with this consideration, it seems now as though the category of necessity stands so completely in the service of the structure of outer reality that it could have no place in art, since art aims at establishing the world of the mind. But it needs to be considered that, as certain as it is that all cognition aims at necessary conjunction, it is just as certain that a thoroughgoing necessary conjunction is cognitively unattainable. It portrays the ideal of reality but one that is only attainable for an epistemological fiction, for "the human being generally," for the "absolute ego" or the world spirit. A world conceived through and through as necessary towers as much over the factual structure of reality [*Realität*] that we possess up till now, as a world thoroughly given up to contingency would fall short of it. And here art enters. We seek the sense and interconnectedness of what happens; reality does not supply it. We must first create it, but we *must* do so. Art supplies it. In art's microcosms it feigns the unattained and unattainable ideal as something attained. Here it flatters the soul's fundamental intellectual need, even as it flatters all of the soul's most irrational inclinations. Although agreeing here in its orientation with the procedure of science, in its fulfillment it nonetheless goes so far beyond science that it expresses, again, an element of the *mental* world (directly opposed to outer reality).

At the same time, in addition to satisfying this supreme intellectual demand, the necessity afforded by art satisfies a deep ethical need. For since it is precisely human beings' actions and fates whose necessary conjunction art puts on a display, it simultaneously affords, along with the intellectual reassurance, the moral reassurance that springs specifically from submission to—and conviction of—the fact that the law and a vocation guide the life of an individual and that every blind stone that destroys a life is a tool in the hand of God or fate.

Necessity should thus be chalked up to the paradigmatic truth of a wish not only in an intellectual, but also in an ethical respect; that is to say, it is to be numbered among those contents of art that are true because they manage to express the inner world of wishes, the wishes or demands of the soul.

(c) We saw that the necessary conjunction of representations is an |487| entirely essential element for the construction of objective reality, so much so that the subjective side of this conjunction was distinguished from the objective side more through nuances than in terms of the matter itself. But now we come to a form of conjunction of representations that remains completely confined to the mental world since this form of connection is not guided by any sort of representation of a purpose and is subject solely to the natural course of associations and to feelings. This kind of conjunction of representations finds its expression in lyric poetry.

Conjunctions of representations in keeping with the most common associations, with the similarity of the sounds of the words, and with spatial or temporal contiguity are particularly prevalent in folk songs and children's songs, the latter leading to simple nonsense.[44] But usually the impression of truth in lyric poetry rests on the fact that the course of representations is exclusively determined by a dominating feeling instead of a logical viewpoint. Gottschall even demands that the particles in lyric poetry be pushed into the background since they mostly designate a direct logical interconnection.[45] Lyric poetry naturally also helps itself to the most general logical forms: linking together what is similar, placing what is opposed in opposition, restricting the universal, universalizing the particular, and so forth—no other sensible combination of words is even possible. But it helps itself to these forms somewhat as numerology helps itself to the four species.[46] For

---

[44] Compare "Kinderpredigt [Children's sermon]": "*Quibus, quabus*, die Enten geh'n barfuß" [the ducks go bearfoot], and so forth from *Des Knaben Wunderhorn*. [Landmann-Kalischer is citing the work by Achim von Arnim and Clemens Brentano, first published from 1805 to 1808; see *Des Knaben Wunderhorn: alte deutsche Lieder* [The Boy's Miraculous Horn: Old German Songs], München: Müller, 1908, p. 540.]

[45] Rudolf von Gottschall, *Poetik*, Breslau: Trewendt, 1870. [See ibid., pp. 175, 177].

[46] [Landmann-Kalischer is referring to the four species of plants used in the celebration of the Jewish holiday of Sukkot, the festival of the tabernacles.]

the conjunctions of representations in lyric poetry, everything objective is present only insofar as it has some significance for the feeling. Thus the odd capriciousness of folksongs that tell a story. While the most exact details of time and place are customary in every epic narrative, they are nowhere to be found in lyric poetry. It is satisfied with the most general indications: 'then,' 'soon,' 'already,' 'alongside,' 'above,' and so forth. The comically un-lyrical effect of Heine's stanza:

> In the year eighteen hundred and seventeen
> I saw a girl, wonderful[47]

is like an *experimentum crucis* for this peculiarity of time-details in lyric poetry.

The interconnectedness of the representations is not only *dominated* by the feeling but is frequently only intelligible at all on the basis of it. Analyze, for example, the sequence of representations in: |488|

> Death is the cool night
> And life the sultry day
> It's already growing dark; I am sleepy
> The day has made me tired.
>
> Over my bed a tree rises and
> In it a young nightingale warbles
> Singing of nothing but love
> And I hear it even in dreams.[48]

The interconnectedness of [the representations in] the poem is only intelligible via the detour of feeling. But the entire inner truth of this poem rests on this interconnectedness!

And what else makes up any *simile's* deep artistic truth than the mastery with which the most heterogeneous things are put on the same level with one another because *mentally*—for the intuition or the feeling—they have the same value, regardless of whether, as things, they have as little to do with one another as stars and flowers, birds and humans, death and night or

---

[47] From "Jenny" in *New Poems*. [Heinrich Heine, *Neue Gedichte*, Hamburg: Hoffmann und Campe, 1844.]

[48] [Heinrich Heine, "Die Heimkehr [The Return Home]," in *Buch der Lieder* [Book of Songs], Hamburg: Hoffmann und Campe, 1868, p. 248.]

even drawers, church graveyards, and sphinxes![49] Even the degree to which similes may be implemented is determined by the mental equivalence of the representations or elements of the representations. Any simile that violates this equivalence feels untrue to us, whether it be because the representations that are compared contradict one another in terms of their intuitive content or their effects on our feelings, or because the simile that is supposed to illuminate, embellish, or forcefully accentuate the representation works for only one of its elements,[50] but blurs the others or obscures them through the simile's own obscurity. When Lohenstein says: "These gifts [of Duchess Hermildis] drew various heroes into the court like the gagate stone [*Agtstein*] draws chaff,"[51] the attractiveness of these gifts is not equivalent in this way to that of gagate, first, because we know something indeed of the latter but not of the former and, second, because the representation of chaff evokes a feeling that contradicts the representation of heroes. Further, every mistake in the equivalence of the feelings' *intensity* that is triggered by the comparison of the representations can be felt as untrue in the most palpable way. When the young Schiller claims to stand there like a statue, inanimate and turned to stone by Laura's mastery of the piano,[52] this has the effect of a hollow exaggeration; by contrast, the utmost correctness, |489| purity, and sureness that we find straightaway in Goethe's employment of such similes do not make the slightest difference to the great truthfulness of his poetry.

Thus the truth of similes, those "strange representations whose probability is grounded in an emotional deception,"[53] is explained by the general essence of artistic truth. We should not draw conclusions for actual contexts, as the Romantics did, from contexts peculiar to art. Bernhardi may have found in the metaphor the expression for the notion that a secret bond binds the sensory and the supersensory world together and that their separation from one

---

[49] Compare Baudelaire, *Fleurs du mal. Spleen LXXVIII. J'ai plus des souvenirs que si j'avais mille ans* [I have more memories than if I'd lived a thousand years].

[50] Compare Johann Jakob Breitinger, *Kritische Abhandlung von der Natur, den Absichten und dem Gebrauch der Gleichnisse* [Critical Essay on the Nature, Aims, and Use of Similes], Zürich: Orell, 1740, pp. 465f.

[51] Ibid., p. 465 [Landmann-Kalischer is citing the Swiss literary critic's paraphrase of a line from Daniel Caspar von Lohenstein's novel *Großmütiger Feldherr Arminius* [Magnanimous Commander-in-Chief Arminius], Leipzig: Bledit, 1689–90, Bl. 144.]

[52] [Landmann-Kalischer is referring to the opening lines of Schiller's poem 'Laura am Klavier' [Laura at the piano]: "Wenn dein Finger durch die Saiten meistert / Laura, itzt zur Statue entgeistert, / Itzt entkörpert steh ich da" [When your finger, Laura, exerts its mastery over the keys / then I find myself standing there / stunned, like a lifeless statue, and disembodied]; Friedrich Schiller, *Sämtliche Werke*, Band 1, München: Hanser, 1962, p. 41.]

[53] Breitinger, *Kritische Abhandlung von der Natur*.

another is only apparent. But as *for us*, in order to do justice to all the different contents that are felt to be true in art, we have to be satisfied with seeing in the metaphor the linguistic expression for the equivalence in our minds of the representations that are compared. If in *Zerbino* it is said:

> All that the decision of the gods otherwise enviously separated
> God has united together here in phantasy
> So that the knell here knows its color
> And a sweet voice shimmers through every leaf,[54]

what is first expressed in this unification of sense impressions that are separated in reality is *not*, as Tieck would have it, the mystery of a higher life but instead the mystery of our own soul. The world-order that holds in the "Garden of Poetry" mirrors the scaffolding of the inner world.

5. Feelings

As we pass from representations over to feelings,[55] we cannot pose the question as precisely as was done earlier. Representations formed the material for the construction of external reality. We noted the differences that inherently mental representations displayed in their content and flow, in contrast to those that were cognized as true and were elevated to the status of being a component of the really existing world (in keeping with principles that we do not have to investigate here). These differences were mirrored in the relationship of artistic truth to objective truth. These differences do not exist for feelings. We have already begun to see that wherever feelings participated in the construction of external reality, religious and poetic elements |490| were smuggled into it. For the construction of the world that we designated as 'reality' in the narrower and strict sense, these elements accordingly had to be excluded in turn. Hence, feeling does not cross over into the outer world and if art uncovers the mental world of feeling as well, then this cannot be characterized through its contrast with objective reality.

---

[54] [Ludwig Tieck, *Prinz Zerbino oder die Reise nach dem guten Geschmack* [Prince Zerbino or the Journey to Good Taste], *Werke in einem Band* (Hamburg: Hoffmann und Campe, 1967), p. 440 (Act V, scene 4).]

[55] By 'feeling,' in what follows, I mean the practical side of consciousness generally, thus also will, strivings, drives, and so forth.

But although feeling is not worked on for purposes of cognition, it nonetheless does not remain fully captive of its original form of existence, the inner world. The law of the world of expression makes its elementary power obtain in feeling, too. There is an expression of feeling in life, first in predominantly passive feelings as a *physiologically-physiognomic* expression, then in the more active feelings expressed in *actions*. One could think of verbal expression as well but, as is easily seen, compared with these elementary and relatively adequate forms of expression, it is no expression at all but instead merely an approximate reference to a reality [*Realität*], a means for human beings to come to some understanding with one another and, beyond this, a means, indeed, of assisting representations along with the expression that the latter also possess in objective reality.

Every feeling brings with it its physiological and physiognomic expression so infallibly that some have wanted to make this, its outer form of existence, directly into its essence.[56] But this expression, insofar as it is adequate, is an involuntary expression. Turning pale, blushing, quivering, crying, laughing, and having a fit are not objectifications for the person filled with the corresponding feelings. It is probably an alleviation of the feeling at that instant, but not a *portrayal* of it, something that is attempted much more through words, albeit in vain. In addition, while there is a momentary bodily expression of this sort for emotions, the feelings that extend over a longer stretch of time and space assert themselves as an expression only imperfectly, in conflict with the customary manner of living and with other, opposed feelings, consolidating themselves only gradually in facial color, posture, and gestures. And the expression of weaker feelings in general can ultimately be ascertained only by plethysmographs and the like. The physiological-physiognomic expression of feeling is thus never pure in life; it cannot be so and, at most, it comes to be adequate in grand individual moments—moments in which life attains to art.

Insofar as the artistic portrayal of the feeling follows and depicts this natural expression, its truthfulness is subject to the same conditions as any artistic portrayal of real events is. Here, too, memory will |491| isolate the natural expression that is distorted in many respects and give the expression its typical form of appearance. The actor will elaborate a character's typical gesture; the portraitist will elaborate the contour of the head, indicating the

---

[56] [Landmann-Kalischer may be thinking of theories of emotions developed by Carl Lange and William James.]

expression of the soul. Even when the lyric poet, the dramatist, or novelist reproduces the flow of representations characteristic of an emotion, this can still count as a depiction of the natural expression of feeling.

But art goes even further in this correction that it makes to the reality of life in the interest of artistic truth. Feeling is given to us not only indirectly through its "accompanying appearances" but also directly through inner perception. And through inner perception we know not only the feeling itself, but also the wish, the urge, the will to express the feeling that dwells in it [the feeling] and that in life is never realized in its full range. A purer elaboration of the factually perceptible expression of feeling (that is dependent upon a thousand external conditions) thus does not suffice for art. It goes beyond the depiction of the factual expression of feeling to the completely novel creation of an adequate expression of feeling and it succeeds at this, to be sure, by going back to the *elements* of the physiological expression. By securing such elements that can be altered in their own right, it achieves an individualization and intensification of an expression, which may be called the "truth wished-for in the expression of feeling" [*die Wunschwahrheit des Gefühlsausdrucks*], since it corresponds not to reality but only to the longing.

As *elements* of the physiological expression of feeling, we must consider all those artistic means of expression that appear at first to be unconnected with the factually perceptible natural expression. This includes, above all, music's entire means of expression, but then also the pictorial artist's colors, lines, surfaces, proportions of space and weight, as well as the poet's rhythms and rhymes. This is not the place to investigate the details of what underlies the power of expression of these means, e.g., the colors. In any case we have to suppose that in the end colors—like rhythms, melody, and harmony—can be understood on the basis of physiological elements of the expression. But we may also actually "grade the pitch in terms of human lungs and grade the sound's duration on our innate metronome, the heart beat."[57]—The fact that by these means the most complicated sequences of feeling can find adequate expression is a discovery of art and a mystery |492| that at this juncture we can only register but cannot discuss. Art not only discloses a truth to us here, it imparts this truth to us in an entirely new language and it seems that the expression of this truth is possible only in this language.

---

[57] See Hugo Riemann, "Die Ausdruckskraft musikalischer Motive [The Power of Expression of Musical Motifs]," *Zeitschrift für Ästhetik und allgemeine Kunstwissenschaft* I/1: p. 57.

The second natural form of expression of feeling, an action, is directly attached to the physiological expression. It is initially a reflex-motion, and it is also like this in its effect. The angry person who sees the glass that he threw to the ground shattered is soothed by this visible expression of his anger. But the immediate expression of feeling is then curbed the moment that a conscious act of will emerges from the predominantly reflexive motion.

An action is initially subject to the purely external constraints of life, the resistance of other human beings, the conflict with other feelings, but then to the constraints of reason as well. Just as—on the theoretical side of consciousness—not only the outer world of naive consciousness but also the rigorous concept of objective reality developed from it stands over and against mental reality, so, too, here, in the practical domain, not only the complexity of external life but also the law of ethical consciousness developed from it confront the immediate expression of feeling through actions. Just as representations are modified for cognitive purposes, so the expression of feeling is modified for ethical reasons. Just as theoretical consciousness assaults its individual elements in order to set forth objective reality's interconnectedness, so, too, practical consciousness does not allow action to express a single, momentarily dominating feeling. Instead the law that actions should express a determinate relationship of feelings to one another—a relationship essentially prescribed by *society*—presides over the expression of feeling. Just as in theoretical consciousness the cognitive purpose is so dominant that at times there is scarcely any consciousness of the natural mental make-up of representations and perceptions, so, too, in the practical sphere the ethical law is so forceful that the feelings contradicting it and their natural expression are often completely erased. Custom and ethical life, pride and shame hold us back a thousand times over from the action that would express our feeling adequately. The greater the height the ethos climbs to as a whole, i.e., the more the spontaneous expression of feeling in actions is inhibited by reinforced feelings of humanity, justice, self-respect and respect of others, and the less the demand for such expression can be satisfied in life, the more a people will be in need of art. |493|

In the artistic portrayal, every feeling can attain the expression adequate to it, uninhibited by other, opposed feelings, by duty, custom or convention in actions, speech, and gestures. Art shows the human being as he is alone with himself and the feeling as it is for itself alone. Just as in the case of perceptions art ignores the particular cognitive purposes through which they are improved and altered, so, too, here, in the case of feelings, it cancels every moral purpose, every limitation that emerges from the complexity of the personality and from its will for unity. The individual feeling alone stands out and acquires that immediacy of expression that often lends children's expression of feeling such a convincing honesty.

Here once again art also provides either the typical expression of what is a matter of fact or a truth wished-for. In particular, the drama which, *ex verbo*,[58] has actions as its object contains sometimes the one truth, sometimes the other truth. The reason that the heroes present on stage generally appear magnified, in contrast to real human beings, lies for the most part in the fact that their feelings, their inner essence in general is expressed so decisively in their actions. Here as elsewhere, the classic poets, who saw in drama an expression of character more than of feeling specifically, are the representatives of the paradigmatic truth since they frequently portray precisely the conflict between an expression of feeling that is really possible and one that is wished for. By contrast, for others, such as Molière, Hebbel, or Ibsen, the expression of feelings in actions is magnified to a degree that leaves behind any possibility of natural expression and is only conceivable as a truth wished for. A human being is no longer a human being, but instead the personification of greed, jealousy, love-frenzy, adventurousness, or resoluteness. One need only think of Brand.[59] Or take a figure like that of Kandaules in *Gyges und sein Ring*.[60] It is probably difficult to find a man in history whom pride and the need to communicate drive to such an extreme that he would give up his wife's beauty to the gaze of others. And if he were to be found in reality, his action would still contradict probability so much that an artistic portrayal of it would to that extent seem untrue. Nonetheless, Kandaules' deed seems true as an expression of a tendency, a potential, a universally human feature. Poetry works here like a magnifying glass. Hilde Wangel from the *Baumeister Solneß*[61] has a similar effect. From the standpoint of possibility, her entire appearance and manner of action can only |494| be characterized as that of someone unbalanced. Yet as an expression of longing for an action that would give expression to her innermost dream and belief, the figure is

---

[58] [Literally, 'from the word'; less literally, 'from what the word itself means'; Landmann-Kalischer is flagging the Greek root 'δρᾶμα' signifying an act or deed.]

[59] [In Ibsen's 1865 verse tragedy by that name, Brand is an idealistic and uncompromising priest whose tragic fate is bound up with those very qualities.]

[60] [Kandaules is the king whose pride is responsible for his downfall in this 1854 drama by Friedrich Hebbel, based upon sources in Plato and Herodotus.]

[61] [In this 1892 Ibsen play *The Master Builder*, Solness who suffers from vertigo nonetheless climbs to the top of the scaffolding of a tower at the urging of the much younger Hilde Wangel, only to fall and break his skull.]

true in the deepest sense. The behavior of Käthchen von Heilbronn[62] also has the same character of a truth wished-for, with the sole difference that Kleist sought at the same time to preserve the truth of what is probable, in this case through the girl's naiveté on the one hand and through recourse to the wondrous and the pathological on the other.

4. Results: The Relationship of Artistic Truth to Scientific Truth, in Particular to the Truth of Psychology. The Kinds of Artistic Truth. The Relationship of Artistic Truth to Beauty

If we survey the foregoing considerations, the result is that nothing new has been maintained here about art itself. The notion that art affords us the nature that forever runs through human beings, that it gives matters of the soul a sensory expression, that it animates the sensory dimension, has become a commonplace. Our investigation has also been concerned not with matters of facts in and for themselves but with showing that the *truth* of art rests upon these facts. The nature of the artwork is such that it cannot take up the object immediately but instead must get to it first through the phantasy of the artist, allowing it to re-emerge in the phantasy of the observer. From this nature of the artwork it follows that the cognition conveyed by it can also in no way be scientific or philosophical cognition *of something objective*. The cognition conveyed by the artwork is instead exclusively psychological cognition. This concept of artistic truth needs to be formulated and clarified in detail.

From this construal of artistic truth, both its interconnectedness and its contrast with scientific truth become clear. On the one hand, it becomes clear how art can at times be on the road as it were to scientific truth, namely, by coming closer, through its paradigmatic portrayal, to a conceptual cognition or by anticipating an ideal of scientific research through the necessary conjunction of its elements. On the other hand, it also becomes clear how, in fabrications of phantasy, in the fairytale, in the poetic composition of a wish in general, art can be a slap in the face of every reality and objective truth and, nonetheless, it overwhelms us in case after case with the same impression of truth. Thus, one cannot say that artistic truth is |495| one with scientific truth or that it outshines the latter—"revealed in advance to the childlike

---

[62] [*Käthchen von Heilbronn* is the central figure in the 1810 Kleist play by that name.]

understanding."[63] Nor can one say that art, by its very sense and essence, is a lie, an exaggeration, an embellishment. It is rather both if we measure art, intent on attaining its own truth, against objective truth since the mental reality that it expresses encompasses both the side of consciousness that coincides with scientific cognition and the side that is turned away from [objective] reality.

If in keeping with this consideration it is clear that artistic truth can stand in no relation at all or in a merely contingent relation (see p. 475 above) to the contents of scientific or historical truths, then it nonetheless seems as though we would have to exempt from this general judgment a science that seems to have the same content—according to our definition—as artistic truth has: psychology. Completely like artistic truth, psychology seems to have the task of uncovering the distinctive reality of the mind. If, for example, natural science (in the broadest sense) has the objective stimulations of the senses as its object, then psychology, completely like art, has to do with the subjective phenomena of the senses. Hence, it seems that we would have to allow the same relationship to hold between artistic truth and psychological truth that was once assumed to hold between artistic truth and scientific truth generally, namely, that the content of both truths is the same and only the form in which these contents were expressed by science and art is different. On this view, scientific truth would be discursive; artistic truth intuitive.

Is this really only a difference in form? And what does this mean? What does a formal difference consist in?

If there is no sort of causal explanation and deduction contained in the artistic cognition, what alone justifies us speaking of artistic *cognition* at all is solely the feature of agreement contained in this concept. But precisely this feature of their agreement is different in the two sorts of cognition.

Like any science, psychology translates something intuitively given, in its case, something intuitively given to inner perception, into concepts. It analyzes the complex phenomena of consciousness, classifies their elements, and draws up lawful relations between them. By contrast, art merely makes what is given to inner perception accessible to another organ, to outer perception; it makes perceptible for eye and ear what was only |496| present to "inner sense." More precisely, art gives the sensory perception a shape that agrees with representation; it makes the content of an abstract representation present in a way that can be sensed. It gives feelings an audible or

---

[63] [From Schiller's poem *Die Künstler* [The Artists].]

colorful shape; it embodies those feelings in representations that correspond to them. Like art, science fashions agreements, draws up equations. But by producing agreements between *concepts*, science elevates all elements of the given equally into another region. Art fashions an agreement by fashioning an image that is the counterpart to what is mentally given, leaving it as it is, as when someone attempts to produce the same color as a given one. What one understands in science by a poetic or artistic manner of conceiving things is just conceiving things through analogy, the sort of conceiving that explains one object through comparison with another. Every artwork is to a certain extent a hypothetical construction that subsequently proves to be correct or false, depending in each case upon whether the feeling of agreement enters in or not. In this respect art is like the proof procedure of geometry. Within what can be perceived via the senses, it constructs for sensory perception something corresponding to memory's or phantasy's representation, doing so just as, within actual space, geometry constructs for the intuition of space some hypothetical configurations corresponding to predetermined concepts. Psychology investigates in detail the difference between a representation in memory and a representation in perception. Art constructs the corresponding remembered representation and portrays it intuitively. By producing an agreement between concepts, science makes clear what was given in a confused way. Art illumines it by fashioning an image as a counterpart to something given. If one acquires scientific cognition, it is as if one is stroking a Chladni plate: little pieces of sand jumbled together scatter in various directions before arranging themselves into regular figures.[64] But artistic truth is like a light that suddenly illuminates a dark object.

The significance that art possesses for an individual human being consists in this light that it casts on our inner life, as does all the happiness, all the enrichment, but also all the unsavory effects that proceed from it. We know all the more through art. It refines our sense of hearing; it makes us attentive to a thousand things in the visible world that we would have heedlessly passed over. But because it also makes us more aware of the life of our feelings and makes our feelings more acute, it can lead to an ill-fated existence directed inward, the sort of existence that inhibits everyday life. |497|

---

[64] [Chladni discovered that sand strewn on a glass plate arranges itself into definite figures as the disk, stroked by a violin bow, swings; see Ernst Chladni, *Entdeckungen über die Theorie des Klanges* [Discoveries in the Theory of Sound], Leipzig: Weidmann, 1787.]

From what has been said about the relationship of scientific to artistic truth, it follows that artistic truth is more polymorphous than scientific truth precisely to the extent that representations of objects are more polymorphous than the objects themselves. Since artistic truth consists solely in the agreement of what is given in inner and outer perception, individual truths are thus independent of one another. While the truth of judgments rests on their interconnectedness, artistic truth—like beauty itself—can only be affirmed in an individual judgment. Thus, different truths about the same object, like those of probability and those of what is wished for—images of things that are directly opposed to one another—nonetheless do not exclude one another in art since they belong to different spheres of consciousness.

We distinguished the truth of perceptions and that of representations and combinations of representations and here we distinguished in turn the truth of memory's representations (which is expressed in what is paradigmatic, characteristic, and probable on the one hand, and in the unity of the feeling and the style on the other) and that of fantasy's representations (which was essentially the truth of a wish). As for the latter, it was different, depending upon whether it gave expression to intellectual postulates (such as those of the animation of nature and necessary conjunction) or to tendencies of feeling and willing. Finally, art disclosed its own truth in the adequate expression of feeling accessible only to its resources.

Now it is clear that of these various kinds of truth, only those combinations that are on hand in the mind come across as true. An aria, for example, can contradict the truth of the natural expression but can possess for all that the supreme truth of the adequate expression of a feeling that is peculiar to art. Every truth regarding what is typical excludes the truth of the fairytale. Each of these spheres of consciousness has its own consistency within itself, and whenever one sphere, by spilling over into another, violates this consistency, it immediately comes across as less than truthful (see above p. 479). In many an epoch and among many groups of people, either memory's representations or perceptions or phantasy's representations or feelings are so much in the foreground of consciousness that a truth corresponding to the other spheres of consciousness is not sensed or felt as such and its lack is not missed. Thus, the early Middle Ages were sensitive too much to the literary and too little to the visual to feel the lack of "the truth of nature" in its imagistic portrayals.[65] |498| In the past year on the occasion of the Jubilee for

---

[65] On this subject, see André Jolles, *Zur Deutung des Begriffes Naturwahrheit in der bildenden*

Schiller, as writers of the most diverse sort commented on him and the figures in his dramas, several agreed that his figures are true only for the very young and for the very mature, for those who are not yet acquainted with life, for those who no longer seek it, and for all those for whom the general rhythm of life suffices. Indeed, in contrast to the representation of human beings deepened by the experience of living, what is expressed in Schiller's figures is a representation that individually lacks determinateness, having become vague and silhouette-like for being far-away. As a result these figures are felt to be true only by the sorts of persons in whom the zone of such general representations is strongly developed. These different kinds of artistic truth also explain the relative justification for such different currents in art like those of naturalism and idealism, which are indeed in opposition precisely regarding artistic truth. If, according to the doctrine of naturalism, art is supposed to show us the world as it is and if, by contrast, according to the doctrine of idealism, it is supposed to lift us up into a higher sphere of purer reality, these are merely different zones of consciousness, which they demand that art portray. Both forms of portrayal can be true or untrue. If naturalism seeks the truth of what is characteristically the case, then idealism demands of art the truth of what is wished for.—Likewise, specific *combinations* are necessary at one time that are impossible at another. A truth wished for stood in the foreground for the "Romantic" Kleist but he was nonetheless unable to dispense with probability in the figure of Käthchen. The "Naturalist" Ibsen fleshed out his heroes in a consistently Romantic fashion but was nonetheless able to give them so much force of being true, that they could not fail to be part of a milieu that was shaped completely in keeping with what is typically true. To correspond to every sphere of consciousness, without falling into contradictions, that is the secret of the completely great ones. Goethe's figures, true in *every* connection as they are, mirror the tremendous equilibrium of his soul's powers. To see this, one need only place his Mignon next to Hilde Wangel or Kätchen von Heilbronn.

Next to the individual and temporal differences in the reality of the consciousness, what determines the particular kind of artistic truth that finds expression in a work is its place in the system of arts. |499| We have already made mention of the particular form of truth of tragedy and lyric poetry, likewise of the different kinds of art which are the result of different possible

Kunst [On the Interpretation of the Concept 'Truth of Nature' in Pictorial Art], Freiburg in Breisgau: Harms, 1905.

artistic standpoints, i.e., from the difference in the mind's stance towards the object (naive and sentimental poetry). Aristotle has already suggested something of this sort for the difference between tragedy and comedy.[66] Humboldt has expanded on this in a very interesting manner for the fairytale, lyric poetry, the epic, and drama.[67]

The question arises finally of how the truth of the |500| artwork relates to its beauty, whether it is identical with it or with one of its elements, whether it is a consequence or presupposition or mode of it.

By way of anticipation, it is from the outset clear that being true cannot be regarded as a modification of the beautiful in the way that the tragic, the comic, sublime, graceful, and so forth are. Even if each beautiful object as a matter of fact comes in one of these modifications, none of them is essential to the beautiful while being true is. Moreover, each modification of the beautiful can and must be true; indeed, the kind of artistic truth that an artwork contains is determined quite essentially by the modification of the beautiful that it portrays. Thus, we saw that the tragic, in order to be able to have its

---

[66] To be sure, he grounds it initially on the diversity of the object [Aristotle's *Poetics* 4 (1448a1)]. Tragedy imitates σπουδαίους [the noble], the comedy φαύλους [the ignoble]. But he is aware, too, of the artists' dispositions that drive them to imitate one or another sort of human being—the εὐτελέστεροι [more vulgar] and σεμνότεροι [more serious] (ibid., 1448b, pp. 245–27). So that the difference in genera in the end still comes down to the difference in the standpoint toward the same object. For naturally human beings are not diverse in so pure a sense that, considered from a given standpoint, the same human being could not be attributed to one sort as well as another or, in other words, could not be made the hero of a comedy or a tragedy.

[67] See *Hermann und Dorothea*, published by Hettner, 1888. Since Humboldt's construal, in terms of its basic thought, has a kinship with what is expounded in the text and since his construal is well-suited to illuminate it further, the relevant passage is cited here in its entirety: "One can define poetic truth in general through the agreement with nature as an object of imagination in contrast to historical truth as the agreement with it as an object of observation. What is historically true is what stands in no contradiction with reality; what is poetically true is what stands in no contradiction with the laws of the imagination. The imagination either merely leaves itself over to the arbitrariness of its own play, which it merely executes artistically, or it follows the inner laws of the human mind or the outer laws of nature. Depending upon which one of these directions it chooses, poetic truth becomes a mere truth of phantasy or an idealistic or pragmatic truth. The former is usable only in the fairytale.... All that remains in question for such an arbitrary procedure is merely whether the imagination is in a position to summarize these features in one constant series, in *one* image. The idealistic truth is the preferred property of the lyric writer and tragedy. It takes up as completely valid everything in it that is thinkable according to the general constitution of the mind, according to the general laws of changes in it, however so distant, moreover, it be from nature, however so seldom it may be found in experience. The more rigorous pragmatic truth, by contrast, rejects everything that does not lie within the usual course of nature and attaches itself precisely to the laws of nature, the physical as well as the moral, insofar as they agree with it. It directly demands the natural and if it does not exclude the extraordinary and unusual, it must still always agree perfectly with the course of nature as a whole, with the generic concept of humanity... But this is the domain of the epic poet." (p. 170/171). [See Wilhelm von Humboldt, *Aesthetische Versuche über Goethe's Hermann und Dorothea* [Aesthetic Essays on Goethe's *Hermann und Dorothea*], mit einem Vorwort von Hermann Hettner, Braunschweig, Vieweg, 1888; as indicated here, Hettner wrote the foreword but is not the publisher.]

effect, demanded its own form of truth, namely, necessity. Hence, while the modifications are material additions to the beautiful (its forms of appearance, so to speak), truth is an inherent feature of the beautiful itself.

In the history of aesthetics the beautiful has been traced back to truth[68] and artistic truth has been traced back to beauty.[69] In fact, both concepts partially coincide. The concept of artistic truth, as it has been interpreted in the accounts offered here, directly coincides with the Kantian explanation of the beautiful in terms of subjective purposiveness. What we called 'the truth of the artistic portrayal' was at bottom nothing other than its subjective purposiveness, taking this word not only in the Kantian sense as "agreement of the powers of our soul with some cognition in general," but in the expanded meaning of living out the mind's tendencies, fulfilling laws of the mind in general.[70]

If we briefly run through the "elementary aesthetic objects"[71] from this viewpoint, it is immediately apparent that, for simple sense-impressions and for gestalts, what we called 'the *truth* of their artistic portrayal' was nothing other than the portrayal's conformity to laws governing the mind [*psychische Gesetzmäßigkeit*]; hence, their beauty. Correctness |501| of the segment, the arrangement, the perspective makes up not only the painting's sensory truth but also its sensory beauty. Thus Schopenhauer traces what is harmonious and even everything that is satisfying about the impression of nature to the truth and consistency of nature and the "brain-phenomenon" corresponding to it.[72] "Every modification, even the gentlest, that an object acquires through its position, reduction, occlusion, distance, illumination, linear perspective, aerial perspective, and so forth, is without fail provided and precisely calculated by its effect on the eye. The Indian proverb 'every kernel of rice casts its shadow' is corroborated here. Thus, everything

---

[68] ". . . thus we see at once what the poetically beautiful consists in. It is, namely, a brightly illuminating beam of the true that penetrates our senses and disposition with such force that we cannot prevent ourselves from feeling it, no matter how heavily an inattentiveness weighs upon us." Johann Jakob Breitinger, *Kritische Dichtkunst* [Critical Art of Literary Composition], Zürich: Orell, 1740, p. 112.

[69] By the most diverse writers. "The inner truth springs from the artwork's consistency" (Goethe). "Truth is entirely and really a matter of style" (Wilde). "We call an artwork 'untrue' whose parts fall apart" (Dessoir).

[70] [Landmann-Kalischer likely has in mind Kant's account of 'subjective purposiveness' and the 'agreement' of imagination and understanding, as powers of 'cognition in general' (§9) in the *Kritik der Urteilskraft* [Critique of the Power of Judgment].]

[71] Compare Witasek, *Grundzüge der allgemeinen Ästhetik*.

[72] Arthur Schopenhauer, *Welt als Wille und Vorstellung* [The World as Will and Representation] II, Book Three, Chapter 33, Leipzig: Brockhaus, 1859, p. 459.

manifests itself here in a manner thoroughly consistent, exactly appropriate, coherently and scrupulously correct; here there are no tricks. If we consider the sight of a beautiful view merely as a brain-phenomenon, among the complicated brain-phenomena it is the only one that is without fail completely appropriate, faultless, and perfect. All the rest, especially our own operations of thought, in being formal or material, are beset with deficiencies and improprieties, more or less." It is likewise clear in the case of *norm-compliant beauty* [*Normschönheit*] that if an artistically portrayed object does not correspond to the concept of its genus, it is not only not true but also aesthetically ineffective or repugnant. And just as the beauty relative to a norm consists in nothing other than conformity to a norm, i.e., the typical truth of what is portrayed, so, too, the *beauty of an expression* [*Ausdrucksschönheit*] is to be sought in nothing other than the adequacy of the expression. Wherever instead of stirring we feel rhetoric, instead of emotion a straining for effect, the aesthetic effect of the expression is lost along with its truth. What concerns finally the beauty of the *objective*, we have already seen above that inner probability and necessity in the conjunction of events and actions have been put forward as an aesthetic requirement from the beginning.

From the standpoint of the artist as well in the course of creating, his work's truth presents itself as a question of his aesthetic capability. If someone has not mastered the *means* of expression, he cannot express even the most sincere feeling adequately. The expression of any incongruity between idea and execution, as takes place, e.g., in the case of any inconsistent treatment of a dramatic character (Wieland's Alceste!), comes across as untrue. And so, too, from the other direction, an artist who does not honestly mean it |502|, who does not grasp and implement his theme in a completely determinate and consistent manner will come across not only as *not true* but also *as not beautiful*.

Joined together with this last consideration is a final series of thoughts that leads to the same result.

The claim that art discloses its own truth entails the further claim that this truth can be conveyed *only by art*. In the course of considering the expression of feeling we already saw that art cultivates means that are not available to the natural expression of feeling, that it fashions a new language of its own in order to attain the adequate expression. We must suppose that it is precisely these peculiar, completely abstract forms that first enable the feeling to be established truthfully at all. Those limitations of the expression spoken of above, the enfeebling counter-effects that they are known to have on feelings themselves, the modifications in the mind [*die psychischen Moden*] that elevate one feeling while suppressing another, the habit finally that gradually dulls the natural effects of objects [*Gegenstände*] on feeling -- all this has as a consequence the distortion of the life of feelings. If the artist is the discoverer here, uncovering the *nature* of the mind, then he indeed does so, paradoxically, precisely through the form [of the art]. How else would it be possible to explain that peculiar connection that obtains between the intensity and peculiarity of a feeling and the rigorousness of the form by means of which it is expressed, that connection that articulates itself purely externally such that lyric poetry, whose object [*Objekt*] is quite genuinely the expression of feeling, has as its form a discourse that is *bound* in some way and such that music, the art of expressing feeling par excellence, possesses the most rigorous forms of all the arts. The more rigorous rhythmic forms in lyric poetry, even rhyme, have frequently been attacked for leading down the wrong path, to untruth. Rhyme, it has been sometimes assumed, bends the thoughts, occasioning the poet to say something other than he originally wanted to say. For artful kinds of play like acrostic this is without doubt on target; even in forms like Ghaselen and Sestina the temptation may be present to satisfy the form at the cost of the thought. But opposite this tendency, there is an enormously stirring force that the form exercises on the content to be shaped [by it], the concentration, the compression that the form forces on it, acting on the feeling to be expressed like a press acts on a piece of fruit, so that everything slack, hollow, conventional, mendacious, usual, and dull remains in the background and nothing but the essence, the purest essentiality, the individuality of the feeling is driven to the forefront. Everything |503| then that presses in the mind for expression also seeks a form in which it can crystallize, as the strongest [impulse] presses for the most rigorous [expression] [*das Stärkste nach der strengsten*].

And is it not possible for us to ascertain something similar for the remaining forms of artistic truth as well? We saw that the segment and the arrangement of what is portrayed in painting correspond to the confines of consciousness and that perspective corresponds to the laws of seeing. But is not the necessity or idea of the segment, of the arrangement, of the perspective originally called for by the technical conditions of painting in general what it depends upon in order to capture something spatial on a limited surface? Theodore Poppe has attempted to demonstrate that if poetic truth is analogous to the image in memory and phantasy, [it is because] this is required by the technical form of the art of literary composition: by the nature of language.[73] R. M. Meyer seeks to make the living truth of poetic gestalts dependent upon the conditions of the effectiveness of the poetry, namely, on whether our phantasy is stirred or not to reproduce it.[74] In particular, probable and necessary conjunctions are also mandated by the nature of the artwork since the work is subject, in its isolation, to conditions |504| other than reality for its construal.[75]

Hence, far from doing damage to the truth, the form would first bring out the truth and it would be truth not beauty in whose service what is called 'form' stands.

In keeping with all of this, the contents of the concepts of truth and beauty partly coincide. They stand to one another in a correlative relationship. Art needs truth in order to be able to have an effect; psychological truth needs art in order to be discovered. Art's capacity to have an effect rests on this, namely, that what is given by the senses corresponds to the laws of the senses and what is to be awakened in representations and feelings corresponds to the life of representations and feelings. For its part, psychological truth needs artistic forms in order to come to light, and these forms are themselves the expression of psychological laws. Stylistic unity, for example, is not only a law of artistic form but, as an expression of the confines of consciousness

---

[73] See "*Von Form und Formung in der Dichtkunst* [On Form and Forming in the Art of Literary Composition]" in this journal, *Zeitschrift für Ästhetik und allgemeine Kunstwissenschaft* I, 1, pp. 88–112.

[74] R. M. Meyer, "Lebenswahrheit dichterischer Gestalten [The Living Truth of Poetic Forms]," *Neue Jahrbücher für das klassische Altertum*, VIII. Jahrgang, 1905, Bände XV und XVI, 1. Heft. In the course of his exposition, the author mixes the psychological up with the formal. In the negative part of his claims, he comes into complete agreement with our accounts of the matter. This agreement occurs when he says: "The analogy of the actual circumstances does not in turn suffice as an answer (why some situations appear compatible [*vereinbar*], while others do not). For our contingent experience can neither decide with certainty what is psychologically possible nor can it be denied that there is a good deal that can be demonstrated to be intelligible that in its poetic execution is nonetheless not convincing to us" (p. 53). ". . . . Even the weaker effect of 'minor' [*chargierten*] or monotone characters can in no way be derived from analogy with our experience of living objects. For there are enough people who are always completely the same and there are still more that we at least always see in the same situation. And if one calls Harpagon a pathological figure, there are also some just like him; there are enough monomaniacs and persons who consider everything under the same viewpoint of a specific political idea." The positive counterpart to this negative claim would be this, that in objective reality there are, indeed, such people. But in mental reality they occupy no space of any breadth; hence, their artistic truth is less. Instead of coming to this conclusion, R. M. Meyer springs from the objective reality immediately over into the aesthetically formal dimension: "A character representing only bravery or spirit or evil appears unnatural to us, not because it could not occur but instead because it does not prompt phantasy to reproduce it" (p. 61). This would be, as emerges from what is said in the text, a consequence of its artistic, i.e., psychological untruth; but the untruth itself does not consist in this.

[75] [Landmann-Kalischer may be appealing to the modal difference between possibility, reality, and necessity. Earlier she made the point that the writers of comedy and tragedy, while not writing about what really happened, are constrained by what is probable and necessary respectively.]

and of the concentration of feeling and interest, it is also a requirement of artistic *truth*. If one begins with art and assumes that beauty is its goal, artistic truth is a necessary means for it to have an effect. If one begins with artistic truth, with the reality of consciousness, art is the sole path on which it can be discovered and established. Beauty drives truth to the forefront, truth drives beauty to the forefront. If a determinate relationship obtains between the means through which representations are stirred and the representations stirred by this means—a relationship that arouses the feeling of beauty—then these representations, the results of the process of contemplation, are also true. If representations are psychologically true, then between them and the impressions through which they were aroused a relationship obtains that is characteristic of the contemplation of the beautiful.

If these concepts then are correlates in terms of their *content*, beauty is still the more encompassing concept in terms of *scope*. For an artwork simply not to contradict laws of the mind is one thing, for it to correspond to them in a positive way is quite another. In the history of art there are streams that aim so exclusively at a specific effect of art that the truth that their works contain becomes irrelevant to the main effect. Medieval art in its entirety and all strictly ecclesial art are intent on devotion, on ceremonial emotion, and in part on instruction. An artwork can aim at splendor, at shocking, at purely sensuous bliss, at virtuosity in the treatment of an external form; its ultimate refinement can consist in the |505| harmony with which all its elements work together. Of Italian art, in contrast to Nordic art, one can in general say that it is more intent on beauty than truth. In order to be able to have an effect, its works must also be true, but their effect does not lie in that truth. This holds for the "elementary aesthetic objects," especially also those of sense-impressions and 'gestalts,' whose aesthetic effect one can probably trace back to truth, but which in terms of their *impression* lie beyond [what is considered] true and false. Truth is thus one time an aesthetic minimum; at another time, however, a positive aesthetic category. It is a necessary component of beauty but one whose existence is sometimes cognized only in its later development, like the differentiations within a seed that appears homogeneous.

This relationship already follows from the fact that, as we saw, it is not the artwork as a whole that can be true but only what is portrayed, the result of the process through which we make it our own. This process as a whole yields the impression of beauty. But in order for this process to able to get started, representations must be stirred up in us by the artwork, representations that correspond to what exists in the mind, i.e., representations that are artistically true. To this extent, then, beauty presupposes truth. The more differentiated the process becomes, and the more it ascends from the realm of perception into that of representations and feelings, the more distinctly the element of truth thus emerges in it, so much so that, under certain circumstances, truth can become the chief effect of the artwork. Truth concerns the content, beauty the portrayal as a whole; the former only the result, the latter the relationship of the means to that result.

But how, one will perhaps ask, can concepts that are supposedly correlates in terms of their content be different in terms of their scope? I answer: beauty as a whole bears (psychological) truth in itself as a necessary element (analytically). But this truth, should it come to light, spins out of itself, like a silk worm, a greater web in which and on which it unfolds, yet it is a web that has for its part its own value and of which it [the truth] is itself still only a part, even if—perhaps—the main part, the seminal and core point.

Philosophy of Values

Table of Contents[1]

First Part

Critical Discussion of Münsterberg's *Philosophy of Values*[2]
- (1) General characterization of the new doctrine of values — 2
- (2) Metaphysical derivation of values — 5
- (3) The doctrine of the four worlds — 12
- (4) Logical value's realm of validity — 22

Second Part

I. Introduction — 31
II. On the psychology of the emotional sphere — 34
- (1) Feeling's subjectivity and character as a state — 34
- (2) Connection of feelings to the I; emotions — 36
- (3) Dependency of feeling on the individual and the moment — 42
- (4) Reproducibility of feelings — 44
- (5) Independence of feelings from peripheral stimuli: universality of the stirrers of feeling — 49

III. Objectivity of value judgments — 53
- (1) Sense of objectivity: objectivity as a task — 53
- (2) The task of sciences of value — 62
- (3) The fulfillment of the task — 70

IV. The place of values in being — 83
V. The relationship of values to one another — 88

---

[1] [For an introduction to this article see §6 of Matherne's Introduction.]
[2] See Hugo Münsterberg, *Philosophie der Werte. Grundzüge einer Weltanschauung* [Philosophy of Values: Basic Features of a Worldview], Leipzig: Barth, 1908 (hereafter: "MPV"). Review in the "Literature Report" of this journal [*Archive für Psychologie*, XVIII], p. 10.

First Part

Critical Discussion of Münsterberg's "Philosophy of Values"

(1) General Characterization of the New Doctrine of Values

There is the good as the pinnacle of all human thinking and the ultimate cause of all being, "like the sun" that not only warms but also animates everything on earth, and then there's the good as a social convention with changing content, a weapon in class conflict, signifying nothing of the inner connectedness of all beings or the unfolding of what happens, [nothing but] a bit of foam on a wave--the more recent philosophy of values moved between these extremes of the Platonic and the sophistic world-view.[3] In every transcendent picture of the world, the place of values is given in the Platonic sense. Like God, they dwell above being and, like the heavens, above humanity and the earth. By contrast, every immanent view of the world with a natural scientific orientation was compelled to incorporate values as a secondary phenomenon into the flow of what happens naturally and emphasize their dependence upon the human being. In itself, nothing is either good or evil; incorporated into the subject, values lose their cosmic significance. No longer the supreme being, only fleeting shadows and lights above things firmly grounded and complete without them. Their absolute, metaphysical significance sinks down to a merely relative and biological significance.

As the question of values begins today to move once again back into the center of philosophical work, the new school is turning against the degradation of values that is the result of the mechanistic and positivistic direction of thinking. It was the critical philosophy, however, that offered the positive and fertile thought that seemed to enable a mediation between the extremes. Here was a possibility of countering the naturalistic derivation of values just as Kant countered the corresponding Humean construal of causality. Values are, indeed, subjectively conditioned, but *subjectively* in the critical sense. |3|

Once the Copernican reversal was implemented, once the idea was conceived that subjective elements, precisely through their subjectivity, constituted the objective world, one needed then only to look closer at the psychological character of this a priori of the world and it could not help but become clear that all these forms of intuition and categories psychologically

---

[3] [See §6.1 of Matherne's Introduction for background on Münsterberg and an overview of the First Part of this essay.]

display the norm more than the reality of thinking.[4] That is to say, they display the law to which we have to bow, the 'should' we are obliged to realize. Consciousness of the norm [*Normalbewußtsein*] confronts the actual process of thinking. "The rules of thinking drawn up by logical consciousness . . . are determinate sorts of conjunction that are possible *alongside* others in a process naturally necessary and they are distinguished from other conjunctions precisely through the value of being the norm [*Normalität*]."[5] "The human being's natural thinking has an indestructible proclivity to meander [literally, 'to go for a walk': *Spazierengehen*]" (*Präludien*, 248), but the naturally necessary, generalizing associations are only permitted under completely determinate conditions; the "axiom of implication," the principle of non-contradiction, the principle of sufficient reason, and so forth can only be derived from the "purpose of being universally valid" (*Präludien*, 318). A judgment is not only a conjunction of representations or the analysis of an entire representation; in contrast to representing, it is characterized much more by the fact that it rejects or accepts this analysis or this combination.

If correct thinking stands under the sway of a norm, a value, so, too, the reality whose a priori this thinking exhibits is also dependent ultimately on a value and not only on this or that form of thinking. Theoretical thinking itself is conditioned by a practical factor. A value reveals itself as the form of the forms of thinking. In keeping with this point, the value of truth can no longer be derived from being; being is, again in keeping with this point, far more dependent on the value.

This thought bore fruit for the general problem of value. Kant started out from the claim to universal validity that logical judgments make. And he carried out the critical thought as the solution of the problem in the strict sense only for logical judgments. The forms of thinking |4| are universally valid because they constitute the world, because experience first becomes possible through them. By contrast, the constitutive significance of ethical judgments already acquires for Kant a sense that has been transferred [from logic's experience-enabling function] since they constitute, not the empirically real world, but instead a transcendent world. In addition, much as the moon receives its light only from the sun, aesthetic value has for Kant only

---

[4] [Landmann-Kalischer is referring to the 'Copernican reversal' that Kant details in the Preface to the second edition (1787) of the *Kritik der reinen Vernunft* [Critique of Pure Reason], *Kants gesammelte Schriften*, ed. Deutschen [formerly, Königlichen Preussichen] Akademie der Wissenschaften, Berlin: De Gruyter, 1902, p. Bxvi.]

[5] Windelband, *Präludien*, Tübingen: Mohr, 1903, p. 266.

an indirectly constitutive significance. We are in Kant's debt for decisively drawing the boundary of the aesthetic domain opposite the logical domain and no one has elaborated its peculiarity quite like he did. Nevertheless, with regard to the question of what the validity of the aesthetic judgment rests upon, he makes the aesthetic domain dependent upon the logical. To be sure, it is not cognition that the beautiful conveys but it is still a form of "cognition in general." And he grounds aesthetic judgments' claim to universality on this formal agreement with the logical domain. Here [those with] modern ambitions draw the consequences. They are more Kantian than Kant himself. They want to implement the critical thought in every domain of value. The logical judgment is a value judgment. If the logical judgment's claim to universality has its legitimacy from constituting reality, something of a corresponding nature must be demonstrable for the remaining values as well. It must be possible to legitimize the good, the beautiful, and the holy in the same way with respect to their value. They, too, are values for this reason, that each of them is a condition of the existence of a world.

It is already almost a generation ago when Windelband composed his prelude in this key. The book by Münsterberg is the artful fugue that builds upon the themes struck at that time.[6]

What is characteristic of this new attempt to justify the dignity of values lies in placing all domains of value on the same level relative to a constitutive significance; what is characteristic of the attempt is, in other words, the "doctrine of the four worlds," as we intend to name this theory for short.

As we look to characterize the new doctrine of value in a general way, the following four points need to be emphasized:

(1) Values are posited by the subject. The doctrine thereby differs from the objective idealism of Plato and all Platonism.
(2) As subjectively conditioned, values are nonetheless nothing personal |5| or relative since they are not a product of what is [*Seiendes*] but its presupposition. In contrast to every mechanism and materialism, this doctrine is critical.
(3) Value can become the world's presupposition because thinking is also dependent upon value, upon a norm. The new doctrine goes

---

[6] [In this paragraph Landmann-Kalischer plays on musical metaphors, beginning with the title of Windelband's book *Präludien* [Preludes] and its "key" [*Tonart*], followed by Münsterberg's "fugue" that builds upon the themes "chimed" or "struck" [*angeschlagen*] by Windelband.]

beyond Kant by uncovering the practical element within the theoretical sphere.

(4) The remaining values are not dependent upon the theoretical domain but are instead autonomous. Each value forms the a priori of its own particular world that has nothing to do with the other worlds. One may not distinguish only two worlds and by no means an empirical and a transcendent world; instead one has to distinguish four worlds that are on the same footing with one another in relation to empirical reality. By means of this doctrine of four worlds, the spokespersons for this newer doctrine distinguish themselves especially from Fichte who also taught, to be sure, that being first comes to have its standing through a value—through duty—but who had the theoretical world emerge from the practical world and thus taught a monism of value.

(2) Metaphysical Derivation of Values

Setting up a value as an a priori element always involves more than the purely logical concept of the a priori. Each judgment presupposes certain logical axioms. Only psychological investigation discovers in the judgment the necessity of acknowledging it, the act of affirmation and denial, the truth value that one *strives for*. Here the a priori is no longer grasped logically but instead psychologically and, indeed, voluntaristically.

Münsterberg arrives at his thesis by seeking the place of the unconditioned values. He finds it neither in nature nor in the make-up of a person; not in nature since its thoroughgoing causal conjunction excludes value, not in a person's make-up since personal pleasure and displeasure cannot justify any absolute value. He concludes—without weighing further possibilities—that values must belong to the supra-personal and profoundest being of the world.[7] Values can |6| display nothing but the satisfaction of pure willing. But he determines the concept of pure willing as follows: the feeling of pleasure is an automatic personal reaction to a stimulus; with respect to its content, it is completely indifferent: a sum of sensations of activity, postponements of attention, and so forth. What is pleasing is not the pleasure but the stimulus. But if this is the case, then it is absurd to maintain that we would be

---

[7] We come back later to the issue of whether Münsterberg's proof that personal pleasure cannot justify any absolute value is successful.

working, through our willing, toward the production of pleasure. The aim of willing is not the pleasure but the realization of the stimulus [that happens to be] pleasurable [*lustbetont*]. The satisfaction afforded by the fulfillment of the will is only the realization of something represented, thus something independent of pleasure and displeasure. Hence, it is clear that the *aim* of the will stands in no relation to pleasure and displeasure. But how do we come to want something that is unconnected to pleasure and displeasure? How can such a *motive* of the will come about? Here Münsterberg seizes on an arbitrary supposition: "there is a fundamental act of will that we do not want to let go of and that nonetheless has nothing to do with generating pleasure and pain: the will that there is a world and, hence, that the content of our lived experience must not only count for us as lived experience but maintain itself independently in itself. From this vantage point everything is necessarily illuminated. Here is the one original action [*Tathandlung*] that gives our existence its eternal sense and without which life is a shallow dream, a chaos, a nothing" (MPV, 74). In contrast to Windelband, Münsterberg stresses that no "ought" intrudes here. The entire sense and the true significance of the act [*Tat*] reside precisely in the fact it is an act of freedom. For someone who does not want to perform this act, there is nothing but personal sensations, nothing has self-standing content, and nothing has its own significance. But there cannot be any need to go beyond this since all truths, beauties, duties, and sanctities of the world are necessarily themselves dependent upon the requirement that there is a world. "The singular act of affirming an independent world necessarily includes all values" (MPV, 75).

With these observations, Münsterberg goes beyond Windelband at the decisive point. For Windelband, too, value is grounded in the ultimate depths of the world's reality itself. But he links its validity to the questionable concept of universal validity and its immediate evidence. "The ideals |7| of feeling, willing, and thinking represent [*repräsentieren*] only the demand for what is worthy of universal acknowledgment. This worthiness naturally cannot be read off the acknowledging as a factical process; it possesses immediate evidence with which it enters into factical validation in individual consciousness when some consciousness of it has come about with respect to any arbitrary, empirical content."[8] The norm is a principle of selection in keeping with a determinate purpose, but this purpose is universal validity. One sees that we are moving in a circle. Even in the case of Münsterberg, all

---

[8] Windelband, *Präludien*, p. 312.

values, the norms of our acting, are derived from a purpose. But this purpose is, on his part, unambiguous and inescapable; it is the structure of the world. Here we need no belief in something universally valid or in its capacity to be known in empirical consciousness. Instead it means clearly that whoever wills the world must acknowledge the values.

Closely connected with this is the fact that the opposition between natural law and normative force that Windelband posits so abruptly has practically vanished for Münsterberg. Windelband still started out from the contrast between judgment [*Urteil*] and evaluation [*Beurteilung*]. "All cognitive propositions already contain a combination of judgment with evaluation." [By contrast,] Münsterberg, for whom 'existence' itself is only one value next to others, can construe even logical judgment only as an evaluation.

Windelband's "purpose of universal validity" seems almost of necessity to give way to willing the structure of the world. Meanwhile, the new, clear, and positive conception [provided by Münsterberg] brings new difficulties with it. We will have to content ourselves with adopting an autonomous supposition here whose justification necessarily lies in what it accomplishes for the explanation. Yet the difficulties of this hypothesis [of his] probably lie chiefly in the facts that it remains obscure who carries out this action and that to speak of a free action here makes as little sense as speaking of an ought. Münsterberg counters that values present an ought and that no other [sort of] wanting stands opposite this ought. After all, a criminal could indeed want to perform a criminal act for the sake of its pleasurable value but not on account of its lack of ethical value. |8| Yet even to assume freedom makes sense only where there is a possibility of choice. A will that wanted to stand pat in the chaos of lived experiences is unthinkable since it would be canceling itself. Precisely for this reason perhaps the entire conception of the will here makes no sense. Münsterberg argues: the world is. It exists through a will that constructs it, i.e., the presupposition of its being is the will to it. It is itself the aim of willing and, hence, valuable.

But just this, that the interconnections among what is given, which form the logical presupposition of the world, should be elaborated by a will whose aim is explicitly directed at it—this is an arbitrary metaphysical assumption. In it a similarity to the dubious course of thoughts in the ontological proof of God is discernible since a necessity in thinking is made here into a reality [*Realität*]. Wanting to know is a *conditio sine qua non* of epistemology [*Erkenntnistheorie*]. But a necessity in thinking is hypostasized when one makes a metaphysical-psychological reality out of this wanting to know. The world tends to be more complicated than our thinking. Just as we do not eat [simply] because we want to preserve ourselves, and we do not exist [simply] because two human beings willed to produce us, so, too, it is likely that the existence of our lived experiences came about, independent of us, through a more sophisticated mechanism than through a sublime, pure will construed ad hoc.

But let us go further. The aim of willing, so we heard, is not pleasure but the realization of a represented stimulus. This realization awakens satisfaction. That is not pleasure. It is nothing like a feeling, nothing like a willing. Münsterberg apparently has in mind a unique [*eigene*] psychological category, a unique mental formation, the presupposition of which is the transition from the wanted to the attained. This transition is called 'realization.' As the source of satisfaction and the object of pure willing, realization is valuable. Now, between what is wanted and what is attained an identity of content must hold sway. Consequently, every identity of two lived experiences is [an instance of] realization and, hence, valuable. "Whoever here wants his lived experiences to count as an independent world must grasp each lived experience and demand that it maintain itself in the stream of lived experiences as they rush away.... This maintaining of itself, however, can consist for us only in this, that |9| each recurs in a new lived experience, that thus a new lived experience, serving new purposes, is posited as one with the old one—but that was precisely the connection that we became acquainted with as realization" (MPV, 75).

Should we acknowledge the trenchancy of this demonstration—and not be forced to assume that the thinker has slipped here into the logical pitfall: 'all *A* are *B*, *C* is *B*, therefore *A* is *C*,'—we are left with only two ways of construing it.

Either Münsterberg seeks to completely reduce the concept of the 'realization' of what is wanted to the concept of the identity of the content of two lived experiences, to the process of recognizing something represented in something perceived. Each specific activity of willing would then be excluded; it would be exhausted in "holding fast to a representation." Each simple case of recognizing would be a source of satisfaction of the will. Now we certainly will not dispute the kinship of both mental processes; we certainly do not want to forget in particular the pleasure that every case of recognizing awakens as does the mere 'quality of being acquainted with something.' But it would still mean consciously departing from characteristic distinctions if we wanted to equate realization and recognizing, satisfaction of the will and pleasure in recognizing. This equation would, furthermore, contradict Münsterberg's own concern to distinguish "satisfaction" from all merely personal "pleasure."

Or we ourselves realize our demand for identity in our lived experiences. Münsterberg has in mind the will that includes an earlier lived experience with the demand of finding it again in a new one. Can this will actively work towards its satisfaction? If so, it would have to produce the lived experiences themselves. If it cannot do this, then it can only recognize the old lived experience in the new one. To be sure, it can have been a wish, a longing for this recognizing. But is fulfilling a wish identical with satisfying the will? Is the sense of being blessed by having a prayer granted identical with the satisfaction of having attained through one's own work a goal that one had long striven for? Here, too, the kinship of the two lived experiences is enormous. It is only that Münsterberg will once again unfortunately want to see the joy in having a wish fulfilled conflated with the satisfaction of pure willing.

Everything depends upon the degree to which he |10| is in a position to grasp the concept of satisfaction actively. But precisely on this point less than full clarity reigns. Values are supposed to be connections of identity that the human being who wants to expand his lived experiences to the world posits himself. Values are supposed to be tasks. But when Münsterberg speaks of the original world of immediate lived experience and of the given, there seems to be no space for arbitrary positing of identities. In fact, he later speaks directly of the "lived experience" [*Erlebnis*] of realization when we confirm the experience [*Erfahrung*] of the one sense through that of the other [or] one's own perception through that of someone else. The concept of satisfaction is grasped just as passively in the place where it is a matter of the existence of another being [*Wesen*]. "The other being has existence, not because I find it in my lived experience or because it comes up in other lived experiences, but instead because precisely the same thing that I find recurs as something identical in the other. This recurrence rewards our holding fast to something and fulfills our expectation, and precisely this recurrence generates that satisfaction that we call 'value,' in this case the value of existence" (MPV, 113). It seems to occupy a mediating standpoint; the identities are indeed given or located in the lived experiences, but we must find them. "To discover an historical interconnection means *elaborating* identities of willing." We are thus actively involved in the identity. Nevertheless—what we are supposed to elaborate must be already hidden in the given. Identities are somehow "given." Satisfaction regarding them is not fully separate from the pleasure in the given.

It was necessary for me to dwell longer on this point because it is the decisive place on which everything that follows is built. The thesis of the entire book, that existence is a value, depends on the equation of realization and identity. That "existence," what Kant calls 'experience' [*Erfahrung*], presents a process of working on our lived experiences [*Erlebnisse*] in the sense of finding an interconnectedness in them, that the world and life hang on the fact that the tangle of our lived experiences does or will maintain itself independently of us, and that every interconnection can be traced back to identity—all of this we will be able to grant.—But that identity or interconnectedness do not count in and for themselves as a priori, that identity is supposed to be at the same time a pure value, namely, the source of the pure satisfaction of the will, this characteristic entanglement |11| of concepts, the positing of the logical and the emotional spheres as one, this would rest precisely on that course of thought that has not proceeded, so it seemed to me, in a way that is free of objections or is at least clear. Let us consider after all that even the downgrading of existence to a value, one value next to others, also rests on this!

One can concede each of the claims individually: 'The world emerges through elaboration of identities.' 'Each value rests upon an identity-connection.' Both are certainly very valuable and very fruitful thoughts, and one will read Münsterberg's account of them in his book each time with pleasure and edification. One could even link the second proposition to the first by adding a 'therefore' to the second proposition. But the fact that Münsterberg makes the *post* into a *prae*, that he is not content with deriving the dignity, the validity of values from the composition of the world but undertakes instead to ground the world on values—therein lies the fatal unraveling[9] of the knot that already contains in itself *in nuce* the tragic outcome of this drama of thought.

How fatal this entanglement of concepts becomes is already immediately evident in the division of the [respective] domain's facts. Within each of these four domains, Münsterberg divides the lived experiences into those of the outer world, the shared world, and the inner world.

---

[9] ['Unraveling of the knot' [*Schürzung des Knoten*] is a German dramaturgical term for the key moment in the play where the plot takes the decisive turn.]

The will accordingly finds not only a jumble of lived experiences but their separation into the surrounding world, the shared world, and the inner world. "As a self that wills, I find myself connected not only in relation to the outer world, but *from the outset* to the shared world as well. In the immediate lived experience I assume a position towards friend and foe...." (MPV, 90). One sees that a point of departure is afforded for value that is different from that for being. If one starts out from value, one can in fact start the investigation, as Münsterberg does, from the ego that empirically wills in its connections to the world, to its fellow human beings, and to itself. If, however, one takes value as an a priori of being, then one can only *begin* with "elements," in any case with "lived experiences," but never with spheres of existence that have already been cleanly separated from one another. In order to acquire value as an a priori of being, he constructs the pure will. In order to investigate values, |12| he must start with the empirical I with its wants, the I that finds itself already opposite diverse worlds.

(3) The Doctrine of the Four Worlds
The theses of the theory of the four worlds are as follows:
"Every valuing emerges with an equally fully valid claim from the immediate certainty of life. To grasp the world in its agreement with itself, both in its progression and in what it brings about, is no more and no less an ultimate value than to understand it in its harmony and beauty or to have cognition of it in the certainty of its existence and in its law-governed character."

"Existence is not here earlier and more fundamentally than being good or being one" (MPV, 441).

"The valuation of cognition that requires laws and the valuation of ethical life that requires freedom do not refer to the same world at all" (MPV, 440).

Two sorts of claims are contained in these theses:

First: every value is autonomous. None radiates from an alien light. Each pure value is a value by virtue of itself.

Second: The different domains of value have equal *dignity*. None is more original than the other; there is no scale of values, no ordering of one over the other; all have the same weight, the same weightiness in relation to the whole and the interconnectedness of the world; *all* are directly anchored in the deepest dimension of being; *all* acquire their claim on validity from their constitutive significance.

Self-Sufficiency of Values

I see the main significance of Münsterberg's book in his treatment of the first claim. The uniqueness and self-sufficiency of all domains of values have perhaps never been elaborated to the extent that they have been here. That an aesthetic consideration can be no sort of—even if imperfect—cognition, that virtue cannot be [the same as] knowledge, that God can be no object of a proof and that, on the other side, the good cannot be a cause of being, that love cannot hold the world together and the law of beauty cannot determine the course of the stars—all that is grounded as a matter of principle in Münsterberg's system. But the uniqueness and fecundity of his thought [13] is specifically expressed in the fact that far *more* self-sufficient values make their appearance than were previously assumed. I do not want to speak here of what I regard as the unfortunate introduction of economic values into the system of pure values.[10] But it should be emphasized that Münsterberg rescues the self-sufficiency and uniqueness of the very values that had previously derived their validity as values solely from aesthetic or ethical values. That love as the agreement of different beings, happiness as the agreement of all inner drives, and self-development as the preservation of the self-identical will in [the course of] being different—that these are values in and for themselves, independent of aesthetic and ethical viewpoints—that is a truly liberating sort of cognition. Since the principle of identity is also the same for whatever relationships in which it emerges, pure, unconditioned values can manifest themselves in all these objects, however personal and sensory they may appear. The agreement of two beings is a value "even if it is a beggar, off the beaten track, who has become one with the young, demanding being, the child at her breast" (MPV, 223). The old, difficult question of how desert and happiness are linked can only be treated phenomenologically if at all. Our own life and our construal of other human beings is expanded and liberated when we know that even the most natural contents of our striving are valuable in and for themselves, when we no longer have to ask anxiously whether our happiness also contains some ethical value, whether our love contains more than personal pleasure. Happiness remains a value even if, from an ethical standpoint, we are unworthy of it, and even if it is not an "ethical" happiness. Unhappiness remains a disvalue regardless of how much it purifies us ethically. If love is valuable for philosophers like Kant and Hegel only as

---

[10] [See Landmann-Kalischer's remarks about economic values in "On the Cognitive Value of Aesthetic Judgments," p. 272.]

an empirical principle of ethical life, for poet-philosophers like Empedocles and Hölderlin it acquires dignity and significance as the principle holding the world together. And so it is its own, self-sufficient value, indifferent to both logic and ethics.

Self-sufficiency is one thing, independence another. Magnetism does not become a form of electricity by the fact that it can be produced by an induction-current. [14] Values can be autonomous while their emergence, the very object in which they appear, is bound to other values. Values can be self-sufficient individuals and can nevertheless stand in a relation of super- and sub-ordination *toward one another*, like the members of a state. Had Münsterberg wanted to present merely the self-sufficiency of all domains of values opposite one another, then he would have dug all too far by anchoring them for that reason in the deepest dimensions of the world's reality. As much as we have to admire his principle of the self-sufficiency of all values and his implementation of that principle, we shall have a hard time being able to follow him all the way—down to the maternal sources [*Mütter*] to which he traces them collectively.

The Relationship of Values to One Another

(1) *Identity is solely a logical concept*. It cannot help but be striking at first, already from a mere glance at the construction, that Münsterberg grounds four groups of values that are independent of one another on one fourfold concept of identity. There are not species [*Arten*] of identity; differences of identity can only be differences in the groups of objects between which it occurs. But then identity itself is always the same concept and, to be sure, a logical concept. Identity is cognized. If it is felt, then in this case the feeling is only an imperfect cognition. There is no reason to think that [*Es ist nicht einzusehen, warum*] the identity which obtains between the parts of one and the same lived experience or between the stages of its development should be something fundamentally its own that remains completely alien and unconnected to the identity that a part preserves with itself in the changing course of lived experiences. The partial agreement of objects, human beings, and drives in what a human being itself wills is logically knowable as an identity. It is a logical value of interconnectedness that can be intuited or felt, moreover, as love, happiness, or beauty.

In Münsterberg's beautiful segment on aesthetic values this point can become particularly clear to us. Since the "pure experience [*Erfahrung*]" from which Münsterberg starts contains only the opposition between wanting and wanted, but not between physical and mental, what is beautiful in the immediate experience is for him not an optical perceptual image or a sensation of sound but the sound itself, the rushing, tempestuous, overflowing waterfall itself. [15] Münsterberg sets aside the psychological explanations of empathy [*Einfühlung*] because, in the spirit of "pure" aesthetics, sympathizing [*Nachfühlen*] with the sorts of volitions that come upon us in regard to the beautiful is a real, fundamental relationship for which nothing further in the way of explanation is needed. The beautiful never stands across from us initially like an object of natural science but instead as a free expression of strivings and volitions. The moon of the poet imbues bush and valley with a silver glow; it is not at all the rigid body whose craters the astronomer studies with his telescope.—We can hail all these observations with the greatest joy: the moon of the poet is neither a merely psychological object nor an object of natural science. However— and here is the decisive point—it cannot stand *alongside* the moon of the natural scientist; it can find no limitation in the latter. For the moon, aesthetically construed, belongs to the world of immediate lived experience, as much as what is optically seen does. What we feel in regard to the beautiful is not the agreement of volitions, since that agreement is in no way immediately contained in the impression; it merely underlies the latter. An agreement cannot be directly felt at all. Science confirms that wherever we perceive beauty, an accordance occurs, just as it is a finding of science that the air makes so many vibrations per second when we hear the sound of a C note. We are able to grasp the agreement of judgments as an agreement directly and we can grasp them in no other way. The agreement exhibits itself to us in no other form. By contrast, when the sort of agreement that we become aware of through "surrender" to it appears to the organ through which we perceive it, it does so in a completely different gestalt, precisely as beauty, and the interconnectedness of beauty with that accordance can subsequently be ascertained by the intellect only as an equation, only as a value of existence. In the immediate aesthetic experience [*Erfahrung*] we encounter representations, to be sure, but no agreements.

On the basis of this fact that the aesthetic value cannot itself ground a world of its own, it seems to me that its unassailably peculiar and a-logical character (that Münsterberg has seized upon and portrayed in such a lively manner) cannot be juxtaposed with the logically formed existence but belongs instead to the realm [16] of the originally given that also spans the world of colors and sounds around us. Logical value cannot affect these worlds; it can only affirm interconnections that it finds between them. The moon of the poet and the moon of the natural scientist lie on different levels. The former belongs to immediate experience; the latter exhibits the results of logically working on all the optic, aesthetic, and, in some cases, acoustic data that are related to the moon as their cause, their bearer, or their unified center. It is nonetheless only the latest stage of natural science that has excluded beauty along with visibility from the real [*realen*] nexus of being.

"Only where a willing preserves itself in a manifold, where the stirrings in all their diversity demonstrate themselves as a singular striving, only there do we experience a world holding sway." This must be granted completely. Only there do we *experience* [*erfahren*] it. And we can go further: becoming aware of this accordance accordingly gratifies us. We give it a value accordingly. If the validity of aesthetic value cannot be derived from the fact that it grounds a world of its own, it can nonetheless be traced back to the fact that beauty or goodness is an identity perceived by a different organ. With Kant we can ground the aesthetic value on its formal agreement with the logical value, on subjective purposiveness. But we cannot identify our experiencing of a world with the constitution of precisely this world.

(2) *The other values presuppose existence.* In truth all those worlds that are supposed to be ranked alongside 'existence' already presuppose it. Münsterberg thinks that all those worlds arise from the experience still not worked on and they arise precisely through being worked on, i.e., through elaboration of identity, albeit in different directions. In fact, however, several of these worlds cannot be acquired at all without the world that has already been worked on logically. Harmony, love, and happiness are relationships of identity, not between the experiences still not worked on at all, but between factors that, indeed, are given, on their side, as outer world, shared world, and inner world by virtue of first having been logically worked on. The elements of the outer world itself between which harmony [17] occurs are not pure intuitions but such that are already judged as objects, just as each art fully presupposes the world of objects. The architect requires representations of purpose, acquaintance with mathematics and physics. Painters and sculptors may start out with the focus so much on form and color as such, but insofar as they portray figures they presuppose the logical representation of an object—not to speak of the writer who possesses concepts as his material, regardless of how musically he endeavors to work on it.

It is superfluous to expand further on how the values of development are dependent upon the values of existence. It follows already from the concept of them. The one who itself wants to be something else is something logically formed; the community that we construe as a group obtaining for itself, the self that remains one with itself in its willing—in order for it to be able to be construed as something that wills this or that, it must first be an entity that exists.

Münsterberg assumes that the value of interconnectedness—nature as mechanical happening—and the value of development—nature as willing—are equally elaborated from the primitive lived experience [*Erlebnis*]. But he seems to overlook that this process of working on nature in different directions first sets in with values of culture. For in no conceivable experience [*Erfahrung*] is there is anything logically unformed at all. The nature of native peoples or cave dwellers insofar as they have wills is objective in the same manner as that of the natural scientist, i.e., it is logically formed, *existing* in the same manner. The counterpart to our willing can become nature for us only if it already exists as logically formed and, thanks to natural science, nature is for us today "material for action" in a much higher measure than it could be for primitive human beings. Language itself points to existence as the presupposition of other values. It cunningly contradicts the philosopher when he says that existence is not there earlier and more fundamentally than *being* good or *being* one (MPV, 441).

(3) *The concept of constitution makes sense only for logical value.* What then does constitution of a "world" mean? By virtue of logical values, by means of the will to identity, we build the world of things [18], fellow human beings, even ourselves out of a chaotic jumble of lived experiences. On the basis of that single logical axiom, we erect—according to Münsterberg—the edifice of all the sciences, logic, ethics, aesthetics, dogmatics, dialectics, and mathematics from the world of the immediately given. If there is one presupposition on which all this depends, then it makes good sense to speak of the constitutive significance of this principle. All that we do also builds upon the results that are gained by working on material logically. But what kinds of worlds do the remaining values generate? Beauty generates beauty; ethical life generates ethical life. If, conscious of some goal, we make nature into the material of what we do, the economy emerges but the economy is precisely nothing other than that process of working on nature; if we preserve our Selves [*Selbst*] in the course of the different claims made on us, we gain our Selves. But nothing more. If natural science is not permitted to find the will to grow that may slumber in every germ of wheat (something

that will still need to be discussed), then the consideration that finds that will is unable to construct a world for it. Or can nature as the counterpart of our willing, the nature that is supposed to be created by that consideration, really be called a world in the same sense as the causally conjoined nature? Growth, progress, economy, right, and ethical life are values—can they be called self-sufficient worlds? Can right—as "the order by means of which the realization of the common will [Gemeinschaftswillen] is consciously and purposely [zielbewußt] secured in the intercourse of the members of the community with another"—be placed alongside and independent of the order that arises as *existence* from working by means of logical axioms on everything given? Is the order of right not permitted to have its place *within* existence instead?

At the outset Münsterberg could rightly maintain that the values of preservation hold absolutely for any consciousness at all *that wants a world*. But, now, a consciousness that does not want a world is unthinkable. No human being can withhold acknowledgement of existence. By contrast, a consciousness that does not want a divine world is thinkable. *Deniers* of God are possible. Can the value of the holy thus be called constitutive in the same sense as that of truth? |19|

It seems as though the doctrine of the four worlds has arisen from an inversion of the argument. In the case of identity as self-preservation it meant that the logical principles must be acknowledged as unconditionally valuable because they constitute reality and science. In the case of self-agreement [Selbstübereinstimmung i.e., its harmony with itself] and self-unfolding, it can only mean that these interconnections must respectively constitute a world of its own because they are valuable. In opposition to this [last inference] we must hold fast to the notion that every agreement may be valuable but not every agreement constitutes a world.

Even psychologically the difference between value and a necessity on which our world depends seems to hold. Beauty, love, happiness are pleasing; hate, ugliness, being torn apart on the inside are repulsive. It is naturally necessary for us to seek the former and flee the latter. By contrast, there is no relationship between the consciously pleasing value of truth and the absolutely compelling character of our need to acknowledge, seek, and follow the truth. The researcher's intellectual ecstasies hold only for the truth that is newly discovered or needs to be discovered. In daily life truth is such stale bread that we often diabolically take pleasure in a lie and error instead. A chief ingredient of comic effect is freedom from logical constraint [Zwang], something that is *only* temporarily possible, that is, only temporarily not binding. The constraint here is absolute since logical value is constitutive. It is, by contrast, typical for the other values that they exist essentially as ideals. Their greater felt-value is perhaps connected with this fact. The logical values represent [*repräsentieren*] the minimum of existence. That the world preserves itself is a condition of one's own existence. But life is possible without happiness, without beauty, without ethics. Failing to fulfill an ethical demand does not cancel our existence. The community in which the individual subordinates his will to that of the collective is, to be sure, no ideal community but the *possibility* of a social life can nevertheless be achieved by coercion. If I do not act as I want, I checkmate my *self*, to be sure, but I continue to exist. If I do not seek the ultimate unity of all values, I do not of course have the world that the religious human being possesses but I can live a rich, bountiful life even without this. All this was cited by Münsterberg to illustrate the independence of |20| values from one another—but it proves only the independence of the values of existence from the rest; this independence is not reciprocal. Or how could I be good without being here? When other values are canceled, only the world made up of them is canceled; they can only cancel themselves. When the value of existence is canceled, all being, all thinking, and every other value are canceled with it. It is also not possible for there to be anything but unanimity about logical axioms. By contrast, the views regarding what is to be valued as good and beautiful have diverged considerably from one another and continue to do so. It would be bad, indeed, for a world should it be constituted by these values.

What Münsterberg calls a 'world' is only a specific content of lived experience that follows its own laws. To name any content of a value a world, in analogy with the value of existence, is a metaphor.

If I cancel the value of beauty, the world of beauty sinks away; but this is an identical claim. If I cancel logical value, then nothing exists at all any more, and even this claim of non-existence does not hold, and so forth. This value cannot be canceled for an instant; it would unhinge the world—the aesthetic, religious, ethical world no less than the existing world.

(4) *Relationship of the values of life to the values of culture.* Finally, the fact that the remaining values cannot be put on a par with logical values in regard to constitutive significance is also evident from the fact that the relationship of the intentionally elaborated values of culture to the immediate values of life is shaped in a completely different way from that of the logical

values. It is an important and fruitful thought running through the book, one that is indeed also already expounded by Avenarius, namely, that the human work of culture consciously re-enacts those accomplishments that primitive human beings exercise unconsciously and instinctively in immediate lived experiences. Now it is clear: If a value has a constitutive significance, that is to say, if a world is actually constructed by fulfilling the task that the value presents, then every subsequently acquired value must either confirm or correct that earlier acquired value. For only through the connection of the values of one domain of value to another, only through the work of interweaving individual values, can a whole arise that |21| deserves to be called a 'world.' This connection of values to one another will necessarily become particularly clear where the step is taken from instinctual valuation to elaborating values in a conscious and fully planned manner. But this relationship of the values of culture to the values of life takes place for Münsterberg only in the case of logical values; as for the rest, the values of culture are completely disconnected from the values of life. One can perhaps grant that music has for its content the task of harmoniously shaping a human being's inner world, and that the connection of human beings to one another is a theme of literature. But does really *the same thing* that is instinctively love, once it is consciously and intentionally worked on, become art (literature)? It remains to be seen whether this aesthetic portrayal of the values of life is a further development of them in the same sense in which right is the intentional continuation of social progress or a capitalist economy is the continuation of the economy of the hunters and fishermen who made up peoples naturally. The relationship between values of life and those of culture takes shape differently in turn with regard to the final values [*Abschlußwerte*]. The way of consciously working on values is supposed to "invert" the instinctive act here. While in religion a world is erected over all values, a world in which they are all fused in a unity, philosophy seeks the foundation of all worlds, the uniform root from which they all proceed.

Hence, on all these domains of value the values of culture, although they arose from the same drive to which the values of life owe their existence, nonetheless exhibit opposite the latter something completely new, all its own, and self-sufficient—albeit something new through which what is posited more primitively is by no means supposed to be canceled and in no way encroached. Matters are completely different, however, for the relationship between the values of existence and those of various interconnections. Scientific thinking is the conscious exercise of those mental functions that are already requisite for the most primitive orientation in the world. But precisely for this reason the values of existence are subordinated here to those of interconnections; that is to say, where both do not agree, the value of culture [including science] must supersede the value of life. Where logical judgments hold at all, opposite judgments cannot both be true. Either the rod in water is broken or it isn't. The world scientifically conceived must rectify the primitive judgments of perception. Here |22| Münsterberg's general determination of the matter has its place: the contrast of the instinctive and immediate, on the one side, with the conscious and planned, on the other. Only here can there actually be talk of "re-enactment and continuance" [*Fortführen*]. Only here does the constitutive significance of a value give notice of itself. Here it becomes clear once again that Münsterberg's conception is tailored to the value of truth, that the determinations holding for logical values are transferred and merely retrofitted to the other values, and thus can hold for the latter only in a completely vague, analogous sense.

Let us summarize what has been discussed in this chapter. Münsterberg's doctrine of four worlds, i.e., his placement of values of unity, values of development, and final values on a par with logical values, does not seem tenable for the following reasons:

(1) because identity, to which he traces all values, is a logical concept;
(2) because aesthetic, ethical, and conviction values [*Überzeugungswerte*] presuppose logical values;
(3) because the concept of constitutive significance to which he traces the unconditioned validity of values, makes sense only for logical values; and
(4) because an actual continuation of the values of life into the values of culture takes place only in the case of logical values.

(4) Logical Value's Realm of Validity

While Münsterberg, by placing aesthetic and ethical values on the same level as logical values, elevated them, on the one hand, to a height that, it seemed to us, is not warranted, the elevation of the one brings with it, on the other hand, a lowering of the other: logical values are restricted in their validity by the doctrine of the four worlds. The domain of logical validity is reduced.

It is immediately striking in Münsterberg's construction that logical value counts for him as the "value of existence" and, indeed, as the value of existence in the narrowest sense, namely, as the core concept of being, fundamentally free from all other values. It is nature, mechanistically construed, that counts for him as the domain of logical value. Yet logical thinking grounds not only what is but what is valid [*nicht nur das Sein sondern auch das Gelten*]. It is not only nature, it can also be God, it can be beauty or goodness, what is here |23| or not here. By virtue of this circumstance—Münsterberg makes this objection himself—the equal justification of values is canceled once again, the whole is ultimately subordinated to cognition, thus to logical valuation. Münsterberg answers this objection with two arguments (p. 443). First, he says, the interconnectedness, e.g., of truth and beauty, may itself have the value of being true but the interconnected values themselves would thereby still be conceivable as equally justified. We have already acknowledged this above by way of differentiating the self-sufficiency of values from the independence of them from one another and we can grant it here all the more since, according to the objection, as Münsterberg himself continues, an ultimate prerogative would nonetheless still remain for the evaluating proper to thinking [*das denkende Bewerten*]. But Münsterberg also does not want to allow logical value this ultimate primacy. He could only allow this, so he opines, "if logical cognition of the interconnectedness really were the concluding action of the I" [*die abschließende Handlung*]. "But obviously," so he continues, "this action is conclusive only for those who as such are seeking cognition, while the I encompasses more than a striving for cognition. Even for the thinker who has attained such a conclusive value of thought, the manifold of life still contains, alongside this valuing of truth, the valuing of beauty, of ethical life; in short, we stand then anew before a plurality for which we once again think a unity and yet we would find this thinking once again only as one valuation in us alongside others" (MPV, 443f).

In response to this, the following needs to be said. The psychological fact that the one thinking can, at the same time, also be the very one who values aesthetically or ethically is not something that can come into consideration for the question lying before us. It cannot be considered since this personal union of values does not cancel the fact that while it is possible to assign value or lack of value to an object in each individual case only on the basis of a logical judgment, the logical value is not subject to such a dependence on other values. "The ultimate primacy of the evaluating proper to thinking" cannot be disputed further. Its realm of validation precisely encompasses the realm of all other values, reaching farther than that of any other value.

One could object that even logical thinking can be ethically and aesthetically evaluated, but in the first place this evaluation is then |24| carried out in the form of a logical judgment, and in the second place, while I *can* indeed impose these criteria on thinking, I do not need to. Ethical and aesthetic evaluating [*Bewerten*] has eyelids, the logical does not; everything is necessarily subject to logical evaluation [*Beurtheilung*]; mystics have made vain attempts to withdraw from the tyranny of logical thinking. Logical formation reaches down into the most primitive perception. As a function of the interconnectedness of things, thinking can leave no element of consciousness isolated; it must assign each element its place in the whole. Every element must welcome thinking's intrusion, but they are also able to since its function is purely formal. One can always make the will or whatever is irrational the master or the core of the world—but one must acknowledge that it is the intellect that installs it as master. The worldly master is crowned by the spiritual [*geistlichen*] master. With the acknowledgment of the Pope's approval, the Kaiser loses his power. We said at the start that identity is a logical concept. The entire process of world creation, as Münsterberg thinks it, is accomplished by elaborating identities. However, the organ for the cognition of identities, the function that according to Münsterberg thereby posits the world as world, is the intellect.

It is not only that logical value does not by itself justify nature; it also does not justify a nature conceived mechanically, as Münsterberg would have it. The realm of thinking is not only greater in scope but also far more polymorphous in content. He needs his four worlds only because he arbitrarily constricts the one world. With the requirement that the world preserve itself and be coherent in itself, the program for the system of all the sciences and philosophy is given; with this requirement, logical thinking justifies existence as a whole and not only a partial domain of cognition—[e.g., that of] modern natural science.

We come here to a core point of the system. For Münsterberg the mechanistic consideration of nature is no science alongside others; instead it is for him the system that necessarily results from the nature of our cognition and the system that is alone permissible and consistent in terms of its method. The sphere of concepts of the natural scientist is for him the world of cognition |25| in general. 'Logical' is for him synonymous with 'mechanistic.' No purposive force is supposed to be able to enter into the causally interconnected nature. "Development and the *scientific interconnectedness* of things are contradictory in their basic presuppositions" (p. 313). "The world devised by natural science is fundamentally without a goal, an aim, a development" (p. 315). In the system of nature there can be no progress. "The will to become otherwise oversteps the *natural scientist's* sphere of concepts," and "The will to become otherwise can never enter into the interconnectedness of things in nature insofar as it is supposed to be an object of *cognition*." "The vitalism that would rank forces striving towards a goal alongside physical-chemical forces in order to explain vital processes is untenable and *logically* irresponsible" (p. 307). All these sentences are based upon Münsterberg's identification of causal cognition and cognition in general. These sentences are correct as long as, by 'cognition,' one does not understand any system of random interconnections that merely do not conflict with logical laws, but intends instead to allow only what has been joined together through some logical interconnection to count as cognition and correspondingly as existing. Not only formally, also content-wise, in keeping with the nature of interconnections among them, all "lived experiences" should be worked on in a way that corresponds to logical laws.

Now this ideal makes sense only as long as one believes in the possibility, in principle, of a formula for the world [*Welt-formel*]. But if one does not share this belief, if one sees in the fact of formulas proof that the world is more than the content of formulas, if the only consequence of this expansion of logic's competence is that one seeks to emancipate entire masses of lived experience from the laws of logic, one must also remember that here a logical maximum was demanded hypothetically. Is it then necessary that the interconnections whose formal correctness logic oversees be themselves of a logical nature? The type of interconnections can be determined anew in each case materially through the nature of what is to be known. Hence, the assertion about an interconnection nonetheless always remains a form of cognition; hence, it is still subject to the logical law.

That the question of causes is not the only question that can be posed regarding the value of an interconnection was, for Münsterberg himself, something that already resulted from the science of history. Since |26| the historian has to do, not with objects [*Objekte*], but with subjects instead, he has to elaborate identities of willing. But entities who will this or that [*Wollende Wesen*] cannot be linked through the causality of nature because their reality does not lie within time; and it does not lie in time since the will posits time but does not fill it out. To elaborate identities of willing thus means grasping the individual entity in its historical position thanks to the fact that, in its lived experiences of willing, the willing of other subjects is really rediscovered.

This says, in effect, that where a new object [*Gegenstand*] of cognition presents itself, new principles of cognition must be applied. Indeed, the question then is precisely this, whether, with respect to nature, particularly living nature, we have to deal with subjects or objects [*Objekte*]. The mechanistic construal of nature treats it exclusively as an object, the biological as a subject. But we have to assume that a plant, considered as a subject, is an entity that develops toward determinate goals. The identity that we have to elaborate relative to it is that of the posited goal and the realization of what has been posited. Such a consideration would remain completely within the framework of the value of an interconnection. I fail to see in this a "logical irresponsibility" any more than in Münsterberg's consideration of history. We can assume the "will to grow" as a hypothesis just as well as movements of atoms, if this assumption would explain the interconnectedness of animate nature. We can consider the plant as a subject and, like the historian, investigate "the sense, the significance, the aims, and the inner connections" of its actions without constructing another world, a world other than the very one that proceeds from the value of an interconnectedness. Growth, progress, self-development, economy, right, and ethical life are, to be sure, united by the fact that they treat subjects or, better, that they look upon an outer world and inner world as subjects, namely, as instances of willing. On this presupposition, however, Münsterberg treats the relationship of wills to one another, of the will to itself and to its fulfillment as the value of an interconnection precisely as in history. That each individual entity as a member of society becomes the bearer of pure evaluation, that the individual volitions out of which the daily work of living is put together do not contradict one another (since otherwise the self should collapse into a series of sequences unconnected to anything else), that |27| nature is rendered of service to human beings, that the common will is realized in the exchange among members of the community, that the action carried out agrees with the action willed—all this can be ascertained without the question of the freedom of the will even being touched upon, without someone impartial even coming upon the thought that there would be a world of its own here, with its own laws, a world that would supposedly have nothing in the slightest to do with existence and reality.

It is arbitrary and means that the bow has been stretched too tightly if one allows only one form of explanation to hold. Like the history of the sciences, the natural development of a human being displays an entire series of forms of explanations, each of which nonetheless conveys cognition. For naive minds the fact that something *was* is already sufficient reason for [the presumption] that it still *is*. 'Cognition' can mean subordinating the individual to the universal, the part to the whole, the means to the end, the subsequent to the foregoing, the conditioned to the conditioning, the consequence to the ground. To be sure, in a unified picture of the world the relationship of the forms of explanation to one another needs to be determined. But there is no lack of such determinations. Thus, Lotze, C. E. v. Baer,[11] Franz Erhardt,[12] and W. Stern[13] have investigated the relationship of the teleological consideration of nature to the mechanistic consideration of it and at least laid out clearly the possibility of their obtaining along with one another.

Münsterberg places enormous emphasis on the fact that value-free nature, causally interconnected in a thoroughgoing way, is an act of the mind. It is for him something first elaborated on the basis of the lived experience of what is originally real *and thus*, in his view, only one of many possible worlds. It is for him an act of the mind in the service of a valuable purpose—it would necessarily be possible for other worlds to be constructed under the reign of other purposes. That things in reality are physical bodies without wills does not constitute an objection to [the view] that nature confronts us as something with a will: "We know that reality was first transformed into physical bodies in nature through laborious re-thinking in the service of |28| explanation" (MPV, 197). But the epistemological [*erkenntnistheoretische*] reflection on the historical emergence of a world picture is no *carte blanche* for the merely relative assessment of it. Recalling that atoms are "merely" thought is, as Münsterberg himself emphasizes, no proof that they are nothing but products of thinking. It seems to me to be an historical injustice if one puts forth the mechanistically conceived nature as complete in what it accomplishes while attacking it, on the other hand, as one-sided in its tendency. Following that tendency, the trains of thought looking for causes also went after the whole, the structure of the world; but, of course, like Münsterberg, one should not assume that value-free, mechanistically conceived nature was really the final act [*letzte Tat*] in the sense of that valuable purpose, that this lies incontrovertibly and conclusively before us. The nerve of Münsterberg's accounts is completely the same as that of Eucken and others. It is the battle against the

---

[11] "*Welche Auffassung der lebenden Natur ist die richtige?*" [What Construal of Animate Nature Is the Correct One?] *Aus Baltischer Geistesarbeit: Reden und Aufsätze* [From Baltic Studies: Talks and Essays], Riga: Jonck & Poliewsky, 1908.
[12] *Mechanismus und Teleologie*, Leipzig: Reisland, 1890.
[13] *Person und Sache* [Person and Thing], Leipzig: Johann Ambrosius Barth, 1906.

mechanistic construal of the world. They place the second and the third and fourth world opposite this one world. But they thereby demonstrate nothing other than the fact that they attribute to the mechanistically conceived world a significance far greater than is coming to it. That reality is more than a system of natural objects is proven for Münsterberg by "the fact that natural science makes claims." But is it necessary to bring on such a heavy defense, to go beyond the domain of natural science altogether in order to prove that? Mechanistic explanation is today recognized everywhere to be full of holes; natural science itself already offers us different principles of explanation. "The mechanistic atomic theory cannot explain even the simplest cases of physical happening."[14] Münsterberg and adherents of the same philosophical orientation proceed completely in lockstep with modern natural science. They unite with it in the battle against mechanism. Their significance consists essentially in having elevated beyond any doubt the underivability of values, too, from a mechanistically conceived nature. Yet the inference that they have drawn from this cognition, namely, that nature is subordinate to the world of values, |29| does not seem compelling to me. From the same bit of cognition one can draw the opposite conclusion, namely, if it is apparent that values have no place in the world conceived by natural science, this demonstrates that there is something missing in the construction of this world and a new draft of the structure of the world must be attempted. This construction is then invalid not only for values but also for nature. The separation of values from nature exhibits an overestimation of the mechanistic principle, the likes of which it has only in the camps of the mechanists themselves. If we free ourselves, however, from this spell, if we may assume that cognition does not necessarily come to mean a mechanistic construction, then we can also try to locate values in the whole of a world conceived in a unified way. No longer sworn to mechanism, we no longer need to split up the plurality of experience into enormous gaps for whose unification—since the teachers of the two and four worlds also do not let go of the world's unity—enormous bandages (i.e., final values) will be necessary.

But even these bandages do not suffice, Münsterberg concedes; the world is valuable only if it maintains itself in the transition from one of its configurations to the other. The more securely, however, the equivalence of the various worlds stands fast for him, the clearer it becomes for him that the conflict cannot be removed on the basis of their own essence. We need

---

[14] John B. Stallo, *La matière et la physique modern* [Matter and Modern Physics], Paris: Alcan, 1899.

to search for the final value of the whole that produces the unity of the world once again. But can this task be fulfilled at all? One can join together what is separated—can one reconcile what is contradictory? The same human being cannot be a tiny growth on the earth's crust and at the same time the one for which nature takes the trouble so that he may live out his life in freedom. The same nature cannot be a completely different one, depending upon whether it belongs to the interconnectedness that can be understood or the one that can be known. Religion cannot resolve these contradictions; to the contrary, it only adds new contradictions to them. A miracle is not supposed to cancel the laws of nature, "since the only interconnectedness in which it has significance is not the order of nature at all, but an interconnectedness of wills instead." But both orders also intersect in the same object here. The dead as an object of nature cannot stand up and wander about. In the realm of freedom it can do so. To which realm then does it belong? |30|

Putting a plurality of values together as one should be the true test of divinity. But this concept remains a postulate that cannot be fulfilled. The divine world can put some domains of value together only at the cost of ignoring or denying the value of existence and interconnections [among things]. Restricting the value of truth leads in this way not to putting it together with other values on a higher level but instead only to its multiplication, not only to the old twofold but to a fourfold truth instead.

The attempt to maintain the unity of the world with the assumption of the equivalence of all worlds of value seems to me *prima facie* something that has to be considered a failure. The world's unity presupposes the primacy of logical value.

In spite of all the philosophical protests, the mechanistic kind of thinking has taken hold of heads with such brash ruthlessness that perhaps no reaction to it could be too radical. With Münsterberg we will greet with the greatest joy the disposition "that presses forward again from laws to ideals, from pleasure and utility to pure duties, from dead things to a free will, from the world of facts to the world of eternal values." But precisely where the heart is in play, it is mandatory for conscience to be twice as vigilant. We saw that two theses were united in Münsterberg's doctrine. He grounded the validity of all values on their constitutive sense and he traced the values themselves back to identity-connections. In our previous discussion, it was necessary for us to emphasize precisely the first of these theses, the one that appeared to us as the most characteristic and thus also the most contestable. For those who are acquainted with the author or even those who have merely read the review to the end, there is no need to say what qualities the book possesses, even apart from that thesis. While we need not explicitly refer to the excellence of its expositions in detail, it still deserves to be stressed that the *Philosophy of Values* presents the most encompassing, unified, and fecund system of values possessed by us and that its posing of the task alone—the treatment of all domains of value from the standpoint of one unified thought—already signifies a powerful impulse within the present constellation of philosophical labors. |31|

Second Part

I. Introduction

The critical consideration of Münsterberg's system has led us to the result that constitutive significance can well be ascribed to logical values but not to ethical, aesthetic, and religious values. But now the constitutive sense of these values was the recourse seized upon by those who did not want to assume the supra-individual [*überindividuelle*] validity of ethical and aesthetic values as some incomprehensible phenomenon but instead wanted to explain it on the basis of the reasons for it [*aus seinen Gründen*]. The entire elevation of ethical and aesthetic values to constitutive values sprung from the wish to justify the claim of value judgments to supra-individual validity. If we deny the possibility of constitutive principles in this domain, the question then arises anew: How do we justify value judgments' claim to validity?

Every rationalist epistemology [*Erkenntnistheorie*] is grounded on the contrast of the material and form of cognition. Because the idealistic philosophy of values based itself on the critical doctrine of cognition, it had to assign values their position in one of the two realms. On what side are values to be found? Are they like space, time, and categories, the forms by virtue of which we work on the given, or do they belong to the domain of the material of cognition, to the given itself? For modern philosophy, there is no doubt that values lie on the side of the form, that they exhibit the process of working on the given, indeed, the principle of all work done on the given, the a priori of the world.

In the first part of this work we have developed reasons why this intuition can appear unsustainable for non-logical values. Should we now attempt to assign the values to the other realm of the critical philosophy, to the domain of the material of cognition? It is typical for Münsterberg as well as for every system proceeding from Kant |32| that we hear a great deal about forms, wills, and purposes by virtue of which we form the given. But of the 'given' itself, of the world of immediate lived experience [*Erlebnis*], the raw material of all experience [*Erfahrung*], the primal ground from which four different worlds are supposed to be developed—of this world we experience virtually nothing. And we also cannot experience anything of it. For there is no reality not worked on; that is something beyond experience. It is tacitly presupposed that sensory sensations—in a state that cannot be represented, i.e., devoid of any gestalt, without a temporal or spatial arrangement—and personal drives, emotions, feelings—once again without a temporal marker—belong to this primal world.[15] Even in this realm we will not encounter value. Some aesthetic values that refer to mere sensations may perhaps still reach down into this realm below; but the great majority of aesthetic values as well as all ethical values presuppose the logically formed world. What form the presupposition of ethical and aesthetic judgments are objects [*Gegenstände*] and their manifold connections to our life of feeling, actions, and their motives that are at times quite complicated. Finally, logical values whose objects [*Objekte*] are combinations of representations likewise presuppose these very representations and the forms of their combination, i.e., a categorial processing of the 'given.'

If we thus find no space for values in the construction of the world that the rationalistic epistemology projects, we will attempt to refrain from every construction and to leave values initially there where we find them. But we find values as properties of things. By virtue of the category of substance the good and beautiful, no less than being sweet, black, or hard, are ascribed to a thing as the bearer of qualities. And the values, to be sure, are not some sort of abstract properties that we ascribe to things on the basis of comparisons and subsumptions; instead we call things 'valuable' on the basis of an 'immediate feeling that they arouse in us, just as we call them 'green,' 'sweet,' or 'hard' on the basis of an immediate

---

[15] ['Sensory sensations' is a translation of *Sinnesempfindungen*, i.e., the sensations proper to a particular sense organ as opposed to sensations more aligned with feelings [*Gefühlsempfindungen*], a distinction made by Stumpf, glossed by Landmann-Kalischer in the following section. Otherwise Landmann-Kalischer mostly but not invariably follows the convention of employing *Empfindung* for sensation and contrasting it with *Gefühl* [feeling]. See Carl Stumpf, *Über Gefühlsempfindungen* (1907), in *Carl Stumpf—Schriften zur Psychologie*, ed. Helga Sprung, Frankfurt am Main: Peter Lang, 1997: pp. 296–344).]

sense impression. Hence, values count for us as lived experiences, not as the principle by virtue of which the lived experiences [*Erlebnisse*] are formed into an experience [*Erfahrung*]. While they cannot belong to the underworld of the material of cognition since they |33| presuppose in part the world already formed, they are nonetheless placed on a par with sensations thanks to the immediacy with which they emerge in that already formed material. They form a kind of sensation of a higher order, qualities of things that are bound to other qualities of the same thing. For different qualities are not grasped together in a thing in the form of a flat surface. Each thing is an artful layer [*Geschicht*] within which a complicated system of dependencies takes place. Each representation of a thing is familiar with the contrast of essential and accidental, primary and secondary qualities. According to the mechanistic representation, the qualities of the sense of touch form the basis on which the remaining sensory properties of a thing rest. Just as these properties then are constructed on the sense of touch, so are the values. And not only the secondary qualities, even the developed representation of a thing and its connection to other things presuppose values—at least partially. They are therefore not some 'merely' subjective addition, merely an 'evaluation' that enters upon things that are complete without them. This claim is mistaken since many objects, e.g., artworks, are so little 'complete' without their 'value' that their existence can only be conceived on the basis of this quality essential to them. Values are instead properties that only appear in a thing that is complete on various sides, somewhat like the way certain phenomena (teething, growing hair, and molting) first make their appearance in the mature state of an organism.

The conjecture, therefore, is that we ascribe value to objects on the basis of feelings that they arouse in us, just as we attribute colors, odors, and so forth to them on the basis of sensations; that is to say, that we objectify feelings in the same way as we objectify sensations and with the same legitimacy or illegitimacy.

On the assumption that this standpoint is capable of being sustained, we want to attempt to determine whether it is possible from here to explain the peculiar constellation presented by the validity of value judgments: their claim to universal, unconditioned validity, and their validation that is in fact always only empirical, temporally and individually conditioned. |34|

II. On the Psychology of the Emotional Sphere

(1) Feeling's Subjectivity and Character as a State

At the outset, psychological considerations clash with the insertion of values into the world of the empirically given. Values are determined by feelings and desires, but feelings and desires are subjective in nature; indeed, they are the haven, the content of subjectivity, the occasion thanks to which, according to Wundt, the subject detaches itself from the world that was previously inseparable from it.

Now it is beyond doubt that feelings—over against the will as well as sensations—exhibit their own distinctive group of mental phenomena. Far be it from us to have any intentions of erasing this clarity finally gained in the 18th century. Yet whether feelings give notice of their uniqueness precisely by being closed off in the subjective dimension is subject to justified doubts. The inner perception that tends to be called upon here as a witness would itself first have to be investigated for its credibility.

Thus some years ago I embarked on an indirect path of investigation by testing the relationship of judgments of feeling to judgments of the senses.[16] The result was a complete parallelism of the two sorts of judgments. All the sorts of deceptions that judgments of the senses are exposed to—physical, physiological, as well as psychological deceptions—can be recognized in the case of value judgments. Feelings thus seemed to me, in terms of their immediacy, to stand completely on a par with sensory sensations, on the one hand, and with what can be evaluated and worked on, on the other.

Meanwhile, Stumpf has proposed the name 'feeling sensations' [*Gefühlsempfindungen*] for everything that was previously called a 'sensory feeling' [*sinnliches Gefühl*].[17] He did so because sensory feeling seemed to him to point to a series of properties that also apply to sensory sensations |35|. Recently, Külpe has dropped subjectivity as a criterion of feeling in general.[18] He also acknowledges that the non-localizability of feelings does not distinguish them from representations or from sensations, that sensations

---

[16] "On the Cognitive Value of Aesthetic Judgments," *Archiv für die gesamte Psychologie* V (1905), p. 263.

[17] Carl Stumpf, "Über Gefühlsempfindungen [On Sensations of Feeling]," Vortrag auf dem II. Kongreß der Gesellschaft für experimentelle Psychologie, Würzburg, Ende April, 1906. *Zeitschrift für Psychologie*, Bd. 44.

[18] "Oswald Külpe, "Zur Psychologie der Gefühle [Towards a Psychology of Feelings]," *Referat für den Genfer Internationalen Psychologenkongreß*, 1909.

exhibit polar opposites (light and heavy, hot and cold, bright and dark) just as much as feelings, that feelings are also related to an object different from them, and that sensations can also directly trigger motor reactions. And finally, doesn't a sensation display a subject's reaction to a stimulus just as much as a feeling does?

Feelings, so it has been said, are states [*Zustände*] [that consciousness finds itself in], whereas sensations and representations are contents of consciousness. But seeing is also a state, and a feeling can also be considered content. Instead of neatly dividing up the life of the soul into subjective and objective elements, into elements that have the character of states [*zuständliche*] and elements that are contents, it is more correct for us to distinguish a subjective and an objective side in every lived experience. Sensing, representing, feeling, and willing are, in each case, a mental, subjective lived experience; the sensed, represented, felt, and willed are something objective [*Objektives*] or in any case want to become as much. Rightly or wrongly, they are objectified; they are the material out of which, seeing and testing, we construct the objective world. The difference between what is characteristic of a state [*Zuständlichen*] and what is objective [*Gegenständlichen*] is, to be sure, an ultimate difference that cannot be traced back to something else. But precisely because it is so far-reaching, it cannot be connected to individual elements of consciousness. Act and content can be distinguished not only within the sphere of representation but in every mental lived experience [*psychisches Erlebnis*].

What perhaps particularly leads to the assumption of feeling's status as a state is its property of radiating, under certain circumstances, over the entire consciousness and pervading every representation and sensation. But this property does not apply to all feelings without exception and seems to be exclusively a function of intensity.

It will be objected further that it is feelings' indirect connection to their objects that characterizes them as states. Feelings are connected to causes, sensations |36| are immediately transposed to the place that stirred them [*Erregungsstelle*]; one is delighted about something, but one sees something.

To this objection, what needs to be said is that the way of construing the form in which feelings and sensations are connected to stimuli is dependent upon the philosophical interpretation. For Schopenhauer sense impressions are transferred, by virtue of an unconscious causal inference, from their effect in consciousness to their cause in space. So, too, the assumption that feelings are connected to their stimuli as to their causes proceeded from the pre-conceived belief that each is a state [that consciousness finds itself in]. But if we examine the facts of consciousness, we find that an entire series of feelings are transposed to the place where they are stirred no less immediately than colors or odors are, and that the consciousness of these places as simultaneously the causes of feelings and sensations springs here, as it does there, only from a subsequent reflection, an act of knowing. We judge immediately '*this is* beautiful, disgraceful, ugly, good' just as we judge 'this is blue, salty, smooth, and so forth.' Hence, the notion that a feeling is merely a state cannot be proven by referring to the feeling's indirect connection to the object since this indirect connection is itself merely a theory based on [the supposition that] feelings are states. What lent this theory so much plausibility is the fact that it is indeed valid for a determinate domain of the life of feeling. Our next task is to separate this domain from pure feelings.

(2) Connection of Feelings to the I; Emotions

Don't feelings stand in a much closer relationship to the I than sensations do? Don't they precisely characterize the subject? And are they incapable, precisely for this reason, of asserting something about the object [*Objekt*] to which they refer?

This question certainly deserves to be affirmed for a part of the sphere of emotions. It is clear that only the *pure* feelings that are immediately connected to objects [*Gegenstände*] can acquire objectivity [*Objektivität*] and reveal properties of things. These 'pure' feelings [*Gefühle*] are to be distinguished from those that are grounded on the relation of objects [*Objekte*] to the subject, that is, from emotions [*Affekten*].

We come here to the old distinction of disinterested |37| gratification from any 'interested' consideration. A judgment about a thing's *being* in relation to one's own being is constantly the presupposition, the stimulus, if it is a matter of an emotion.[19] A disgraceful action, as long as it is considered purely as such, arouses a disliking [of it]: a pure feeling that, once objectified, grounds the action's disvalue. The same action stirs up hate, revenge, rage, i.e., emotions, as soon as it is considered an assault on my rights, on my life, or on whoever is close to me. Compassion is likewise an emotion that refers to the connection

---

[19] In this way both Meinong and Stumpf characterize the "movements of the mind" (value-feelings) as "judgments of feeling" in contrast to pure feelings ("feelings of representations").

or similarity with me of the human being who suffers and to the *reality* of his suffering. The presupposition of the emotion is thus the relation of an object [*Objekt*] to the subject; the emotion is the felt [or feeling befitting: *gefühlsmäßige*] expression of this connection.

Given this characterization, it is clear that the emotion can convey no cognition of the object but instead only about its connection to the subject. Since the I is an essential condition of the emotion's emergence, it is conjoined with the I in the closest possible way. In the disinterested feeling, by contrast, it is a psychological fact that all judging, all knowledge of being and non-being, of the I and what is not I, is suspended and the feeling latches onto the represented object itself. Thus it is characteristic not of the I but of the object. To be sure, every stirring in the soul exhibits a reaction of the subject to an object. But in sensation and in the 'pure feeling,' this connection is *created* since marks of the object are taken up by the subject; in emotion, by contrast, the connection of the object to the subject forms the content, the presupposition of what is happening in the soul.

Hence, what has been asserted of feelings simply, their character of being states and their subjectivity, can only be legitimately asserted of emotions but not of pure feelings.

Now, indeed, there can be no doubt that for emotions, too, it is possible to find a law-governed character [in them]. What is pleasurable or not through its connection to human needs |38| is also designated—indeed, *only* this is explicitly designated by some—as a value or a good and a system of these values can also be drawn up.

For all intents and purposes, ancient ethics, taken as a whole, set out for such a system. Döring has recently made a deliberately methodical and well thought through attempt in this direction.[20] "The doctrine of goods—on the elementary level—is the science of the values or goods holding for all, i.e., the core concept of all universally valid, singular value judgments;—on the level that brings everything together, it is the science of all the value resulting from these elements, holding for all; that is to say, it is the science of all the value of the relationships making up human life or fate, i.e., the science of the possibility of happiness, the universal value-judgment" (p. 7). Döring uses a far-reaching measure of universal validity for the value-determinations holding for the individual. "Certainly, the judgments of popular consciousness in

---

[20] August Döring, *Philosophische Güterlehre* [Philosophical Doctrine of Goods], Berlin: R. Gaetner, 1888.

regard to individual goods are sporadic, unmethodical, incomplete, and contradictory, but to bring these value judgments of popular reflection into view, to free them from their fluctuations and contradictions, and to elevate them to scientific validity through a methodical, deliberate, controllable procedure is precisely the task of the doctrine of goods" (p. 8).[21]

In contrast to this attempt to put the chaos of human desires into the form a scientific system, our own attempt |39| to demonstrate the possibility of objective validity merely for the pure values appears shamefully modest. Still, as audacious as the execution of such an undertaking must presently appear to us, it has to be said that the objectivity that can be secured for these personal goods, is precisely circumscribed. These goods express, as we saw, the I's connection to things; thus, they can be expressed quite universally and objectively, albeit not as determinate properties of determinate things but instead merely as a concept of a relation. The very same objective state of things, for example, the death of a human being, is a misfortune for his friends, a bit of good fortune for his enemies, and the friend will no more expect the enemy to mourn with him than the enemy will expect the friend to celebrate with him. The same political event is victory for the one party, defeat for the other. Indeed, even if I define [*bestimme*] love in a generally formal way, with Münsterberg, as the agreement of two beings [*Wesen*], this is then the objective definition of a value, but a value that always holds only for two distinct beings. For political, ethical, or aesthetic reasons, a third person can likewise see a value in this agreement but this is then just a different value, not the value of love. If, by contrast, I call an action 'good,' then every being who is capable of grasping it can feel and acknowledge this same value, and I can expect everyone to do this. Hence, the pure value can be an objective determination of an object, whereas what is emotively valued can be exhibited objectively only in relation to a subject.[22]

---

[21] The analogy of value judgment with judgments of the senses has also occurred to Döring: "The primitive impression, the individual sensation corresponds in the theoretical domain to the feeling as a value-judgment. Through the ordering activity of unconscious, theoretical thinking, the individual sensation joins together [with others to form] constant intuitions or individual representations and, further, representations of types and universal representations, yet without any systematic completeness. Just as the individual sensation does this, so popular reflection in the domain of value judgments produces the representation of constant individual goods and coherent complexes of goods but without a fixed, systematic resolution. And just as the thinking schooled by logical rules is first in a position to bring the entire sum of representations into a conclusive, systematic order, so the entirety of value judgments first achieves completeness, making up a systematic unity, in the elementary doctrine of goods" (ibid., p. 9).

[22] Döring overlooks this distinction when he also grounds the pure values on needs and places these—for example, the soul's sensory need to occupy itself, the need that is supposed to ground the pleasure taken in the beautiful—on a par with all other needs.

If one keeps this distinction in view, construing objective value judgments as developing from immediate feeling judgments loses the look of a paradox. From personal pleasure and displeasure, we can never climb up to unconditioned values; such is Münsterberg's contention. Münsterberg and others are concerned with purging ethical norms of self-centered [*selbstisch*] motives; they say that a willing that is determined by physiological-psychological conjunctions, by calculations of pleasure and displeasure, by the power of the stronger, by the utility for everyone or something else of this sort ultimately |40| does not go back to a norm that, as the inner fact attests, is removed from everything personal, from every pleasure-displeasure [calculation]. But precisely this purity of the ethical norm, the removal of the will, something not determined by desire at all is much more likely to be encountered in simply finding something pleasing than in that action of the I invented by Fichte, devised artificially and explicitly for this purpose as it is. Münsterberg discusses in passing the view that the subjective evaluation may transpose values from out of oneself into a sphere beyond oneself. "Objective nature is constructed from our own sensations in precisely this way." But pure values, in his view, could not be only projections of personal desires, they could not be merely what is unqualifiedly agreeable, useful, consoling. Ethical action is in itself valuable without regard for enhancing happiness. But, then, as he himself concedes (MPV, 447), freeing feelings up from our contingent I never means the cancelation of the connection to the I altogether. "To the contrary, the value was a value for personalities [*Persönlichkeiten*] generally, only not for these and those but instead necessarily for every thinkable personality." The values are given in a [place] beyond experiences "that acts impersonally in us ourselves as a basic force" (MPV, 452). 'In us ourselves.' Hence, within our person, as a personal feeling, there must still be a sphere that is independent of the particularity of the individual, of its desires and inclinations, and that exhibits a pure reaction of feeling to a stimulus. What is valued purely by finding it pleasing can be projected as a law beyond the human being, since from the very outset, already within the personality, it was cut off from their particular interests. But why shouldn't a personally felt pleasure or displeasure indicate something universal? Why turn psychology on its head instead of affirming the simple, internal fact that each human being distinguishes within himself between the individual and the universal sense of an inner action? Whereby the merely individual and the universally valid pleasure are, however, each time the same personal feeling. Just as thinking rightly and thinking falsely is each time the thinking of a person.

"Every psychological state"—so we must acknowledge with Bergson—"mirrors the entire personality by the fact that it belongs to a person. There is no sensation, even if it were |41| the simplest sensation, that would not virtually include the past and present of the entity that feels it."[23] If the simplest sensation is thus a personal sensation and its connection to the object can nonetheless be objectively valid, then personal feeling must also be able to acquire universal significance.

This distinction should not be misunderstood as though we underestimated the significance that is owed to the emotional entity and the individual for the *discovery* of new values. Emotions and abnormal states of mind can unsettle the elements of the world picture in a mind so thoroughly that completely new values become visible. It is not only that the emotion has moments of a free outlook, moments in which the intensification of the entire mental state makes a person clairvoyant—as Jean Paul puts it, "at the spot where you are in the deepest despair, you are aware of every blade of grass." It is also that the object of the emotion reveals to gazes passionately directed at it completely different properties from those seen by the sober eye. Not only hate sharpens the eyes; love does, too. A unique individuality has an effect in the same direction. What sort of philosophy one has depends, of course, on what sort of human being one is. But these words do not have the frivolous sense and interconnection in which they were uttered. They do not mean that one must hold back from making an arbitrary, personal decision when one knows no way out of a theoretical dilemma. They designate instead the fact that, for the cognition of certain truths, determinate ethical or aesthetic beauties, certain characteristics appear predestined. A personality is so little a hindrance to establishing pure values that the discovery of new values far more often proceeds only from great and unique personalities. But all this is not to be understood as though it is the individual in us that cognizes pure values. All this is instead only the condition, the psychological presupposition of pure valuation, the material so to speak that is presented by the person to the suprapersonal eye of our soul. |42|

(3) Dependency of Feeling on the Individual and the Moment
But now, according to the most widespread representation of things, feeling is bound not only generally to the subject in contrast to the object

---

[23] Henri Bergson, *Einführung in die Metaphysik* [Introduction to Metaphysics], Jena: E. Dietrichs, 1909, p. 15.

but specifically to the individual I. It allegedly characterizes not only human beings instead of things [*Sachen*] but the peculiarities of one human being in relationship to other human beings. And ultimately it is also allegedly still dependent to a high degree on the momentary state of the subject to a high degree. On this view feeling can be directly characterized as a reaction of the I in the moment to a stimulus.

"In the course of the periodic functions of the organism, the same outer behavior is possible: activity or inactivity, sometimes intensively pleasurable, sometimes not pleasurable." . . . "Under the same outer circumstances, the same sensory impression is one time pleasurable, another time indifferent, a third time absolutely repugnant." "In addition to the properties of the objective causes initially occasioning them," feelings "are co-determined by the respective state of the organism and its functions."[24]

Do these sentences really express a characteristic property of feelings? Is it really the case that these relationships have only a "weak analogy" to the phenomenon of adaptation in the domain of sensing by the senses [*sinnliches Empfinden*]? It seems to me that one can claim what is said word for word for sensations, too. "Under the same outer circumstances, the same temperature is one time warm, another time indifferent, a third time quite cold."

Sensation is dependent upon the make-up of the organ taking it up, just as the feeling is. One can speak here at most of a gradual difference but in no way of an intrinsic difference. One need only recall after-images and phenomenal contrasts for every organ of sense. The general state of the subject also further influences not only the degree, sharpness, and number of sensations but also their quality as is shown by abnormalities of sight, taste, and temperature of those ill with a fever. And, |43| finally, representations can also influence the sensation. We hear what we expected to hear. In spite of all these phenomena, one does not hold sensations to be hopelessly subjective but instead concedes without further ado that one can abstract from these conditions of the moment and, in spite of them, can arrive at objectively valid judgments. So, too, then, the reaction to a feeling, a reaction conditioned by the momentary state of the subject, will also not be completely at the mercy of the moment. We will also be able to attain a normality value here. After all, we tend often to suspend an ethical or aesthetic judgment, when we are moved by the fact that we would have been able to evaluate the object only in this or that

---

[24] Hermann Ebbinghaus, *Grundzüge der Psychologie* [Basic Features of Psychology], Leipzig: Veit & Comp., 1902, pp. 541, 549.

emotionally influenced state or in a state influenced by unfavorable points of comparison.

The claim that feeling reveals individual differences among human beings seems more important. But then there can likewise be no doubt about the individual differences in *sensations*. What differences could be greater than those differences between the sensations of a composer listening to a symphony and those of a completely unmusical person doing the same? In spite of these immense individual differences, objectively valid judgments about sounds have become possible and, to be sure, by the fact that one has produced exact scales of stimuli that one could use as an objective measure to test the value of individual judgments. Far from sensations having been banned, with a sympathetic shrug, into the sphere of the merely-subjective on account of the individual differences, those differences have come to signify far more the task (for the psychology of the senses) of first ascertaining the law-governed connections between stimulus and sensation. The same must then be possible for feelings as well. The fact that we dwell on the individual differences in feelings' reactions proves nothing else than that the discovery of the objective law-governed character is long overdue here.

Are we really supposed to stand pat with the frivolous proposition 'there can be no dispute about taste'? It is a matter of the most ardent seriousness and the best that there is in a human being that he can be worked up about this. We tend today to smile about the quarrels that differences in valuation have called up between individuals as well as peoples. But as false as someone's |44| valuations may be, as clumsy as his possibilities of mounting a proof may be, the human instinct that says to him that it is possible to ascertain a truth about these matters is just as right. After all, isn't he learning everyday himself? Doesn't everyone experience in his life how his value judgments develop and doesn't he constantly deem the later judgment to be the more correct one? Are we seriously supposed to assume that a judgment that condemns the Straßburg cathedral as a work of barbaric ornateness has objectively as much justification as another judgment that devoutly reveres this cathedral as a miracle of beauty? Should it even be possible for our ethical and aesthetic conscience to content itself with this, our logical conscience would not permit beauty and ugliness to be ascribed simultaneously to the same object or goodness and badness to be ascribed to the same action. As a matter of fact, the current dispute everywhere about aesthetic taste, about the 'right' ethical feeling, proves that human instinct here demands an objectivity as emphatically as it does for sensory phenomena [*Sinneserscheinungen*]. And even for logical values, moreover, this objectivity is achieved and expounded even though individual differences in logical cognition (at least in relation to detail and clarity) cannot easily be thought to be greater than they are.

In a subsequent section[25] we will cite the causes that are responsible for the fact that human beings' ethical and aesthetic judgments seem to agree with one another so much less than the judgments of the senses. But it is precisely the historian who is cognizant that the allegedly unfathomable [*unübersehbar*] manifold of personal intuitions regarding art is more of a phantom than a fact.[26] Moreover, only the view in our time that is concentrated with passionate interest on individuals and on everything individual could lose sight of the clear lines that describe the development of judgments of taste, the enormous uniformities and sorts of law-governed character that prevail here.

(4) Reproducibility of Feelings

Another distinguishing mark that is supposed to be proper to feelings and to limit their significance to the subject and to the moment |45| is this, that feelings do not leave behind any residues in representation and they could not be reproduced.[27]

First, concerning the residues in representation, we must, it seems to me, also assume for feelings what is in keeping with the analogy of every physical as well as mental event. There is nothing that, once having happened, would not leave behind traces. (*Rein ne se perd avec Dieu*.[28]) The facts of educating and habituating feelings also speak for this. Similar to what happens in the life of representations, a facilitating link seems to be implemented in the case of feelings in the sense that once a feeling has been experienced it enters in more easily, *ceteris paribus*, than a feeling not yet awakened. A habit, a predisposition to certain feelings is created, an attitude, an accentuation. Only in this way, it seems to me, are the modes of feeling that emerge in history explicable. Every sphere of culture creates a certain *convenu* [agreement] in regard to those feelings that, of all possible feelings, are given preference as the feelings that ought to be brought to consciousness and cultivated. For the Greeks in the Classical Period, the desire for perfection was such a

---

[25] See III, (2) The task of sciences of value.
[26] Kurt Breysig, *Kulturgeschichte der Neuzeit* [History of Modern Culture], Berlin: Bondi, 1901, Band I, pp. 115ff.
[27] See Külpe, "Zur Psychologie der Gefühle."
[28] ["Nothing is lost with God."]

dominating emotion that Aristotle was able to base God's relationship to the world on it (κινεῖ ἐρωτώμενος[29]). Christianity brought the orgy of compassion, love, and suffering and the stone steps of churches were hollowed out by the tears that nuns poured out for Christ's passion. In 18th century France, cheeriness was the fashionable emotion to such a degree that one even went to one's death with a smile on one's lips. Rousseau, the mood of an Ossian, the fever of a Werther—all brought with them an orientation to a new sentimental feeling, and so forth.

Now whether the arousal of a residuum in a representation, a residuum that we must also assume for feelings, yields a reproduction or an actualization of the feeling, depends, it seems to me, upon the extent to which the reproducing elements are similar to the stimuli that first called forth that feeling.

The question has been discussed repeatedly in recent times, as much in psychology as in aesthetics. The view that seems to be generally accepted consists in the fact that non-reproducibility distinguishes feelings from |46| sensations, but that this non-reproducibility is ascribed not to feelings alone but to all centrally aroused phenomena. Everything centrally aroused is not reproduced but instead actualized.[30]

Should one take this separation as an ultimate factum? Should one make a particular place for sensations opposite the entire rest of the psyche? It is not difficult, I believe, to derive from the nature of the phenomena themselves

---

[29] [Landmann-Kalischer may be citing, a bit incorrectly, *Metaphysics* Lambda, ch. 7, 1072b: κινεῖ δὴ ὡς ἐρώμενον: "it moves by being loved."]

[30] Arthur Wreschner, *Die Reproduktion und Assoziation von Vorstellungen* [The Reproduction and Association of Representations], Leipzig: Barth, 1907, p. 9: "The concept of 'representation' ought to be limited to those traces of earlier sensations or perceptions that have become conscious again." Ibid., p. 10: "It matters only for a secure distinction between the world of perceptions and of representations; within the processes that are only centrally aroused, such a distinction loses its meaning or acquires a completely different sense." Wreschner comes to this clear and decisive standpoint because he sees the only secure—objective—mark of differentiation between the actual lived experience and its representation in the presence or the lack of the outer cause or peripheral arousal. But his mark still seems to me to be the solely secure and objective one only when one already is starting out from the relationship of the sense impression to the representation. If one starts from the soul as a unity, the peripheral arousal is only the particular form in which the adequate stimulus appears for sensations. Even for feelings, their adequate cause can be given, only with the proviso that this is then no outer cause but instead is to be sought in something mental, in judgments, representations, or sensations.

I also cannot accept the other argument that Wreschner cites against represented feelings. The content of a representation cannot be qualitatively contrasted with that of the perception corresponding to it, and, when we remember with joy a suffering that we have withstood, were this joy really then the content of the representation, then we would not be able to see any represented feeling in this memory. But this joy is still not the content of the representation! It is far more the completely current, present feeling that has as its presupposition the representation of the earlier suffering and its contrast with the present, better condition. The representation of the earlier suffering is the occasion of a new feeling that now enters alongside that represented feeling.

the operative differences here, differences that are not by any means to be covered over, while construing the soul in a completely unified way.

As for what concerns representation first, it is necessary to say that every representation tends toward actualization [*Aktualisierung*]. There is no thought that does not want to find words, no representation of movement that does not yearn to become an actual movement. It is doubtful whether a rigid, qualitative opposition can still be upheld at all, whether one |47| would not be able to define representations in general as tendencies to actualization. The profound, ultimate difference that obtains between representation and sensation in terms of their content should not be diminished or denied. But beyond this declaration of the facts of the matter we can get clear about their interconnectedness and significance. And here we must register the following point: everything mental leaves behind a residuum in a representation. Every reproduction is a tendency to the renewal of something earlier. But now this renewal can only take place where the relevant phenomenon can be centrally aroused. It is clear that what is aroused peripherally cannot be re-actualized through an arousal of the residuum in a representation. Hence, in contrast to sensations, the residuum here must come to have a life of its own. That this is, however, an exceptional state—a state that does not persist in itself but indicates instead only an unstable balance—emerges from the fact that a merely imagined pain burns no less than one peripherally occasioned, that in the case of a strongly developed capacity of representation the representation in fact passes over into sensation in the form of a hallucination and illusion, or that, where this is not possible, the human being with his own hands goes about portraying what he carries in himself as a representation, portraying it through the work of his hands so that it may be actualized. Everyone who leads an intensive life of representations will be able to testify to the compulsion for realization that every lively representation bears in itself. For art and literary composition there is psychologically no more decisive cause of its emergence. The possibility of realization is so decisive for the representation that it has been claimed at times that every reproduction of sensations happens only through the kinetic sensations attached to them. A sound, for example, could only be reproduced in the key in which it would, of course, still be singular while in each case, for the reproduction of sounds, the muscle sensations of the larynx or the neural impulses [*Innervationen*] for these movements played a decisive role.

Representations are thus not copies of sensations; in terms of quality, content, and so forth they must be characterized as self-sufficient formations of their own. Viewed from the standpoint of the entire organization of the psyche, however, they must be characterized as unstable formations, having emerged from the unique constellation such that residues of representations of sensations, on account of their peripheral |48| emergence, cannot be re-actualized like those of all other mental contents.

If the renewal of *sensation*, on the one hand, has the tendency to actualize the same sensation, the renewal of *feeling*, on the other, cannot invariably be regarded as an actualization. Certainly, the difference stands fast: while the stimuli that produced the *sensations* cannot be reproduced centrally, it is, by contrast, at least thinkable that the same or similar representations that called forth the feeling are reproduced in consciousness. In this case the feeling is actualized. And not only in this abnormally favorable case but even otherwise, representations (the present psyche's state of consciousness [*Bewußtseinslage der heutigen Psyche*]), regardless of how removed those representations may be from an earlier state, nonetheless have that very similarity with one another that representations have among themselves in general. Thus, one is perhaps right in a way to find in every reproduction of a feeling a progressively weaker degree of actualization. The degree of reanimation of feelings depends, however, precisely on the degree to which its presuppositions are repeated. If feelings directly latch on to sensations, they participate in the non-actualizability of these sensations. The more purely a sensation was what exhibited the stimulus of the feeling, the weaker the reanimation of the feeling. This explains the familiar experience that acute bodily pains are so easily and completely forgotten. And conversely, if within the complex of perception preference goes to the element of representation that the feeling is attached to, it [the feeling] is able to be re-actualized to the degree to which those representations can be centrally aroused again. So, too, for the formal elements of a visual impression that one can make clear to oneself conceptually or can envision through mimetic movement, the course of a melody, sequences of harmony in a musical piece. The shattering character of a shattering event will be re-actualized as often as the representations are present again. By contrast, an emotion that is grounded on the connection of an event to the I at a given moment, cannot be re-actualized from the moment the I has become something else, from the moment time and circumstances or powerful transformations have called forth an adaptation to that event. |49| So, too, the impressions of childhood cannot be re-animated since the I has become something else.

From this it follows that if the re-animation of earlier feelings is to be conceived not in the form of reproduction but instead in that of an actualization, regardless of how feeble the latter form is, this difference of feelings in contrast to sensations is grounded on their dependence upon mental stimuli. The non-reproducibility of feelings is another name for their tertiary nature. Feelings can be actualized because and to the extent that the mental processes that form their presupposition are each time the same as or similar to one another. Sensations cannot be arbitrarily actualized since their presuppositions cannot be reproduced centrally.

Regarded in this way, the non-reproducibility of feelings cannot amount to a reason to contest the possibility of their objectification. In order to be further processed and compared with one another, it is only necessary that feelings leave behind a residuum in a representation. That the arousal of these residua mostly has an actualization of the feeling as a consequence presents itself as a consequence of their dependence upon mental stimuli and is accordingly explained by this distinguishing mark of them. With this observation we come to the final and sole characteristic feature that separates the life of feeling from that of sensation: its tertiary nature.

(5) Independence of Feelings from Peripheral Stimuli: Universality of the Stirrers of Feeling

Objectivity presupposes law-governed connections. But precisely these sorts of connections seem to be denied by the chief peculiarity of feelings. Külpe expresses the independence of feelings from the periphery in a positive, direct way as the universality of what can stir feeling [literally, the universality of the stirrers of feeling: *Gefühlserreger*]; everything that enters into our consciousness at all could elicit feelings.[31] Since, moreover, wherever several feelings work together, a resulting unified feeling arises as their effect, the connection of feelings to determinate stimuli seems to be made endlessly more difficult.

The life of feeling, however, is not the only source of our familiarity with a result that is the collective effect of several stimuli. Only a musician |50| can distinguish all the sounds and all the instruments that work together in one chord played by the orchestra. Even sensations of different domains of sense like smell, taste, and touch go together in indistinguishable unities. The sensations either fuse into a new unity or one of the elements dominates and impresses its character on all the others.

---

[31] Külpe, "Zur Psychologie der Gefühle."

In entirely the same way, the positive or negative complete impression of a personality or an artwork is determined sometimes by a single dominating impression, sometimes by many moments of pleasure and displeasure working together in a way that can be difficult to analyze. Indeed, in every artwork as in every action so many efficacious moments are joined together that any unified [*einheitlich*] judgment can only be construed as their result. But for the more practiced eye analysis is no less possible here than it is in the domain of the senses. It has happened to me that I disputed with other persons in the liveliest way about accepting or rejecting a poem, but that in the course of a more precise analysis we came to agree fully in our individual judgments about its idea, intuition, image, rhythm, resonance, and word-order. Yet the moments of pleasure provided the decisive impulse for one party's judgment as a whole, while moments of displeasure provided the decisive impulse for the other's.

The amount of things that arouse feelings can no more deter us from searching for their adequate stimuli than can the ways they co-operate and fuse with one another. Just as any content of consciousness can bring forth feelings, so, too, can the entire spatial world produce sensations of light and color. If in spite of this it was possible to orient oneself in the latter case, we want to attempt to determine whether it is not also possible in the former case.

Now one can hold fast, it seems to me, to pleasure and displeasure as the only qualities of feelings and yet distinguish different feelings. In fact, what we experience when we speak of a noble action and what we experience when we hear a Bach fugue are so *toto genere* different [generically so completely different] that it seems to be an abstraction that has been driven too far and thus is senseless to detach only one and the same feeling of pleasure as identical in both cases. Beyond being distinguished by their quality, feelings are still distinguished by other identifying marks. And here, of course, the following viewpoints are possible: |51|

(1) Mental phenomena that are qualitatively the same can nonetheless be distinguished in terms of *intensity*, *duration*, and *expanse*. By the 'expanse' of a feeling, I understand here the scope of the soul that a feeling can lay claim to, how widely and how deeply, as it were, the soil of the psyche is washed over by a wave of pleasure or displeasure. Whether a gentle titillation on the periphery forces the mouth into a smile or whether the contrast of the greatest and most rousing groups of representations calls forth side-splitting laughter.

Now since each of these criteria—intensity, duration, and expanse[32]—can be stratified only gradually, no single one of them is equipped by itself alone to make it possible to differentiate feelings of pleasure or displeasure distinctly. By contrast, characteristically different formations of feeling seem to me in fact to emerge from combinations of these inherent features. One need only envision some of the formations that afford themselves in this way: short, weak pleasure limited to a sense impression or a representation (a pleasant taste, a gift placed in view); likewise limited and short, but strong pleasure (a sudden wave of an appealing fragrance carried by the wind, succeeding with a fortunate rhyme); likewise limited and strong, lengthy pleasure (inhaling the smell of a rose, reading a suspenseful novel); extended, strong, and lengthy pleasure (the greatest forms of happiness in life); extended, strong but short pleasure (the great aesthetic enjoyments are of this sort); extended, long but weak pleasure (humble fulfillment of a duty); extended but short and weak pleasure (the glimmering of a weak shimmer of hope in a state of misery).

One sees that, according to this, qualitatively similar and yet characteristically different feelings afford themselves and feelings of displeasure can be differentiated correspondingly.

(2) The synthesis that feeling enters into with the representations it presupposes is so tight that in the classification of the presuppositions we may also be looking at a classification of feelings.

It lies in the nature of the mental stimuli that they themselves |52| form an essential component of what they stir up [*erregen*]. Since, at every moment of consciousness, all its contents are fused together in an innermost unity, what stirs up and what is stirred up cannot stand side by side as though they were alien to one another.

So, too, then, the realm of feelings has been repeatedly subdivided in terms of its presuppositions precisely by those representing pleasure and displeasure as the only qualities. Feelings of willing, feelings of value, intellectual feelings, and sensory feelings have been distinguished. And so, too, the feelings that we have our eye on here have been characterized already before and after Kant in terms of their peculiarity and their presuppositions as pure, disinterested feelings or feelings of a representation.

---

[32] These moments do not coincide with what Külpe assumes as "types of feelings"; see Külpe, "Zur Psychologie der Gefühle," p. 5.

Thus, Witasek, for example, starting out from pure pleasure and displeasure, has nonetheless divided the aesthetic domain even further.[33] Within the complex of feelings triggered by an artwork, a complex often full of contradictions, it will be possible for everyone enjoying the artwork aesthetically to distinguish the pleasure or displeasure that refers to the beauty of the gestalt, the beauty of the expression, or that of the norm. Everyone will likewise be able to distinguish from this pleasure the different pleasure that is directed at the consideration of an action or a decision of the will and those pleasures in turn that refer here to the moral force as such or to the harmonious mix of the will's tendencies or to the disposition. One may not object that all these are objective distinctions that have nothing to do with the actual diversity of feelings. The feelings that trace back to diverse stimuli are precisely the distinctive feelings that any normal human being can distinguish, resulting both from that combination of inherent features that we presented and from their fusion with the stimuli. One may always say that it is invariably only pleasure; but pleasure is nonetheless only the inherent feature that is qualitatively the same in all pleasures. The pleasure afforded by a disposition is still a different form of pleasure from the pleasure afforded by a color; the displeasure over something that goes against the norm is a displeasure different from that of a musical disharmony. One pleasure cannot take the place of another; someone who has never experienced the one has not experienced something quantitatively less but instead has not experienced something qualitatively distinctive.

If in this way, while maintaining the simple differences in quality, we succeed |53| nonetheless in distinguishing diverse forms of feeling, the assumption of the universality of the stirrers of feeling loses, I believe, the force of its argument in regard to the question that concerns us. There can be talk of universality in the strict sense only if each representation could stir up [erregen] each feeling, as is, of course, the case for the assumption of pleasures and displeasures that are qualitatively the same [respectively]. If we find, however, that each representation of a determinate sort can only stir up a determinate feeling in its concrete gestalt, then we can regard law-governed connections between feelings and the things that stir them up as possible in principle. We are then able to seek adequate and objectively determinable stimuli for pure feelings connected to objects no less than for sensations. With this conclusion, the last objection from the side of psychology to the objective significance of feelings falls to the wayside.

---

[33] [Landmann-Kalischer also discusses Witasek's aesthetics in "On the Cognitive Value of Aesthetic Judgments," pp. 270–71 and "On Artistic Truth," p. 482.]

III. Objectivity of Value Judgments

(1) Sense of Objectivity: Objectivity as a Task

Because our account is oriented to sense impressions, it also becomes clear in what sense we are able to speak of objectivity and objectification of feelings.

(1) It is not possible here for us to think of a reality that certain lived experiences would enter into consciousness, equipped with.[34] The reality that Hume ascribed to sensations in contrast to representations exists nonetheless only as a *feeling* of reality. Someone may say: "only sensations produce the matter of what we call actuality; what the sensation for its part as a mental stimulus arouses in the subject can only be of a subjective nature"—but that person might recall the synthetic character of all actuality and that even the claim of sensations to objective validity is fulfilled only if they stand in a law-governed connection to their stimuli. What makes up the objectivity of the judgment is not the "real" object to which it refers; instead the immediacy and law-governed character of the connection expressed in the judgment justify the [claim to] reality. Even if one starts out from the "first" world already shaped into reality, the validity of the *judgments of perception* is in need of universal |54| *laws*, "according to which we necessarily connect the subjective sensation to objective reality."[35] Even the qualities of touch that for a long time have counted as the basis of all objectivity owed this valid character not simply to their own peculiar make-up but to the circumstance that all other sensations can refer to them in a law-governed manner.

But the objectivity that is defined as an independence from the human being also cannot be meant here. Without aesthetic and ethical feeling certain forms would not be beautiful, certain actions would not be good; yet without eye and ear certain vibrations would be neither colors nor sounds.

And finally, the universal agreement of judgments also cannot count as objectivity; indeed, it has nothing to do with objectivity at all. The judgments of the deaf and color blind alter nothing when it comes to the objective sense of sensations of sounds and colors, and objectively false judgments enjoy the most universal agreement. As clouds draw by, in the front of the moon, the

---

[34] [In the following paragraph, all instances of 'real' and 'reality' are translations of *reale* and *Realität*, while 'actuality' is a translation of *Wirklichkeit*.]

[35] Christoph Sigwart, *Logik*, I (second edition), Freiburg: Mohr, 1889, p. 398.

sensory judgments of all human beings agree that the moon is moving more quickly than the clouds.

(2) In terms of its aim, its sense, the primary value judgment, like the primary judgment of the senses, is objective; that is to say, it contains the connection of a feeling (sense) impression to an object. To be sure, the value judgment like the judgment of perception can be articulated—as a judgment of inner perception—in a subjective form. But this is nonetheless rather the derivative, skeptical form of it. In its naive form the value judgment is not voiced as "this pleases me" but instead as "this is good" just as the child's judgment of the senses is not voiced as "I see blue here" but instead as "this is blue."

Yet this objective sense of the primary value judgment is not identical to the objectivity of its content. Like every judgment of perception, so, too, every primary value judgment *means* something objective. It asserts a perceivable property of an object and is thereby a theoretical judgment. But the objective *sense* of a judgment does not automatically make it an objectively valid judgment ("ambiguity of truth"). In order to arrive at objectively correct judgments on the basis of what is objectively meant, |55| the primary judgments need to be carefully *worked on* in a way that is often difficult and lengthy. The objectively valid values are not given; instead they have to be won [*zu gewinnen*]. We judge the truth and falsity of a combination of thoughts, its value or lack of value, on the basis of an immediate feeling, incapable of being further analyzed, an intuitive cognition; we first become aware of beauty or goodness through an immediate feeling. But the warrant for the correctness of this primary judgment of feeling is not given with the immediacy of the judgment. Subjective evidence attaches to deceptions no less than to correct judgments. The correct judgment is often only the result of working on something at length.

Many disagreements have arisen, it seems to me, from mistaking this twofold character of objectivity—the objectivity intended and the objectivity acquired or that remains to be acquired [*erworben*]. Truth is, as one party teaches, an immediate feeling that accompanies certain combinations of representations (Rickert).[36] Truth, another party teaches, is something produced in the course of experiences, much as health, wealth, and physical strength are produced (James).[37] Should truth be nothing other than a feeling

[36] Heinrich Rickert, *Der Gegenstand der Erkenntnis* [The Object of Cognition], second and improved edition, Tübingen: Mohr, 1904.
[37] William James, *Der Pragmatismus*, translated by Wilhelm Jerusalem, Leipzig: Klinghardt, 1908 [Landmann-Kalischer lists the date as "1907," perhaps citing the date given by the translator at the end of his Foreword].

of the necessity of a judgment, how then do we arrive at a system of what is true? What becomes then of a combination of representations that it would be compelling to accept today and no longer compelling to accept tomorrow? But if truth is not supposed to be an immovable property of a representation in which it inheres, if the representation first becomes true, if it is made true by events, if it is a happening, a process, and, to be sure, the process of its self-confirmation, its verification—how then is the immediate distinction of the true and the false to be explained, a distinction that is, indeed, an undeniable fact? Should a truth or untruth be given to *every* representation "on credit"? At least for representations that surface as completely novel, this is not possible.

Each of these opposed doctrines leads to contradictions. But every contradiction disappears as soon as we take up both and see in the second the natural development of the first. |56| Truth is a property of certain representations. Certainly. The sense of my assertion, when I call that judgment true, is certainly and really that this judgment has that property. But perhaps I am mistaken. Perhaps the result of testing this judgment, comparing it with others, is that I accorded it that property incorrectly. In this case the judgment first gets ahold of its truth or untruth gradually, in the process of thinking. Truth is something found in advance as a provisional assumption; as an ideal, it is something that needs to be produced. A truth can never be produced if it were not the case that every individual judgment already contained within itself a tendency towards it [truth]; we could never be certain of the intuitively grasped truth if we did not know how to produce it. The primary value judgment, like a sensory judgment, brings its evidence along with it; working over the judgment first verifies it.

Within this process of working on it, we must—again following the path indicated by sensory judgments—distinguish two stages or forms. The primary value judgment can already be corrected through comparison and experience. The ultimate warrant for its validity, however, lies only in the objective determination of its adequate stimuli.

The supreme objectivity that we want to attain and claim for values consists in the following. We want to determine what is valuable in its distinctiveness that can be expressed without the concept of value. Just as what we perceive as color cannot, to be sure, be established in its distinctiveness independently of the human being but can be so established independently of the eye, so, too, what underlies values should be expressed independently of the valuing. Ethics, logic, and aesthetics are the sciences that accomplish or are supposed to accomplish for values what optics and acoustics have already accomplished for sense impressions. They construct not only a psychology and physiology of value stances, not only something corresponding to Goethe's doctrine of colors, but something corresponding to Newton's doctrine.

The result of comparing the various judgments of feeling with one another and then ascertaining their adequate, objectively displayable stimuli is a world of norms to which immediate feelings are subordinated just as the world of sense impressions is subordinated to the world of concepts and laws. The norm is related to the individual feeling like the color numbered in the spectrum is related to the optical impression |57| that different individuals under different circumstances can get from it [the color]. What is objectively valuable and what is subjectively pleasurable do not always go hand-in-hand; indeed, they do so no more than physically determinable colors and sounds constantly agree with what is seen and heard. From the progressive comparison of countless individual judgments arises the anomaly that norm and concept, which are developed solely from the primary judgment of feeling and perception [respectively], can nonetheless come to contradict the latter. Thus, the praxis often seems to contradict the theory that is nonetheless only praxis expanded and thought to the end.[38] But if it makes good sense to speak of a correct or false seeing and hearing on the basis of physical concepts, one may also no longer reject as absurd the claim of a correct or false feeling.

Only when we become familiar with the stimuli of feelings and the scales of those stimuli in as precise a fashion as we are with those of sensations, will we be able to ascertain the actual, individual differences of feelings and the constant deceptions in regard to feelings. But then it will not be possible any more to doubt the possibility of objectively valid judgments of feeling. Just as objects have a determinate, physical weight, independent of how light or heavy they seem to one or the other person today or tomorrow, so, too, they have a determinate inner weight, an objectively determinable value, independent of how light or heavy they may be found to be by X or Y in the 9th or the 19th century.

(3) This construal of value judgments as subject to the concept of truth could be interpreted as rationalism. Yet a greater rather than a lesser significance is

---

[38] John Stuart Mill (*Die induktive Logik*, translated by Jacob Schiel, Braunschweig: Vieweg, 1849, p. 429) calls attention to the seeming paradox that a universal judgment which is derived from a particular judgment is often more certainly true than one of the particular judgments from which it is inferred by induction. He explains this paradox by the fact that each of the particular judgments contains an inference that can be false in the individual case but not in all cases.

ascribed to the irrational elements here. To be sure, logical value does not find its limitation in the other values as is the case for Windelband and Münsterberg but it finds it in the |58| lived experiences of feelings, like those of the senses, that have not yet been worked on. The rational loses its overriding position when one grants the world of the given a broader reality, when one accords it its own set of laws that the intellect merely finds and draws out.

In place of a mystical, "immediate evidence of normative universal validity" that suddenly "*springs forth*" at some point or other of consciousness, in place of a higher necessity that "*breaks through*" in the naturally necessary movements of empirical consciousness, a necessity that is in no case derived from anywhere but only shown, a necessity that cannot be produced but only brought to consciousness[39]—in place of this mystical necessity we obtain in this way a derivable and producible truth.

Strangely enough, it is conceded by some that the objective valuations in logic, aesthetics, and ethics proceed from an ideal I and are distinguished from valuations by the momentary I, by immediate feeling. But they would rather not see that the former [valuations] display the conceptual, normal development of the latter; they take refuge in the most presumptuous, metaphysical representations in order to explain the valuation by the ideal I and to explain this I itself; and they would rather not see the simple fact that feelings have been worked on and objectified or, better, corrected by countless peoples [*Geschlechter*] in a process that has been as long and painstaking for feelings as it has been for sensations.

And yet this construal of values would do justice to both: on the one hand, to the empirical manifoldness and only subjective validity of value judgments, their derivation from the mental constellation of the person valuing, their immediacy; and on the other hand, to value judgments' claim to universal validity, their objectivity. Value judgments' claim to universal validity is none other than that of all judgments of perception that intend to be more than a subjective declaration.

If it sounds strange today that the intellect is supposed to be the only judge of moral and aesthetic values no less than of logical values, it is possible that this strangeness springs only from the current constellation of philosophical orientation. But it may bring to mind one of the oldest and ever-recurring definitions of philosophy, namely, that philosophy |59| is the doctrine of the highest good "insofar as reason strives to make it into a science."

---

[39] Windelband, *Präludien*, 1903, pp. 47f.

Sensory judgments are the great exemplar that shows us the way even for the sublimest value judgments. Is it not remarkable that we doubt the objective sense of a value judgment in general because we discover contradictions and obscurities among the primary value judgments, while the corresponding facts in the domain of the senses do not lead us astray in the cognition which the senses can provide? But perhaps this different behavior corresponds to the difference in what has been attained so far. After all, even sensory cognition was discredited because of the compelling evidence that deceptions also introduced. That first source of all our cognition was scorned and disdained long before the attempt was made to render harmless the occasional murkiness of its waters. Just as the cultivation of the physical sciences slowly produced a transformation here, so, too, the cultivation of the sciences of value will free us from our radical doubt concerning value judgments. Only we may not behave then like fools and children who want an answer on the spot and with complete precision to questions that the wisest individuals of all times racked their brains over. The lung is the organ that allows us to breathe but the fact that it can also suffocate us makes it no less so. What is right for the senses should be the same fare [*billig*] for values. The objectivity of sensory judgments and value judgments is no fact but instead a demand lying in them, a task.

Fulfilling this task for ethical and aesthetic values is, of course, confronted with the difficulty that, where it is possible for them to agree with one another, they do so far less than sensory judgments do. Their presuppositions are more complicated since they are more dependent upon representations and not only upon those momentarily aroused but also upon latent masses of representations. Hence, for research directed at the objective sense of value judgments there arises as preliminary work the task of testing ethical and aesthetic judgments for their reliability, of working on the primary value judgment in such a way that its most immediate object, the adequate stimulus of the feeling, comes to light. Once the sources of deception are discerned, it will be possible, if not |60| to eliminate them, at least to have them compensate for one another or to take account of them. At this juncture I prefer not to enter into the investigation of the various forms and sources of value-deceptions, although it is of the utmost importance for the question that concerns us. Here I must refer to an earlier work in which I sought to prove in detail that the sources of value deceptions possess their exact analogue in those of sense deceptions.[40]

---

[40] See above, PV 145/34, note 16. [See Chapter 4 of "On the Cognitive Value of Aesthetic Judgments."]

Here I can only draw attention to one of the most important sources of deception, the exhibition of which at the same time methodically suggests the way science can prepare objective findings in this domain.

Every value judgment contains the connection of a feeling to an object. But precisely this connection is the source of countless errors. Even if we assume that individuals had arrived at unanimity regarding the categories, the standards of the judgment, it is still always possible for a dispute to arise as to whether these categories were connected to this or that object correctly or incorrectly. A value judgment is then incorrect because its immanent object (what is closest to it, what it means) does not agree with the factual object that it is connected to. There is no dispute regarding logical axioms from the moment that they are clearly elaborated. Contradictory judgments can nonetheless be considered true when one falsely applies the category of agreement to them; i.e., when one completely fails to perceive the contradiction contained in them. So, too, one can make ethical or aesthetic judgments without getting clear about what ethical or aesthetic stimulus in the narrower sense the judgment is directed at. Did someone who panned that picture *see* at all those inherent features that transported others into a state of ecstasy? Did someone who thought highly of that human being ever observe the small-minded envy that dictated others' low esteem of him?

Countless judgments that agree with one another in relation to the categories, the standards of judgment, part ways because these categories are falsely applied, over-generalized, or mixed up with one another. Smoothness is no doubt |61| a quality to be valued positively as a property of human skin or as sheen of wood or stone. The layperson who admires it in a statue of Canova incorrectly transfers this standard to a sculptured figure. The familiar judgments about Goethe's moral character are off base not for valuing fidelity and altruism positively and the opposite of them negatively but for claiming an absolute and exclusive validity for categories that are of course valid within a limited sphere of life. This exclusive, ethical valuation of altruism is perhaps merely the form in which human beings who are unacquainted with and do not grasp a life devoted to objective purposes, revere the human being who goes beyond himself, subordinating the personal to something else.

This is obviously connected, furthermore, to the particular energy that is the mark of sensation in contrast to all other mental contents,[41] such that

---

[41] See William James, *The Principles of Psychology*, New York: Holt, 1890, Chapter 2. [Landmann-Kalischer is likely using *Psychologie*, übersetzt von Marie Dürr, Leipzig: Quelle & Meyer, 1909.]

the most complicated masses of representation are still always connected to the sensory impression that may have quite contingently occasioned its reproduction. Whoever utters the words 'this pleases me' can be subject to the same deception as the one who, while intently eavesdropping, hears in a way that injects [*hineinhört*] all sorts of possible occurrences into a barely perceptible noise. The creaking of a floorboard can appear to us to be whispering, to be steps, someone passing through a doorway, and so forth. Many things come to have their value or lack of value in the same way as the floorboard comes to have all the possible occurrences that are supposed to be playing out on it. What is contingently present in a sensory way provides the scapegoat that is supposed to be responsible for whatever enters into our consciousness precisely as good, beautiful, or evil. Recently, the antinoise club published a rectangular, sparkling white card on which were the words, printed a little bit crookedly and in common letters, "Quiet is noble." The speculation was completely correct. The fact that the content of this sentence triggered lively sympathy among the large bulk of club members sufficed so that this tasteless form was not seen at all and this card appeared as something beautiful. It is the same process that allows countless, deplorable verses, house blessings, wax Napoleons, etc. to awaken fervor, edification, and enjoyment. |62|

Adding to this is finally the fact that all ethical and aesthetic categories designate not simply quality but also intensity. How far we are from the ideal of objectivity in this domain becomes shockingly apparent from the desperately simple language that completely fails here to express factual qualitative and gradual differences. (A scientific language can freely create here without regard for the "customary use of language.") Thus, it happens that someone accustomed to the higher degree of goodness, truth, or the expression of beauty already feels the lower degree of these categories negatively, as a deficiency precisely of these values, as non-value. And vice versa. "I know no writer of lines, the most miserable of his caste, on whose products something of the splendor of a poet does not fall for a fully unspoiled eye, for a phantasy suffocating in the aridness of a hard life, regardless of how undeserving of this splendorous light that writer may be."[42]

---

[42] Hugo von Hofmannsthal, "Der Dichter und diese Zeit," *Die Prosaschriften gesammelt*, I ["The Poet and this Age," *Collected Prose Writings*, I], [Berlin: S. Fischer], 1907, p. 19.

The objects [*Gegenstände*] of ethical and aesthetic judgments are thus so complicated that even the schooled judgment does not always succeed in singling out and recognizing the adequate stimulus that conditioned the feeling. Systematically tracing judgments of feeling back to their immanent objects [*Objekte*] will thus make it possible to bring numerous [otherwise] contradictory judgments into agreement with one another.

(2) The Task of Sciences of Value

(1) There are two contrasting ways of construing the object [*Gegenstand*] of logic, ethics, and aesthetics. One way sees in them a branch of psychology whose task would be to describe what is; the other way sees in them normative sciences whose task would be to determine what ought to be. From the concept of objectivity as we developed it in the preceding chapter, it follows that in the sciences of value we are looking at neither sciences of thinking, feeling, and acting nor even sciences of how, in view of some higher purpose, one is supposed to think, feel, or act. Instead we have to determine logic, ethics, and aesthetics very simply as sciences of the true, good, and beautiful. Psychology would accordingly be merely the presupposition, |63| merely the preparation for these objective sciences; normative science would be merely the consequence, merely the application of them.

It is beyond doubt that there can be sciences of thinking and acting which describe and explain this thinking and acting, completely independent of whether it is correct, whether it is good. Indeed, a purely phenomenological treatment of thinking or acting would be conceivable to the degree that it could determine precisely in advance which actions under given circumstances will be performed, which thoughts will be thought (Mill's ethology). In contrast to this approach, we first have to establish that it is not actual thinking, acting, and feeling but instead only the thinking, acting, and feeling that is deemed valuable that can possibly matter for the sciences of value. The immediate objects of these sciences are stances toward values [*Werthaltungen*] and their expression: value judgments.[43]

But now none of the sciences mentioned has *de facto* stood pat with the psychology of value stances. From the comparison of value judgments with

---

[43] Segal has, in my opinion, rightly emphasized, against Jonas Cohn, that the respective objects of the sciences of value do not suffice to make them normative sciences; Jakob Segal, "Psychologische und normative Ästhetik" [Psychological and Normative Aesthetics], *Zeitschrift für Ästhetik und allgemeine Kunstwissenschaft* 2 (1907): pp. 1–24. On the norm character, the authoritative validation already of the value primarily posited, see pp. 92f below.

one another and from the examination of everything individually deemed good, beautiful, and true, each has sought instead to determine those actions, objects, and combinations of representations that underlie all the individual, positive value stances and that could thereby be designated as the adequate stimuli of feelings. Logic comes to its determinations through consideration not only of thinking but also of all the sciences' manners of proceeding; aesthetics investigates not only aesthetic feeling but also artworks; ethics considers not only the motives of the will but also right and custom.

Acoustics sets up a system of sounds, on which every individual instance of hearing can be measured. Similarly, logic, ethics, and aesthetics seek to set up the system of the true, the good, and the beautiful respectively, towards which individual logical, ethical, and aesthetic judgments can orient themselves. Now, to be sure, this system is a norm insofar as it is the rule "that is valid for certain phenomena without the latter actually [*wirklich*] following the rule in all cases," |64| but it is not a norm that makes demands. It is instead one that articulates the general essence of the phenomenon. The universality and necessity that pertain to objective values is no particular, normative universality and necessity; instead it is the sort of universality and necessity that each law has opposite all individual phenomena from which it is derived. Windelband, Sigwart, and others have derived the norm deductively from purposes that stand fast a priori. The objective values, by contrast, are supposed to be derived, according to the general laws of scientific procedure, from the value stances empirically at hand.[44] Norms stand opposite the actual individual value stances, independent of them and providing them direction. So, certainly, do objective values. But while the norm is opposed to the reality, the objective value contains only the innermost reality of valuing.[45] The sciences of value have fulfilled their task when they succeed in providing a picture of the objective sense of values that would be as unified as the physicist's picture of nature. What results from these sciences, the fruitfulness that practical life can experience through them, is for them just as much a secondary consequence

---

[44] On the objections that Husserl has raised against any derivation of the norm, see pp. 75f below.

[45] I register the agreement of what has been presented here with C. F. S. Schiller's "axioms as postulates" in *Personal Idealism*, edited by Henry Sturt, London: Macmillan, 1902, p. 124: "The ideals of normative science must be developed out of the facts of descriptive science... the logical account of postulation is an idealised version of the course of actual postulating. But for this very reason it has a guiding power over the actual processes, which the fancy processes of an abstracted logic, legislating vainly in the void, can never claim."

and application as technology is for natural science. For it is not the law but the cognition of the law that can be, as Husserl emphasizes, the power determining our thinking or acting.[46]

(2) The possibility of thinking of objective values developing from immediate judgments of feeling, what are at first perhaps individually conditioned judgments, is cut off from the outset when, in a rigid dualism, one sets up a contrast between *natural law* and *normative force*. From the psychologically unmistakable difference between "natural" thinking and thinking determined by a purpose, Windelband infers two |65| laws that are inimical to one another: "No natural law compels a human being always to think, will, and feel just as he is supposed to think, will, and feel according to logical, ethical, and aesthetic necessity!" (Windelband, *Präludien* I, 44). The natural law is subject to the normative force. We have three criticisms of the introduction of this contrast:

(a) This contrast is directed at a rift that does not in fact exist.
(b) This contrast displaces the point of departure of the sciences of value.
(c) This contrast places in opposition to nature a norm that cannot directly have an effect on it at all.

(a) As illuminating as Windelband's explanations appear, insofar as they explain the difference between two laws, they are powerless, it seems to me, to prove what they want to prove, namely, that different worlds are expressed in these two laws, that only the one is nature, but the other a norm. The thought here seems to me to shoot past its target. To be sure, with a norm a new law sets in. But must it be on another star? Is it not possible for two spheres of nature to meet here together?

One tears open this rift between nature and value because nature behaves indifferently or inimically toward our positings of value. But this behavior is merely a particular expression of the completely universal, mutually hostile relationship that obtains between nature and the human being in general. By taking control of plants and animals for his purposes, a human being behaves toward the inner will of these organisms with just as little consideration and understanding as these behave towards him. Just as we regulate streams,

---

[46] Edmund Husserl, *Logische Untersuchungen* [Logical Investigations], Halle: Niemeyer, 1900, p. 66.

so streams at times also regulate our irregular settlements. Boring a tunnel through a mountain is no slighter assault on nature than an earthquake is on the world of human beings.

Furthermore, this indifference of the one law of life towards the other is found not only in the human being's relationship to nature but also within nature beyond the human realm no less than within values. An earthquake does not only destroy human values; it destroys the germinating seeds, the trees ripening with fruit no less. A flood breaks into the country |66| and challenges its place on the earth's surface. The sun's glow that produces organic life can also make it wither. The caterpillar must come to an end, if the butterfly is to develop. And is it otherwise within values? The moral law and the desire for happiness, sensual happiness and peace of soul must battle one another again and again. Christian fervor destroyed the works of ancient beauty; and not only can aesthetic, ethical, and religious values unfold in ways that are alien to one another or come into hostile contact with one another; even within the same domain of value, different values necessarily come into conflict with one another. Love of neighbor is a virtue but being stern with oneself and others is no less a virtue. Conformity to a norm is beautiful but the passionate expression that destroys it is no less beautiful. "In vitium ducit culpae fuga...."[47]

Since everything in nature is battling one another, why precisely should values be in harmony with the other spheres of nature? What needs to be stressed, it seems to me, is not that what runs counter to norms springs from our essence just as necessarily as what conforms to norms, but instead that, as the Stoics taught, what conforms to norms lies as much within our essence as what runs counter to norms, that it is just as much nature. For Windelband, Eucken, and others, this antinomy-like co-existence of the norm and what runs counter to it in the same consciousness presents the problem of all problems. But it emerges in a readily conceivable manner, it seems to me, from the complicated state of organic essences and human essences in particular in which diverse spheres of nature intersect. In regard to ethics, Marie Luise Enckendorff has recently expounded the thought that what we ought to do is itself a law of our being, that what we ought to do is a law of nature no less than the sap that pushes upward in a tree and that is not, therefore, other than nature because it works, of course,

---

[47] [Horace, *Ars poetica*, l. 31: "The flight from one fault [*culpae*] may lead to another [*vitium*]."]

against the law of inorganic nature, the weight of the masses [making up the tree].[48]

Thus, one not need transpose the different values, on account of their often hostile relationship to one another, into metaphysically different worlds and this is also no less necessary when it comes to the difference between nature and value. Even more: it is not permissible. For the roots |67| of norms can be tracked down to the realm of nature and the roots of something natural can lie in a norm. Anyone who sets altruism up as an ethical law must concede that it is already placed in the human being as a drive. On the other side, the most subtle demands of the moral law have become nature in the beautiful soul. The thinking that consciously subjects itself to the norm of what is correct stands under the sway of the same law that already acts as a "hidden inference" in the simplest judgment of perception. The logical law of nature acts in turn in cultivated thinking. Graceful movement can be natural and learned movement can become "second" nature. If the one can in this way pass over into the other, then they must have more kinship with one another than an a priori form and an empirical given can have.

But is the dignity of values thereby undermined? Are they robbed of the authority of the power that they exercise on our life? Is this dignity better preserved by making values the condition of all reality and making nature into a subordinate, partial domain of value or by conceiving value as reality, as nature itself? Construing value in the latter way gives it all the power of a force of nature and, furthermore, the sort of power that could prevail over all others. The tyranny of a value sets itself up in us as a force of nature against nature. To be sure, one thus perhaps removes the invincibility of the individual norm. It no longer dominates by God's graces; instead it does so by virtue of its own inner power. Since one may put its power to the test anew and confront it with new forces—we cannot wish for anything better than this for the best norm to prevail, the one best suited to the respective human condition. While the rigid opposition of nature and norm ultimately leaves the development of norms as something incomprehensible, the other construal takes it up into the flow of natural development. The content of the norms must then develop just like that of all other forms of theoretical cognition.

(b) This contrast appears to us to be not only drawn too deeply but also extended too far. Between natural thinking and true thinking lies the sort

---

[48] Marie Louise Enckendorff, *Vom Sein und Haben der Seele* [On What the Soul Is and Has], Leipzig: Dunker & Humblot, 1906. [Marie Louise Enckendorff is the pseudonym of Gertrud Simmel (née Kinel).]

of thinking that is, to be sure, acquainted with the concept of truth but deficient in it. What matters is |68| contrasting the "idea" of the true with what is held to be true, but not with thinking that does not seek the true at all. Feeling spontaneously tells us at every moment how we should think, how we should act. But whether it tells us what is right, this is what ethics and logics are supposed to examine. The contrast that matters for the sciences of value can be neither the contrast between natural law and normative law as Windelband conceives it nor that between natural law and ideal law as Husserl conceives it ('ideal law' in the sense of a lawfulness grounded purely in concepts, not empirical). Instead what matters is the contrast between the natural law of the thinking that is striving for the value and the natural law of the values themselves. Every science is accustomed to presupposing the object with which it concerns itself, taking it up as given. It is not part of geometry's subject matter to speculate about the emergence of space and it is not part of psychology's subject matter to speculate about the emergence of the soul.

So, too, in my opinion, the sciences of value should start from the fact of value as something given to them and make it their task solely to determine it objectively and more precisely. I say 'should' but they have in fact constantly done this. Only the more modern, psychologizing consideration has pressed the questions of the origin of the ethical, aesthetic, and religious feeling into the foreground. For logic it was always epistemology that worked on the question of the sense and origin of the concept of truth. But it is clear that questions of empiricism, apriorism, and so forth lie beyond the framework of logic and ethics as sciences of the true and the ethical, respectively. They lie outside them just as speculations about the emergence of the organs of sense lie outside the psychology, physiology, and physics of sounds. If we want to gather what is objectively true and ethical from what is empirically held to be true and ethical, this does not touch the question of how we come to consider something true or ethical at all; thus it does not decide whether and in what sense absolute validity [*Geltung*] can be coming to what objectively holds [*Geltenden*]. Whether the axioms are impressed on our mind by experience, whether they belong to the inveterately persisting structure of our mind, whether they spring from a need of our nature, whether they are applied experimentally |69| and only elevated after a while from postulates to the rank of axioms—these questions reach back to the emergence of perception itself, to the problem of how we come to hold anything at all to be true or ethical. They have no bearing on the fact in which we see the point of departure for the sciences of value, the fact that we find truth and ethics from the outset as a property of certain sentences and actions. This fact does not, for example, contradict an empiricist or humanistic construal of axioms as postulates. The entire sensory organization of our soul can be construed as a product of development; it can be construed as a question that we put to nature. "Not only our delusions but also our perceptions depend on what we come prepared to perceive" (Schiller, *Personal Idealism*, 63n). But none of these are strictly *logical* questions, ethical questions.

(3) While no theoretical cognition is completely fruitless for our action, it is especially the sciences of value that will stand in a particularly close relationship to praxis, since the realization of values is a necessary goal of our striving.[49] Every cognition of a value can become a prescription but it nevertheless comes to have this prescriptive character only indirectly, mediated by a mental mechanism as a consequence of which we necessarily seek every value and flee every non-value.

Thinking in the ethical domain should—according to Sigwart—"investigate how we should act so that we act well and in the consciousness of objective necessity."[50] Logic [in his view] should likewise say how we must think so that we think in a true and universal manner with consciousness of objective necessity. These demands, it seems to me, overreach since they cannot be fulfilled. Someone can indeed indicate to us the means that lead to our ends [*Zwecke*] but a prescription of how one is supposed to act or think seems to me as little capable of being realized and thus as senseless as prescribing how one should hear or see. The nature of that mechanism, which we considered above, entails that cognition of what is objectively valuable cannot act immediately on our current |70| value stances. Certainly, given the extremely high malleability of our feeling, this influence has never been denied. But it still depends on the organ how far our judgment can be modified by theoretical cognition. By knowing that and how diverse sounds lie before it, a hearing that is malleable and not deficient by nature can also be gradually brought to the point of really distinguishing these sounds. But one can communicate a hundred times over to someone with crude sensibilities the objective difference between c^1 and c^2 or between c and g or c and d—and he will continue to *hear c^1* as c^2, c as g, c as d. The acquaintance with the

---

[49] On this point, compare pp. 92f below.
[50] Christoph Sigwart, *Logik*, II [Freiburg im Breisgau: Mohr, 1893] (second edition), p. 732.

objective difference can perhaps lead him to skeptically withholding judgment relative to his own perceptions, but it cannot change his perceptions themselves. So, too, a new objective determination of what is good will not only not help overturn a human being's evil urges; it will also not prevent our feeling from holding fast to the old good as good. After Nietzsche set up the tablet with the command "Become hard!" many of us have perhaps observed that this determination was correct and have made judgments correspondingly; many have attempted to act correspondingly but of those for whom it was not already natural previously, only the fewest had any success in feeling hardness as good, and scorning compassion, mildness, and goodness. In order to make an object of theoretical cognition practically effective, what is first necessary is a long *habit* of thinking or a conscious, pedagogical system. Thus, theoretical cognition of value comes to have the character of a norm or a prescription only in an entirely *indirect* and belated fashion.

(3) The Fulfillment of the Task
(a) Logic

If we look now to see how far the task of presenting the objectivity of values is fulfilled already, we find, initially for logic, in the axioms and in the doctrine of implication a series of propositions that provide the conditions of the feeling of truth. In the axioms we see pure judgments, freed of any possibilities of deception because they are free of any material components. These pure judgments present the adequate stimulus for the feeling of value, the very propositions that in a thousand |71| individual cases underlay our acceptance and rejection of judgments. The axioms are not immediately given but acquired through reduction. "The universal principle must first be carved out from a determinate application and elevated in its pure gestalt into the clear consciousness of it."[51] We see in this derivation of axioms the same procedure that, when applied to sensory judgments, has led to ascertaining the adequate sensory stimuli. The validity of axioms thus presents itself to us as something attained by working on judgments that are immediately held to be true.

Now the validity of axioms is justified in two ways, from behind or from the front, so to speak. Either one grounds their validity in their constitutive significance or in the immediate evidence of them.

---

[51] Sigwart, *Logik*, II (second edition), p. 294.

Our construal of the matter (a construal that takes sensory judgments as paradigmatic) cannot entirely agree with either of these doctrines. As far as the first is concerned, then it must be said that logical value has, of course, the widest conceivable domain of application. What elevates the significance of logical values so far above the remaining value judgments and sensory judgments is that, as properties of judgments or, more precisely, as properties of the form of judgment, they find application to all judgments and thereby to being as a whole and its contents. Hence, their significance is of a constitutive sort. But, now, this constitutive significance is nothing other than the particular result that working on the primary logical judgments leads to, precisely as a consequence of their wider domain of application. Münsterberg takes the constitutive significance of the value of truth as his paradigm in order to ground the validity of all other values on a constitutive sense to be ascribed to them. The constitutive significance of the value of truth is for us, by contrast, only the particular form of objective validity that is to be acquired for all other value judgments as well; it is only the particularly stringent result of a method that, oriented to working on sensory judgments, sets forth the objective validity of other value judgments as well.

According to the second prevailing doctrine, a particular kind of evidence is ascribed to axioms, one that immediately distinguishes them from all other judgments. They are not supposed to derive their validity |72| somehow from the particular propositions from which they were gathered; instead they are supposed to become principles only by virtue of the fact that they bear their necessity within themselves and "are immediately true."[52] One assumes this immediate truth as given to inner perception and warranted by it. The evidence or insight is supposedly different from blind judgments whose truth is believed "instinctively and mechanically." To be sure, even blind assumptions are often not doubted in the slightest but they are made in an obscure urging and "they have nothing of the clarity that is proper to the higher manner of judgment."[53]

These distinctions seem to me untenable for the following reasons:
(1) Even if it is granted [zugegeben] that axioms are really signaled out in inner perception by a particular sort of evidence, their validity would nonetheless not be grounded on this evidence of them. If the psychological work

---

[52] Ibid.
[53] Franz Brentano, *Vom Ursprung sittlicher Erkenntnis* [On the Origin of Ethical Cognition], Leipzig: Duncker & Humblot, 1889, p. 19. ["Landmann-Kalischer writes *ethischer* in place of *sittlicher* but refers to the same edition.]

of the last decades has yielded any assured result—and a result that is of the most far reaching significance precisely in a philosophical sense—it is this, that it has shaken our belief in the evidence of inner perception, that it has proven that inner perception is not credible. What has psychology not trotted out as facts to prove this—the psychology of the assertion and comparison, the psychology of feelings, dreams, hypnosis, depersonalization, automatism. The credibility of inner perception was lost from the moment that it became clear how slight a part of mental life falls within the scope of consciousness at all. Things appear to us as fully new that we have demonstrably not only seen or heard but also apperceived. Things appear to us as familiar, as déjà vu, that have never entered into our visual field. Every judgment of inner perception exhibits a construal of the inner happening that is to be explained, for its part, on the basis of the respective mental constellation and is accordingly subject to critique. Such a judgment can be assumed to be correct once and for all only in a hypothetical form: |73| I believe that I am noticing this. I believe that I do not hear a sound. It is clear that the assertion of a witness so compromised cannot provide warrant for the validity of propositions that form the basis of any part of our cognition.

(2) Even if it is granted that the difference between evident and blind judgments is given in inner perception, this still does not affect the very judgments that Brentano wants to single out by virtue of their evidence. The judgments of outer perception are subjectively no less evident than those of inner perception. What normal human being will take his judgment that the sun shines to be blind but the judgment that he sees light to be evident? The subjective evidence of the axiom is likewise the same as that of the propositions from which it is derived. That A cannot be B and not be B at the same time has no greater subjective evidence than the application that one finds of this evident proposition, in unpurified form, in a statement like "On the night of the theft, A cannot have been in X, since it can be demonstrated that he was in Z on this night."

(3) Although Brentano wants the evidence in inner perception to be recognized to be separate from blind judgments, he was ultimately himself able to characterize it through nothing other than the correctness of what was grasped evidently. It emerges, from his examples, that he makes the correctness of judgment the criterion of evidence. Hence, he obviously moves in a circle when he then wants to ground the objective correctness of what is judged [*Beurteilten*] through evidence on a particular, "higher" manner of judgment. But the

passage from Descartes that he himself drew on clearly shows the way for us to get out of this circle. The natural light distinguishes itself for Descartes from the spontaneous, blind urge to hold something to be true. But it distinguishes itself not by a peculiarity unique to it and given to inner perception but by the fact that "quaecumque *lumine naturali* mihi ostenduntur (. . .) nullo modo dubio esse possunt, quia nulla alia facultas esse potest, cui aeque fidam ac lumini isti, quaeque illa non vera esse possit docere."[54]

With this observation we come to our thesis: The subjective evidence of axioms is initially nothing other than that of judgments of perception. If they hold objectively, this happens not because they are evident but instead because they are examined. Their objective validity |74| can be grounded, not on their subjective evidence but only on reflection; not on inner revelation but on intellectual work and deliberations.

Some will accuse us of a *petitio principii* here. If merely working on the primary sensory judgments and value judgments justifies the objective validity of these judgments, this process of working on them consists in nothing other than applying the logical axioms to them. If now we want to acquire these axioms themselves by working on judgments primarily held to be true, we are merely tracing their validity back to them themselves, i.e., we already presuppose the validity of them that we wanted to prove.

This circle seems to me to be, not a refutation, but instead a proof. Thinking that works on thinking must lead, as a matter of necessity, to propositions that underlie the very thinking that is doing that work. These propositions are absolutely undeniable since their denial itself acknowledges them, "quia nulla alia facultas esse potest . . . quae illa non vera esse possit docere."[55] But this attempt to deny them, this cognition that it is impossible—what else are they then reflections through which we convince ourselves of the validity of the axioms?[56] The circle that the thinking leads to is the warrant of absolute validity. The circle of thinking finds closure in the axioms. [Consider] the function of working out the objective reliability of all other judgments; the

---

[54] [Whatever is shown to me by the *natural light* (. . .) can in no way be doubtful because there can be no other faculty that is equally faithful and would be able to teach whatever is shown by that light to be false.]

[55] [Because there can be no other faculty . . . that would be able to teach whatever is shown by that [natural] light to be false.]

[56] See, too, Joseph Delboeuf, "Logique Algorithmique," *Revue Philos.* (1876), p. 231: "Il y a donc une évidence légitime et une évidence illégitime . . . On nous dira peut-être qu'avant de se prononcer sur le caractère de l'évidence il faut mûrement réflèchir . . . Mais qu'est-ce cela sinon se démontrer à soi-même la vérité de ces propositions que l'on dit être indémonstrables, parcequ'elles seules, croit-on, rendent possible la démonstration des autres vérités?" [So there is a legitimate evidence and an

axioms acquire this function not by virtue of a unique sort of objective validity that has already been guaranteed them from somewhere else. Instead absolute validity is ascribed to the axioms precisely and only because they fulfill that function. The validity of the axioms results as it were *per exclusionem* ['through exclusion,' i.e., through a process of elimination]. Where there is no plaintiff, there is no need for a judge. No conceivable experience can enter into contradiction with the principle [*Satz*] of contradiction since it is itself the principle [*Prinzip*] of anything being valid.

Recently Husserl has explicitly opposed any derivation and derivability of logical axioms as a matter of principle.[57] |75| There is, as he explains it, an essential, absolutely unbridgeable difference between ideal sciences and real sciences. The former are a priori, the latter empirical. Every law that stems from induction is a law for facts; every law for facts stems from induction. But now induction can never justify the validity of a law but only the more or less high *probability* of its validity. Thus it cannot justify the apodictically evident, supra-empirical, and absolutely exact laws that make up the core of all logic. These are all valid a priori; they cannot be justified and legitimized through induction but only through apodictic evidence.

To this view we must reply, from our standpoint, that, certainly, pure logic does not proceed on the basis of psychological facts. "The true significance of the forms of inference emerges most clearly when we articulate them in equivalent *ideal incompatibilities*." But couldn't these ideal incompatibilities that are, to be sure, the goal of logic, be derived from empirically felt incompatibilities? The derivations of logical axioms that Husserl so rightly opposes were lacking in that they derived the status of being valid [*Gelten*] from arbitrarily selected [*beliebig*] mental lived experiences; [his point is that] the validity of the principle of contradiction cannot be derived from experiencing opposites. But should one not be permitted to derive laws of validity from *facts of validly obtaining*? Consider the obviously supra-empirical validity and apodictic certainty of logical laws, could they not be the result into which such an empirical derivation of these principles would flow?

To be sure, even the facts of validly obtaining [*des Geltens*] are facts, even the propositions derived from them are valid only *cum fundamento in re*

---

illegitimate evidence.... One will perhaps says to us that before pronouncing on the character of the evidence, it is necessary to reflect carefully.... But what is that if not to demonstrate to oneself the truth of those propositions that are said to be indemonstrable because they alone, one believes, render possible the demonstration of the other truths?]

[57] Husserl, *Logische Untersuchungen*, pp. 178, 62, 76, 190, and passim.

[with a foundation in a thing], but we can hardly lay claim to another sort of validity for aesthetic and ethical values. The fact that *logical* laws are elevated to a higher form of validity, that they acquire apodictic certainty, does not prevent them, it seems to me, from being derived in the same way as the laws of other values. Their supra-empirical validity ensues only from the particular *result* to which |76| their derivation leads: from the singular circumstance that thinking has its own contents as its object (see p. 74 above). For the legitimation and justification of logical laws we find Husserl ultimately still referring us only to that evidence that he himself reproaches as an accessory feeling that accompanies certain judgments contingently or as a matter of a natural law. In what he himself lays claim to as evidence, he seems to me to fail to move out beyond that circle that we already pointed out in the case of Brentano. He speaks of the kind of insight that we experience only in the domain of the purely conceptual (p. 91),[58] of the unwaveringness that we feel in inferring but that one is, indeed, not permitted to mix up with the genuine logical necessity that belongs to every correct inference, and that says and may say nothing other than how the ideally lawful validity of the inference is to be known as a matter of insight (although it is not really known by everyone who makes a judgment) (p. 107). Evidence is a lived experience of the truth. "Truth is an idea the individual instance of which in an evident judgment is a current lived experience" (p. 190). Evidence is the lived experience of the accord between the experienced sense of the assertion and the experienced state of affairs. Do we really move with this account beyond an accessory-psychological determination? Is it really impossible for a lived experience of the accord to take place where the accord does not in fact obtain? Husserl concludes his critical treatment succinctly as follows: "The feeling of evidence can have no other *essential* precondition than the truth of the respective content of the judgment. For just as it is self-evident that where there is nothing there is also nothing to see, so it is no less self-evident that where there is no truth, there can also be no discerning of this or that as true, in other words, no evidence." Is this really self-evident? Just as it happens that something is still seen where there is nothing, so it may well happen that something is discerned as true where there is no truth.

But if it could nonetheless be assumed that evidence and truth were really correlative concepts, how could evidence then "justify and legitimate" the truth? Truth is indeed then demanded in turn for the justification of the evidence.

---

[58] [All instances of 'experience' as a verb in this paragraph are translations of *erleben*.]

With the derivation of the laws of validity from what factually counts as valid [or what as a matter of fact validly obtains: *dem tatsächlichen Gelten*], we do not want to limit logic to a psychology of what counts as valid, a "psychology of evidence." |77| In the first place the facts of counting as valid [or validly obtaining] are not only of a psychological nature; there are also the validations objectified in the sciences. Secondly, the listing of the axioms as well as also the figures of syllogism as the adequate stimulus of the feeling of truth has only a preparatory character. In terms of what it accomplishes for logic, it does not go beyond what, for example, the psychology and physiology of the sense of taste have accomplished for taste. In [what is labeled] "logistic" [or 'symbolic logic'] (*Logistic*)[59] logic possesses an objective doctrine of what is logically valuable, a doctrine that could be designated as a physics of the true.

It seems an obvious objection to the symbolic display of logical operations that nothing could be contained in the symbol that is not contained in the symbolized, that a mere display of the facts in another language neither is nor could afford new cognition. But it can also be maintained that acoustics expresses in numbered oscillations in the air the same thing that we perceive by ear. It says the same thing as the ear, only with other words. Contained in these other words is the knowledge of the principle that underlies all our perceptions. What the oscillating string was for acoustics, what the prism was for optics, the principle of substitution was for logic. Just as the oscillating string was able to rectify the ear's perceptions, so the logical calculus was able to rectify the forms of inference.[60] What optics and acoustics have accomplished for the psychology and physiology of hearing and seeing, this is precisely what symbolic logic offers for logic. It gives logic more firmness, precision, and exactness; it removes from logic several causes of error, delivering more secure and quicker solutions (Delboeuf). "Boole a étendu la puissance et le champ de la logique."[61]

---

[59] The name for the new symbolic or algorithmic logic, a name proposed by Couturat, Itelson, and Lalande at the Second International Congress for Philosophy; see [Couturat] *Revue de métaphysique et de morale* (1904), p. 1042.

[60] Delboeuf, "Logique Algorithmique," p. 547: "C'est par là que j'ai été conduit à soupçonner d'abord et à reconnaître ensuite avec la plus grande évidence la fausseté des règles aristotéliennes du syllogisme. J'étais presque éffrayé de ce résultat, et j'ai été plutôt satisfait que mécontent de constater qu'en ce point aussi je n'étais pas le premier qui eût fait une découverte analogue." [It is from there that I was led first to suspect and then to recognize with the greatest degree of evidence the falsity of the Aristotelian rules of syllogism. I was almost afraid of this result and I was far more satisfied than annoyed to note that on this point I was also not the first to have made a similar discovery.]

[61] Louis Liard, *Les logiciens anglais contemporains* [Contemporary English Logicians], Paris: Germer Baillière, 1878, p. 101: "Boole wanted . . . to expand the field and increase the power of deductive logic."

Along with this accomplishment of symbolic logic, what is essential is at the same time given, |78| namely, that it displays the general determinations of the true detached from the feeling of truth and detached from thinking.

The logical laws do not hold as laws of thinking; instead, like other value judgments and like sensory judgments, they express something that objectively is [*ein objektiv Seiendes*]. Since, however, the value of truth applies to all judgments and thus to all the contents of being [*Seinsinhalte*], logical values cannot, like sensory judgments, also find their objective expression in this or that make-up of beings [*Seienden*]. Instead they find it only in the general properties of actual or possible being in general [*Sein überhaupt*]. In terms of its object, logistic is "pantic" or "pantology." Itelson was the first to express this important thought (International Philosophy Congress, 1904).

Itelson, meanwhile, does not conceive his "pantic" as a doctrine of values. Instead the concepts of true and false belong for him to epistemology and he excludes them as such from logic. "*La Logique ne s'occupe même pas du vrai et du faux, car le vrai et le faux sont des qualités de la pensée et non des objets.*"[62] "*On ne peut faire la théorie de la connaissance sans Logique, tandis qu'on peut faire de la Logique sans théorie de la connaissance.*"[63] But, further below, for the certainty of logic he draws on the argument that logic is the most naive of all sciences since one cannot criticize the laws of thinking: "*l'esprit ne peut pas plus s'élever au dessus de l'esprit que l'aéronaute ne peut s'élever au dessus de l'atmosphère,*" and "*si l'on ne veut pas admettre la jurisdiction de la Logique, il faut encore faire de la Logique.*"[64] Yet he concedes, on the other hand, that symbolic logic is no other logic than traditional logic: "*elle est simplement la forme moderne de la Logique formelle, et elle englobe la Logique aristotélienne et scolastique* [and it encompasses the Aristotelian and Scholastic logic]."[65] When he makes all these claims, he must also concede that the "pantic," as he understands it, developed at least from a logic that, of course, had thinking and, to be sure, correct

---

[62] [Couturat] *Revue de métaphysique et de morale* (1904), p. 1039: ["Logic is not preoccupied with the true and the false because the true and the false are qualities of thought and not of objects."]

[63] Ibid., p. 1041: ["One cannot do epistemology without logic while one can do logic without an epistemology."]

[64] Ibid., p. 1042: ["The mind can no more rise above the mind than a flyer can rise above the atmosphere" and "if one does not want to admit the jurisdiction of logic, it is necessary to make use of logic again."]

[65] Ibid.

thinking, as its object. Aristotle derived his logic from laws of thinking and speaking, and when he distinguished the correct from the false forms of inference, he presupposed the concepts of true and false. It remains for this reason no less true that in logic one should not think on the basis of thinking; in the highest, objective form |79| that logic can acquire, there is in fact as little talk of thinking as there is talk of hearing in acoustics or of the perception of space in geometry. Once the general rules that perception follows are established, its objective being is then knowable according to its own laws with so much certainty that every possible perception can be calculated in advance. What remains for it is only the content of the truth itself, no longer the elaboration of the true from what is held to be true. Just as acoustics is no longer the science of hearing but that of the properties of oscillations in the air, so, too, logic is, in its completed form, no longer a science of thinking but instead of the most universal properties of every being and possibility [*alles Seienden und Möglichen*]. The laws of correct thinking become universal relationships that can be abstractly displayed.

(b) Ethics

Ethics has advanced far less than logic in completing its task as a science of values. In view of the way the ethical amalgamates, on one hand, with the religious; and, on the other hand, with social and legal questions, and finally with problems of the doctrine of goods [*Güterlehre*] in particular, with the domain of what is valued affectively, it was not possible for the work to remain concentrated on the question of the ethical content. From the amalgamation with religious concerns, an entire complex of problems arose, those of theodicy, the question of the necessity of grace, and the dispute over Pelagianism; from the amalgamation with the doctrine of goods, the problem of the relationship of virtue to happiness ensued; from the combination with social interests, the result has been a stress on altruism and the evaluation of action in terms of its consequences for a collective whole. All these objects form necessary limit-questions [*Grenzfragen*] of ethics; but it is clear that the question of what place, for example, the ethical occupies in the context of the world—how the latter must be conceived in order to explain the phenomena of ethical life—corresponds to the question of the emergence of consciousness. As such, it has as little to do with ethics as a science of values as the investigation of the emergence of the soul has with scientific psychology.

For the objective determination of the content of ethical life |80| the most propitious point of departure was naturally offered by those ethical schools

[a] that took up the intuitive grasp of the ethical dimension as a predisposition grounded in our natural make-up [*Organisation*] and not further derivable and [b] that were also clearly aware of the co-operation of the intellect in clarifying and developing what was grasped in this way (Butler, Clarke, Hutcheson, later Herbart). But even earlier already, even on other foundations, the question of the content of the ethical dimension had been treated again and again alongside the more general problem of the origin of the ethical and its interconnectedness with the law of the world, alongside the practical doctrine of virtue and duties. An entire series of objective determinations emerged; whether one located the ethical dimension in the activity of reason, in rational self-love, in submission to the divine will, in the cultivation of harmony within the state of a person, in disinterested benevolence, in the drive for revenge, in the respect for the law or in the realization of freedom, one believed oneself to be in possession of the principle that underlies all ethical judgments.

Thus there was never any lack of attempts to determine the objective content of the ethical dimension; yet the views of the sense of this objectivity nonetheless departed widely from one another. In the principles mentioned, sometimes one saw axioms, sometimes results of reflection, sometimes 'ideas,' sometimes properties of things. Moreover, if some were able to regard principles like the harmonious cultivation of a person and disinterested benevolence as similar, they thus overlooked the difference between qualities of the moral sense and objective determinations of the properties of objects underlying these qualities. Finally, ethical life has been quite generally conceived—except by Herbart and a few others—too exclusively and directly as a uniform concept. The modes of the ethical dimension, the various spheres of ethical life that need to be conceived as originally differentiated, separate qualities of the moral sense, continued to be neglected.

(c) *Aesthetics*

Aesthetics has always concerned itself far more than ethics has with the particular dimensions of its domain, with the modifications, forms, |81| types, elements, ideas, and concrete stages of the beautiful. Differences that force themselves on it from all sides—the differences of the arts, those of art and nature, the genres of poetry, the comic and the sublime, and so forth—prevented aesthetics from devoting itself to the investigation of "the beautiful" as exclusively as ethics devotes itself to the investigation of "the ethical." Qualities that are diverse in a purely aesthetic sense, the adequate stimuli of the aesthetic sense, have recently been elaborated more and more on the basis of all these modifications.

Yet aesthetics has also worked for ages on determining what is beautiful independently of taste and it has not done so entirely without success. There have been attempts to determine the absolutely gratifying line mathematically, be it as a circle, a golden segment, or a serpentine line. Lipps has investigated in terms of their objective make-up the relationships of form that are felt to be beautiful through *empathy* [*Einfühlung*].[66] Since the days of Polycleitus, the proportions of the human gestalt that are considered beautiful through *conformity to a norm* have been set down by Leonardo, Dürer, and others in such a way that work was done in different schools of painters and artists according to such a "canon." The effort to determine gratifying relationships of sounds objectively and numerically has already succeeded for the art of sound just as completely as the exhibition of sounds as air vibrations has for acoustics. Even for poetry, when it comes to the objective portrayal of what is pleasing, things are not so bad. Aristotle has set down the basic features of how an action must be constituted if its unfolding is to be pleasing, and classical French tragedy depends on what he has prescribed. Aesthetics, like physics, has its false theories. When the inapplicability of the corpuscular theory of light and that of the assumption that heat is impenetrable matter became known, it did not lead to doubts about the objective sense of light and heat. It is impossible to see why something objective should be tied only to the reaction of sense organs, why the reaction of feeling should say so much less about the make-up of things than the reaction of sound, light, or touch.

(d) Dogmatics

Finally, the same thing that logic, aesthetics, and ethics have achieved for the immediate feeling of truth, for aesthetic and ethical feelings, theology—in Church Dogmas |82|—has done for the immediate religious feeling. "Religion must indeed be a thing of the heart; but in order to elevate it from the region of subjective caprice and wayward-ness, and to distinguish between that which is true and false in religion, we must appeal to an objective standard. That which enters the heart must first be discerned by the intelligence to be true. It must be seen as having in its own nature a right to dominate feeling, and as constituting the principle by which feeling

---

[66] [Landmann-Kalischer is likely referring to Lipps's *Grundlegung der Ästhetik* [Foundation of Aesthetics], Hamburg: Voss, 1903, pp. 506ff. See her review in *Archiv für die gesamte Psychologie*, V, 1905: pp. 213–27.]

must be judged."[67] The feeling itself, however, is presupposed. Theology is the science of God and divine things. Precisely for this reason, the existence of God is its point of departure. God cannot be proven if he is not believed. "Reason cannot produce and it cannot guarantee belief, it can only expand and circumscribe it, lending it words and increasing its believability."—Hence, we have here the same relationship as in the case of the other sciences of value: the value as a fact given to immediate feeling, and the science purging these facts of contradictions, clarifying and objectively determining them.

We cannot enter here into the discussion of how far theology has succeeded in setting up objectively determinable properties of God and how far the different confessions exhibit, as it were, different theorems, erecting themselves on similar facts of feeling and developing with these—corresponding to the new experiences of religiously inspired human beings.[68] Here we want only to point to this, namely, the paradigmatic clarity with which the authoritative character of systematized knowledge comes to light here in contrast to intuitive cognition. Acoustics says that the unmusical person hears badly and the Church that the heretic believes falsely. The Catholic Church's organization that fully corresponds to its belief of being in possession of absolute truth is the paradigm of any complete science of value. Were |83| it conceivable that we might have cognition of the beautiful in all its forms as certain as the [cognition the] Roman Church alleges to have of the content of belief, then this cognition would have to be systematized and prescribed as the law of the "wise" [in these matters] just as the rules of belief were by the prophets. Every individual aesthetic judgment would then have to be subordinated to this law just as today every logical judgment is already subordinated to logical laws. And, of course, this submission would have to be blind, as the Church demands. [It would have to be blind] since that higher cognition would not be able, as we saw, to modify the individual judgment immediately; it would only of necessity denounce as an individual imperfection everything not agreeing with it.

---

[67] John Caird, *Einführung in die Religionsphilosophie* [An Introduction to the Philosophy of Religion, London, 1880], cited in James, *Die religiöse Erfahrung in ihrer Mannigfaltigkeit* [*The Varieties of Religious Experience*, London: Longman, Greens, 1902, p. 434], übersetzt von Georg Wobberstein, Leipzig: Hinrichs, 1907.

[68] H. Fielding, *The Hearts of Men*, London: Hurst and Blackett, 1902, second edition, p. 313: "The creeds are the grammar of religion.... Speech never proceeded from grammar, but the reverse. As speech progresses and changes from unknown causes, grammar must follow."

But this is a dream. The imperfection of our cognition demands at all times the acknowledgement of the Protestant principle: respect for the individual experience since only on the basis of it can cognition support itself in order to become complete.

IV. The Place of Values in Being

If we see in values something given, if we classify them as lived experiences [*Erlebnisse*], incidents, elements, or whatever we want to call the given, this is not to say that they disappear in the mass of the given without distinction. Rather the task arises for us of deriving from their distinctive character the role that they play in the world as a whole. Even sensory qualities differ from one another in their epistemological as well as biological significance. Some form the basis of our existence; others appear to be almost completely useless; some count as the foundation of reality; only a phenomenal significance is accorded to others.

When we seek correspondingly to determine the function of values, an essential difference between values and the other qualities given to us becomes apparent. They stand closer to the end result of each perception, the reaction. The feeling shows a Janus face. On one side it is turned to perception; on the other it is turned to the will. It combines both. It is the link between them [*Zwischenglied*] that, awakened by perception, itself acts immediately on the will. |84| For this reason, values are what lead from what is to what will be. The positive value judgment, working on the will, becomes the norm of acting. Thus what secures values their decisive and distinguishing significance opposite the other qualities is this, that the human picture of the world and the future configuration of the world, insofar as it is a work of human beings, directly depends on them.

Someone would have to be blind to want to deny the influence of values on reality. One can, however, acknowledge this significance that values have for the whole and at the same time equate them, as something given, with all other qualities.

When we investigate the significance that individual positions and classes of occupations have for what is essential to a state [*Staatswesen*], we find that an occupation whose exercise is an indispensable condition for the preservation of society, in no way needs to be distinguished in regard to the conditions of its exercise from another occupation that could perhaps be missing without any harm worth mentioning. The most important work can be performed by the most vulgar of men, while a superficial or irrelevant work is performed, by contrast, by a person who calls the most ancient nobility, the most exceptional endowment, the rarest education her own. Indeed, it can be said that the self-preservation of society demands an organization in which the most important sorts of work are *not* in need of exceptional and thus rare powers.

Something similar can be claimed for the qualities we are investigating, those with, to different degrees, a high significance for the world's interconnectedness. Anything given to us can be of fundamental significance for this; but that says nothing about its lineage, its dignity, its place within or outside the world. Were one intent on venturing a priori a conjecture about this, it could only be that the fundamental, universal condition of the world must be precisely of the most common material [*Stoff*] that consciousness is acquainted with; I have in mind a material that places the slightest demands on the mind and that could also be assumed on the lowest levels of consciousness.

This reflection holds now not only for those values that determine human productions and actions but also for those without which the existence of a world cannot be thought at all. |85| With the idealistic philosophy, we can recognize in logical value the a priori of the world and, in spite of this, while holding fast to the *purely logical* concept of the a priori, we can also consider this value as something given or found in advance [*Vorgefundenes*]. We find representations in advance [i.e., already there] that bring with them the feeling of the judgment's necessity and others in which the compulsion to deny them lies. We have here an act of affirmation and negation that can be traced to the most primitive constitution of the soul and that is given simultaneously with the first stirrings of the life of representation.

A constitutive principle is one such that the cancellation of the world would follow from denying it. As soon as one places such a principle as a formal principle opposite all the rest of the world, one invariably founders on the reef of schematism.[69] It remains forever inconceivable how the lived experiences given to the subject are interconnected with a priori concepts and which concepts are supposed to work on which occurrences. As soon as one assumes more than a pre-established harmony here, as soon as one assumes the concept of triggering, one immediately enters onto empirical terrain. We escape this difficulty when from the start we refrain from elevating logical value above everything else given, when we let it inhere in the same world

---

[69] [Landmann-Kalischer is likely referring to the chapter on 'schematism' in Kant's *Kritik der reinen Vernunft* [Critique of Pure Reason], A137/B176–A147/B187.]

within which it plays its decisive role, when it is for us nothing other than a *primus inter pares* ['first among equals'] since all being depends upon it.

What we can claim is nonetheless merely a purely logical relationship of dependency. We commit a μετάβασις εἰσ ἄλλο γένος,[70] when we make something on which something else is logically dependent into something somehow temporally thought as prior; i.e., when we make it into something metaphysically of a different sort that we allow to act on what is dependent, to "work on" it, to "produce" the reality. The fact that truth is constitutive since every attempt to deny it presupposes it, is the oldest, ever-recurring and irrefutable refutation of all skepticism. This is all that underlies the idealistic philosophy of value. Everything that it claims beyond that about these matters is a metaphysical gloss of a logical relationship found in advance, a gloss, to boot, that first intends to justify the empirical reality through empirical concepts like 'production,' 'form-giving,' and 'working on.' It thus seems to us appropriate for the time being to stand by the concept of |86| dependency, to affirm it and take it up. The being—that of values no less than that of things—is dependent upon the truth-value of the judgment. What follows from this for the place of this value? Is not one thing also dependent upon another otherwise within the world? Is the sun less a part of nature because of the fact that the life of everything living hangs on it? Is not dependency perhaps only possible at all among objects of one sort? (Like cause and effect?)

And finally: of what sort then is the dependency of being on value? It seems to me that, in the initial joy of the discovery, one has overestimated this dependency and overextended its significance. "The value of the existential judgment," as Münsterberg puts it, "is synonymous with the value of the existence of the world." From the premise "we call 'real' what should be acknowledged by judgment to be real," Rickert concludes: "thus, reality becomes a particular sort of truth and the concept of reality presents itself as a concept of value." Correspondingly, one would have to argue: "we call 'ethically valuable' only what should be acknowledged by judgment to be valuable." Thus, in this way the ethical value becomes a particular sort of truth and the concept of the ethically valuable presents itself as a logical value. This argumentation [mistakenly] identifies the means and the content of cognition, organs for construing an object and conditions of its existence. The same over-valuing of the means is found in Fichte: "The entire world of

---

[70] [If, in a putative argument, there is a change from one genus (category) to another, the argument does not hold; hence, this change (μετάβασις) is traditionally labeled 'a category mistake'; see Aristotle, "Posterior Analytics," I, p. 75a39.]

the senses, reality, arises only through knowing and is itself our knowing. But knowing is not reality precisely because it [knowing] is knowing."[71] It is difficult to follow this logic. The subjectivism reveals itself by the fact that it ignores even the grammatical object. Without doubt, the organ through which we grasp reality co-determines the character of this reality. But the fact that we cast shadows when we stand in the sun is not only our fault but just as much the sun's fault as ours. Instead of saying that knowing is not reality precisely because it is knowing, it should be said conversely that reality that is not our knowing is precisely for that reason no reality. For we can think away ourselves and our knowing, think them as it were out of the world, just as little as we can any other component of |87| the world. We could just as well ask: how would the world be without air? The earth without plants?

What depends completely on judgment such that it is nothing but the content of the judgment is not being but an error. What Rickert and Münsterberg claim about judgment in general holds only for a judgment that is false. And perhaps they are right when they hold that ultimately all judgments declared to be true [i.e., articulated as true, *als wahr ausgesprochen*] are false. Being, as it is mirrored in our heads, exists perhaps only as the content of a judgment. But we must uphold the transcendent sense of the judgment, the truth that it intends, opposite any error that it may contain *de facto*. What Rickert and Münsterberg claim by equating the existential judgment with existence [*Dasein*] can be reduced to the formula: *esse = judicari* [to be = to be judged]. What we would like to maintain, in contrast to this, is that what obtains *only* as the content of a judgment is precisely something that is not the case [*Nichtseiende*]. For while, for example, in the case of ontological, mathematical, or moral dependency, what is dependent cannot be or cannot be in a certain way without what it depends upon, we invariably presuppose that the content of a judgment would exist even without our judgment or if we were to judge otherwise. The world whose make-up changes overnight, depending respectively upon our cognition of it, is not the world meant by a judgment, the world that we mistakenly believe to be reaching through a judgment. This is perhaps like the horizon that always moves away from us just as much as we come closer to it, but is nonetheless the fixed borderline that we never lose sight of and that we are always advancing towards.

---

[71] J. G. Fichte, *Werke*, ed. J. H. Fichte, Berlin: Veit, 1845/46, Volume I, p. 246. [All instances of 'reality' in the remainder of this paragraph, including the quoted material, are translations of *Realität*.]

Even if it is conceded that a "should" [*ein Sollen*] is the object of the judgment, we nonetheless find what compels the affirmation of one combination and the denial of another already there as a property of determinate combinations of representations. The judgment carries out a mandate contained in its object. The urge to rationalize being's irrational elements is inherent in them. We find combinations of representations already on hand that urge us to posit them as being the case [*als seiend*].[72] If being is thus, to be sure, dependent upon what is supposed to be the case [*Sollen*], the latter is nonetheless dependent, for its part, upon irrational elements of being. Hence, the value of truth displays itself—and, indeed, precisely from this extreme standpoint—as a perceived quality, as do the other values. The fact that |88| the other qualities can be worked on in terms of their truth values does not keep them from belonging to the same genus. To human beings in prehistoric time the stone that was suited to working on wood afforded itself in the same manner as the wood itself. And in both cases the sovereign is a human being.

V. The Relationship of Values to One Another

We see that logical value has a wider domain of application than any other value since even thinking's ethical or aesthetic evaluation can itself be affirmed only via thinking, in the form of a judgment. Nonetheless, as we already saw in the first part, the self-sufficiency of values opposite one another remains intact. Indeed, the construal of values as a given, as a quality of things, provides an informal explanation of this self-sufficiency. The beautiful and the good are reducible to one another or dependent upon one another as little as what is colored and what makes sounds are. They may be metaphysically or genetically unified; just as color, noise, and warmth are dependent upon vibrations, so all values may rest upon an agreement. But the agreement is each time an agreement of different objects and is thus perceived each time by another organ, just as the "final apparatuses" developed to photograph airwaves are different from those developed to photograph much quicker and more granular vibrations of ether. A human being who has the most cultivated sense for the agreement of judgments and could not tolerate any logical obscurity can nonetheless be someone who fails to

---

[72] [The literal meaning of these last two sentences is that the irrational elements and the combination of representations "want" [*wollen*] to be rationalized and posited as being, respectively.]

take offense at the lack of harmony of sounds or colors and is incapable of feeling the unity of a picture or a personality.

The irreplaceability of one value by others follows from this consideration. No amount of goodness or moral rigor relieves us from taking account of aesthetic values, no wisdom can take the place of acting morally, and even the highest level of aesthetic refinement cannot replace the moral sense— and also cannot kill it. Such is the lesson of the battles that generations of Parnassians, savages, and others have waged for the hegemony of aesthetic value. I believe that we can say without qualification that they have ended in |89| defeat. The irreplaceability of one value by another reaches all the way down to the demands of the senses. When Lord Henry in *Dorian Gray* observes that yellow satin could compensate for all life's misfortunes and that all seven cardinal virtues together could not excuse pasties served cold, the reader, shuddering, feels a premonition of the tragic end of the man who lives what he teaches.[73] For while the cardinal virtues can never excuse an awful pasty, the world's best pasties will also not be able to atone for a single mortal sin.

The different values have absolutely nothing to do with one another. All the sounds of the world cannot produce a color. Thus, it also appears to me to be an arbitrary, metaphysical assumption, not corresponding to experience, when Münsterberg alleges that there is genuinely nothing absolutely at odds with value, that each violation of value in one domain of values is valuable in another domain, and that the conflict of values remains unresolvable only in the limited experience of the I.[74] This thought of a compensation cancels once again the self-sufficiency of values opposite one another, stressed so much by Münsterberg, and it is ultimately senseless. After all, what is the claim that this aesthetic disharmony is perhaps logically valuable supposed to mean? It is as though one wanted to ask whether this grey, since it is no genuine color, perhaps for that very reason yields a sound or a taste.

But what produces the illusion of values compensating for one another is the fact that within the limitations of a personality not all values can be

---

[73] [Oscar Wilde, *The Picture of Dorian Gray*, New York: Dover, 1993, Chapter 9, p. 80: "Well, I am not like that young man you told me of when we were down at Marlow together, the young man who used to say that yellow satin could console one for all the miseries of life." Ibid., Chapter 11, p. 104: "Even the cardinal virtues cannot atone for half-cold 'entrees', as Lord Henry remarked once, in a discussion on the subject, and there is possibly a good deal to be said for his view. For the canons of good society are, or should be, the same as the canons of art."]

[74] Münsterberg, *Philosophie der Werte*, p. 472.

developed to the same extent. While Münsterberg teaches that the conflict of values remains unresolvable only in the I's limited experience, I would like to claim, to the contrary, that it can be resolved only within the limited experience of the I. The reason is that here, where one must give way to the other, one must also be subordinated to the other. We must take sides, choose, and learn to be humble. This human being is loveable not only on account of his beauty; perhaps he is loveable on account of his goodness or his wisdom. Where it concerns the value of a matter or a human being, a single value will always, as we have already seen, |90| swing the balance for the entire judgment. Precisely because of the lack of connection of values to one another, their disparateness, it is extremely unlikely that all values should be realized in a positive sense in the same matter or person.

What value swings the balance for the entire judgment is dependent not only on personal taste, not only on what sense just is most developed in the one judging, but essentially depends instead upon the biological significance of the values and is thus subject, in each cultural milieu, to a fixed rule. Each society generates a *scale* of values: the affairs of state may stand, for instance, above those of the individual; right stands above happiness; religion above beauty; morality above wisdom. In the first part we saw that the thought of a scale of values does not contradict the self-sufficiency of individual domains of value. Nevertheless, in the shocking arbitrariness of the determinations mentioned and in their being the opposite in different periods, one sees that a genuine scale of values cannot be gathered from the biological viewpoint. The diverse values have, like the diverse senses, a diverse and historically changing significance for our life, for its advancement and preservation. But one may not confuse these differences in utility, i.e., the connections of values to the respective relationships of individuals or peoples, with differences of value.

A scale of values can be grounded on values' empirical interconnectedness in the person valuing as little as it can be on their diverse biological significance, respectively. In each act of cognition an ethical accomplishment is also expressed more or less; every ethical doing presupposes some cognizing. But this co-operating and self-conditioning of values merely corresponds to the co-operation roughly of optic and haptic perception for the uniform representation of space. It rests, just like the apparent compensation, on values coming together within the boundaries of an individual person. It is reciprocal dependency of the valuing, not of the values.

A scale of values grounded in the essence of the values themselves can only result when it is successfully proven that |91| other values are contained in one value, hence, that one value has other values as an object.

If we look around to see whether and where we meet up with such a relationship of values to one another, we find it realized, as far as I see, in three places and, indeed, in a different form each time: (1) in the relationship of logical values to the remaining values, (2) in the relationship of the cultural values to the values of life, and (3) in the relationship of pure values to what is affectively valued.

The first relationship is purely *formal*. A prerogative of logical value resulted, as we saw, from the fact that the validity of even the remaining value judgments depends upon the logical value. But this dependency nonetheless obtains for ethical and aesthetic judgments only insofar as they are judgments; only their logical correctness, their being in accordance with one another or contradicting themselves, is subject to the jurisdiction of logic. The ethical or aesthetic value itself, the matter of cognition, withdraws from the logical evaluation. These values can be incorrectly connected to a theme [*Gegenstand*]; thus logic decides about their validity in each individual case. But if their immanent object [*Objekt*] is established in a logically unobjectionable manner, no logic in the world has power over them.

In the second case it is a matter of the relationship of judgments within one domain of value to one another. The more mature judgment takes the place of the blind judgment. Since the evaluation of the earlier judgment on the basis of the new judgment invariably happens from the viewpoint of the truth-value, this relationship is reducible to the logical domain. The process of systematically thinking through a theme must correct those judgments previously assumed to be true which sprung merely from contingent, fragmentary, and rough acquaintance with the theme. We can call this subordination of the earlier judgment to the more mature judgment an *organic* subordination because it is comparable to the process of growth in which the higher level always supersedes the lower level.

Matters are otherwise in the third case. In the relationship of pure values to what is valued affectively, a *material* subordination takes place. And with the latter we come to an important determination.

In and of itself [*An und für sich*] there is no reason to let what is valued by diverse spheres of ourselves be dependent upon one another. |92| A scale within pure values is as senseless as proportioning the value of satiation to that of morality. Love and happiness are values by themselves [*durch sich selbst*]. When one puts pure values, on account of their universality, on a higher level than personal values, one is transferring an epistemological interest to the philosophy of values. The ordering of logic and that of practical striving are different from one another and the slighter objective sense of the latter's values in and of themselves could not have any bearing on it. But now the state of things is as a matter of fact such that all our actions and strivings, indeed, even already our feelings, form the *object* [*Gegenstand*] of a pure valuation, namely, ethical evaluation. Hence, it is possible here for a conflict to arise; the same good the possession of which signifies the highest value for a person can appear to ethical consciousness to be opposed to value. And here there can be no doubt about what it must subordinate itself to. An affective valuing can never make the ethical value its object; the latter is removed from its sphere. By contrast, the very same action that exhibits the value *affectively* also forms the object of the *pure* evaluation. The presupposition here of the pure value is accordingly another value. It can likewise be something already valued affectively, something that has become cherished out of habit, a thinking guided by fervent wishes, regarding which the value of truth sets itself up as the judge.

With this observation we have, as I believe, answered a question that, although lying outside the framework of this work, had to be touched on a number of times.[75] We have assumed value as something given to us. We have construed the process of *striving for* values as a mental mechanism in accordance with which all our actions are oriented toward the side of pleasure and turned away from displeasure. But the following question cannot help but force itself upon our investigation: How can this construal obtain together with the fact that we not only *want* what is valued positively but also *should* want it? How does it happen that the pleasure [that one takes] in the good or in the truth contains an authoritative validity opposite any personal pleasure? |93|

Intuitive ethics founders on this question. When Butler and Price allowed the capacity for the determinations of value, *in keeping with its nature*, to be superior to all other drives, when they allowed obligation to reside already in the concept of the ethical, they simply pushed back the question; they then traced conscience as the intuitive source of everything ethical back to God. Our construal of the relationship of values to one another enables us to offer

---

[75] See above pp. 63, 69.

a simple explanation here: the authoritative validity of pure values emerges from the relationship of values to one another. As soon as being pleased in a disinterested manner has as its object something that pleases in a way accompanied by an interest, it must also possess a higher level of validity than the latter. Since it provides the value of an evaluation, our highest and deepest willing must emerge from it. Here is the same limit that we touched on in the logical domain (see above, pp. 73f). *There is no instance by which the pure value, for its part, would be valued further.* Hence, our willing must be *inviolably* tied to this value. Where it collides with wanting something else, it will make apparent to consciousness its ultimate necessity as something that ought to be.

Whether now a material subordination can also take place within pure values, whether, in the course of working on all values systematically, it is possible to succeed in establishing one value that unites all other values in itself, whether and to what extent we are able to see in religion or philosophy the doctrine of the highest good—this question reaches beyond the framework of an investigation whose sights were set on the distinction of true and false value judgments, the real [*real*] content and the objective determination of everything valuable.

Translator's Afterword

Mention, as opposed to use, of English words in what follows is indicated by single quotation marks. Mention of individual German words is signaled by italicizing them. The purpose of this afterword is to sketch the approach that I have taken to the translation and some decisions made in translating key terms, decisions that might not be gathered from review of the Lexicon alone. In general, I have tried to translate German terms fairly uniformly, albeit without hamstringing word selection when the German term and its context dictate one connotation rather than another. For example, in some cases the use of *wollen* is equivalent to English uses of 'willing'; in other cases, to that of 'wanting'. Similarly, while *erhalten* typically means the same as 'to get' or 'to receive', there are times when its meaning coincides with 'to preserve'. So, too, depending upon the context, *beurteilen* is translated 'judge' or 'evaluate'.

'Lived experience' is used to translate *Erlebnis* and 'experience' to translate *Erfahrung*. When both terms surface in close proximity to one another (e.g., in the same sentence or in successive sentences), I indicate the German word in each case respectively (see AT 469; PV 10, 15, 17, 32, 83).

'Object'

In most cases 'object' is used to translate *Gegenstand* or *Objekt* since they are often synonymous in Landmann-Kalischer's text (as they seem to be at times for Kant; see CV, n. 35). However, when both terms appear in close proximity to one another (e.g., in the same sentence or in successive sentences), mention is made of the German word translated as 'object' in each case (see CV 268, 272, 275, 290; AT 502; PV 26, 32, 36, 62). In some contexts (e.g., CV 317, 318; PV 91) where both German terms appear, I maintain the difference by translating *Gegenstand* as 'theme' and *Objekt* as 'object'. This use remotely echoes Meinong's distinction between *Gegenstand* and *Objektiv*, where 'God exists' and 'God does not exist' have the same *Gegenstand* but different "objectives."[1]

'Cognition' and Related Terms

'Cognition' is principally used to translate the noun *Erkenntnis* and the nominalized verb *Erkennen*, while 'knowledge" and 'knowing' are reserved for *Wissen*. I translate the different verbal forms of *wissen* invariably with a form of the verb 'know'. But I render the different verbal forms of *erkennen* variously with 'cognize', 'discern', or 'come to know' and their cognates. Verbal and nominative instances of *Wiedererkennen* are rendered by grammatical forms of 'recognize' and 'recognition' respectively. To translate *anerkennen* and its cognates (e.g., *Anerkennung*), I employ 'acknowledge', 'acknowledgment', and 'accept' or 'acceptance' (when contrasted with words for 'deny' or 'rejection' [CV 267, PV 3: *Verwerfung*; PV 50: *Ablehnung*]).

'Stir' and 'Arouse'

In order to differentiate uses of the cognate terms *anregen* and *erregen*, I translate the grammatical family of terms affiliated with *anregen* principally with the verbs 'stir', 'stir up', and 'prompt' (e.g., *angeregt* is usually rendered 'stirred up'), while generally reserving 'arouse' and 'arousal' for the family affiliated with *erregen*. However, there is one exception here: I render *Gefühlserreger* as 'stirrers of feeling' and, in the context of the discussion of the latter, occasionally translate *erregen* as 'stir up'.

'Gestalt' and 'Configure'

Since 'gestalt' is now a common term in English, I do not translate it. But I use 'configure' and 'configuration' principally to translate *gestalten* and *Gestaltung* accordingly.

---

[1] Alexis Meinong, "Über Gegenstandstheorie," *Untersuchungen zur Gegenstandstheorie und Psychologie* [Investigations of the Theory of Objects and Psychology], hrsg. von A. Meinong (Leipzig: Barth, 1904): p. 6 and "Über Urteilsgefühle, was sie sind und was sie nicht sind [On Judgments of Feelings, What They Are and What They Are Not]," *Archiv für die gesamte Psychologie* 6 (1905): p. 33.

'Reality' and 'Actuality'

Since Landmann-Kalischer uses *Wirklichkeit* far more often than *Realität* and since 'reality' is far more common in English than 'actuality', I use 'reality' and 'real' to translate *Wirklichkeit* and *wirklich*. In departures from this practice—typically cases where both German terms occur within the same context (the span of a paragraph or page)—the German terms are flagged with parentheses.

'Representations'

Vorstellung is rendered 'representation' instead of 'presentation', as Brentano's and Husserl's translators often render it. This rendering is based upon Landmann-Kalischer's use of the Latinate verb *repräsentieren* to characterize *Vorstellung* in her 1923 work *Transcendenz des Erkennens*. Criticizing the English empiricists' view of a *Vorstellung* as a kind of faded intuition, Landmann-Kalischer contends that a *Vorstellung* "represents [*repräsentiert*] the full intuition, that it points by means of its incomplete content to the complete content" (*Transcendenz des Erkennnens*, Berlin: Bondi, 1923, p. 11). The possessive constructions 'memory's representations' and 'phantasy's representations' are used to translate *Erinnerungsvorstellungen* and *Phantasievorstellungen*, respectively, in order to underscore that Landmann-Kalischer is discussing representations that make up memory and phantasy rather than representations of memory or of phantasy where 'of' indicates an objective genitive.

There are instances where the same English word is used to translate two different German words. For example, I translate *Dichtung* 'poetry' in some instances but 'poetic composition' in others, but I use 'poetry' alone to translate the less used *Poesie*.

Lexicon

An asterisk indicates that the English word in question, while used to translate the respective German word, is more often used as a translation for another German word, also cited in the Lexicon. For example, an asterisk is added to 'mood' as the translation for *Laune* since 'mood' is more often used as a translation for *Stimmung*. Similarly, an asterisk is added to 'outcome' as the translation of *Ausgang*, since 'outcome' is more commonly used to translate *Ergebnis*. And so on.

Absicht	intention
Abstufung	nuance
Äquivalenz	equivalence*
Affekt	emotion
Akt	act
anerkennen	acknowledge, accept
Anerkennung	acknowledgment
anführen	cite
angenehm	pleasant, pleasing, agreeable
angeregt	stirred up, stirred, animated
Anlage	disposition, predisposition
Anordnung	organization
anregen	prompt
anregend	stirring
Anregung	prompting, stirring up
Ansatz	starting point
anschließen	link up with, adhere to, latch onto
ansinnen	expect
Anspruch	claim
antasten	encroach
Art	kind
Aufbau	construction, structure*
aufbauen	construct, build upon, erect*
Aufeinanderfolge	succession, sequence

204 LEXICON

auffassen	construe, grasp, take up
Auffassung	construal, view, conception, grasp, take
Aufforderung	mandate (n.)
aufheben	cancel, supersede
aufrechterhalten	uphold
Aufregung	excitement
aufstellen	set up, draw up, put forward
auftreten	occur
Augenpunkt	ocular point (a vanishing point in perspective), ocular perspective
ausbilden	cultivate
Ausdeutung	gloss
Auseinandersetzung	critical treatment
ausführen	carry out, expand on
Ausführung	account, execution
Ausgang	outcome*
ausgebildet	cultivated
ausgeführt	expanded on, expounded
auslösen	trigger, elicit
ausmachen	make up
ausreichend	sufficing
ausschalten	set aside, suspend
Aussage	assertion
Ausschnitt	segment
Auswahl	selection
Banne	spell
Bau	structure
bauen	build, construct*
Baukunst	architecture
bearbeiten	work on
bedeuten	signify, mean
Bedeutung	significance, meaning
bedingt	conditioned, based
Befriedigung	satisfaction
beglückt	blessed
begrenzt	limited
begründen	establish, ground
Begründung	justification, explanation

beilegen	confer
beimessen	attach
beliebig	arbitrary
beschränken	limit (v.), confine
Beschränkung	restriction
beseelt	inspired, animated
bestehen	consist, obtain*
bestimmt	definite, determinate, specific
betonen	stress, accentuate
Betrachtung	consideration, observation
beurtheilen	judge, evaluate*
bewahrt	intact
beweisen	prove
bewerten	evaluate
Bewertung	evaluation
bewußt	conscious, deliberate
beziehen	connect
Beziehung	connection
bezug ('in bezug auf')	in relation to
Boden	terrain
darlegen	present
Darlegung	explanation*, presentation
darstellen	portray, exhibit, display, present
Darstellung	portrayal, exhibition, presentation
Dichter	poet
Dichtkunst	art of literary composition
Dichtung	poetry, poetic composition, composition
dulden	tolerate, allow
durchführen	implement, draw and sustain
Durchführung	treatment, implementation
durchgehends (wohl)	overwhelmingly
Eigenart	uniqueness, unique property, idiosyncracy
eigentümlich	peculiar, distinctive
Einfühlung	empathy
eingefallen	occurred [to someone]
eingeschränkt	restricted
Einheitspunkt	unifying point
Einschränkung	restricting, qualification

Einstimmigkeit	accordance
Empfindnis	sentiment
Empfindung	sensation
Enge	narrowness, narrow confines
erarbeiten	work out
Ereignis	event
erfahren	experience (v.)
Erfahrung	experience (n.)
erfassen	grasp
erfinden	invent, devise
erfolgen	come about, materialize
erforderlich	requisite (adj.)
Erfordernis	requisite (n.)
erfreuen	enjoy, be delighted about
erfüllen	fulfill, complete (v.)
Ergebnis	outcome, result
erhärtet	supported, corroborated
erhalten	get, come to have, receive, obtain
erhalten (sich)	preserve
Erinnerung	memory
Erinnerungsvorstellung	memory's representation, memory-representation
erkennen	cognize, discern, know, come to know
Erkennen	cognition
Erkenntnis	cognition
Erkenntnistheorie	epistemology
erlangen	succeed
erleben	experience
Erlebnis	lived experience, experience
ermitteln	ascertain
Erniedrigung	belittlement
erproben	put to the test, examine
erregen	arouse, stir up*
Erregung	arousal
erreichen	attain, reach
errichten	erect
erweisen	show
erwerben	acquire*
erzielen	arrive at

faktisch	factical
Fassung	rendition
Feinheit	refinement
fertig	complete
festgelegt	set down, established
festhalten	capture, hold fast, uphold
festlegen (sich)	commit, devote oneself to
feststehen	stand fast
feststellbar	determinable
feststellen	ascertain, register, maintain, establish
Feststellung	finding, determination
Folge	consequence, sequence, result
Folgerung	inference*
Forderung	demand, mandate, require
fortfahren	continue
fortführen	continue, reenact
Gebäude	edifice
gebieten	mandate (v.)
Gedächtnis	recollection
Gefallen	being pleased by, finding pleasing
gefallen	please
Gefühlserreger	stirrers of feeling
Gefühlsinhalt	felt content
Gegenstand	object, theme
gegliedert	divided, subdivided
Geheimnis	secret, mystery
Geist	mind, spirit
Geisteszustand	state of mind
gelten	hold, count, count as valid
Geltung	validity, validation
Gemeinschaftsglieder	members of the community
Genuss	enjoyment
Gerätschaft	device
Geschehen	happening
Geschichte	story, history
gesetzlich	lawful
Gesetzlichkeit	lawfulness, set of laws
gesetzmäßig	law-governed, law-like

Gesichtspunkt	viewpoint
Gestalt	gestalt, figure
gestalten	configure
Gestaltung	configuration, configuring, design
Gestaltungskraft	creativity
Gestaltungsprinzip	principle of configuration
Gewähr	warrant (n.), guarantee
gewähren	afford, provide
gewährleisten	warrant (v.)
Gewahrwerden	becoming aware
Gewaltsamkeit	ferociousness
Gewertete	valued
gewinnen	acquire, secure (v.), gain, gather
Gewirr	tangle, jumble
Gleichberechtigung	equal justification
gleichgültig	immaterial
Gleichnis	simile
Gleichsetzung	being put on the same level
Gleichstellung	being placed on a par with, parity
Gleichung	equation, equivalence
Gleichwertigkeit	equivalence
Glieder	members
gliedern	divide, subdivide
gliedern (sich)	be divided
Gliederung	arrangement, division
Grad	degree
Grenze	boundary, limit
grob	gross, coarse
gröbst	most rough and ready
Gültigkeit	validity*
haften	link (v.)
Handlung	action
hemmen	inhibit, curb
Hemmung	constraint, inhibition
herausarbeiten	elaborate
herausstellen	establish, exposit, highlight
Herausstellung	highlighting
Herrschaft	reign (n.), sway

herrschen	reign (v.)
hervortreten	stand out, emerge
hineinbauen	build into
hineintragen	introduce, smuggle
Hineintragung	importing
Hort	haven
knüpfen	link, tie
konstatieren	affirm
konstruieren	devise
Konstruktion	construction*
Kunterbunt	mishmash
Laune	mood*
liebäugeln	flirt
Lust	pleasure
Lustspiel	comic play
Lyrik	lyric poetry
leisten	accomplish, achieve
lückenhaft	fragmentary
Machwerken	shoddy works
Moment	inherent feature, respect, moment
meinen	mean, allege
Mißfallen	dislike, disliking
Mitleid	compassion
nachdrücklich	insistently
Nachfühlung	sympathy
nachweisen	demonstrate
Naturvölker	peoples more at home in nature
Normgemäße	what conforms to the norm
Normzwang	normative force
Objekt	object
offenbaren	manifest
Persönlichkeit	personhood, personality
platt	shallow, uninspired
Poesie	poetry*
Psyche	psyche, mind
psychisch	mental
psychische Welt	mental world, world of the mind
real	real*

Realität	reality*
rechtfertigen	justify
regelrecht	appropriate
Reihe	series, par, series of sequences
Relation	relation
repräsentieren	represent*
Richtung	direction, orientation, axis
roh	crude
sachlich	material
Sachverhalt	state of affairs
Satz	proposition, sentence
Schätzung	assessment
schaffen	fashion, generate
Schilderung	depiction
Schlaraffenland	land of milk and honey
Schluß	conclusion, inference, implication
Schrank	limitation
Schwankung	fluctuation
sicherstellen	secure
Sittengesetz	ethical law
Sittlichkeit	ethical life
Stand	position, status, standing
Stimmung	mood
Stück	portion, piece
Tat	deed, act, work
Tatsache	fact
tatsächlich	factual
Täuschung	deception, illusion
trachten	endeavor
Typisch	typical, paradigmatic
Typus	paradigm, type
Überdruss	weariness
Übersichtlichkeit	clearly visible design
übertragen	transfer
Übertragung	transference
Umdichtung	rewriting
Umgestaltung	reconfiguration
Umschlagen	turnover (n.), flip over (v.)

Umstand	circumstance
umständlich	laborious
umwandeln (sich)	transform
Unabwendbarkeit	inevitability
ungezwungen	informal
Unlust	displeasure
unschlichtbar	unresolvable
Unterschied	distinction, difference*
unverbraucht	unspoiled
Urteil	judgment
verarbeiten	process (v.), work over
verfälscht	distorted
Verhältnis	relationship, proportion
verhalten (sich)	behave, conduct, comport, or relate itself to
verklären	glorify, embellish
Verknüpfung	conjunction
verlegen	transpose
verlogen	fake
Vermutung	conjecture, supposition
Verquickung	amalgamation, conflation
verschieden	different, diverse, various
Verschiedenheit	difference, diversity
Verschränkung	entanglement
versetzen	transport
verwischen	blur, erase
vollziehen	draw out, implement, enact, carry out
Vorgang	process (n.), occurrence
vorkommen	happen
Vorkommnis	incident, occurrence
Vorschub leisten	foster
Vorsprung	prerogative
Vorstellung	representation
Vorwurf	theme
Wahl	choice
wähnen	mistakenly believe
Wahrheit	truth
Wahrheitswert	value of truth, truth-value
walten	hold sway
werten	value (v.)

Wertung	valuation
wiedererkennen	recognize
Wiedererkennen	recognition
wiederholen	repeat, recur
wiederkehren	recur
Wille	will
willkürlich	deliberate(ly), arbitrary, voluntarily
wirken	act, work, come across as
wirklich	real, actual
Wirklichkeit	reality, actuality
wirr	muddled, jumbled
wissen	know
Wissen	knowledge, knowing
Wohlgefallen	gratification, gratify, liking
wollen	will, want
Wollen	willing
Wollung	volition
Wucht	brute force
Würdigung	appreciation
Wunschdichtung	poetic composition of a wish
Wunschwahrheit	truth wished for, truth of a wish
zergliedern	analyze
Ziel	goal, aim, destination, target
zubilligen	allow
zugeben	grant, concede
zugestehen	grant*
zukommen	come, pertain, accrue to
zumessen	attribute
zusammenfallen	coincide, fall together
zusammenhängen	join together
Zusammenhang	interconnection, context, link, nexus
Zusammenstimmung	accord (n.)
zusammentragen	gather together
Zusammentreffen	coincidence
zuschreiben	ascribe
zusprechen	accord (v.), attribute
Zustand	state
Zwang	compelling character, constraint, compulsion
Zweck	purpose, end

Bibliography

Ach, Narziß. *Über die Willenstätigkeit und Denken*. Göttingen: Vandenhoeck & Ruprecht, 1905.
Allesch, Christian. *Geschichte der psychologischen Ästhetik*. Göttingen: Verlag für Psychologie, 1987.
Allesch, Christian. "Fechner, Brentano, Stumpf. A Controversy on Beauty and Aesthetics." *Paradigmi. Rivista di critica filosofica* 3 (2017): pp. 11–23.
Arnim, Archim von, and Clemens Brentano, eds. *Des Knaben Wunderhorn: alte deutsche Lieder*. München: Müller, 1908.
Avenarius, Richard. *Der menschliche Weltbegriff*. Leipzig: Reisland, 1892.
Baer, C. E. von. *Aus Baltischer Geistesarbeit: Reden und Aufsätze*. Riga: Jonck & Poliewsky, 1908.
Baudelaire, Charles. *Les Fleurs du mal*. Paris: Poulet-Malassis et De Broise, 1857.
Baumgarten, Alexander Gottlieb. *Aesthetica*. Frankfurt an der Oder: Kleyb, 1750.
Baumgarten, Alexander Gottlieb. *Aestheticorum, Pars altera*. Frankfurt an der Oder: Kleyb, 1758.
Bechstein, Ludwig. "Die verzauberte Prinzessin." In *Das Märchenbuch*. Leipzig: Wigand, 1879: pp. 24–29.
Beiser, Frederick. *The Genesis of Neo-Kantianism*. Oxford: Oxford University Press, 2014.
Bergson, Henri. *Einführung in die Metaphysik*. Jena: E. Dietrichs, 1909.
Bodmer, Johann Jakob. *Critische Abhandlung von dem Wunderbaren in der Poesie*. Zürich: Orell, 1740.
Braitmeier, Friedrich. *Geschichte der poetischen Theorie und Kritik*, I. Frauenfeld: Huber, 1888.
Breitinger, Johann Jakob. *Kritische Abhandlung von der Natur, den Absichten und dem Gebrauch der Gleichnisse*. Zürich: Orell, 1740.
Breitinger, Johann Jakob. *Kritische Dichtkunst*. Zürich: Orell, 1740.
Brentano, Franz. *Vom Ursprung sittlicher Erkenntnis*. Leipzig: Duncker & Humblot, 1889.
Brentano, Franz. *Descriptive Psychology*. Translated by Benito Müller. London: Routledge, 1995.
Brentano, Franz. *Psychology from an Empirical Standpoint*. Translated by Linda L. McAlister. London: Routledge, 2014.
Breysig, Kurt. *Kulturgeschichte der Neuzeit*. Berlin: Bondi, 1901.
Brunetiere, Ferdinand. *Évolution de la poésie lyrique en France au dix-neuvième siècle*, II. Paris: Hatchette, 1895.
Caird, John. *An Introduction to the Philosophy of Religion*. New York: Macmillan, 1880.
Calker, Friedrich. *Denklehre oder Logik und Dialektik*. Bonn: Weber, 1822.
Cassirer, Ernst. *Kant's Life and Thought*. Translated by James Haden. New Haven, CT: Yale University Press, 1983.
Chladni, Ernst. *Entdeckungen über die Theorie des Klanges*. Leipzig: Weidmann, 1787.
Clewis, Robert. "Aesthetic Normativity in Freiburg: Jonas Cohn as an Alternative to Kant." *History of Philosophy Quarterly* 39(2) (2022): pp. 183–97.

Cohn, Jonas. "Beiträge zur Lehre von den Wertungen." *Zeitschrift für Philosophie und philosophische Kritik* 110 (1897): pp. 219–62.
Cohn, Jonas. *Allgemeine Ästhetik*. Leipzig, Engelmann, 1901.
Couturat, Louis. "Logique et Philosophie des Sciences: Séances de Section et Séances Générales." *Revue de métaphysique et de morale* 12(6) (1904): 1037–77.
Dahlstrom, Daniel. "Edith Landmann-Kalischer." In *The Oxford Handbook of Nineteenth-Century Women Philosophers in the German Tradition*, edited by Kristin Gjesdal and Dalia Nassar. Oxford: Oxford University Press, forthcoming.
Delboeuf, Joseph. "Logique Algorithmique." *Revue Philosophique de la France et de l'Étranger* 2(9) (1876): pp. 225–52.
Dessoir, Max. *Ästhetik und allgemeine Kunstwissenschaft*. Stuttgart: Enke, 1906.
Döring, August. *Philosophische Güterlehre*. Berlin: R. Gaetner, 1888.
Ebbinghaus, Hermann. *Grundzüge der Psychologie*. Leipzig: Veit, 1902.
Ehrenfels, Christian von. *System der Werttheorie*. Leipzig, Reisland, 1897.
Eisler, Robert. *Studien zur Werttheorie*. Leipzig: Duncker & Humblot, 1902.
Erhardt, Franz. *Mechanismus und Teleologie*. Leipzig: Reisland, 1890.
Eschenbach, Gunilla. *Imitatio im George-Kreis*. Berlin: De Gruyter, 2011.
Fechner, Gustav. *Elemente der Psychophysik*. Leipzig: Breitkopf und Härtel, 1860.
Fechner, Gustav. *Vorschule der Ästhetik*. Leipzig: Breitkopf & Härtel, 1897.
Fichte, Johann Gottlieb. *Sämtliche Werke*, Band I. Edited by J. H. Fichte. Berlin: Veit, 1845.
Fiedler, Konrad. "*Moderner Naturalismus und künstlerische Wahrheit.*" In *Wissenschaftliche Beilage der Leipziger Zeitung* (1881); reproduced in *Schriften zur Kunst*, edited by Hans Marbach. Leipzig: Hirzel, 1896: pp. 133–82.
Fielding, Harold. *The Hearts of Men*. 2nd ed. London: Hurst and Blackett, 1902.
Goethe, Johann Wolfgang von. *Aus meinem Leben: Dichtung und Wahrheit*, Bände 1–3. Tübingen: Cotta; 1811–14.
Gorodeisky, Keren. "19th Century Romantic Aesthetics." In *The Stanford Encyclopedia of Philosophy*, edited by Edward N. Zalta. https://plato.stanford.edu/archives/fall2016/entries/aesthetics-19th-romantic/, 2016.
Gottschall, Rudolph von. *Poetik*. Breslau: Trewendt, 1870.
Gottsched, Christoph. *Versuch einer critischen Dichtkunst vor die Deutschen*. Leipzig: Breitkopf, 1729.
Greenwood, John. *A Conceptual History of Psychology*. 2nd ed. Cambridge: Cambridge University Press, 2015.
Greve, Felix Paul, ed. *Die schönsten Geschichten aus 1001 Nacht*. Leipzig: Seemann, 1914.
Grimm, Jacob, and Wilhelm Grimm. *Kinder und Hausmärchen*. Halle: Hendel, 1812.
Grimm, Jacob, and Wilhelm Grimm. *Kinder und Hausmärchen*, 32. Auflage, Berlin: Bardtenschlager, 1906.
Gurlitt, Cornelius. *Die deutsche Kunst des neunzehnten Jahrhunderts: Ihre Ziele und Thaten*. In *Das Neunzehnte Jahrhundert in Deutschlands Entwicklung*, Band II, edited by Paul Schlenther. Berlin: Bondi, 1900.
Guyer, Paul. *Kant*. London: Routledge, 2006.
Guyer, Paul. "What Happened to Kant in Neo-Kantian Aesthetics? Cohen, Cohn, and Dilthey." *The Philosophical Forum* 39(2) (2008): pp. 143–76.
Guyer, Paul. *A History of Modern Aesthetics*, Vol. 3. Cambridge: Cambridge University Press, 2014.
Hahn, Johann Georg von. *Griechische und Albanesische Märchen*. Leipzig: Engelmann, 1864.
Hauptmann, Gerhart. *Die versunkene Glocke: ein deutsches Märchendrama*. Berlin: Fischer, 1897.

Heine, Heinrich. *Neue Gedichte*. Hamburg: Hoffmann und Campe, 1844.
Heine, Heinrich. *Buch der Lieder*. Hamburg: Hoffmann und Campe, 1868.
Herbart, Johann Friedrich. *Lehrbuch zur Einleitung in die Philosophie*. Leipzig: Voss, 1850.
Hildebrand, Adolph. *Das Problem der Form in der bildenden Kunst*. Strassburg: Heitz, 1893.
Hillman, Susanne. *Wandering Jews: Existential Quests between Berlin, Zurich, and Zion*. ProQuest Dissertations & Theses Global, 2011.
Hofmannsthal, Hugo von. "Der Dichter und diese Zeit." In *Die Prosaischen Schriften gesammelt*, I. Berlin: S. Fischer, 1907: pp. 1–51.
Humboldt, Alexander von. *Kosmos* II. Stuttgart: Cotta, 1847.
Humboldt, Wilhelm von. *Aesthetische Versuche über Goethe's Hermann und Dorothea*. Braunschweig: Vieweg, 1888.
Husserl, Edmund. *Logische Untersuchungen*. Halle: Niemeyer, 1900. Translated as *Logical Investigations*. Translated by J. N. Findlay. London: Routledge, 1973.
Husserl, Edmund. *Ideas for a Pure Phenomenology and Phenomenological Philosophy: First Book: General Introduction to Pure Phenomenology*. Translated by Daniel Dahlstrom. Indianapolis: Hackett, 2014.
James, William. *The Principles of Psychology*. New York: Holt, 1890.
James, William. *Die religiöse Erfahrung in ihrer Mannigfaltigkeit*. Translated by Georg Wobberstein. Leipzig: Hinrichs, 1907.
James, William. *Der Pragmatismus*. Translated by Wilhelm Jerusalem. Leipzig: Klinghardt, 1908.
Jolles, André. *Zur Deutung des Begriffes Naturwahrheit in der bildenden Kunst*. Freiburg in Breisgau: Harms, 1905.
Kant, Immanuel. *Kritik der reinen Vernunft, Kants gesammelte Schriften*, Bd. 3. Edited by Deutschen [formerly, Königlichen Preussichen] Akademie der Wissenschaften. Berlin: De Gruyter, 1902.
Kant, Immanuel. *Kritik der Urteilskraft, Kants gesammelte Schriften*, Bd. 5. Edited by Deutschen [formerly, Königlichen Preussichen] Akademie der Wissenschaften. Berlin: De Gruyter, 1902.
Klein, Carl August, ed. *Blätter für die Kunst*, 7. Folge, 1904.
Kreibig, Josef. *Psychologische Grundlegung eines Systems der Werttheorie*. Wien: Hölder, 1902.
Kreibig, Josef. "Über den Begriff 'Sinnestäuschung.'" *Zeitschrift für Philosophie und philosophische Kritik*, 120(2) (1902): pp. 197–203.
Külpe, Oswald. *Grundriß der Psychologie*. Leipzig: Engelmann, 1893.
Külpe, Oswald. "Der assoziative Faktor in der neueren Ästhetik." *Vierteljahrsschrift für wissenschaftliche Philosophie* 23(2) (1899): pp. 145–83.
Külpe, Oswald. "Zur Psychologie der Gefühle." *Referat für den Genfer Internationalen Psychologenkongreß*, 1909.
Laas, Ernst. *Idealismus und Positivismus: Eine kritische Auseinandersetzung, Dritter Theil: Idealistische und positivistische Erkenntnistheorie*. Berlin: Weidmann, 1884.
Liard, Louis. *Les logiciens anglais contemporains*. Paris: Germer Baillière, 1878.
Lichtwark, Alfred. "Urteile über Böcklin." *Zukunft* 22 (1897): pp. 245–51.
Lipps, Theodor. *Grundlegung der Ästhetik*. Hamburg: Voss, 1903.
Lohenstein, Daniel Caspar von. *Großmütiger Feldherr Arminius*. Leipzig: Bledit, 1689–90.
Mardrus J. C., and E. P. Mathers, eds. *The Book of the Thousand Nights and One Night*, Vol. 2. New York: Routledge, 1990.
Matherne, Samantha. "Edith Landmann-Kalischer on Aesthetic Demarcation and Normativity." *British Journal of Aesthetics* 60(3) (2020): pp. 315–34.

Mayer, Eva. "Anfänge des Frauenphilosophiestudiums in Graz ab etwa 1900 am Beispiel der Meinong-Schülerin Auguste Fischer (1867–1958)." In *Logical, Ontological, and Historical Contributions on the Philosophy of Alexius Meinong*, edited by Mauro Antonelli and Marian David. Berlin: De Gruyter, 2014: pp. 161–82.

McDowell, John. "Values and Secondary Qualities" and "Aesthetic Value, Objectivity, and the Fabric of the World." In *Mind, Value, and Reality*. Cambridge, MA: Harvard University Press, 1998: pp. 131–50.

Meier-Graefe, Julius. *Der Fall Böcklin*. Stuttgart: Hoffman, 1905.

Meinong, Alexius. *Psychologisch-ethische Untersuchungen zur Werttheorie*. Graz: Leuschner & Lubensky, 1894.

Meinong, Alexius. "Über Gegenstände der höheren Ordnung." *Zeitschrift für Psychologie* 21 (1899): pp. 182–272. Translated as "On Objects of Higher Order and Their Relationship to Internal Perception." In *Alexius Meinong Gesamtausgabe*, Vol. II, edited by Rudolf Haller and Schubert Kalsi and translated by Schubert Kalsi, 1978: pp. 137–208.

Meinong, Alexius. "Für die Psychologie und gegen den Psychologismus in der allgemeinen Werttheorie." *Logos. Internationale Zeitschrift für Philosophie der Kultur* 3 (1912): pp. 1–12.

Meinong, Alexius. *Über emotionale Präsentation*. In *Sitzungsberichte der philosophisch-historischen Klasse der Kaiserlichen Akademie der Wissenschaften in Wien*, Vol. 183 (1917): 415–16. Translated as *On Emotional Presentation*. Translated by M. L. Schubert Kalsi. Evanston, IL: Northwestern University Press, 1972.

Meinong, Alexius. *Philosophenbriefe. Aus der wissenschaftlichen Korrespondenz*. Edited by Rudolf Kindinger. Graz: Akademischen Druck- u. Verlagsanstalt, 1965.

Meinong, Alexius. "The Theory of Objects." In *Realism and the Background of Phenomenology*, edited by R. M. Chisholm. Atascadero, CA: Ridgeview, 1991: pp. 76–117.

Meyer, R. M. "Lebenswahrheit dichterischer Gestalten." *Neue Jahrbücher für das klassische Altertum*, XV. Jahrgang, 1905. Edited by Johannes Ilberg and Bernhard Gerth: pp. 46–62.

Mill, John Stuart. *Die induktive Logik*. Translated by Jacob Schiel. Braunschweig: Vieweg, 1849.

Moland, Lydia. *Hegel's Aesthetics: The Art of Idealism*. Oxford: Oxford University Press, 2019.

Moland, Lydia and Alison Stone, eds. *Oxford Handbook of American and British Women Philosophers in the Nineteenth Century*. Oxford: Oxford University Press, forthcoming.

Moore, G. E. "Review of Hugo Münsterberg's *Philosophie der Werte*." *International Journal of Ethics* 19(4) (1909): pp. 495–504.

Münsterberg, Hugo. *Philosophie Der Werte; Grundzüge Einer Weltanschauung*. Leipzig: J. A. Barth, 1908.

Münsterberg, Hugo. *On the Witness Stand: Essays on Psychology and Crime*. Garden City, NY: Doubleday, 1908.

Münsterberg, Hugo. *The Eternal Values*. Boston: Houghton Mifflin, 1909.

Münsterberg, Hugo. "The Opponents of Eternal Values." *Psychological Bulletin* 6(10) (1910): pp. 329–38.

Münsterberg, Hugo. *Psychology and Industrial Efficiency*. Boston: Houghton Mifflin, 1913.

Muther, Richard. *Geschichte der Malerei im 19. Jahrhundert*, Bd. III. München, Hirth, 1893/94.

Nassar, Dalia. *The Romantic Absolute*. Chicago: University of Chicago Press, 2013.

Nassar, Dalia, and Kristin Gjesdal, eds. *Women Philosophers in the Long Nineteenth Century: The German Tradition*. Oxford: Oxford University Press, 2021.

BIBLIOGRAPHY 217

Nassar, Dalia, and Kristin Gjesdal, eds. *Oxford Handbook of Nineteenth-Century Women Philosophers in German Tradition*. Oxford: Oxford University Press, forthcoming.
Norton, Robert. *Secret Germany: Stefan George and His Circle*. Ithaca, NY: Cornell University Press, 2002.
Novalis. *Hymnen an die Nacht, 2* in *Schriften. Die Werke Friedrich von Hardenbergs*, Band 1. Stuttgart: W. Kohlhammer Verlag, 1960-77.
Oelmann, Ute, and Ulrich Raulff, eds. *Frauen um Stefan George*. Göttingen: Wallstein Verlag, 2010.
Orth, Johannes. *Gefühl und Bewußtseinslage*. Berlin: Reuther & Reichard, 1903.
Paul, Jean. *Vorschule der Ästhetik*. Stuttgart: Cotta, 1813.
Philipp, Michael. "Die Thematisierung des 'Jüdischen' im George-Kreis vor und nach 1933." In *"Verkannte brüder"? Stefan George und das deutsch-jüdische Bürgertum zwischen Jahrhundertwende und Emigration*, edited by Gert Mattenklott, Michael Philipp, and Julius H. Schoeps. Hildesheim: Georg Olms Verlag, 2001: pp. 201-18.
Pojman, Paul. "Ernst Mach." In *The Stanford Encyclopedia of Philosophy*, edited by Edward N. Zalta. https://plato.stanford.edu/archives/win2020/entries/ernst-mach/, 2020.
Poppe, Theodor. "Von Form und Formung in der Dichtkunst." *Zeitschrift für Ästhetik und allgemeine Kunstwissenschaft* I, 1 (1906): pp. 88-112.
Raspa, Venazio, ed. *The Aesthetics of the Graz School*. Berlin: De Gruyter, 2013.
Raulff, Ulrich. *Kreis ohne Meister: Stefan Georges Nachleben*. München: Beck, 2009.
Reicher, Maria. "Value Facts and Value Experiences in Early Phenomenology." In *Values and Ontology*, edited by Beatrice Centi and Wolfgang Huemer. Frankfurt: Ontos, 2009: pp. 105-35.
Reicher, Maria. "Ästhetische Werte als dispositionale Eigenschaften: 1905-2014." *Deutsches Jahrbuch Philosophie* 8 (2016): pp. 961-74.
Reicher-Marek, Maria. "Dispositionalist Accounts of Aesthetic Properties in Austro-German Aesthetics." *Paradigmi. Rivista di critica filosofica* 3 (2017): pp. 71-86.
Rickert, Heinrich. *Der Gegenstand der Erkenntnis*. 2nd ed. Tübingen: Mohr, 1904.
Riedner, Johannes. "Edith Landmann als philosophische Interpretin und Zeugin Stefan Georges. Zu Problemen der Assimilation im George-Kreis." *Marburger Forum* 3(4) (2002): pp. 1-14.
Riehl, Alois. *Philosophische Studien aus Vier Jahrzehnten*. Leipzig: Quelle und Meyer, 1925.
Riemann, Hugo. "Die Ausdruckskraft musikalischer Motive." *Zeitschrift für Ästhetik und allgemeine Kunstwissenschaft* I/1 (1901/2): pp. 44-64.
Rollinger, Robin. *Austrian Phenomenology: Brentano, Husserl, Meinong, and Others on Mind and Object*. Berlin: De Gruyter, 2008.
Rosenkranz, Karl. *Ästhetik des Häßlichen*. Königsberg: Kornträger, 1853.
Ruge, Arnold. *Neue Vorschule der Aesthetik: Das Komische*. Halle: Waisenhaus, 1837.
Salice, Alessandro. "The Phenomenology of the Munich and Göttingen Circles." *The Stanford Encyclopedia of Philosophy*, edited by Edward N. Zalta. https://plato.stanford.edu/archives/win2020/entries/phenomenology-mg/, 2020.
Schasler, Max. *Aesthetik: Grundzüge der Wissenschaft des Schönen und der Kunst*. Leipzig: Freytag/Prag: Kempsky, 1886.
Schiewer, Gesine Lenore. "Das Problem des Politischen in der Philosophie Edith Landmanns. Diskussionen im Umfeld von Wertphilosophie, Gestalttheorie und Wissenssoziologie." In *Das Ideal des schönen Lebens und die Wirklichkeit der Weimarer Republik. Vorstellungen von Staat und Gemeinschaft im George-Kreis*, edited by Roman Koster et al. Berlin: Akademie-Verlag, 2009: pp. 77-96.

Schiller, C. F. S. *Personal Idealism*. Edited by Henry Sturt. London: Macmillan, 1902.
Schiller, Friedrich. "Über Anmut und Würde." *Neue Thalia*, 2. Jahrgang, 1793: pp. 115–230.
Schiller, Friedrich. *Die Künstler*, translated as "The Artists." In *The Poems of Schiller*, translated by Henry Wireman. Philadelphia: Kohler, 1879: pp. 82–97.
Schiller, Friedrich. *Sämtliche Werke*, Band 1. München: Hanser, 1962.
Schnaase, Carl. *Geschichte der bildenden Künste*, Zweite, vermehrte und verbesserte Auflage; Vierter Band. Düsseldorf: Buddeus, 1871.
Schönhärl, Korinna. "'Wie eine Blume die erforen ist'—Edith Landmann als Jüngerin Stefan Georges." In *Stefan George. Dichtung—Ethos—Staat. Denkbilder für ein geheimes europäisches Deutschland*, edited by Bruno Pieger und Bertram Schefold. Berlin: Verlag für Berlin-Brandenburg, 2010: pp. 207–42.
Schopenhauer, Arthur. *Die Welt als Wille und Vorstellung*, I. Leipzig: Brockhaus, 1844.
Schopenhauer, Arthur. *Die Welt als Wille und Vorstellung*, II. Leipzig: Brockhaus, 1859.
Schultze-Naumburg, Paul. "Die Gestaltung des Arbeiter-Wohnhauses." In *Die künstlerische Gestaltung des Arbeiter-Wohnhauses*, Zentralstelle für Arbeiter-Wohlfahrtseinrichtungen, 14. Konferenz (1905). Berlin: Heymann, 1906: pp. 29–47.
Schumann, Friedrich. "Beiträge zur Analysis der Gesichtswahrnehmungen." *Zeitschrift für Psychologie* 30 (1902): 331f.
Schwarz, Hermann. "Gefallen und Lust." *Philosophische Abhandlungen, R. Haym gewidmet* (1902): pp. 407–506.
Segal, Jakob. "Psychologische und normative Ästhetik." *Zeitschrift für Ästhetik und allgemeine Kunstwissenschaft* 2 (1907): pp. 1–24.
Sibley, Frank. "Aesthetic Concepts." *Philosophical Review* 68(4) (1959): pp. 421–50.
Sigwart, Christoph. *Logik*, I. 2nd ed. Freiburg: Mohr, 1889.
Sigwart, Christoph. *Logik*, II. 2nd ed. Freiburg: Mohr, 1893.
Simmel, Georg. *Philosophie des Geldes*. Leipzig: Duncker & Humbolt, 1900.
Smith, Barry. "Pleasure and Its Modifications: Witasek, Meinong and the Aesthetics of the Grazer Schule." In *The Philosophy of Alexius Meinong*, edited by L. Albertazzi. *Axiomathes* 7(1–2) (1996): pp. 203–32.
Smith, Norman Kemp. "Avenarius' Philosophy of Pure Experience: I." *Mind* XV (57) (1906a): pp. 13–31.
Smith, Norman Kemp. "Avenarius' Philosophy of Pure Experience: II." *Mind* XV (58) (1906b): pp. 149–60.
Spinoza, Baruch. *Tractatus de Intellectus Emendatione. Opera, quae supersunt omnia*. II. Edited by H. E. Gottlob Paulus. Jena: In bibliopolio academico, 1803.
Stallo, John B. *La matière et la physique moderne*. Paris: Alcan, 1899.
Stern, William, ed. *Psychologie der Aussage mit besonderer Berücksichtigung von Problemen der Rechtspflege, Pädagogik, Psychiatrie und Geschichtsforschung*, Band 2, Nr. 3. Leipzig: Barth, 1905.
Stern, William. *Person und Sache*. Leipzig: Johann Ambrosius Barth, 1906.
Stumpf, Carl. *Tonpsychologie*. Leipzig: Herzel, 1883.
Stumpf, Carl. "Über Gefühlsempfindungen." *Zeitschrift für Psychologie und Physiologie der Sinnesorgane* (1907) 44: pp. 1–49.
Sulzer, Johann Georg. *Allgemeine Theorie der schönen Künste*, Band 2. Leipzig: Weidmann, 1774.
Taine, Hippolyte. *Nouveaux essais de critique et d'histoire*. Paris: Hatchette, 1909.
Tetens, Johannes. *Philosophische Versuche über die menschliche Natur*, I. Leipzig: Weidmann, 1777.
Tieck, Ludwig. *Prinz Zerbino oder die Reise nach dem guten Geschmack, Werke in einem Band*. Hamburg: Hoffmann und Campe, 1967.

Twardowski, Kazimierz. *On the Content and Object of Presentations*. Translated by R. Grossmann. The Hague: M. Nijhoff, 1977.
Überweg, Friedrich. *Philosophische Bibliothek. Grundriss der Philosophie*, Vols. 1–2. 7th ed. Berlin: Mittler, 1886–88.
Vendrell-Ferran, Íngrid. *Die Emotionen. Gefühle in der realistischen Phänomenologie*. Berlin: Akademie Verlag GmbH, 2008.
Vendrell-Ferran, Íngrid. "Tatsache, Wert und menschliche Sensibilität: Die Brentanoschule und die Gestaltpsychologie." In *Feeling and Value, Willing and Action*, edited by Marta Wehrle and Maren Ubiali. Cham: Springer, 2014: pp. 141–62.
Vendrell-Ferran, Íngrid. "On the Analogy between the Sensing of Secondary Qualities and the Feeling of Values: Landmann-Kalischer's Epistemic Project, Its Historical Context, and Its Significance for Current Meta-Ethics." In *Philosophy of Value. The Historical Roots of Contemporary Debate: An Overview*, edited by Beatrice Centi, Faustino Fabbianelli, and Gemmo Iocco. Berlin: De Gruyter, forthcoming.
Vischer, Friedrich Theodor. *Das Vorträge, erste Reihe: Schöne und die Kunst*. Stuttgart: Cotta, 1898.
Wachenroder, Wilhelm Heinrich. *Herzensergießungen eines kunstliebenden Klosterbruders*. Berlin: Unger, 1797.
Walther, Gerda. *Toward an Ontology of Social Communities*. Edited and translated by Sebastian Luft and Rodney Parker. Berlin: De Gruyter, forthcoming.
Weber, Max. "Die 'Objektivität' sozialwissenschaftlicher und sozialpolitischer Erkenntnis." *Archiv für Sozialwissenschaft und Sozialpolitik*, 19 (1904): 22–87.
Whitaker, Paul. "A Key to Südermann's 'Die drei Reihefedern.'" *Monatshefte* 48(2) (1956): pp. 78–87.
Wiggins, David. "A Sensible Subjectivism." In *Needs, Values, Truth: Essays in the Philosophy of Value*. Oxford: Blackwell, 1987: pp. 185–211.
Wilde, Oscar. "The Decay of Lying." *Intentions*. Engl. Libr. Nr. 54. Leipzig: Heinemann & Balestier, 1905: pp. 3–45.
Wilde, Oscar. *The Picture of Dorian Gray*. New York: Dover, 1993.
Winckelmann, Joachim. *Geschichte der Kunst des Alterthums*. Dresden: Walther, 1764.
Windelband, Wilhelm. *Präludien*. Tübingen: Mohr, 1903.
Witasek, Stephan. "Wert und Schönheit." *Archiv für systematische Philosophie* VIII (1902): pp. 164–93.
Witasek, Stephan. *Grundzüge der allgemeinen Ästhetik*. Leipzig: Barth, 1904.
Witasek, Stephan. "Über ästhetische Objektivität." *Zeitschrift für Philosophie und philosophische Kritik* 157 (1915): pp. 87–114, 179–99.
Wreschner, Arthur. *Ernst Platner und Kants Kritik der reinen Vernunft*. Leipzig: Pfeffer, 1893.
Wreschner, Arthur. *Die Reproduktion und Assoziation von Vorstellungen*. Leipzig: Barth, 1907.
Wundt, Wilhelm. *Beiträge zur Theorie der Sinneswahrnehmung*. Heidelberg: Winter, 1862.
Wundt, Wilhelm, ed. *Philosophische Studien*. Leipzig: Engelmann, Bd. 8 (1893) und Bd. 9 (1894).
Wundt, Wilhelm. *Vorlesungen über Menschen- und Tierseele*. Leipzig: Voss, 1897.
Wundt, Wilhelm. *Grundriß der Psychologie*, 4. Auflage. Leipzig: Engelmann, 1901.

Index

For the benefit of digital users, indexed terms that span two pages (e.g., 52–53) may, on occasion, appear on only one of those pages.

acoustics, 171–72, 183, 184–85
action, 17–18, 49, 64–65, 90–91, 92–93, 99, 101–3, 119–20, 121, 131–32, 142–43, 147–48, 149–51, 159, 170–71, 176, 196–97
activity, 119–20
actualization, 156–58
aesthetics, xx, 3–63, 84, 109, 117–18, 127–28, 155, 170–72, 186–87
  German, xxxii–xxxvi, xlii–xliii, 64
  Hegelian, 65–66
aesthetic
  categories, 41
  drive, 66
  experience, xxxiii–xxxiv, 127–28
  feeling, 17–18, 20, 21–22, 32–35, 39–41, 58–63, 67, 162
  impression, 34–35, 44–45, 84–85, 113
  judgment, xxxiii, 4–63, 65–66, 135–36, 170
  process, 59–60, 61–62, 113–14
  threshold, 40–41
agreement, 51–52, 127–28, 154–55, 162–63, 193–94
altruism, 174
a priori, the, 119
architecture, 54–55, 75
Aristotle, 52–53, 70, 90–91, 107–8, 154–55, 184–85, 187
art, xlii–xlvi, 26–28, 38–39, 50–51, 52–53, 54–55, 64–66, 70, 76–77, 100, 132–33
  Classical, 82–83
  Italian, 113
  Japanese, 35–36, 72
  Medieval, 113
  Nordic, 113
art critic, 27
artist, 29, 30–31, 38–40, 66, 81–83

artistic expression, 77, 100, 102–3, 110
artwork, 26–32, 35–36, 38–39, 66–67, 72–73, 77, 78, 83–85, 90–91, 103, 111–12, 113–14, 143–44, 159, 161
attention, 119–20
Avenarius, R., 56, 76, 132–33

Baer, C., 138–39
Balzac, H., 32–33
Baudelaire, C., 36, 96–97
Baumgarten, A., xxxiv, 65–66, 67
beautiful sciences, 64–65
beauty, xx, 4, 16–18, 24, 32, 35–36, 38, 53, 58–63, 64, 65–66, 70, 106, 108–14, 117–18, 127–29, 130–32, 134–35, 143–44, 153–54, 161, 163, 186–87
  Apollonian, 30–31
  determinate form of, 32
  Dionysian, 30–31
  experience of, xxxix–xlii
  of expression, 109–10
  forms of, 58–59
  norm-compliant, 109–10
  objective, 35
  qualities of, 59
being, lvii–lviii, 8, 116, 125–27, 128–29, 134–35, 148, 184, 189–93
Bergson, H., 150–51
Bernhardi, F., 97–98
Beuve, St., 32–33
Blätter für die Kunst, xxiv
brain-phenomenon, 109–10
Brentano, F., xvii–xviii, xix, 4–5, 74, 178, 179–80, 181–82
Brunetière, F., 33, 43
Butler, J., 197

Cassirer, E., xiv
categories of understanding, 74
Catholic Church, 188
character(s), 89, 92, 102–3
children, 35, 72, 85–87, 88–89, 101–2, 157, 163
choice, xvi, 121
Christianity, 30–31, 154–55, 173
cognition, xlix–l, lii, 12–20, 29, 43, 64–66,
    74–75, 82–83, 94, 99, 103–4, 126–27,
    134–40, 142–44, 148, 151, 153–54,
    163, 167, 171–72, 174–77, 188–89,
    191–92 and *passim*
  artistic, xlv–xlvi, 64, 100, 104
  conceptual, 65
  object of, 136–37
  objective, 13–14
  psychological, 103
cognitive drive, 66
cognitive purpose, 74–75, 101–2
cognitivism, xxxiv
Cohn, J., 6, 7–8
color, xxxvii, 15–18, 100
comedy, 35–36, 92–93
common sensibility, 6
comparison, 50, 104–5
compassion, 147–48
consciousness, xxix, 12–13, 67–68, 101,
    104–5, 112–13, 120–21, 131, 146–47,
    157, 159, 162, 185
  content of, xxix, 146, 168–69
  objects of, xxix–xxx, xxxi, 146
Consensus Gentium, 45, 56
constitution, 130–32
constitutive significance, lvii–lviii, 117–18,
    125, 130–31, 132–34, 142, 177–78
constraint, 131–32
contemplation, xxxv–xxxvi
content, lv
contrasting phenomena, 33
Copernican reversal, 116–17
correctness criteria, 47–49, 167, 168–69
counterpart, xlv–xlvi
culture, xlix, 35–36, 132–34, 154–55

death, 96–97, 149, 154–55
deception(s), 24–41, 44, 53, 56–57, 68,
    167–69
  aesthetic, xxxviii

  emotional, 97–98
  intensity, 40–41
  in judgment, 24–26
  memory, 75
  physical, 37–40
  physiological, 28–37
  psychological, 26–28
  sensory, 71, 72–73, 74, 145
Delboeuf, J., 183
Descartes, R., 8, 179–80
desire, 8–9, 10, 19, 43, 145, 150–51
development, 130, 138–39
dignity, 125, 174
disinterested, xxxiii, 10, 30–31, 80–81,
    147–48, 160, 197–98
divine world, 131, 141
dogmatics, 187–89
Döring, A., 148–49
drama, 28, 35, 36–37, 52–53, 102–3
dream, 85
duration, 34, 159
duty, 119

Ebbinghaus, H., 152
economic values, 12, 126–27, 130–31,
    132–33, 138
Eisler, R., 6, 22
Eleatics, 14–15
emotion, xlv, 29, 30, 80–81, 82–83,
    97–98, 99, 124, 142, 147–51, 154–55,
    157. *See also* feeling: subjectively
    conditioned
emotional sphere, liii–liv
empathy, xxxv, 60, 127–28, 187
Empedocles, 126–27
Enckendorff, ML., 173–74
epistemology, xxiii–xxiv, 13–14, 121–22,
    184–85
  rationalist, 142, 143–44
Erhardt, F., 138–39
essence, 82–84, 110–11
ethical action, 150–51
ethical feeling, 17–18, 21–22, 28–29, 162,
    187–88
ethics, lvi–lvii, 131–32, 164–65, 166, 170–
    72, 173–75, 185, 186–87, 196–97
  ancient, 148–49
Eucken, R., 139–40, 173–74

evaluation, 121, 135-36, 143-44, 196-97
evidence, 179-80, 181-82
evil, 116
existence, 121, 124, 125, 129-32, 133-35, 138, 192
expanse, 159
experience, 47-49, 117-18, 119-20, 122-24, 127-28, 142-44
explanation, 138-39

fairytale, 85-89, 103-4, 106-7
fashion, 38
Fechner, G., 38, 40-41, 54-55, 57-58
feeling(s), xxxix-xli, xliii-xliv, liii-liv, 5, 8-19, 21, 28-30, 36-37, 59-63, 66-67, 68-69, 80-82, 84, 85-87, 93, 96-97, 98-103, 105-7, 110-11, 142-61, 162, 163, 165-66, 167, 170, 174-75, 177, 187-89, 196-97 and *passim*
  expression, 99-100, 110
  and judgment, 10-11
  for nature, 53-54
  objectively conditioned ('pure'), liv-lvi, 15, 147-48
  of reality, 162
  representations, 61
  reproducibility of, 154-58
  sensory, 145-46
  subjective, 12-13, 145-47
  subjectively conditioned, liv, 15
Fichte, J., 82-83, 119, 150-51, 191-92
Fiedler, K., 66, 67
folksong(s), 95-96
form, 112
four worlds, the, l, 118, 119, 124, 125-36, 139-40, 141, 142-43
freedom, xv, 120-21, 125, 138, 140-41, 185-86

genre, 93
geometry, 104-5
George-Kreis, xxiv-xxv
George, S., xxiv-xxv
German Idealism, xv-xvi, xxxiv
gestalt, 71-74, 80-81, 109-10
  quality, 17-18
given, the, 123-24, 130-31, 142-43, 189

God, xlix-l, li, 94-95, 116, 121-22, 126-27, 134-35, 154-55, 174, 187-88, 197-98
  deniers of, 131
Goethe, J., 9, 65, 81-82, 96-97, 106-7, 165
Gottschall, R., 95-96
Gottsched, J., 64
Graz School, xxviii-xxix, xxx-xxxi
Grimm, H., 85-87
growth, 138
guilty pleasure, 27-28

habit, 74, 110, 154-55, 176-77, 196-97
hallucination, 44-45, 156
happiness, 126-27, 129, 131-32, 150-51
harmony, xlix-l, 6-7, 113, 129, 131, 173-74, 185-86
hedonism, xxxix-xlii
Hegel, G., xv-xvi, xxxiv, 65-66, 126-27
Heine, H., 95-97
Herbart, J., 52-53, 58-59, 185-86
history, 138, 139-40
Hölderlin, F., 126-27
holy, 117-18, 131
human nature, 103
Humboldt, H., 107-8
Hume, D., 162
Husserl, E., xiv, 171-72, 174-75, 181-82
Hutcheson, F., 17-18, 185-86

Ibsen, H., 102-3, 106-7
idealism, xlviii, 106-7, 142. *See also* German Idealism
identity, xlix-l, 123-24, 126-29, 134, 138, 141-42
illusions. *See* deception(s)
imagination, xlv
imitation, 64
individual, the, 151-54
inference, 12, 181
intellectualism, 19
intensity, 40, 159, 169
intentionality, xxix
interconnectedness, 16-17, 96, 116, 124, 125, 127, 130, 131, 133-38, 140-41, 185-86, 195
intuition, xlv, 65, 78-80, 96-97, 104-5, 116-17, 142-43
  artistic, 65

Itelson, G., 184–85

James, W., xlvii, 99, 163–64
Judgment, xx–xxi, 42–50, 117–18, 119, 121, 145, 148, 152–53, 167, 192–94, 195, 196 and *passim*
　cognitive, xxxix, 4–5, 8, 12
　ethical, 117–18, 135–36, 170
　objectively reliable, 21, 25–26, 42–43, 44, 46, 49–50, 56–57, 162
　primary value, liv–lv, 10, 12, 163–64, 167
　scientific, 42–43
　secondary value, liv–lv, 10
　sensory, 4, 19–25, 41–58, 164, 177
　subjective 20–21, 22–23
　systems of, 46–47

Kant, I., xv, 4–5, 6, 10, 13–14, 18–19, 28–29, 46, 51–52, 65–66, 109, 116, 117–19, 124, 126–27, 129, 142–43, 160
knowing, xv–xvi, xxxiv, 146–47, 191–92
Kreibig, J., 6, 7–8, 11
Külpe, O., 12–13, 34–35, 145–46, 158

Laas, E., 47
landscape, 29, 72
language, 111–12, 130, 169
law
　ideal, 174–75
　moral, 174
　natural, 121, 174–75, 181–82
　of the world, 185–86
life, 125, 131–34, 173
Lipps, T., 61, 187
lived experience, xlix, 122–25, 127–28, 130–31, 132–33, 136–38, 139–40, 142–43, 165–66, 189
　subjective and objective sides, xxx, 146
Locke, J., 13–14, 62–63
logic, xli, 117–18, 126–27, 128–29, 133–34, 135–37, 174–85, 196–97
logical value, xlix–l, lii, 128–29, 130–33, 134–42, 190–91, 193–94
Lohenstein, D., 96–97
Lotze, H., 16–17, 138–39
love, xlix–l, 126–27, 129, 131–32, 149–51, 194–95

Maeterlink, M., 36–37
Marburg School, xvi
masterpieces, 50
Meinong, A., xx, 5, 7–9, 10–11, 20–21, 147–48
memory, xliii–xliv, 39–40, 74–85, 89–90, 99–100, 106–7, 111–12
mental phenomena, xxix, 159
method, xviii–xxi, xxviii–xxix, xxx–xxxi
Meumann, E., xviii
Meyer, 111–12
Mill, JS., 170
mind, 75–76, 110–11, 139–40
mirroring, xliii–xliv, 70–89
moment, the, 151–54
mood, 26–27, 30, 35, 36–37, 53–54
motive, 119–20, 142–43, 150–51
Müller, M., xxvi–xxvii
Münsterberg, H., xlvi–lii, lvii–lviii, 116–43, 149–51, 165–66, 191–92, 194–95
music, 60, 73, 132–33, 158
Muther, R., 32–33

National Socialism, xxiv
naturalism, 27–28, 64, 76, 106–7
natural science, xvi, 104, 127–29, 130–31, 136–37, 139–40, 171–72
nature, 53–54, 77–78, 130, 134–35, 136, 137–41, 172–75
　mechanistic understanding of, 136–37, 138–40, 141–42, 143–44
　teleological consideration of, 138–39
necessary, the, 89–98, 166
Neo-Kantianism, xiv
Nietzsche, F., 16, 30–31, 176–77
norm(s), 116–17, 118–21, 165, 171–74
Novalis, xv–xvi, xxxiv, 9, 93
numerology, 95–96

object, 13, 14, 28, 54–55, 60, 137–38, 148, 149
　aesthetic, 37, 53, 54–55, 59–60, 109–10, 113
　'construed' [*aufgefaßte*], 37
　psychological, 127–28
objectification, 63
objective reality, xliii, 67–71, 72–74, 76, 89, 95, 98–99, 101, 162

objective reliability, 24–41
objectivity, xlii, 14–15, 46, 62–63, 67–70, 84, 109–10, 147, 149, 153–54, 158, 162–89 and *passim. See also* 'objective reality'
   conditioned feelings (*see* feeling(s): objectively conditioned)
   natural, 49–50
   sense of, 162–70
   as a task, 162–70
object theory, xxviii
observer, appropriate, xxxviii
observation, 30
odor, 24–25
organ(s)
   aesthetic, 34–35, 36–37
   sense, 4, 14, 17–18, 20, 21, 45, 53, 59, 63, 152–53
orientation, 30–32

pain, 59–60, 156, 157
painting, 72–73, 82–83
paradigm, 77–80, 82–83, 103–4
perception, 16–19, 20–21, 45, 47–49, 71–76, 82–84, 104–5, 135–36, 163, 166, 174, 175–76, 180, 183, 184–85, 189, 195
   inner, xxx, 10–11, 20–21, 22, 70, 99–100, 104–5, 145, 163, 178–80
   outer 104–6, 179
personality, 150–51, 159, 194–95
perspective, 72–73
phantasy, xliii–xliv, 85–89, 111–12
phenomenology, xiv, 126–27, 170
Philosophy of Values (Münsterberg), xlvi–xlvii
Platner, E., 17–18
Plato, 10–11, 16–17, 52–53, 116, 118
pleasing, 28–29
pleasure, xxxiii, 10–11, 24, 52–53, 57–58, 61, 63, 119–20, 122–23, 150–51, 159–61, 165, 197
   aesthetic 43
poetic justice, 93
poetic theme, 82–83
poetry, xxiv–xxv, 64–65, 69–70, 82–83, 88–89
   lyric, 89–98, 110–11

Poppe, T., 111–12
positivism, xvi, 116
praxis, 176
Prévost, A., 87
Price, HH 197–98
pride, 101
probable, the, 89–98
property, 4–5, 13–14
   objectively conditioned, xl, 14–15
   response dependent, xxxviii–xxxix
   sensory, 16–18
   subjectively conditioned, xxxvii–xxxviii, 14–15
Protestantism, 189
psychology, xvii–xviii, xix, 104–5, 116–17, 119, 150–51, 155, 161, 165, 170, 175–76, 178–79, 183 and *passim*
   'assertion', 75–76
   descriptive, xvii–xviii, xix
   of emotion (*see* emotion: psychology of)
   experimental, xix
purpose, 120–21
purposiveness, 65–66, 109, 129

quality, 16–18, 143–44, 161
   of the aesthetic sense, 59
   primary, 143–44
   secondary, xxxviii–xxxix, 143–44
Quandt, H., 32–33

rationalism, 165–66
realism, xx
reality, 46, 94, 99, 119, 121–22, 191–92
   consciousness of, 67–68
   empirical, 191
   external, 70, 88–89, 98
   mental, 68–71, 101
   objective, xliii, 67–70, 76, 85–87, 95, 99, 101, 103–4
   subjective, xliii, 67–74
   of thinking, 119
realization, 122–24
reason, 101
recognition, 122–23
recollection, 75–76
redemption, 88–89
relativism, xx–xxi
relic, 28

religion, 131–33, 140–41, 142, 185, 187–89
repetition, 78
representation, xliii–xliv, 17–18, 35–36, 39–40, 44–45, 47–49, 64–65, 68–70, 77, 78–80, 89–98, 101, 104–7, 116–17, 122–23, 145–46, 152–53, 154–57, 163–64, 167, 168–69, 193 and *passim*
reproduction, 156, 157–58
residuum, 156
revaluation, 30–31
rhyme, 110–11
Rickert, H., 163–64, 191–92
Riehl, A., 76
Romanticism, xv–xvi, xxxiv, 28–29, 65–66, 88, 97–98, 106–7
Rosenkranz, K., 60
Rousseau, J., 154–55
Ruge, A., 58–59

satire, 35–36
satisfaction, 123–24
Schasler, M., 58–59
Schelling, F., xv–xvi, xxxiv, 65–66
Schiller, F., 58–59, 64–65, 82–83, 96–97, 106–7, 171, 175–76
Schlegel, F., xv–xvi, 83–84
Schnaase, K., 54–55
Schopenhauer, A., 59–60, 82–83, 109–10, 146–47
Schwarz, H., 10–11
science, 15–16, 69–70, 82–83, 85–87, 94, 104–5, 127–28, 130–31, 136–37, 139–40, 148–49, 166–67, 170–72, 174–76, 181, 183. *See also* 'natural science'; 'science of value' and *passim*
    ideal, 181
    normative, 170
    objective, xxxi
sciences of
    the beautiful, xxxi, 170–89, 193–94
    the good, xxxi, 166, 170–89, 193–94
    mental phenomena, xxix
    the true, xxxi, 170–89
science of value, xx, 148–49, 167, 170–77
secondary quality analogy, xxxvii, 10, 62–63

self, 130–31
sensation, 13, 14–15, 18–19, 24–25, 34, 40–41, 46, 47–50, 62–63, 73–75, 119–20, 142–44, 145–47, 150–51, 152–54, 156–58, 162, 168–69 and *passim*
sense(es), 53
    aesthetic, 50–53, 55, 59
    of color, 53
    expression, 103
    impression, 47–50, 61, 69–70, 71–76, 78–80, 109–10, 157, 162, 165
sensitivity, 40–41
sensory qualities, xxxvii, 4, 8, 13–14, 15–18, 19–20, 62–63
sensory states, xliii–xliv
sentiments, 14–15
shame, 101
significance, 116, 134
Sigwart, C., 20–21, 171–72, 176–77
simile, 96–97
Simmel, G., xxii, 5, 6–7, 40–41, 46–47
skepticism, 191
society, 101, 127, 189–90, 195
soul, 34–35
sound, 24–25, 95–96, 127–28, 156
Southwest School, xvi
Spinoza, B., 25–26, 42, 62–63, 94
state, 189–90
Stern, W., 138–39
stimulus, 34, 47–49, 119–20, 122, 145–46, 147–48, 150–51, 153, 162, 165, 167, 168, 177
    aesthetic, physical, and physiological, 37–40, 52
    peripheral, 156, 158–61
Stumpf, C., 21, 24, 47–49, 142–43, 145–46, 147–48
style, 60, 80, 112–13
stylization, 65, 78
subject, 13, 137–38
subjective reliability, 20–23, 26, 56–57
subjectivism, xxxvi–xxxvii, xxxix, 116–17, 192
subjectivity, 4–6, 12–13, 28, 116–17, 145
sublime, 58–60
symbol, 183
sympathy, 127–28

Taine, H., 32–33, 78
taste, 8–9, 10–11, 18–19, 24–25, 27–28, 50, 57–58, 153–54, 187, 195
taste (flavor), 34
technique, 54–55
tempo, 34
Tetens, J., 15
theme, 54–55, 60, 80–81, 196
thinking, 118–19, 120–21, 135–36, 180–81, 184–85
  forms of, 117–18
  product(s) of, 139–40
  realm of, 136
  scientific, 133–34
  theoretical, 117
things themselves, xix
Tieck, L., 98
tone, 60
tragedy, 92–93, 108–9
transcendence, xxiii–xxiv
transcendent, 116, 117–18, 119
transcendental, xv
truth, xx, 42, 46–49, 56–58, 66, 77, 93, 102–3, 131–32, 163–64, 165–66, 174–75, 177–85, 191–93
  aesthetic, 56–57, 67
  artistic, xlii–xlvi, 64–114
  feeling of, 66, 183
  historic, 82–83, 104
  individual, xlv–xlvi, 56–57
  of nature, 64, 106–7
  objective, 84, 98
  scientific, 7–8, 82–83, 103–14
  wished for, 88, 102–3, 106–7

ugly, 61–62
ultimate warrant, lv–lvi
unity, 64–65, 80–82, 112–13, 134–35, 140–41
  of feeling, 80, 158
universal, the, 95–96, 171–72
universality, 45–46, 51–53, 55–56, 117–18, 120–21, 158–61

validity, 77–78, 120–21, 125–27, 129, 134, 141–42, 144, 148–49, 162, 164, 166, 175–76, 177–83, 196
  of axioms, 177–81

subjective, 166
supra–Individual, 142
value, xxx, 8–12, 39–40, 116–98 and *passim*
  aesthetic, xx, 51, 117–18, 127–29, 134, 142–43, 166, 194
  cognitive, 4
  constitutive, 142
  ethical, xlix–l, liii, 51, 94–95, 101, 121, 126–27, 130–31, 134, 142–43, 191–92, 196–97
  feeling of, 8–9, 10–11
  final, 132–33, 134, 139–41
  metaphysical, xlix–l, 119–25
  objective, xix, 6–7, 162–98
  property, xx–xxi, 143–44
  pure, 126–27, 150–51, 196–98
  relationships among, 127–34, 196
  scale, 118–97
  science of, xx, 148–49, 167, 170–77
  self-sufficiency, 126–27, 131–32, 134–35
  subjective and subjectivism, 4–9
  unconditioned, 119–20, 126–27
value judgment, xx–xxi, liii–lvi, 4–5, 9, 12, 19–58, 142, 145, 150–51, 162–98 and *passim*
valuing, associative and immediate, 28, 34–35
Van Dyck, A., 78–80
Vischer, T., 58–59
Von Ehrenfels, C., 5, 7–9, 14, 18–19, 31–32, 49–50

Wagner, R., 27–28, 40–41
Weber, M., 6, 40, 45
Weber's Law, 40
Whitmer, L., 24
Wilde, O., 87
will, xlviii–xlix, 8–9, 30, 85, 119–20, 121–25, 129–31, 135–40, 161, 189, 197–98 and *passim*
Winckelmann, J., 82–83
Windelband, W., xvi, 116–17, 118, 119–21, 165–66, 171–72, 173–75
wish, 95, 103–4, 123, 196–97
Witasek, S., 10–11, 161
world, xlviii, 116–92
  external (outer), xliii, 6, 69–70, 73, 98, 101, 118–19, 124–25, 129, 138

mental, xliii, 67–69, 70–71, 73, 94, 95, 98
objective, l, 13–14, 68–70, 116–17, 146
primal, 142–43
shared, 129
spirit, 94

world-formula, 137
worldview, 27–28, 69–70
Wundt, W., xvii, 12–13, 24–25, 72, 75–76, 78–80, 83–84, 145

Zionism, xxv–xxvii